D1606615

Being Salvation

Being Salvation

Atonement and Soteriology in the Theology of Karl Rahner

Brandon R. Peterson

Fortress Press
Minneapolis

BEING SALVATION
Atonement and Soteriology in the Theology of Karl Rahner

Copyright © 2017 Fortress Press. All rights reserved. Except for brief quotations
in critical articles or reviews, no part of this book may be reproduced in any manner
without prior written permission from the publisher. Email copyright@1517.media
or write to Permissions, Fortress Press, PO Box 1209, Minneapolis, MN
55440-1209.

Cover design: Alisha Lofgren

Hardcover ISBN: 978-1-5064-2332-6
Paperback ISBN: 978-1-5064-0894-1
eBook ISBN: 978-1-5064-0895-8

The paper used in this publication meets the minimum requirements of American
National Standard for Information Sciences — Permanence of Paper for Printed
Library Materials, ANSI Z329.48-1984.

Manufactured in the U.S.A.

This book was produced using Pressbooks.com, and PDF rendering was done by
PrinceXML.

Contents

Acknowledgments

In this brief space, I would like to express my gratitude to the many people who supported me and contributed to the completion of this project in one way or another. Although the vast majority of my writing occurred while holed up alone in Notre Dame's Hesburgh Library, the ideas and insights which inform it emerge out of conversations with my insightful friends, colleagues, and mentors. I owe thanks to the other members of my systematic theology cohort in graduate school, Daniel Castillo and Kevin McCabe, for providing valuable feedback on various parts of this project and exposing me to promising ideas in their own fields. This project—and my approach to theology in general—has also benefitted from conversations and correspondences with Thomas O'Meara, Brian Daley, Michael Fahey, Richard McBrien, and Todd Walatka, as well as the scholars in the Karl Rahner Society, who have encouraged my work, especially Mark Fischer and Leo O'Donovan. In addition, the friendship and fellowship extended to me by the many graduate students populating the corridors of Malloy Hall have been invaluable. I am also grateful to the philosophy department at the University of Utah for the course reduction in 2016–17 that helped me finalize the manuscript, as well as to Verlag Herder for granting me permission to include a variety of Rahner's texts and images here.

I owe a profound debt to the entire Department of Theology at the University of Notre Dame, which has shaped me profoundly over my eleven years in South Bend. Cathy Hilkert first introduced me to Rahner's thought during my undergraduate studies and adeptly fielded my various and persistent inquiries, sparking my interest in Rahner and bringing me to realize how much there was to learn about Catholic theology. Matt Ashley led me farther down the rabbit hole with a doctoral seminar on Rahner, exposing me to the breadth of Rahner's thought and providing me with a foundational knowledge and set of key texts to which I have returned time and again. Finally, I offer my sincere thanks to Bob Krieg, whose enthusiasm in the classroom, sharp insights, and exceptionally generous and wise support as my *Doktorvater* have formatively shaped me as a theologian.

However, the years spent learning from these bright lights would not have been possible without the love and support of my parents, Barb and Dick Peterson, my teachers from the beginning, from whom I continue to learn. My children, Joshua and Eva, bring me great joy and occasion the most helpful insights about what Irenaeus meant when he spoke of human growth. Finally, in addition to forcing me to learn a thing or two about Aristotle, my wife, Anne, has given me the companionship, dedication, and love that have made our joint journey into the perils of both academia and parenthood a wonderful adventure.

I dedicate this book to my grandparents, Gertrude and Verner ("Pete") Peterson and Lucille and C. Eugene ("Gene") Green, whose lives, each in their own unique way, brought to life Paul's words about faith, hope, and love. May perpetual light shine upon them.

Abbreviations

AH	*Against Heresies*, Irenaeus of Lyons
ANF	*Ante-Nicene Fathers*, Robertson et al (eds.)
CCC	*Cathechism of the Catholic Church*
CD	*Church Dogmatics*, Karl Barth
D	*Enchiridion Symbolorum* (31st ed.), Denzinger, edited by Karl Rahner
DS	*Enchiridion Symbolorum* (32nd ed.), Denzinger, edited by Adolf Schönmetzer
ET	English translation.
FCF	*Foundations of Christian Faith*, Karl Rahner
GS	*Pastoral Constitution on the Church in the Modern World* (*Gaudium et Spes*), Vatican II
KRA	Karl-Rahner-Archiv
LfTK	*Lexikon für Theologie und Kirche* (encyclopedia)
LG	*Dogmatic Constitution on the Church* (*Lumen Gentium*), Vatican II
NPNF	*Nicene and Post-Nicene Fathers*, Schaff et al (eds.)
NRSV	*New Revised Standard Version* (Bible)
PG	Migne's *Patrologia Graeca*
PL	Migne's *Patrologia Latina*
RAM	*Revue d'Ascétique et de Mystique* (journal)
SM	*Sacramentum Mundi*, Karl Rahner
ST	*Summa Theologiae*, Thomas Aquinas
SW	*Sämtliche Werke*, Karl Rahner
SzT	*Schriften zur Theologie*, Karl Rahner

TD   *Theo-Drama*, Hans Urs von Balthasar

TI   *Theological Investigations*, Karl Rahner

ZAM *Zeitschrift für Aszese und Mystik* (Innsbruck journal; eventual renamed *Geist und Leben*)

Introduction

In its explicit formulation the classical Christology of the Incarnation does not give expression in a clear and immediate way to the *soteriological* significance of the Christ event. This is especially true of western Christianity's understanding. Perhaps because of western individualism, the idea of an 'assumption' of the *whole* human race *in* the individual human reality of Jesus is rather foreign to their way of thinking. Within this horizon of understanding, then, the hypostatic union is the constitution of a person who *performs* redemptive activity, provided that his actions are moral and that his accomplishment is accepted by God as representative for the human race. But he does not mean in his very *being* salvation.[1]

About 300 feet to the south of the Main Building at the University of Notre Dame stands a statue of Jesus. A look at the center of Jesus's chest reveals his radiant Sacred Heart, after which the basilica on campus (which also stands about 300 feet away) is also named. His arms are spread widely and extended in a welcoming gesture to the north, greeting those who descend the front steps toward the central part of campus. This statue of Jesus also faces the towering statue of Mary, which stands prominently on the top of the Main Building's golden dome (Figure 1).

This piece of artwork expresses an important soteriological message, one which is particularly poignant during the campus-wide stations of the cross that takes place during Holy Week. During this two-hour procession, a fourteen-foot cross is carried by students, eventually to the penultimate station located directly in front of Mary on the dome, very close to this statue. As at every other station, the people gathered

---

1. Karl Rahner, *Foundations of Christian Faith: An Introduction to the Idea of Christianity* (hereafter *FCF*) (New York: Crossroad, 2007), 292–93 (emphasis original).

intone, "Behold, behold, the wood of the cross, on which is hung our salvation; O come, let us adore." Notably, these words do not refer to Jesus as our *Savior*, the one who brings about our salvation, but rather, as our *salvation itself.*[2] This soteriological message is further underlined by the Sacred Heart statue, beneath which is a plaque which bears the words, *Venite Ad Me Omnes* ("Come unto me All"). The Christ depicted here is not simply dispensing grace which he has merited (i.e., "Receive the fruit of my work"), but is, rather, inviting the observer toward him, beckoning the world into his open arms, where it can enter into his radiant, Sacred Heart.

Figure 1: Sacred Heart of Jesus statue, located immediately south of the Main Building at the University of Notre Dame

This book can be summarized as an argument that the theology of Karl Rahner has this same soteriological insight at its core: Jesus is best understood not just as a super-agent who performs and makes possible our salvation, but as the very locus of salvation itself. Since salvation consists in our existing in the immediate presence of God, partaking in his very life and even nature (2 Pet 1:4), this insight could also be

---

2. The reference to Jesus as salvation itself is confirmed by the phrase which follows, "let us adore." Properly speaking, the wood of the cross is only *venerated*, whereas God alone *adored*. Thus, the object of the second clause is not the wood of the cross, but rather, the salvation (i.e., Jesus) just mentioned.

expressed in Pauline terms: Our eternal life lies in our becoming "members" of the body of Jesus (1 Corinthians 12), the one who is both fully human and fully God (Philippians 2); Christian existence is one of being "in" Christ, who sums up all creation in himself (Ephesians 1), the New Adam (Romans 5).

In order to make the case that Rahner exemplifies this kind of soteriological rationale, I utilize a theological category under the term "representative soteriology." Although the word "representative" has been used in soteriological discussions in a number of ways, I specify the shape of this category by appealing to three particular markers and the way in which they interact, namely: (i) Christ, gathering up the human family in himself, brings us before God, (ii) Christ mediates the presence of God to us, and (iii) Christ effects our salvation in a person-centered, rather than a primarily act-centered, manner (Jesus not only *does* our salvation—he *is* our salvation). In such a model, "atonement" cannot be reduced to a particular feat or accomplishment of "making costly amends"; instead, it is a broader, interpersonal term signifying the reconciliation between God and humanity, a reconciliation encompassed in the Logos incarnate.[3] Paradigmatic instances of representative soteriology occur in the theology of the early church fathers, especially that of Irenaeus of Lyons and his idea of "recapitulation." Representative soteriology differs in very important ways from the idea of "physical redemption," a purely ontological and incarnational theory of atonement attributed broadly to the church fathers in the early twentieth century.

Although the next chapter itself provides a more thorough introduction to the book's outline, method, and objectives, let me say a brief word here about how it unfolds. The first chapter surveys the secondary literature on Rahner's soteriology. In this literature, Rahner's soteriological thought is predominately described as "sacramental," both by his critics (e.g., Hans Urs von Balthasar, who judges the themes of "symbol" and "solidarity" to be theologically insufficient for various reasons) and supporters (e.g., Joseph Wong, who describes Jesus as irrevocably establishing God's salvific will in the word through a sacramental mode). My primary thesis is not that this "sacramental" classification is wrong, but that it only tells part of the story: In Rahner's particular system of thought, sacramental and representative soteriologies necessarily supplement one another. In the second chapter, I

---

3. On this more ancient meaning of "atonement," see Gerald O'Collins, *Jesus Our Redeemer: A Christian Approach to Salvation* (New York: Oxford University Press, 2007), 10–15.

offer an in-depth look at this "sacramental" character of Rahner's soteriology, analyzing its basis in his theology of *das Realsymbol* and arguing that the way Rahner's speaks of Jesus as *das Realsymbol* inevitably
leads to a theologically rich idea of "representation." In the third chapter, I move away from Rahner's writings in order to consider classical,
patristic instances of representative soteriology; here, Irenaeus of
Lyons looms especially large. In chapter 4, I turn to back to Rahner,
examining the soteriology operative in his early writings, which draw
heavily and explicitly upon the patristic categories treated in the previous chapter; in doing so, I focus especially on his theology dissertation, *E latere Christi* ("From the Side of Christ").[4] Finally, the last chapter
examines work from the latter half of Rahner's career, demonstrating
that the representative soteriology which he adopted during his early,
patristic phase continues to have a formative impact on his mature
theology.

It is very important to clarify that although Balthasar's critique
serves, to some extent, as a point of departure for my argument, I
do not intend for this book to be a work in "Rahner vs. Balthasar"
polemics. The contemporary Catholic Church and the theologians
within it are, in my judgment, frequently divided in an excessive and
tribalist fashion, often accompanied by broad (and often politically
charged) labels of "liberal" and "conservative." There are indeed very
important theological differences between Rahner and Balthasar, and
these differences certainly deserve to be studied in a careful and critical way. However, my work here is not primarily concerned with such
differences, and even less is it an exercise in Balthasar-bashing. Rather,
my intention is to point out and elaborate upon a dimension of Rahner's thought which has been significantly underappreciated by his
critics and apologists alike. Since Balthasar's critique provides an articulate and very convenient entry point into how Rahner's soteriology is
typically (and only partially) understood, I have made use of it.

To this point, I should also add a short autobiographical note—
namely, that this Balthasarian critique overlaps to a large extent with
my own suspicious reaction to Rahner upon first encountering his
thought over a decade ago in an undergraduate course called "Christian Anthropology." At that time, I was perplexed as to how Rahner's

---

4. *E latere Christi: Der Ursprung der Kirche als zweiter Eva aus der Seite Christi des zweiten Adam, eine Untersuchung über den typologischen Sinn von Joh 19, 34* ["From the Side of Christ: The Origin of the Church
as Second Eve from the Side of Christ the Second Adam, An Examination of the Typological Meaning of John 19:34"] in *Spiritualität und Theologie der Kirchenväter*, eds. Andreas Batlogg et al, vol. 3
(1999) of *Karl Rahner: Sämtliche Werke* (hereafter *SW*), 32 vols. (Freiburg i.Br: Herder, 1995-), 1–84.

theological anthropology, with its ideas of the "supernatural existential," human freedom, and self-transcendence, made any essential connection to Jesus Christ. I certainly recognized the maxim that "Christology may be studied as self-transcending anthropology, and anthropology as deficient Christology,"[5] but it was unclear to me how Jesus could function for Rahner as anything more than a prime instance of successful humanity. By the end of this undergraduate course, I clearly understood that Rahner's anthropology posited that the free human person's "Yes" to grace was always a "Yes" to Christ, but it would take a couple of graduate courses and further study of Rahner's theology of *das Realsymbol* before I had more than a superficial understanding about why this was the case. It was only later that I discovered that *das Realsymbol* provides *only part* of Rahner's answer to this connection between the believer, grace, and Christ. Thus, this book stands as the next major step in my own quest as a theologian to fully appreciate the role which Christ plays in Rahner's thought.

Throughout the process of research and writing, I have come to appreciate how Rahner's soteriology is, to a large degree, encapsulated by that Sacred Heart statue which I walked by so many times during my studies at Notre Dame. Perhaps it is symptomatic of being overinvested in my own small project, but whenever I return to South Bend and visit this statue that stands at the heart of Our Lady's great campus, I cannot help but hear Rahner's words:

I want to see the pierced side of him who has locked me in his heart and who therefore took me with him when he went home, passing over from this world through death to the Father, so that I, too, am now where only God can be. I want to see the wood of the Cross, on which the salvation of the world, my salvation, hung. Come let us adore him.[6]

5. "Current Problems in Christology," *Theological Investigations* (henceforth *TI*) 1:149–213, at 164, note 24.
6. "Good Friday: 'Behold the Wood of the Cross . . .'," in *The Great Church Year: The Best of Karl Rahner's Homilies, Meditations, and Sermons* (New York: Crossroad, 1993), 149–54 at 154.

1

Christ the Notification?

Critiques and Categorizations of Rahner's Soteriology

Karl Rahner's status as one of the most influential theologians of the twentieth century is uncontested. However, valuations of that impact differ significantly. While many have celebrated his influence on Catholic theology, others have viewed his theology with deep suspicion. The time surrounding the Second Vatican Council exemplifies this phenomenon. In the years leading up to this event, Rahner had garnered enough detractors among the Roman Curia to have him entirely excluded from council preparations.[1] Once he was included, which occurred only after Pope John XXIII's personal intervention at Cardinal Juluis Döpfner's behest, his activities quickly led to the appointment of a Roman censor for all of his writings.[2] While Cardinal Alfredo Ottaviani (the head of the Holy Office) eventually remitted the censor and even gained a deep respect for Rahner over the course of the council, some of his detractors remained steadfastly opposed to his thinking. During the council, a group of "French integralists" published

---

1. Herbert Vorgrimler, "Karl Rahner: The Theologian's Contribution," in *Vatican II Revisited: By Those Who Were There*, ed. Alberic Stacpoole (Minneapolis: Winston, 1986), 32–46, at 38.
2. Günther Wassilowsky, *Universales Heilssakrament Kirche: Karl Rahners Beitrag zur Ekklesiologie des II. Vatikanums* (Innsbruck: Tyrolia, 2001), 93.

a pamphlet identifying Rahner and Joseph Ratzinger as "heretics who ... are worse than Teilhard and the modernists."[3] However, his theological contributions were embraced by enough council fathers to find expression in a multitude of the council's documents, including *Lumen gentium*, *Dei Verbum*, and *Gaudium et Spes*.

In the years following Vatican II, Rahner's detractors continued to criticize his thought sharply. The most well-known of such criticism, perhaps, came not from the Curia or reactionary traditionalists, but was leveled by the Swiss Catholic theologian Hans Urs von Balthasar. Among Balthasar's major concerns were that Rahner jeopardized the demands and truth claims of Christian revelation in an attempt to "accommodate" the contemporary world[4] and that his theory of the "anonymous Christian" was an oxymoron which (among other things) eviscerated evangelism and missionary activity.[5] But along with these worries, Balthasar voiced a concern that for Rahner, Jesus Christ does not actually "do" anything to accomplish our salvation.

This latter concern about Karl Rahner's soteriology is central to the subject of this book. The question of how (and even *whether*) Rahner understands Christ to *effect* human salvation serves as a point of departure for this study of his Christology and soteriology, a study which takes this accusation seriously and attempts to interpret Rahner in such a way as (i) to allay the concerns (namely, insistence upon an authentic and robust christocentricity and on the indispensable place of the Paschal Mystery as the nexus point of salvation history) of those who level it, and (ii) to complexify and supplement the extant apologies for Rahner by suggesting a new approach. Let us turn to these assessments, beginning with those shaped by Balthasar's critique and subsequently considering the apologies and other sympathetic treatments. The outlines of my own interpretation will conclude the chapter and be filled in by those which follow.

---

3. Karl Rahner, "Es ist merkwürdig bei einem Konzil," *Stimmen Der Zeit* 9/2012, 590–96, at 591. English quotations from non-English sources are, unless otherwise noted, my own translations.
4. Cf. Hans Urs von Balthasar, *The Moment of Christian Witness* (San Francisco: Ignatius Press, 1994).
5. Cf. Aidan Nichols, "Rahner and Balthasar: The Anonymous Christianity Debate Revisited," in *Beyond the Blue Glass: Catholic Essays on Faith and Culture* (London: Saint Austin Press, 2002). Note also Rahner's response in "Anonymous Christianity and the Missionary Task of the Church," in *TI* 12:161–78, particularly his observation that Cornelius was baptized *because* he possessed the Holy Spirit (ibid., 171, Acts 10:47).

The Instigating Question: Balthasar

In the fourth volume of his *Theo-Drama* series, Balthasar devotes about 80 pages to a historical outline of Christian soteriology before elaborating his own "dramatic" soteriology.[6] Within this historical outline, he identifies two contemporary soteriological approaches, which he classifies in terms of "solidarity" (e.g., J. Alfaro, H. Küng, E. Schillebeeckx, Rahner) and "substitution" (e.g., K. Barth, W. Pannenberg, J. Moltmann, but also Catholics such as R. Garrigou-Lagrange, M. Blondel, J. Daniélou). Balthasar's own stated course of action is to synthesize these two insights, so that Christ's solidarity *with* sinful humanity extends to a point of taking our sinfulness upon himself, and thus undergoing unique and unprecedented alienation from God; in the words of Jean Galot (of which Balthasar approves), "There is solidarity, it is true, but it extends as far as substitution [*bis zur Substitution*]: Christ's solidarity with us goes as far as taking our place [*unsere Stelle einnehmend*] and allowing the whole weight of human guilt to fall upon him."[7] That is, "the idea of solidarity is insufficient, without that of representative ('vicarious') suffering."[8]

Balthasar insists that any account of "solidarity" ought to (i) encompass human sinfulness (for "the incarnate Son of God's solidarity [is] with *sinful* humanity"),[9] and (ii) "extend" into a unique, unsurpassable, vicarious suffering on the part of Jesus as a result of this sinfulness. However, Balthasar laments, solidarity "easily slides unnoticed into misuse at the hands of a liberal Christology that puts the emphasis on Jesus' solidarity—expressed in his life and teaching—with the poor, sinners and the marginalized and sees the Cross as nothing more than the ultimate consequence of this 'social' solidarity."[10] In this view, "Jesus became the Redeemer, not by his death on the Cross, but by his moral example and his teaching."[11] Balthasar explains that this understanding of solidarity tries to draw on the patristic understanding of the "exchange" between God and humanity which occurred in Jesus, but asserts that this "*commercium* no longer operates at the ontological

---

6. *Theo-Drama* (henceforth *TD*) 5 vols. (San Francisco: Ignatius, 1988–1998), 4:231–316. This section occurs within the third volume in the German original *Theodramatik* 4 vols. (Einsiedeln: Johannes, 1973–1983).
7. *TD* 4:297. The entire phrase "representative ('vicarious') suffering" is Graham Harrison's translation of *Stellvertretung*.
8. Ibid.
9. Ibid., 268.
10. Ibid.
11. Ibid., 268–69.

plane but only on the social and psychological level."[12] At this point, Balthasar concludes his treatment of contemporary solidarity soteriologies with an "excursus" on Karl Rahner.[13]

From the outset, Balthasar portrays Rahner's soteriology as inimical to theories of "representation." "In Scripture, in the Fathers, and in Anselm, the *pro nobis*, preeminently in the Cross of Christ, is interpreted as a representative expiation [*stellvertretende Sühne*]. Rahner rejects this interpretation."[14] As evidence, he cites an instance where Rahner critiques the idea of Jesus taking our place in such a way that "self-redemption" is undercut.[15] Moreover, Balthasar makes note of Rahner's refrain that "God, who is unchangeable, cannot be caused to 'change his mind' by an event in the world like the Cross of Christ; he cannot be changed from an insulted, wrathful God to a reconciled God."[16] In rejecting this extreme view, which—Balthasar (rightly) notes—neither Anselm nor Scripture hold, Rahner is alleged to have thrown out the baby ("representation") with the bathwater (theories of atonement based on changing *God*, rather than *us*), as it were.

Balthasar goes on to say Rahner styles this immutable, saving God as "he-who-is-always-reconciled [*der je-schon-Versöhnte*],"[17] a vision of

---

12. Ibid., 273. Recently, and citing Balthasar, Walter Kasper has made the same point about Catholic proponents of "soft" atonement theories of solidarity collapsing the "metaphysical" in to the "social" in his *Mercy: The Essence of the Gospel and the Key to Christian Life* (New York: Paulist, 2014), 74.
13. For purposes of reference to the original German text, this section can be found in *Theodramatik* (Einsiedeln: Johannes Verlag, 1980), 3:253–62.
14. TD 4:274.
15. Namely, from "The One Christ and the Universality of Salvation" (1975) TI 16:199–2224, at 208. As Balthasar cites it, "This theory 'requires man's place to be taken by Jesus *in a way that is ultimately beyond our powers to conceive*; it contradicts a proper understanding of man's self-redemption'" (TD 4:274, emphasis original. Note: G. Harrison's English translation here differs from the one in *TI*, cited later in this chapter in the subsection, "Inconceivable" Representative Action? Rahner and *Stellvertretung*"). It should be noted that in this passage, Rahner sets Anselmian "satisfaction theory," rather than any account of "representation" (as Balthasar would seem to have it), in opposition to "self-redemption." Rahner explains the term self-redemption in the same article: "If, however, self-redemption means that a man can achieve his fulfilment without God, then any form of self-redemption is foreign to Christian teaching. Christian salvation can only be understood as self-redemption in the sense that a man does not merely receive his salvation in a passive manner but rather realises it with total, and not just partial, freedom. The very possibility of freedom, however, is established by God through nature and grace. To gain a proper idea of this grace one should not conceive of the grace in which a man achieves salvation as an external means but rather as the innermost core of human freedom which is freely constituted by God" (TI 16:206–207). Rahner returns to the term in "The Christian Understanding of Redemption" (1981), where he writes, "it is simply wrong to maintain that self-redemption and redemption from outside are . . . mutually exclusive" (TI 21:239–54, at 241).
16. TD 4:275. As Balthasar notes, Rahner on several occasions (unfairly) attributes such a view to Anselm.
17. Such a description of God is embraced by Hegel in his account of the Christ-event, in which "God has shown himself to be by his very nature reconciled with the world" (*Lectures on the Philosophy of Religion*, 3 vols. (New York: Humanities Press, 1962), 3:99). But cf. Rahner's claim in "Reconciliation

God which renders the "the Incarnation and death of Jesus Christ . . . only . . . a final cause or . . . a 'quasi-sacramental' cause."[18] According to Balthasar, such causality means that "it is not Christ who, in virtue of his uniqueness, embraces and contains mankind [*die Menscheit in sich einfaßt*] in order to reconcile it to God through his suffering—for we have already heard that such 'representative' action [*Stellvertretung*] is inconceivable."[19] While he does not go so far to say that Christ's soteriological significance is, for Rahner, simply that of a moral exemplar, Balthasar repeats that for him, "Jesus could not represent [*stellvertreten*] men in any other way but that in which one man is able to 'be there' for another"; Jesus is one graced man who exists in a weak "solidarity" with others who are not "essentially different" from himself.[20] Rahner's preference for a robust account of personal freedom (interpreted as "self-activation of the subject in its totality") weakens his account of "solidarity," and so, "it remains unclear in what sense—if Christ is to be more than an example—Rahner wishes to speak of 'sharing' [«*Teilnahme*»] in the death of Christ."[21] Balthasar admits that Rahner "[o]ccasionally . . . does speak of a participation [*Teilnahme*] in the death of Jesus," but confusingly "veto[es] against Jesus genuinely 'representing' [*echte Stellvertretung*] sinners."[22] Alternatively, Balthasar suggests that Jesus "on our behalf (that is, as our representative), should *endure* the alienating alienation . . . liberating man from alienation." Such a "genuine 'representation' [*Stellvertretung*] (that is, on behalf of, and in the place of, the sinner)" would, in fact, *enable* rather than *detract from* our own self-actualization.[23]

Balthasar concludes his soteriological concerns by turning to Rahner's more specifically christological writings. It seems, he says, that for Rahner, Jesus's "(hypostatic) unity is only the highest instance . . . of the unity that comes about in the coincidence of the human transcendence toward the divine horizon and God's self-disclosure."[24] That

and Vicarious Representation" (1982) that "God has reconciled the world to himself in Jesus the crucified" (*TI* 21:255–69, at 261).
18. *TD* 4:276.
19. Ibid.
20. Ibid.
21. Ibid., 278–79.
22. Ibid., 280.
23. Ibid., 281.
24. Ibid. Similarly, as Balthasar discusses the incarnate Son as uniquely capable of bearing the world's sins, he remarks that Jesus's "Godmanhood . . . is more than the 'highest case' of a transcendental anthropology" (*Mysterium Paschale: The Mystery of Easter* (San Francisco: Ignatius Press, 2000), 138). Shortly thereafter, Balthasar elaborates his critique in a footnote, diagnosing Rahner's theology as suffering from a "minimalist interpretation" of texts like 2 Cor 5:21 and Gal 3:13, which Balthasar uses extensively in support of his own substitutionary atonement schema (147).

is, "the 'Hypostatic Union' . . . appears to be only the 'most successful instance'" of concrete human nature, to which God is communicating himself.

Balthasar's criticism of Karl Rahner can be summarized as follows: determined to provide a robust account of human freedom, Rahner has constructed an anthropology according to which an immutable God is consistently self-communicating in grace to members of the human race as they, in turn, self-realize by accepting this grace. Within the scheme, Jesus's role amounts merely to existing as the most success-ful case of this dynamic of self-communication and realization. While Rahner infrequently gives superficial lip-service to notions of our "par-ticipating" in Christ, he eschews any suggestion of Christ as our "rep-resentative" from his system, under the historically naïve pretense of guarding against atonement theories which seek to change God rather than us. The result is a rather weak soteriology: "Christ's Passion," Balthasar remarks with Rahner clearly in mind, "is more than a sacra-mental sign that God *is* reconciled to the world and is applying the fruits of this reconciliation to the world."[25] In other words, Rahner's Christ does not so much *do* anything to effect our salvation as he does simply exist as a kind of notification to the world of what God is always and consistently doing anyway.

Balthasarian Critiques

This multifaceted critique raised by Balthasar proved to be quite influ-ential after its publication. Not only was Rahner himself keenly aware of it, as we will see in chapter 5, but Balthasar's criticism exerted its influence on other evaluations of Rahner's Christology and sote-riology. Here, let us briefly consider two critical readers of Rahner whose interpretation of his soteriology overlap extensively with that of Balthasar, turning subsequently to other evaluations that draw on certain of Balthasar's suggestions.

Guy Mansini

The first half of Guy Mansini's *The Word Has Dwelt Among Us* is devoted explicitly to christological considerations.[26] A large swath of this first

25. Ibid., 265. Balthasar's critique of Rahner continues after his explicit "excursus," remarking that "we should not say that the Cross is nothing other than the ('quasi-sacramental') manifestation of God's reconciliation with the world, a reconciliation that is constant, homogeneous and always part of a given" (362).

half deals with the theologies of Rahner and Balthasar, setting the two in contrast to one another in various places. The book's seventh chapter, "Rahner and Balthasar on the Efficacy of the Cross," contrasts the two on the issue of soteriology. At the outset of this chapter, Mansini summarizes Rahner's soteriological *desiderata* as follows: "the Cross is the cause of salvation only in a quite restrained sense, after the manner of a sacrament"; soteriology must "avoid . . . the 'inconceivable notion' that Christ is our representative on the Cross or does anything in our stead," but must instead stand as "an account in which 'self-redemption' has a prominent place"; the "anger of God . . . becomes a minor or even non-existent theme"; and finally, soteriology cannot undermine God's immutability.[27]

Mansini then proceeds to give a more detailed reading of Rahner's later, explicitly soteriological works, relying on Anselm Grün's work as a guide.[28] The way in which Rahner proposes to best realize the above *desiderata*, Mansini suggests, is to propose that Christ's cross effects salvation according to the mode of a sacrament. In doing so, Rahner "equates saying that the death of Jesus 'causes' salvation with saying that it has a 'meaning' for us," for "the Cross is supposed to *cause* simply because it *signifies*."[29] Pointing out that such a proposal may seem to "do nothing more than reduce the Cross to an event of revelation, a sort of demonstration of God's love," Mansini observes that Rahner "tries" to underline the robust *sacramental* character of signifying in this case.[30] Even so, Mansini's language of "tries" as well as "supposed to *cause*" anticipates his own evaluation of Rahner's level of success in styling Christ as an "effective exemplar (*produktive Vorbild*)."[31]

Mansini's explicit evaluation occurs after a lengthy treatment of Balthasar's own soteriology. In that evaluation, Mansini cites Balthasar's own "excursus" on Rahner's soteriology, noting that it can "be argued that Rahner does not do justice to the New Testament foundations of the notion of representation," a notion which Mansini says Rahner "jettison[s]."[32] Mansini suggests that Rahner's insistence on avoiding this term is *not*, in fact, to protect human freedom, as Rahner

26. Guy Mansini, *The Word has Dwelt Among Us: Explorations in Theology* (Ave Maria, FL: Sapientia Press, 2008).
27. Ibid., 94.
28. Anselm Grün, *Erlösung durch das Kreuz. Karl Rahners Beitrag zu einem heutigen Erlösungverstandnis* (Münster-schwarzach: Vier-türme Verlag, 1975).
29. Mansini, *The Word has Dwelt Among Us*, 98.
30. Ibid.
31. Ibid., 98–99.
32. Ibid., 109.

himself claims (and which Mansini suspects to be a false pretense), but rather, is due to Rahner's insistence on protecting divine immutability, combined with Rahner's inability to realize that the cross can change things other than God (namely, "it can work an economic change").[33] Mansini concludes that the cross "is not merely the manifestation of the antecedent salvific will of God (Rahner), but is also a change – but only in the economy."[34]

To be clear, Mansini does not adopt own Balthasar's own soteriological system (indeed, he is quite critical of it), but his critique of Rahner leans significantly on Balthasar's "excursus." Mansini judges Rahner's soteriology to acknowledge the cross's salvific efficacy in only a "restrained" sense, that the Paschal Mystery becomes, for Rahner, simply a "sort of demonstration of God's love," and that Rahner "jettisons" any notion of Christ "representing" humanity.

George Vass

George Vass, who inherited Rahner's own chair at the University of Innsbruck, devotes the fourth volume of his series on "Understanding Karl Rahner" to the topic of "The Atonement and Mankind's Salvation."[35] Although much of this volume is dominated by consideration of the "anonymous Christian," it includes a more general evaluation of Rahner's overall soteriology as well. Vass makes it clear from the beginning that he feels an "uneasiness" with Rahner's account of human salvation, quickly going on to boldly assert that "Rahner has, properly speaking, no theory of redemption" at all.[36] Vass explains,

> What has made me uneasy throughout in presenting Rahner's soteriology is the fact that he seems to explain away this dramatic character of man's redemption by either reducing it to the historical process of man's 'engracement' by Christ, or attributing it to God, whose love is unalterable in his salvific purpose. Of course, these are mediated through Jesus Christ, but mediation in itself means an a-personal function which does not allow

33. Ibid. Interestingly, Mansini is even more critical of Balthasar, deeming that much of Balthasar's constructive soteriology "must be abandoned," due to his confusion over Christ's natures leading him to improperly "import" things into the immanent Trinity (111–12). Mansini's ultimate conclusion is that both giants of the twentieth century are inadequate, and the best soteriological move is to retreat to medieval scholastic theology: "where we are left after we use Rahner to criticize Balthasar, and Balthasar to criticize Rahner, is with the prior tradition, the tradition of St. Anselm and St. Thomas on 'satisfaction'" (113).

34. Ibid., 112.

35. George Vass, *A Pattern of Doctrines 2: The Atonement and Mankind's Salvation*, vol. 4 of *Understanding Karl Rahner*, 5 vols. (London: Sheed & Ward, 1998).

36. Ibid., 16.

the contours of the personal Mediator to appear, the Christ who, because through his deed mankind's fate was basically altered, apparently changes the attitude of God to mankind.[37]

Vass is much more at home with more act-centered, *dramatic* soteriological theories in which the interplay between God, Jesus, and the rest of humanity moves into an open future in which all parties are, in some way or another, changed. By shunning words such as "propitiation" and "ransom," Rahner renders his view a sterile, playing-out of a preordained process, which Vass, at several points, even compares to Hegel's system.[38] As this process goes through the motions, Christ's mediation is simply the result of God's will, the eventual realization of which was really just a matter of course.[39] Moreover, any genuine theory of redemption must have a strong *pro nobis* dimension, with Christ performing "a free deed . . . *on our behalf.* The Mediator was destined by God to do freely something which man was unable to do."[40]

Vass's lament over the lack of an authentic, representative-Mediator is only one of several ways in which his critique of Rahner echoes Balthasar's excursus. Explicitly citing Balthasar, Vass wonders whether, in Rahner's system, there exists "a difference between man and the Incarnate beyond that of degree?"—for it seems to Vass that Christ is, for Rahner, merely a prime instance of successful humanity, and as Balthasar suggests, even Mary could fulfill this function in the same way.[41] In the end, Rahner's soteriology boils down to Christ notifying the world of a salvation which is already occurring: "man's *soteria* through the mediation of Christ's cross is but the manifestation of God's ever permanent loving concern to save mankind."[42]

Vass's assumption that the two ideas of: (i) a representative-Mediator, and (ii) the performance of a discrete, salvific *task* are inextricably

---

37. Ibid., 17.

38. Ibid., 18, 21.

39. "A justifiable suspicion may arise that in Rahner's thought mediation can be reduced to a pre-established, if not necessary, fulfillment of God's self-bestowal on mankind" (ibid., 17).

40. "Rahner seems painstakingly to avoid words connected with or expressing this drama: 'expiation', 'propitiation', 'sacrifice', 'ransom', and their like. . . . Yet, these words seem to have been part and parcel of the traditional faith: Christ's mediation was always thought to be a free deed of an incarnate person – *on our behalf*. The Mediator was destined by God to do freely something which man was unable to do" (ibid., 18).

41. Ibid., 19. Cf. Balthasar's remark in his excursus on Rahner's soteriology, "Furthermore, we would have to ask why the death of Mary (and her life, which was a preparation for it) did not lead to the same hypostatic union. Was she not free, according to Catholic teaching, from all inherited and personal guilt? And, as such, since she was perfect, was her death not of the same quality as that of Jesus?" (*TD* 4:280).

42. Vass, *A Pattern of Doctrines 2*, 21.

bound to one another is an assumption which should be kept in mind as the book unfolds. Indeed, I would suggest that Vass's assumption that Christ's "representation" is bound together with a singular vicarious act is also operative in Balthasar's own similar critique. It is no surprise that both thinkers thus find Rahner's soteriology "inadequate," precisely in its lack of any dramatic element.

Doubts Raised by the International Theological Commission

Several others have raised doubts about Rahner's place for Christ in the story of human salvation. Among the more amicable of such criticisms can be found in "Select Questions on the Theology of God the Redeemer," published by the Vatican's International Theological Commission (ITC) in 1995.[43] The text begins with "an outline of the authentic Christian teaching on redemption and its bearing on the human condition, as the Church has propounded this teaching in the course of her tradition." After anthropological considerations about "the human condition" which is seriously affected by sin, a brief survey of concepts similar to redemption in other major religions, and reflections about the human situation in the modern world, the text moves on to consider redemption from biblical and historical perspectives (Parts II and III, respectively). The latter is of particular interest here. In its discussion of medieval theologies of redemption, the document makes a distinction between a "descending," incarnational dimension of redemption which emphasizes God's initiative, and an "ascending" dimension of "legal restitution" embodied by "theor[ies] of sacrifice" and Anselm's notion of "vicarious satisfaction."[44]

Rahner enters the discussion as a twentieth-century theologian "who wish[es] to restore the sense of God's 'descending' action on behalf of his needy creatures."[45] The whole idea of "expiatory sacrifice"—which the ITC has classified as "ascending"—is identified as repugnant to Rahner's sensibilities.[46] Rather than "expiator," Rahner's Christ is styled as "both God's irrevocable self-communication in grace and the acceptance of that self-communication by humanity."[47] The document does an admirable job of succinctly stating Rahner's asser-

---

43. International Theological Commission, "Select Questions on God the Redeemer," Vatican City 1995, http://www.vatican.va/roman_curia/congregations/cfaith/cti_documents/rc_cti_1995_teologia-redenzione_en.html.
44. Ibid., Part III, nn. 16, 25.
45. Ibid., Part III, n. 30.
46. Ibid., Part III, n. 30.
47. Ibid. Part III, n. 30, citing *FCF*, 194–95.

tion that Christ's redemptive role operates in accordance with "quasi-sacramental causality" (a topic to which we will devote significant attention below) in which "God's salvific will posits the sign, in this case the death of Jesus along with his resurrection, and in and through the sign it causes what is signified"; Christ himself is described as one such efficacious sign, "a symbolic reality."[48] The fruits of the redemption brought about in this way by Christ may, for Rahner, "be obtained through the acceptance of the inner self-communication of God which is given to all, as a 'supernatural existential.'"[49]

In its evaluation of Rahner's contribution to recent soteriology, the ITC praises his emphasis upon God's ("descending") initiative and the human response to that love. It also notes that Rahner is able to circumvent many of the pitfalls associated with popular ("ascending") "legalistic" articulations of redemption.[50] However, it raises some suspicions which echo those voiced by Balthasar, especially concerning "the causal efficacy of the Christ event and especially to the redemptive character of Jesus' death on the Cross." Specifically, it asks, "Does the Christ-symbol simply express and communicate what is antecedently given in God's universal salvific will? Is God's inner word (as 'transcendental revelation') emphasized at the expense of the outer word given in the proclamation of the gospel as good news?"[51] In other words, the ITC expresses the concern that for Rahner, salvation is extended as an offer to all through God's universally operative salvific will and appropriated *via* the "supernatural existential" which exists in the heart of every person; Christ, on the contrary, may "simply express" this widespread and continually ongoing occurrence.[52]

Interestingly, Balthasar's critical evaluation finds another echo in the ITC's evaluation of Rahner. It is noteworthy that after making

48. Ibid., Part III, n. 30.
49. Ibid., Part III, n. 31.
50. Ibid., n. 32.
51. Ibid.
52. The ITC's lukewarm and even wary evaluation, nevertheless infused with genuine respect and praise, bears a remarkable resemblance to an evaluation of Rahner's Christology and soteriology offered by Joseph Ratzinger in *Principles of Catholic Theology* (San Francisco, CA: Ignatius Press, 1987), 162–71. There, Ratzinger discusses the critique that Rahner's idea of universal orientation toward self-transcendence, which is "concretized" in Christ and his church, results in a "Christianity that is no more than a reflected universality" (166). To this, Ratzinger suggests, "Rahner could, of course, refute all this by saying that he, too, takes as his point of departure that which is inconceivably new, the *Event* that *is* the Savior. He could say that what is universal has now become that which saves only because, in this Savior, a universality of being has come to pass that could not emanate from being itself. I prefer to leave open the question of whether this does justice, on a conceptual level, to what is particular and unique in the salvation history that has its center in Christ" (ibid.).

a distinction between "ascending" and "descending" dimensions of redemption, Rahner's own theology is explicitly associated with the "descending" movement (although, if pushed, the authors would likely acknowledge the "human response" element of Rahner's theology as "ascending").[53] In the section which follows its discussion of Rahner, titled "Retrieval of Earlier Tradition," the ITC notes the efforts of "contemporary Catholic theologians [who] are seeking to maintain in tension the 'descending' and 'ascending' themes of classical soteriology." It goes on to offer a "composite" sketch of this growing movement, which draws upon "Irenaeus, Augustine, and Thomas Aquinas" and which typically take the form of "narrative or dramatic" accounts.[54] These accounts, it notes, fulfill their "ascending" dimension not through "legalistic theories of restitution or penal substitution," but rather

> put the accent on what we might call representative headship. . . . Christ identifies himself with fallen humanity. He is the new Adam, the progenitor of redeemed humanity, the Head or the vine into whom individuals must be incorporated as members or branches. . . . The incarnate Word becomes the gathering point for the constitution of a reconciled and restored humanity.[55]

This representative of ours, Christ, the ITC goes on to say, "identifies with sinful humanity and experiences the pain of its alienation from God"—a comment which echoes Balthasar's call for a representative Savior who "endure[s] the alienating alienation."[56]

The presentation of "ascending" and "descending" soteriologies offered in the ITC's "God the Redeemer" implicitly evaluate Rahner in a similar way as Balthasar has—namely, as a theologian whose theory of redemption stands opposite from categorizations of Christ as our "representative." While Balthasar explicitly makes this claim, the ITC document suggests it by deeming Rahner a "descending" thinker and subsequently articulating representation as an alternative to "restitution"

---

53. As we will see below, Joseph Wong notes that Rahner himself makes the "ascending" and "descending" distinctions and that Rahner's Christology and soteriology embody both aspects (although later in his career, Rahner especially emphasized the former).

54. ITC, "Select Questions on God the Redeemer," Part III, n. 57. This latter remark makes it clear that Balthasar, whose *Theo-Drama* volumes discuss soteriology at length, is among the theologians being exposited.

55. ITC, "Select Questions on God the Redeemer," Part III, nn. 38–39.

56. I would argue that this latter qualification about alienation need not be part of a "representative" soteriology, although the elements in the foregoing description quoted from the ITC constitute the very heart of such a category.

within the "ascending" group of soteriological concepts. Although the ITC clearly appreciates much of Rahner's theology on this topic, the document's reader is left with the impression that for Rahner, the heavy lifting, as it were, of the work of redemption is perhaps being carried out by God's salvific will and the supernatural existential, and that the most fruitful path forward in Catholic theologies of redemption lies elsewhere, in a retrieval of the idea of "representation."

Other Assessments of Rahner's Christology

Framing the issue differently but touching on many of the same themes already discussed, Schubert Ogden[57] has contended that Rahner's Christology ends up being "constitutive" (i.e., Christ as the *sine qua non* of human salvation) in name only, and in effect, collapses into normative (i.e., exemplary) Christology.[58] His succinct but overall fair treatment of Rahner (with whom he disagrees but who he still finds to be "ingenious," "subtle," and "nuanced") notes that Rahner tries to avoid two soteriological alternatives which are often presented as exhaustive. On the one hand, most accounts of Christ as constitutive for salvation (in distinction from simply being its norm)[59] are framed in terms of the satisfaction theory, which Rahner believes almost inevitably to suggest that Jesus effects salvation by *changing God* (i.e., mollifying wrath, etc.; this sort of salvific efficacy accords with Gerald O'Collins's description of "propitiation," as it was understood in Greek paganism).[60] On the other hand, merely attributing a normative salvific role

<hr/>

57. Schubert M. Ogden, *Is There Only One True Religion or Are There Many?* (Dallas: Southern Methodist University Press, 1992), 93–95.
58. Ogden uses the descriptor "representative" for what others (e.g., J. Dupuis, J. Wong) have labeled "normative." This usage differs entirely from how we are using "representative" in this book (a usage which *coincides* with constitutive Christology, rather than standing as its mutually exclusive alternative).
59. In discussing a widely read article by J. P. Schineller ("Christ and Church: A Spectrum of Views," *Theological Studies* 37, no. 4 (1976), 545–66), Brian McDermott, summarizes this distinction well: "By a constitutive position he means one according to which salvation would not be a reality if the life, death, and resurrection of Christ had not occurred; Christ is necessary and sufficient as the one who brings about salvation. A normative Christology, on the other hand, sees Christ as the supreme God-given norm, pattern, or example of salvation, in the light of which other legitimate paths to salvation may be illuminated, evaluated, and purified. No Christology can be constitutive without also being normative, but a Christology can be normative without being constitutive" (*Word Become Flesh: Dimensions in Christology* (Collegeville, MN: Liturgical Press, 1993), 283). Typically, conversations about Christ's "constitutive" role in salvation occurs in the context of theology of religions, as theologians argue about the role and extent which Christ and non-Christian religious have in the salvation of non-Christian individuals. See Jacques Dupuis, *Toward a Christian Theology of Religious Pluralism*. Maryknoll: Orbis Books, 1997.
60. This connection, which Rahner indeed makes, is rather unfair to satisfaction theory, but may be more accurately associated with (at least some versions of) penal substitution theory. On "propi-

to Christ is not sufficient for Rahner, who wants to preserve the traditional claim that Christ uniquely causes of our salvation as its *sine qua non*, constitutive source.

As Ogden summarizes, Rahner avoids these two soteriological horns (in some places, at least) by turning to a Thomistic (and, more originally, Aristotelian) distinction between "efficient" and "final" causality. While the Christ-event cannot "efficiently" cause or bring about God's salvific will (which is, rather, eternal and consistent), Jesus Christ *can be*, and in fact, *is* its "final" cause. Rahner explains this latter category by describing Christ as the "primal sacrament" who communicates grace according to the same kind of causality by which the sacraments operate. While Ogden does not elaborate much on Rahner's favored causality, we will explore it in detail in the second chapter.

Although Ogden has a great respect for Rahner's efforts, he, without "claiming to offer an adequate criticism of Rahner's . . . thesis," finds it unconvincing.[61] In Ogden's judgment, Rahner's attempt to split the horns of propitiation and normative Christology ends up crashing into either of the two boundaries. He explains,

> If there is a real and not merely verbal difference in the Christ event's not being the efficient cause of God's saving will, but being its final cause instead, then, so far as I can see, the Christ event is not really constitutive of salvation after all, but only representative [= normative] of it, similar to the way in which sacraments in general are thus representative. If, on the other hand, the Christ event is different enough from sacraments generally not only to represent God's saving will but also really constitute it, then, in my view, there is not a real, but only verbal, difference in its being called the final cause of God's will to save instead of its efficient cause.[62]

In Ogden's final judgment, Rahner's idea of Christ as "primal sacrament" and "final cause" is consistent more with a normative rather than constitutive Christology. (Ogden himself opts for such a normative position and appropriates Rahner's terminology of Christ as "primal sacrament"; he does, on the contrary, claim that "Jesus is constitutive of *Christianity*."[63])

While Ogden recognizes Rahner's (allegedly unfulfilled) desire to affirm a constitutive Christology, J.T. Farmer goes so far as to simply

---

tiation," see O'Collins, *Jesus Our Redeemer: A Christian Approach to Salvation* (New York: Oxford University Press, 2007), 15–18.
61. Ogden, *Is There Only One True Religion or Are There Many?*, 94.
62. Ibid.
63. Ibid., 96–97, emphasis added.

categorize Rahner's Christology as normative. According to such a position, "Salvation, always possible for all humanity even apart from Christ, becomes normatively present in him."[64] Such a position, in fact, matches quite nicely with the criticisms which Balthasar has leveled at Rahner—namely, that Christ, one graced human among many, is merely "the most successful instance" of a humanity to which God self-communicates. Such a normative categorization of Rahner is convincingly rebutted by Joseph Wong in an article cited by Farmer (mistakenly, it seems, in support of) himself.[65]

Finally, a more specific criticism about Christ's efficacy in Rahner's soteriology concerns the role of the cross. Using Rahner, Schillebeeckx, and other twentieth-century theologians as a foil to compare against his own soteriology, Thomist Rik Van Nieuwenhove says that Rahner "fail[s] – or refuse[s] – to attribute any salvific significance to the cross of Christ."[66] Such a critique is at once more specific and more severe than those above. Rather than the salvific efficacy of the entire Christ-event, Van Nieuwenhove hones in on Christ's passion and death. Moreover, beyond accusing Rahner of granting the cross only "normative" meaning rather than the constitutive efficacy of a *sine qua non*, Van Nieuwenhove charges Rahner with denying any positive salvific significance for it *at all*. Against such a position, he retorts that "emptying the death of Jesus of all salvific power contradicts the New Testament witness (including, in all likelihood, the way Jesus himself viewed his passion) and the ensuing tradition of Christian reflection on the cross."[67]

Summary: Critical Evaluations of Rahner's Christ as Savior

These critical assessments of Karl Rahner's Christology and soteriology coalesce around the constitutive place for Jesus Christ as the *sine qua non* of salvation. Almost all of these assessments recognize Rahner's insistence upon Jesus being the symbol or sacrament of human sal-

64. Jerry T. Farmer, "Four Christological Themes of the Theology of Karl Rahner," in *The Myriad Christ: Plurality and the Quest for Unity in Contemporary Christology*, eds. T. Merrigan and J. Haers (Leuven: Leuven University Press, 2000), 433–62, at 455.
65. Joseph H. Wong, "Anonymous Christians: Karl Rahner's Pneuma-Christocentrism and an East-West Dialogue," in *Theological Studies* 55, no. 4 (1994), 609–37.
66. Rik Van Nieuwenhove, "'Bearing the Marks of Christ's Passion': Aquinas' Soteriology," in *The Theology of Thomas Aquinas*, eds. Rik Van Nieuwenhove and JosephWawrykow (Notre Dame, IN: University of Notre Dame Press, 2005), 277–302, at 277. Van Nieuwenhove's entry here overlaps with and expands upon an earlier essay, "St Anselm and St Thomas Aquinas on 'Satisfaction': Or how Catholic and Protestant Understandings of the Cross Differ," *Angelicum* 80 (2003): 159–76.
67. Van Nieuwenhove, "Bearing the Marks of Christ's Passion," 278.

vation, that is, the highest and culminating moment of God's salvific action within human affairs. But his critics' evaluations raise the question of whether such a role grants Jesus Christ a sufficient place within God's plan of salvation.

Balthasar's worry is that for Rahner, God is always already reconciled to humanity; rather than being humanity's "representative" (a role which, in his judgment, would impede on Rahner's particular and mistaken notion of human freedom), Christ is one man among many humans who is not essentially different from them. His role consists of standing as the prime instance of—and thus, grand announcement about—a larger ongoing process in which humans are being saved by God's grace. Unlike a schema of "representation," such a role falls woefully short of deeming Christ the constitutive *sine qua non* of human salvation.[68]

Two other theologians, Guy Mansini and George Vass, produce critical evaluations which resemble and explicitly cite that of Balthasar. Mansini judges that Rahner's "sacramental" theory of the cross's salvific efficacy only grants a "restrained" level of causality, that event of Christ's death is, for Rahner, a mere "demonstration," and that Rahner "jettison[s]" any notion of Christ "representing" humanity. Vass echoes Balthasar in lamenting the lack of any dramatic element in Rahner's soteriology, precisely in his rejection of any "representative" action on the part of Christ, who is merely the locus at which an inevitable, preordained divine plan unfolds as a matter of course. For both Vass and Mansini, the role which Christ plays in Rahner's account human salvation is rather thin, for he fails to "represent" us and functions more or less as a display board which notifies us of God's loving will being carried out.

Also similar to Balthasar (though to a lesser degree), the ITC suggests that for Rahner, Christ merely *expresses* something (namely, the grace of salvation and fellowship with God) which is already available through God's universally operative salvific will. Again, the role of Christ extracted from Rahner's work seems, more than anything else, to be that of "notifier." The ITC also portrays (though less explicitly that Balthasar does) Rahner and "representative" Christology as inhabiting paradigms distinct from one another. And once again, the under-

---

68. Cf. Balthasar's remark about Rahner's God "who-is-always-reconciled": "This does not mean that the perfect Yes to God on the part of the man Jesus is *the condition without which* neither the world nor *salvation would be possible*" (*TD* 4:276, emphasis added).

lying worry appears to be that "expressing" salvation seems like a rather weak role for the constitutive Savior.

Finally, Schubert Ogden (along with J.T. Farmer) explicitly identifies Rahner's Christology as lacking an authentic "constitutive" identity. According to Ogden, Rahner's exchange of Christ's "efficient" causative role (typically associated with staurocentric satisfaction and substitution theories of atonement) for a "final" and "sacramental" causality ends up rendering Christ a kind of "norm" for human salvation: any "constitutive" dimension seems to exist in name only, a dimension desired by Rahner, which his Christology and soteriology never end up fulfilling. Van Nieuwenhove goes even further, saying that in his desire to move away from classical cross-centered soteriologies, Rahner (and many other contemporary Catholic theologians) has left the cross bereft of any salvific significance at all.

There are two major issues which surface repeatedly in these evaluations, the first of which concerns the "constitutive" vs. "normative" distinction. While only Ogden and Farmer raise the issue of whether Christ is for Rahner in fact (and not just in desire) constitutive of salvation, at the heart of each of these objections is a concern that Christ is not the *sine qua non* of salvation. While Jesus may exemplify, notify, and express God's salvation within the world, it is not clear, especially given Rahner's supposed distaste for talk of Christ as "representative," that if the Christ-event[69] never occurred, neither would human salvation. Rahner's Christology and soteriology thus fail to live up to the "christocentric" descriptor which is so often applied to him.

The second main concern involves the notion of Christ's "representing" the entire human family. Balthasar, Vass, and (though to a lesser extent) the ITC all, though to various degrees, envision such representation in "dramatic" categories centering on a discrete, particular *act* performed by Christ in our stead, undergoing the alienation from God properly due to the rest of us. Since Rahner eschews this latter kind of dramatic, act-centered vision of reconciliation via proxy, his soteriology is presented in juxtaposition to the broad category of representation.

---

69. By this term, I wish to indicate the entirety of Christ's incarnation, life, death, and resurrection.

Symbol and Sacrament:
The Standard Classification of
Rahner's Christology and Soteriology

The criticisms above, directed toward a very influential theologian, have certainly not gone unnoticed. Several of them have received explicit, published responses which defend a profound and meaningful place for Christ in Rahner's understanding of human salvation. The standard method by which such apologies are conducted shares a particular evaluation with the criticisms: Rahner's Christology and soteriology are best classified according to the category of symbol and/or sacrament. But while Rahner's critics go on to portray sacramental or symbolic causality as weak and ineffectual, his advocates describe it in far different terms: Christ, the *Realsymbol* and *Ursakrament* is the nexus point of God's self-communication to the world. In other words, the broad apologetic strategy is to accuse Rahner's critics of underestimating the value of positing Christ as the primordial Sacrament of salvation.

Sympathetic Synopses: Edwards and Ryan

Though neither is an apology for Rahner, two of the most succinct and accessible accounts of his soteriology can be found in Denis Edwards's *What Are They Saying About Salvation?*[70] and Robin Ryan's recent *Jesus and Salvation*.[71] Both works address various theologies of salvation from biblical and historical perspectives, and subsequently, focus on accounts of a more recent vintage, including that of Karl Rahner. Let us consider each.

Edwards follows a common approach to explaining Rahner, beginning with some of the early philosophical claims made by Rahner about the *anthropos* drawn from *Spirit in the World* (1939)[72] and *Hearer of the Word* (1941)[73] in order to introduce his later, properly theological work. Without naming it, Edwards makes reference in this introduction to

---

70. Denis Edwards, *What Are They Saying About Salvation?* (New York: Paulist Press, 1986).
71. Robin Ryan, *Jesus and Salvation: Soundings in the Christian Tradition and Contemporary Theology* (Collegeville, MN: Liturgical, 2015).
72. *Spirit in the World* (New York: Continuum, 1994). Originally published as *Geist in Welt: Zur Metaphysik der endlichen Erkenntnis bei Thomas von Aquin* (Innsbruck: Rauch, 1939).
73. *Hearer of the Word: Laying the Foundation for a Philosophy of Religion* (New York: Continuum, 1994). Originally published as *Hörer des Wortes: Zur Grundlegung einer Religionsphilosophie* (München: Kösel, 1941).

Rahner's *Vorgriff*, a term which is notoriously difficult to translate (often "pre-apprehension").[74] The act of knowing finite and limited things occurs, he explains, "along with, or over against, an implicit awareness of the whole range of being that is without limits. We know specific objects against an horizon of infinite mystery."[75] While we do not "grasp" (*greifen*) or have a grasp (*Griff*) upon this infinite, mysterious horizon which exists as the background against which all finite entities are known, we do encounter it in an anticipatory mode of approach through our (even daily) acts of cognition. This relationship to the undergirding, infinite horizon provides a basis for speaking of the human person as "self-transcendent," as a finite creature within the world which is nevertheless oriented and even called toward an existence fully enveloped by Mystery itself, which Rahner identifies as God.

God's offer of salvation, Edwards explains, is for Rahner an offer of nothing less than God's very self through the gift of grace. God's self-offer in grace is ever present through what Rahner calls the "supernatural existential," an invitation toward creaturely participation in God's own life.[76] Sin consists in the rejection of this offer, while salvation is realized through its reception. Such reception (and rejection) of this transcendental offer occurs through and is expressed by our free, historical, and day-to-day acts and choices. Rahner thus, on occasion, even speaks of "self-redemption," signaling not a Pelagian account of salvation apart from grace, but rather, our grace-driven appropriation of "objective redemption" brought about by God—in particular, through Jesus Christ.[77]

Edwards is clear that for Rahner, such appropriation does not consist of merely aspiring to model oneself after an exemplar Christ whose only impact upon us comes by way of "moral influence." An alternative and more robust notion of Christ's salvific causality exists for Rahner's Christ.[78] Moreover, the idea in the popular imagination of Christ's death propitiating God's wrath by somehow altering his mind and will is *not* a viable candidate for such an alternative. Instead, the causal

---

74. For an extended and careful treatment of this term in light of Rahner's theological aesthetics, see the dissertation of Peter J. Fritz, *Sublime Apprehension: A Catholic, Rahnerian Construction*, Diss., University of Notre Dame, 2010, revised and published as *Karl Rahner's Theological Aesthetics* (Washington D.C.: Catholic University of America Press, 2014).
75. Edwards, *What Are They Saying About Salvation?*, 19.
76. Ibid.
77. Ibid., 24.
78. Ibid., 23–25.

impact which Christ has upon our salvation, Edwards explains, is, for Karl Rahner, that of a primal Sacrament.

Rahner's "basic thesis" is that Christ's "death and resurrection are connected to the salvation of all men and women by way of sacramental causality. . . . The cross is a sacramental cause of our salvation in that it is the sign and the mediation of God's salvation. It is the sign of the 'victorious and irreversible' saving activity of God in our world."[79] Edwards makes two main points in this summary of Rahner's "sacramental" soteriology. The first is that as the *Realsymbol* (Edwards uses this German term as an equivalent for "sacrament") of God's salvific grace, the Christ-event, especially the Paschal Mystery, is at once *caused by* grace and the *cause of* grace, in different respects. Insofar as his life and identity perfectly express and unveil God's Reign within the world, Christ the sacrament is *caused by* and has its origin in God's grace.[80] But with respect to *us*, to whom Christ mediates the grace which he embodies in its temporal fullness, Christ the primal sacrament is the *cause of* grace which, like other sacraments, causes precisely that which it signifies or symbolizes. The entire life of Jesus, the *Realsymbol* of salvation, perfectly signifies God's grace; moreover, this life is "recapitulated" and "fulfilled" in Jesus's "free acceptance of death" and his glorious resurrection.[81]

The second point which Edwards makes is that as God's *Realsymbol* or primal Sacrament, Jesus has rendered God's saving will "irrevocable" within the world. The whole of salvation history, he explains, is marked by a kind of "ambivalence," but God chooses "to give concrete and irreversible expression in history to divine saving love." That is, God chooses "to give fixed historical form to the universal will to save" in Jesus Christ, who fully accepts (including *and especially* in his death) God's self-offer.[82]

Although it does not engage in any defense of Rahner, Edwards's account offers resources for answering criticisms that Rahner's Christ exists merely as a "notification" to the world that God is enacting human salvation. If *Realsymbol* or "sacrament" were to be understood simply as a shallow "sign," such a criticism would have merit. However, as the primal sacrament, Christ does not only signify, but *causes* in the

---

79. Ibid., 26.
80. "Jesus had preached the saving nearness of God, and he had claimed that this reign of God was identified with his own person. . . . The resurrection shows that Jesus is indeed the final and unsurpassable self-disclosure of God. He is the absolute Savior" (ibid., 25).
81. Ibid., 27.
82. Ibid.

very act of signifying. Edwards's account of Rahner's "sacramental" soteriology identifies the Christ-event as the primal means by which God's grace is communicated to the world. As such, Jesus's life, death, and resurrection stand as no mere notification of God's salvific action, but rather, is its very conduit.

Robin Ryan's overview of Rahner's soteriology, though likewise suc- cinct, is more expansive than Edwards's treatment. Though he does not use the term "supernatural existential," Ryan mirrors Edwards in beginning his overview with this idea, talking about God's universal self-offer in grace to every human being. Since human beings are not simply spirit but "a unity of spirit in matter," God's self-offer to human beings "is incarnational, even before Christ because it becomes tangi- ble, especially in the people, history, and teachings of Israel."[83] This incarnational "tendency" was directed from the outset, even before sin, toward God's personal incarnation in Jesus, which is "God's gift of Self to us in the most personal way in our human history." As Ryan explains, the reason that Rahner follows Scotus, rather than Thomas Aquinas, on this question of sin and incarnation has to do with the "Greek patristic tradition," which Rahner draws upon as he "argues that ultimately salvation means participation in the life of God."[84] Although he does not explore Rahner's connection to the fathers any further, as we will do in later chapters, Ryan's choice to frame Rahner's Christology with this patristic, incarnational rationale makes a crucial historical connection that is missed by many of Rahner's other com- mentators. For Rahner, salvation is, by definition, realized in the pres- ence of God, given in grace, and so, the ultimate Gift of grace is an inextricable part of the story of the salvation from the outset of cre- ation.

Ryan proceeds to discuss the salvific value of Jesus's ministry, death, and resurrection. Jesus's ministry is characterized by his repeated insistence on the advent of God's Reign, a point that Rahner makes in company with historical critical scholars. Once again mentioning (but not exploring) a point that will emerge repeatedly in this book, Ryan characterizes Rahner's description of this Reign not simply as Jesus's "notification" of an extrinsic occurrence, but rather, as the "nearness of the reign of God [as] inseparably connected with his person."[85] Turn-

83. Ryan, *Jesus and Salvation*, 102.
84. Ibid., 103. In a later chapter, Ryan briefly returns to this connection to the Fathers, noting Rah- ner's appeal to "the patristic language of 'divinization'" (161).
85. Ibid., 104–5. Ryan immediately follows this statement with a quotation from *FCF*, 254, in which Rahner writes that Jesus is "the one who inaugurates the kingdom of God through what he says

ing to Jesus's death, and Rahner's theology of death and freedom in general, Ryan describes Rahner's theology of the cross in sacramental terms: "Rahner views the death of Jesus as the paradigmatic instance of right dying and the means of the transformation of death. Jesus makes a choice for the Father in the face of the darkness of his passion. This choice sums up his life of freedom, of complete self-disposal before God."[86] Not only does Jesus's particular death stand as a kind of symbolic paradigm for death in general, but it "sums up" and mediates his entire life's choices into a single moment, in which Jesus commends his spirit into the Father's hands (Luke 23:46). This finalizing act of self-disposal, in which Jesus's own freedom is entirely oriented toward God the Father, subsumes Jesus's death into discussion of a renewed life—termed "resurrection," the eschatological victory in which God's grace enables one's permanent and fulfilled freedom.

But how does the story of this one, paradigmatic human impact the rest of us? As he concludes, Ryan, like Edwards, explicitly appeals to "sacramental causality" as a way of explaining what Christ has done "for us." Classically, sacraments are understood to "cause" grace through signifying—as Ryan puts it, grace is "symbolled forth." Jesus's death and resurrection effect and communicate God's grace in precisely this way—this singular moment stands as the sacramental cause of the grace operative throughout the world, which Jesus establishes "irrevocably." As he concludes his treatment, Ryan notes that the communication of Christ's grace, which coincides with and is attained by the fullest operation of our own freedom, entails a profound relationship between the believer and Jesus, "in whom and in whom alone immediacy to God is reached now and forever."[87]

Like that of Edwards, Ryan's account is not explicitly apologetic, but it contains resources within it for responding to Rahner's critics. Ryan incorporates Edwards's insight about a robust sense of sacramental causality into his own, but he supplements it with several important points. First, he marks out a rarely drawn line between Rahner's soteriology and that of the Greek fathers. Salvation consists of God's immediate presence rather than simply the forgiveness of sins, an insight which is just a step away from seeing where critiques such as Balthasar's fall short. God's sacramental self-communication in Jesus

and what he does in a way that it did not exist before, but now and does exist *through* him and *in* him" (emphasis original).
86. Ibid., 106.
87. *FCF*, 309, quoted in Ryan, *Jesus and Salvation*, 109.

is not simply about notifying the world about what God is up to and what salvation looks like, but rather, about making God present to the world itself—and by definition, saving it. As Ryan explains, Rahner's Jesus does not simply *announce* God's Reign as a discrete act; he *inaugurates* it in his own person, inviting others as he "symbols forth" God's salvific presence in his ministry, death, and resurrection. As the believer freely responds to God's self-offer, she becomes intrinsically related to the one who made such an offer "irrevocable." These insights, which Ryan mentions but does not elaborate upon in his excellent, brief synopsis, will become centrally featured elements of my own account of Rahner's soteriology. In particular, what I will call the "person-centered" (rather than "act-centered") dimension of Rahner's soteriological role for Christ provides a rich way for constructing a notion of *pro nobis* "representation" which stands as a Rahnerian alternative to Balthasar's *Stellvertretung* that "extends as far as substitution."

A Detailed Study and Defense: Joseph Wong

Perhaps the most thorough and authoritative treatment of Rahner's sacramental Christology and soteriology is Joseph Wong's *Logos-Symbol in the Christology of Karl Rahner*, a revision of his dissertation to which Rahner himself, in his last years, wrote the foreword.[88] In it, Wong explores the origins, workings, and potential utilizations which lie latent within Rahner's idea of *das Realsymbol*, which Wong describes as the "joint concept of a 'sacrament-symbol.'"[89] Wong's insight is that the sacrament-symbol is particularly useful for organizing Rahner's various, disparate, and somewhat *ad hoc* christological writings. In particular, he says that Christ as *das Realsymbol* helps us to understand how Rahner (contrary to the ITC's portrayal above) conducts a profound Christology both from above (the Christ-event as the definitive final Word of the Father *to* the world) and from below (the Christ event as the "self-realization" of the "Son-Saviour" *in* the world). Wong's book also explicitly responds to Balthasar's critique.[90]

Rather than beginning with a "foundational" consideration of Rahner's philosophical underpinnings for portraying Christ as the primal sacrament, Wong identifies Rahner's Ignatian spirituality as the basis

---

88. Joseph H. Wong, *Logos-Symbol in the Christology of Karl Rahner* (Rome: LAS, 1984).
89. Ibid., 34
90. Ibid., 158. Wong describes this two-fold movement accordingly: "The process of God's gradual entry into history reaches its summit in the mystery of the incarnation" (ibid., 157).

for his sacramental Christology (as well as for his sacramental world-view).[91] Following Ignatius of Loyola's call to find God in all things, Rahner's fundamental "mystical insight" is that "God is always mediated through created realities, especially through people and events."[92] But the finite realities which mediate God are, for Rahner, organized so as to depend on (insofar as they flow both from and toward) a single, definitive communication of grace to the world. Wong explains, "If for [St. Ignatius] things of the world are 'sacraments', then Christ is the *primordial* sacrament of encounter with God." Thus, the "sacramental-symbolic" structure of divine–human relationship is, at its core, an "incarnational structure."[93] Rahner's christocentric sacramental imagination is especially active, Wong argues, in his early writings about Jesus's Sacred Heart, which "is a sacramental symbol which effects by signifying (*significando efficit*). It is the incarnation, or realization in human form, of divine love."[94] It is only after these considerations about Rahner's spirituality that Wong goes on to examine the philosophical underpinnings of *das Realsymbol*.[95] Here, Wong's overview is in basic agreement with that of Edwards, as it builds toward Rahner's affirmation of God himself as the "whither" of the *Vorgriff*.

Much of Wong's monograph is organized according to considerations of Rahner's sacramental Christology in its "from above" and "from below" dimensions.[96] Wong introduces the former through an explanation of "symbolic causality," for which Rahner elsewhere uses the synonym "quasi-formal actuation."[97] Rahner is bothered by a common supposition that Jesus's divinity and humanity are only related to one another "extrinsically," as two disparate realities which have been married in the incarnation. A better account of the relationship

91. Following Gustavo Gutiérrez, I use "spirituality" in this book to refer to a way of life, specifically that of "following Jesus," which flows from one's encounter with the Triune God (*We Drink from Our Own Wells: The Spiritual Journey of a People* (Maryknoll: Orbis, 1984), 1–3, 33–37. Similarly, Richard P. McBrien defines Christian spirituality as "Life in the Holy Spirit who incorporates the Christian into the Body of Jesus Christ, through whom the Christian has access to God the Creator in a life of faith, hope, love, and service" (*Catholicism*, New ed., completely rev. and updated (San Francisco: HarperSanFrancisco, 1994), 1251).
92. Ibid., 47. This sacramental worldview accords with the Ignatian insight that "[p]recisely because God is 'really above the whole world' and not merely its 'dialectical antithesis', he is also found *in the world*" ("The Ignatian Mysticism of Joy in the World" (1937) in *TI* 3:277–93 at 291, cited in Wong, *Logos-Symbol*, 105).
93. Wong, *Logos-Symbol*, 56
94. Ibid., 67–68.
95. Ibid., 82–98.
96. Cf. Rahner's own statement, "There is an ascending Christology (proceeding from the human being Jesus) which coincides with the classical descending Christology (God becomes a human being)" ("Jesus Christ—The Meaning of Life," *TI* 21:208–219, at 218).
97. Wong, *Logos-Symbol*, 129ff.

between Christ's two natures (as defined by Chalcedon) mirrors that of the body and the soul. According to the classical hylomorphism which dominates the Catholic tradition (especially after Thomas Aquinas), the soul is not a ghost within a body moving it like a machine, but rather, is the very form of the body itself. That is, the soul operates upon the body by way of formal causality; the body, as Wong explains it, may even be thought of as a type of "emanation" of the soul. Unlike efficient causality (a cause producing a consequence, or effecting a product), formal causality posits an intrinsic relation between the body and the soul.[98]

Rahner thus seeks to implement this sort of "intrinsic" relation within his Christology by suggesting that Christ's humanity simply *is* the "emanation" of the divine Logos within the world of time and space. However, Rahner feels compelled to add the prefix of "quasi" to this relationship of formal causality, not to weaken the intrinsic relation, but to qualify the "automatic" element of this causality (e.g., the body *must* "emanate" from the soul) in order to guard the freedom of the transcendent Logos's act of becoming incarnate.[99] This is all to say that, conducting Christology "from above," Jesus Christ is *das Realsymbol* or primal sacrament of God in the world; when the Logos freely "self-exteriorizes," the incarnate Son is what occurs.

The "from below" counterpart of Rahner's Christology (which, Wong notes, after 1968, he focused upon most heavily[100]) also involves the idea of Christ as symbol-sacrament, in that this approach consists of demonstrating (*not* deducing),[101] through the use of Rahner's transcendental method, that the human person is a possible *Symbol* for the Logos, that is, potentially *the* appropriate bearer of God's self-exteriorization. (It is this component of Rahner's Christology that Rahner's critics, especially Balthasar, have honed in upon.)

Rahner begins to unfold this "transcendental" approach to Christology with anthropological considerations. In particular, he focuses upon the human person's radical "openness to God," a prompting which resides deep within free human persons that points them beyond themselves. This orientation toward "self-transcendence" gives us a

---

98. Ibid., 129–30.
99. Ibid., 131. Paul Molnar remains unconvinced that Rahner's desire to protect God's freedom with such a qualifier actually succeeds, calling the distinction "spurious" and accusing Rahner of a kind of "emanationism" ("Can we know God directly? Rahner's solution from experience," in *Theological Studies* 46, no. 2 (1985), 228–61, at 231–32, cf. n. 15).
100. Wong, *Logos-Symbol*, 35–36.
101. Ibid., 106, 109, 132, 230–31.

real desire (though not an unconditional demand) for grace, which is, for Rahner, the indwelling of the Spirit, or God's very self-gift to us. Almost all of human existence, Wong explains, consists of our actions which, whether we know it or not, respond (either positively or negatively) to this call (termed the "supernatural existential") to self-transcendent fellowship with God. With this anthropological background in place, Rahner can introduce Christology as *perfected* anthropology. For in Jesus Christ, this call-and-response phenomenon occurs flawlessly. In Jesus's life, death, and resurrection, we observe the perfect expression of the human affirmative response to God's invitation to fellowship; in Jesus and his "Yes!" to God, the human person achieves absolute fulfillment.[102]

Rahner thus speaks frequently of Jesus Christ as the "culmination" of humanity, indeed, a sort of "prime-instance." As such, Jesus is indeed an indicator of what human life ought to be, and what it can be. As Wong summarizes, "If man in his infinite openness is conceived as possible symbol of God, in his turn the God-Man as the 'absolute Saviour' is the sign or symbol of man's definitive salvation."[103] Jesus offers us a glimpse into fulfilled human existence and, standing at the end or *telos* of a journey which he (as fully human) shares with us, beckons us toward participation in his "way" through the supernatural existential call to grace that resides within each of our own hearts.

While accurate, this portrayal of Christ's soteriological role addresses only one part of Rahner's vision. Though he is certainly the "prime-instance" of humanity, Jesus is, for Rahner, the primordial *Sacrament* of human salvation. For Rahner, the idea of *das Symbol* is too profound to be reduced to a sign, the role of which is indicative; rather, his theology is built upon the "joint-concept" of the "sacrament-symbol." And so, like Edwards, Wong underlines how Christ is not merely a sign of God's salvation, but a sign that *brings about* ("realizes") what it signifies ("manifests"). Such a sign is, by classical definition, a sacrament.

The Christ-event is a sacrament which "signifies something precisely by rendering it present and renders present by signifying."[104] In emphasizing this point, Wong specifically raises Balthasar's critique of Rahner's soteriology; for taking seriously the sacramental nature of Christ's incarnation, life, death and resurrection exposes a false

102. Ibid., 133.
103. Ibid., 135.
104. Ibid., 161.

dichotomy at the root of Balthasar's evaluation. "Balthasar's objection that according to Rahner man owes his redemption not to the historical event of Christ's death but to the always effective saving will of God, is based on a misunderstanding of Rahner's view of 'sacramental-symbolic causality.'"[105] The either-or opposition between God's universally operative saving will and the Christ-event dissolves when one posits the latter as *das Realsymbol* of the former, related to it not by means of an extrinsic pairing, but rather, intrinsic self-expression. In other words, Jesus Christ is the primordial Sacrament of, and *by which we receive*, God's salvation, for "the saving will of God is 'always effective' precisely *in view* of the event of Christ, both proleptically and retrospectively."[106]

Before exploring how Balthasar's critique overlooked the implications of Rahner's account of sacramental causality, Wong touched on a similar point earlier in the monograph:

> the soteriological function of the absolute Saviour is rooted in his "quasi-sacramental causality as sign." . . . [A]s a sacramental sign, the absolute Saviour both *manifests* and *realizes* in the concrete God's saving will on man's behalf. . . . [T]he absolute Saviour is the symbol of the saving God offered to man through the Logos who is the 'historical expressibility' (*geschichtliche Aussagbarkeit*) of the Father's fidelity.[107]

Although the contents of these sentences, to a large degree, just reiterate the point about Christ's sacramental salvific efficacy already discussed, Wong includes one clause which is particularly interesting—namely, "on man's behalf." Unfortunately, Wong does not expound upon this remark, but the suggestion that Rahner's Christ, as the primordial sacrament, brings about God's salvation on behalf of humanity appears to affirm some kind of representative role for Christ in Rahner's soteriology.

It is important to consider what sort of representative role Wong might see for Christ within Rahner's theological writings. For although Wong does not explicitly explore the representative category (even in relationship to Balthasar's critique, in which the term surfaces sev-

---

105. Ibid., 242.
106. Ibid. Wong continues, "[W]hen one understands properly the concept of quasi-sacramental causality, one can say that man owes his redemption to the eternal saving will of the Father and, at the same time, to Christ the Saviour. He is the 'primordial Sacrament of salvation', inasmuch as he freely and effectively constitutes the 'historically irreversible saving *situation for all*" (ibid., 242–43, emphasis original).
107. Ibid., 138.

eral times), a genuine representative component to Rahner's Christology and soteriology would serve not only to refute a pervasive theme within Balthasar's critical evaluation, but to illuminate precisely *how* Rahner envisions Christ, *as* Realsymbol *and primal Sacrament*, to communicate God's grace.

It is quite clear that by "on man's behalf," Rahner does not mean that Christ sacramentally realizes God's salvation in such a way that we are rendered passive spectators; "on man's behalf" does not signify "our substitute." (As Balthasar emphatically notes, Rahner so values our participation in human salvation that he even speaks of "self-redemption.") Understanding this, Wong's use of "on man's behalf" to describe Christ's sacramental soteriological role seems to reflect a different understanding of "representative"—namely, that it is only through an intimate relationship to *this One* that salvation is attained.

Wong's reading of Rahner is that Christ, the primordial Sacrament, has definitively communicated God's salvific grace to the world, but we, as free humans, must also *receive* this communication. As Wong puts it, "man's salvation consists in freely appropriating this saving 'situation' through a life-long 'conformation' to the death of Christ. . . . [T]he absolute Savior is the symbol-prototype of the redeemed man."[108] Let us consider these words more closely. The importance of (especially Christ's) *death*, for Rahner, as the summative act of human freedom will be addressed more thoroughly in subsequent chapters, so we will set aside a detailed treatment of that matter for now. The claim articulates two soteriological functions for Christ. The first is sacramental: the Christ-event establishes a new saving "situation" of grace into which we can enter. The second is "prototypical": Christ lives (and dies) a way to which we "conform." The link between the two is that entering into or appropriating the saving situation consists in our act of conformation. Once again, the criticisms of Christ functioning as a mere "prime instance" underestimate the first "sacramental" function of Christ here described, reducing Rahner's soteriological vision to the second one. But Wong hints at an even more profound dimension to this vision of Christ bringing about salvation as both symbol-sacrament and prototype.

Referring to this dual role earlier, Wong writes, "Rahner views the absolute Saviour as the prototype or symbol of true human existence," and thus, "Christ is really sought after and encountered in the actual

108. Ibid., 172.

living out of one's human existence, even if one is not aware of it."[109] Here, Wong indicates that Christ does not merely *bring about* a saving situation which we appropriate by imitation, but that our act of "appropriation" is really one of seeking and encountering Christ. One might even say that Christ himself *is* the "saving 'situation'" into which we enter. Drawing out threads within Wong's account of Rahner in this way, we are faced with a Rahnerian soteriology which is heavily relational in character, as Ryan explicitly noted. "On man's behalf" can thus mean that Christ not only creates the "saving 'situation'" for us, but, as the "Sought" of human existence, he actually *constitutes* that "situation"; the act of "appropriating" salvation thus becomes one of more intimately relating to *the Savior*.

Additional "Sacramental" Readings: Vorgrimler and Mulcahy

Rahner's longtime friend and student Herbert Vorgrimler offers an analysis of Rahner's soteriology in his *Karl Rahner: Gotteserfahrung in Leben und Denken*.[110] Focusing on Rahner's late essay, "The Christian Understanding of Redemption" (1981), Vorgrimler offers an exposition of Rahner's soteriology and defends it against its detractors. In doing so, he takes up many of the same themes treated by Edwards and Wong.

The first major point which Vorgrimler stresses is the centrality of human freedom to Rahner's soteriology. He writes that "Rahner anchored the theme of redemption so much in the context of human freedom that the difference between self-redemption and redemption 'from outside' is dissolved."[111] This is because for Rahner, "redemption does not circumvent human freedom, but is rather 'the fullness of this freedom itself.'"[112] Human freedom itself is a gift from God and does not act in opposition, but rather, in and through God's grace, given ultimately in Christ.

Like Ryan, Vorgrimler also notes that Rahner refrains from couching his soteriology first and foremost within the context of human sin and the subsequent debt to God, as has often been the case for Christian theology done in the West. "Rahner refuses to adopt the pessimistic soteriological-anthropological pathos which spanned from Augustine to the Reformation mentality, in which 'the remission of the damning

109. Ibid., 140.
110. Herbert Vorgrimler, "Soteriologie," in *Karl Rahner: Gotteserfahrung in Leben und Denken* (Darmstadt: Primus, 2004), 218–22.
111. Ibid., 219.
112. Ibid., 218.

debt' was felt to be the overall leitmotif of Christianity."[113] This is not to say that Rahner fails to recognize the "absurd darkness of the world," but rather that, for him, the answer *to* that darkness is best understood not in terms of paying a debt with blood, but that "God must become the justified human; what one calls guilt and sin, is to be understood in a world of becoming (rather than event of friction) as a detour in their development."[114] Salvation is the story, full of twists and turns, of humanity coming to full, free development—a story the center of which is God *becoming* this developed human.[115]

Next, Vorgrimler addresses Rahner's assessment of traditional soteriologies, noting his distaste for Anselmian satisfaction theory and the commonly associated idea of Jesus's vicarious-representative [*stellvertretenden*] suffering. According to a common "false understanding" of such an idea, Vorgrimler explains, "it is assumed that Jesus did something in the place [*anstelle*] of other people, something which only he – and not the others – could do."[116] In Rahner's view, Jesus does not "do what I was supposed to do," but makes it possible for us to freely aspire to God in faith, hope, and love. Vorgrimler also notes Rahner's reservations about the popular idea that in dying on the cross, Jesus "changed the mind" of an angry God. On the contrary, Rahner is confident "that the entire history of humanity is engaged from the outset by the merciful love of God."[117]

Finally, Vorgrimler turns to Rahner's critics, naming Balthasar in particular. "There is for Rahner, contrary to the accusation made in bad faith by von Balthasar, a theology of the cross, but it does not stand under a sadistic, masochistic sign. Rahner has also refused to place his theology of the cross under the sign of Jesus' abandonment by God, a move made by von Balthasar and others; Rahner designates the view that Jesus – who devoutly prayed Psalm 22 on the cross – died forsaken by God, as false."[118] Interestingly, Vorgrimler grants a reading of Rahner shared by Rahner's detractors, writing that for Rahner, "the cross is . . . not a reconciliation with God which would not have come about without the cross."[119]

---

113. Ibid., 220.
114. Ibid.
115. This characterization of Rahner's soteriology, reminiscent of Irenaeus's own anthropology, soteriology, and Christology, anticipates a major theme which, while not elaborated upon by Vorgrimler, will be analyzed throughout this book.
116. Ibid., 221.
117. Ibid., 222.
118. Ibid.
119. Ibid. A more accurate statement, I would suggest, is that for Rahner, God's saving will for recon-

Vorgrimler closes his treatment by introducing Rahner's sacramental theology of *das Realsymbol* as Rahner's way of "hold[ing] on absolutely to the traditional beliefs that 'salvation is in the cross' and that the cross is 'the cause of our salvation.'"[120] This is because with *das Realsymbol*, a "relationship of mutual condition exists between 'sign' and 'cause.' The cross of Jesus Christ is 'the effective sign of God's salvific will in the world'. . . . Simply said: The cross brings the previously existing cause of the cross to salvific efficacy. It would thus be an injustice to say of Rahner that for him, the cross is 'only' a sign."[121] Thus, Vorgrimler says in harmony with the other sympathizers considered thus far, those who criticize the cross's salvific efficacy in Rahner's soteriology underestimate the robust sacramental causality posited in his theory of *das Realsymbol*.

It should be noted that, like Wong and Ryan, Vorgrimler touches briefly on themes which will be developed in this book. In his opening statement in "Soteriologie," Vorgrimler writes, "Much of what was contained in the earlier dogmatic manuals as 'soteriology,' following upon 'Christology,' can be found in Rahner's work where he treats Christology, the Trinity, and God's self-communication. This is because he cannot separate the 'being' and 'work' of Christ from one another."[122]

Eamonn Mulcahy's revised dissertation, *The Cause of Our Salvation*, focuses upon the soteriology of four late-twentieth-century British theologians.[123] Nevertheless, his summary of Karl Rahner's Christology and soteriology is important to Mulcahy's work, since one of his major conclusions is that the soteriologies of these British (Protestant and Anglican) figures would have greatly benefited from dialogue with that of Rahner (among other Catholic thinkers),[124] specifically on the issue of symbolic causality (a category which, in Mulcahy's judgment, is the most promising direction for contemporary accounts of how Christ causes our salvation).[125] In fact, Mulcahy wagers that "the most satisfactory answer to this question [of how a saving event in the past can have a transformative effect today] lies along the lines of sym-

ciliation *does not originate with the cross*, though full reconciliation between a sinful world and God will inextricably involve this event.
120. Ibid.
121. Ibid.
122. Ibid., 218, cf. "Brief Observations in Systematic Christology Today," in *TI* 21:228–38, at 233–34.
123. Eamonn Mulcahy, *The Cause of Our Salvation: Soteriological Causality according to some Modern British Theologians 1988-1998* (Rome: Gregorian Univ. Press, 2007).
124. Ibid., 22–23.
125. Ibid., 398.

bolic causality, where a symbol renders present the reality signified."[126] In order to begin exploring this concept, Mulcahy turns to Rahner, according to whom, "soteriology has to turn to another field of theology to borrow a concept of causality . . . namely sacramental theology."[127] Thus, following the pattern we have seen, Mulcahy categorizes Rahner's soteriology as one rooted in the idea of sacrament.

Much of Mulcahy's assessment of Rahner includes ground already covered above. For instance, he acknowledges that for Rahner, Christ should not be said to "cause" God's salvific will as if his death somehow "provoked" it or changed God's mind; rather, if Christ and his cross are saving (and Rahner wants to affirm that they are!), they are *the results* (rather than the origin) of God's desire to save.[128] Claims about Jesus's life and death "causing" salvation are better handled in sacramental terms: Christ causes by signifying.

This is not to "reduce the cross to a merely revelatory event of God's forgiving love as in Abelard's alleged exemplarist theory,"[129] as some of Rahner's critics might have it. Although Christ and his cross "*evoke* in those who behold it the acceptance of a grace always readily available," Christ's "revealing" and "signifying" do not, according to Rahner, save by means of raising "awareness."[130] Rather, in the case of the "real symbol," the reality signified comes to be through the sign, which can even be said to "cause" the (prior) reality within the world.[131]

However, as he concludes his treatment of it, Mulcahy categorizes Rahner's soteriology as "demonstrative," rather than "effective." He elaborates, saying that "the cross does not *provoke* or *produce* any effect (such as expiation or satisfaction or reconciliation), but *evidences*, *shows*, *reveals* something. For Rahner, strikingly, the cross does not produce salvation nor obtain redemption. The cross does not *do* anything at all! It discloses."[132] In this passage, it seems that Mulcahy overstates his case (although he appends a footnote in which Rahner declares Christ to be the "*signum efficax* . . . the efficacious sign of God's salvific will in the world"). A thoroughly sacramental theology like Rahner's

---

126. Ibid.
127. Ibid., 399.
128. Ibid., 398.
129. Ibid., 399–400.
130. Ibid., 400.
131. Ibid.,400–401. This same basic move for defending Rahner against such criticisms can be found in Mark Lowery, "Retrieving Rahner for Orthodox Catholic Catholicism," *Faith & Reason* 17, no. 3 (1991), 251–72. Lowery sees such a defense as more easily accessible in Rahner's writings on *Real-symbol* and less so in his later works, especially *FCF*, 272n44.
132. Mulcahy, *The Cause of Our Salvation*, 401, emphasis original.

does not allow for an either/or dichotomy between categories such as "demonstrative" and "effective," as the term *signum efficax* itself suggests. That Mulcahy seems to understand the unity of the two in sacramental causality makes this categorization all the more puzzling. Nevertheless, the most important categorization which Mulcahy makes consists of his decision to situate Rahner's account of Christ as Savior in clearly sacramental terms.

Mulcahy's treatment of Rahner in his sixth chapter is complemented by a constructive component. In this "modest soteriological proposition," Mulcahy proposes a soteriology which (like Rahner's) focuses on the *whole* of the Christ-event as a counterweight to what he views as tradition overemphasis on Jesus's passion and death—in doing so, he "attempt[s] to elaborate a «relational» soteriology of *communio* based on a *transformational* model of atonement, in the key of a *symbolic* causality."[133] While his own constructive proposal utilizes the "relational" emphasis which operates within what I will call "representative" soteriologies, Mulcahy's use of "relational"[134] or "representative"[135] as descriptors for Rahner's *own* theology are extremely sparse. The Rahnerian elements he sees in his own proposal have to do with symbolic causality, that is, the idea of Christ effecting our salvation in the sacramental mode.

Summarizing the "Sacramental" Assessments of Rahner's Soteriology

The sympathetic summaries above consistently recognize Rahner's distaste for popularized Western soteriologies which center upon the death of Christ initiating eternal and divine consequences. Rahner, as these readers correctly determine, flips this scheme on its head, positing the Christ-event (and particularly, the cross) as the means through

---

133. Ibid., 22.
134. In his summary of Rahner's *On the Theology of Death* (New York: Herder and Herder, 1965), Mulcahy writes, "it is only in death for Rahner that Jesus' reality can become «pan-cosmic», entering into an open, unrestricted relationship with the whole world and hence able to enter into an effective salvific relationship with all men and women" (*The Cause of Our Salvation*, 459).
135. Mulcahy does discuss Christ saving us as our "representative." This terminology occurs mainly when he is discussing Dorothee Sölle, as she treated in the writings of Reformed theologians Colin Gunton (ibid., 88–95, 112) and John McIntyre (308–12). It also occurs in his treatments of Paul Fiddes (as a contrast to the idea of penal substitution, 152, 160) and Vernon White (who, he notes, speaks in a somewhat Patristic key, 248–49). The closest that Mulcahy comes to giving a "representative" reading of Rahner's soteriology is the following remark: "[T]he cross is not merely making known God's saving will. It actualizes in Jesus' «yes» *humanity's own* response to God's will. A symbol renders present" (ibid. 402, emphasis added).

which an eternal, divine will to save communicates itself to the world. Such a movement is properly categorized as sacramental, for Christ, like all other sacraments (of which he is the chief and principal), is the sign which effects what he signifies. These summaries also distance him from an "exemplarist" or purely "moral influence" brand of soteriology, noting that such an identifier shortchanges the profundity of what Rahner means by "symbol."

Wong, in particular, emerges as a strong defender of Rahner. His joint term "symbol-sacrament" itself stands to ward off the "exemplarist" charge. Moreover, Wong has offered on Rahner's behalf the most explicit and thorough response to Balthasar's charges, an apology which turns on taking seriously Rahner's idea of *das Realsymbol* and sacramental-symbolic causality. Although Balthasar too is aware of these terms and concepts, Wong insists that Balthasar, especially in attributing Rahnerian salvation to God's will rather than to Christ and his cross, fails to fully appreciate the *intrinsic* character of "self-expression" which stands at the heart of *das Realsymbol*, a failure which leads to the false dichotomy just mentioned. With a sacramental-symbolic Christology, the identification of Christ as "prime instance" is no reductive move; on the contrary, it is, situated properly within Rahner's theology of *das Realsymbol*, a claim which has profound sacramental and soteriological implications, positioning Christ as the indispensable nexus point of God's saving self-communication.

Though Vorgrimler's apology is not as thorough as Wong's, Rahner's longtime friend and student makes some key observations about Rahner's soteriology in his defense. Among these are the coextensive and noncompetitive nature of God's grace and human freedom (which allows Rahner to use the term "self-redemption" in a non-Pelagian manner), Rahner's distaste for staurocentric soteriologies which misappropriate the idea of Christ's *stellvertretenden* suffering "in our place," and finally, the way in which Rahner's sacramental theology allows him to retain the idea of "salvation in the cross" by rendering the latter *das Realsymbol* of the former.

The majority of these five theologians' commentary concerns the idea of symbol-sacrament and the causality that accompanies it. But one element that is quite important to Rahner's soteriological vision occurs, abridged as it may be, in the writings of Edwards, Ryan, and Wong, in particular. This element is what one might call a "twofold" account of how human salvation occurs. That is, Rahner sees two distinct (but not separated) movements or dimensions to the process of human salvation. Edwards describes it in terms of "objective redemption" brought about by God (especially in the Christ-event) and "self-redemption," which consists of our appropriation (rooted, of course, in God's grace) of the former. Wong similarly describes the definitive, sacramental Christ-event bringing about a saving "situation" which we appropriate in conforming our lives to the Christ-Sacrament. Ryan neatly choreographs these two movements, underlining that for Rahner, freedom and grace grow in *direct* rather than *inverse* proportion, suggesting a deeply relational soteriology. Although this "twofold" account is not the focus of these authors, it constitutes an important part of Rahner's thought. Going a step further, one could note that God's universal salvific will, operative in the supernatural existential, is *directed toward* the saving "situation" or "objective redemption" brought about by Christ. Such a suggestion further serves to undermine the dichotomy in Balthasar's criticism attacked by Wong.

Finally, latent within the accounts of Ryan, Wong, Vorgrimler are indications of a possible basis for speaking of Rahner's Christ as our representative. While none of the theologians here (or any of Rahner's readers of which I am aware) explicitly link him with this term or category, "representative" is, it seems, the best concept for understanding Wong's passing remark that for Rahner, Christ sacramentally realizes God's saving will "on man's behalf." Moreover, Vorgrimler's observations about the intrinsic relationship between soteriology and Christ's "being" offers an (albeit undeveloped) indication of Christ's representative role in Rahner's thought. Finally, although he too omits explicit discussion of *pro nobis* or "representative" soteriological elements, Ryan's characterization of Rahner's theology of salvation as "relational," especially as illustrated in (to use my own language) "person-centered" reading of God's Reign, provides a strong basis for talking in just this way. Ryan's observation about Rahner's connection to the "Greek patristic tradition" is also pregnant with potential for taking his thought in a "representative" direction. Taken together with the twofold movement of redemption just noted, the idea of Christ saving as a representative in whom we participate holds promise as a more robust response to the criticisms leveled by Balthasar and others, as well as for better understanding the profundity of Rahner's nuanced soteriological thought.

A Further Response to Rahner's Critics:
Christ the Representative

While the majority of Rahner's readers, both advocates and critics alike, classify his soteriology as sacramental, I propose here that Rahner understands Christ to bring salvation as our Representative. To be clear, the proposal to understand Rahner's soteriology in this category is *not* a suggestion to jettison the standard symbol-sacrament lens for understanding Rahner. Indeed, the concept of *das Realsymbol* and symbolic causality are clearly at the very foundation of his account of salvation through Christ. Instead of a strict alternative, my suggestion is that "representative" serves as a category complementary to that of "sacrament." In fact, within Rahner's theology, the claim that Christ is the primordial Sacrament of God's salvation *implies and necessitates* his functioning as our Representative, and vice-versa. Although this particular claim will be substantiated in the next chapter, we will conclude the present chapter by explaining what is meant here by representative soteriology, indicating how such a category can effectively respond to critiques such as Balthasar's, and providing a motivating rationale for exploring this topic. First, however, a quick word about why such a suggestion should not immediately be dismissed out of hand.

"Inconceivable" Representative Action?
Rahner and Stellvertretung

The proposal for a representative soteriological scheme within Rahner's theology may initially seem rather surprising, given Balthasar's assessment above. As we have already seen, Balthasar portrays Rahner as *rejecting* the idea of *pro nobis* "representative expiation" found in scripture, the fathers, and St. Anselm's doctrine of satisfaction.[136] In fact, Balthasar asserts that Rahnerian sacramental causality does not posit Christ "embrac[ing] and contain[ing] mankind in order to reconcile it to God . . . such 'representative' action is inconceivable."[137] His textual basis for this judgment is Rahner's remark, "The satisfaction theory requires the ultimately inconceivable notion that Jesus is

---

136. *TD* 4:274.
137. Ibid., 276.

man's representative and is opposed to the correct understanding of self-redemption outlined above."[138] Several things must be noted about this remark. Conveniently, Balthasar omits "satisfaction" from the quotation, implying, from the context which he provides, that Rahner indiscriminately rejects the *pro nobis* formula contained within scripture and the fathers as well as in Anselm. However, Rahner's specific objection, which is twofold, concerns the Anselmian formula which occurs in both "crude" and "subtle" forms, the latter of which supposes "tortuous distinctions." First, Rahner asserts that history has proven satisfaction theory to have "obscured the simple fact that the event of the cross did not originate in an angry God who demanded reparation, but from a God of gratuitous and merciful love."[139] Second, as his preceding remarks show, he believes it to conflict with the notion of (non-Pelagian) "self-redemption," discussed above.

So, in this remark cited by Balthasar, what specifically does Rahner reject? What's translated as "man's representative . . . opposed to . . . self-redemption outlined above" is shorthand for his earlier assertion (to which Rahner alludes) that "a man does not merely receive his salvation in a passive manner but rather realises it with total, and not just partial, freedom."[140] Moreover, the English translation (which is, of course, not Balthasar's) only exacerbates matters: "*die Idee einer letztlich undenkbaren Stellvertretung der Menschen durch Jesus*" could just as well be translated as "the idea of an ultimately unthinkable substitution in the human person's place by Jesus," since "*Stellvertretung*" carries a certain ambiguity[141] (an ambiguity which, in Rahner's usage, is clarified by attending to the surrounding context).[142] So, while Balthasar

---

138. "The One Christ and the Universality of Salvation," *TI* 16:208. The original German reads, "Die Satisfaktionstheorie aber fördert die Idee einer letzlich undenkbaren Stellvertretung der Menschen durch Jesus und steht dem rechten Verständnis der Selbsterlösung entgegen, von der oben gesprochen wurde" (*Schriften zur Theologie* (henceforth *SzT*) 12:262). (Note: *TD* 4 incorrectly cites the page as 26.)
139. "The One Christ and the Universality of Salvation," *TI* 16:208.
140. Ibid., 207.
141. English translations of *Stellvertretung* include proxy, vicar, representation, substitution, and surrogacy, among others.
142. For a critical treatment of Balthasar's own usage of *Stellvertretung*, see Michele M. Schumacher's "The Concept of Representation in the Theology of Hans Urs von Balthasar." *Theological Studies* 60, no. 1 (1999), 53–71. Joseph Ratzinger composed an encyclopedia entry on the notion of *Stellvertretung* which was published in the early 1960s ("Stellvertretung," in *Handbuch theologischer Grundbegriffe*, 2 vols., ed. Heinrich Fries (Munich: Kösel, 1962–1963), 2:566–75; an English translation by Jared Wicks can be found as "Vicarious Representation," in *Letter & Spirit* 7 (2011), 209–20). In it, Ratzinger anticipates the exact point Rahner would make about the necessity of respecting the individual's freedom when affirming the concept: "It is also clear that salvation arising in virtue of vicarious representation does not arrive mechanically in a person, but requires in the recipient

would have us believe that Rahner "rejects" notions of *pro nobis* "representation" outright as "inconceivable," what Rahner finds "inconceivable" is not the broad category of "representation," but rather, the (allegedly) "Anselmian"[143] suggestion of a passively received salvation won by a proxy—that is, one who "fills in" [*Vertretung*] the place [*Stelle*] of another.

Rahner explicitly says as much in another essay entitled, "The Christian Understanding of Redemption."[144] (It should be noted that this essay was originally a lecture in Vienna delivered in February 1981, less than a year after the publication of *TD* 4; thus, Balthasar would not have had access to it at the time of his writing.) There, Rahner actually affirms the statements "the human race is redeemed by the 'vicarious' suffering of Jesus [«*stellvertretende*» *Leiden Jesu*]" and "the human race is vicariously represented by Christ [*Stellvertretung des Menschen durch Christus*]" as "thoroughly valid [*durchaus legitimen*]".[145] In doing so, Rahner explicitly addresses the ambiguity of *Stellvertretung*, affirming one usage and criticizing another.

Consistent with his earlier writing, the usage of *Stellvertretung* to which Rahner objects is one in which Christ does something "in the place" of others as their proxy.[146] He elaborates,

> A conception of vicarious [*stellvertretenden*] redemption in which Jesus does for me, what I actually ought to do myself but am not capable of doing, and which will then be "credited" to me is a conception that I con-

some kind of openness and readiness.... A Pauline type of *pistis* [faith] must somehow be present, but we do not have to determine in detail what this could be. One might then even speak of this attitude of openness as a *votum ecclesiae* [desire of being in the church], but one must not forget that this is only the subjective side of a totality which only has sense and meaning through the objective reality of the vicarious representation of the *Christus totus* [the whole of Christ]" ("Vicarious Representation," 219).

143. Rahner's label is almost surely unfair to Anselm. Though Rahner provides qualifications with his remarks about "crude" and "subtle" versions and "tortuous distinctions," his use of "Anselmian" to describe what appears to be popularized penal substitutionary models of atonement is problematic. To his credit, Rahner seems to have leveled this sort of critique in a more nuanced way in his final years. E.g., "Everyone is aware of the attempt to explain this objective redemption and reconciliation by using the concept of the (vicarious) satisfaction which God's eternal Son has made to God's holy justice by his obedience unto death on the cross, thereby wiping out the 'sins of the world.' No doubt the Son's obedience has an unsurpassable moral value which manifests God's holiness and justice in the world. However, the notion of an exchange of goods or even of guilt being punished in the person of the guiltless Jesus must not be allowed to obtrude itself on the notion of satisfaction for the sins of the world by the Son's obedience" ("Reconciliation and Vicarious Representation," *TI* 21:262).

144. The original German text can be found in *SzT* 15:236–50. Another important essay on this matter is "Reconciliation and Vicarious Representation [*Versöhnung und Stellvertretung*]" (*TI* 21:255–69 [=*SzT* 15:251–64]), especially 264–69 [=259–64].

145. "The Christian Understanding of Redemption," *TI* 21:248; *SzT* 15:244.

146. I.e., "Jesus antelle der anderen Menschen etwas getan hat" (*SzT* 15:244).

sider to be wrong or at least a misleading formulation of the dogmatic truth that my redemption is dependent on Jesus and his cross.[147]

(As before, Rahner explicitly associates this usage of "*Stellvertretung*" with the Anslemian doctrine of satisfaction[148] and the popularized soteriology of an angry God who is pacified by Jesus's execution.[149]) But, at the same time, he provides an alternative understanding of *Stellvertretung* that properly explicates this "thoroughly valid" term. Asserting that there is an "undeniable origin of redemption from Christ," he explains,

> it is precisely through Jesus that it is possible that I myself, by the power of God's self-communication, am really able to aspire to God, to have faith and hope in him and to love him; in other words, that I can really perform the highest act that can be expected of a human being given the highest possible requirements. Through Jesus my own freedom itself contains the possibility of redemption, liberation, and sanctification the like of which cannot be conceived in a higher, more tremendous or more radical way.[150]

That is to say, *in virtue of Jesus*, who is himself the "origin of redemption," each person has a salvific possibility to which her freedom can be directed—namely, God (the *Realsymbol* of whom *in our world* is, precisely, Jesus). Rahner's objection does not concern the idea of Jesus's providing an indispensable possibility for us, nor the claim that Jesus "embraces and contains mankind in order to reconcile it to God"[151]; rather, Rahner denies the suggestion that Jesus does so in a way that renders us passive objects credited with the fruits of his free act as a proxy. It is only *this* suggestion which Rahner finds "unthinkable"; Jesus saving as our "representative," even by way of "*Stellvertretung*" (an even *more* ambiguous term) is by no means denied.[152] In fact, as I

---

147. "The Christian Understanding of Redemption," *TI* 21:248; *SzT* 15:244–45.

148. Ibid.; *SzT* 15:244.

149. "Wherever we find primarily the idea of an angry God who, as it were, has to be conciliated by great effort on the part of Jesus, we have an ultimately unchristian, popular notion of redemption that is incorrect. . . . God so loved the world that he gave his only-begotten Son, and it was not because the Son gave himself that an angry God with great effort changed his mind about the world" (ibid., 249; *SzT* 15:245).

150. Ibid., 248–49; *SzT* 15:245.

151. *TD* 4:276.

152. It is noteworthy that Rahner's earliest usage of *Stellvertreter* is consistent with his later approval of the term so long as *substitution* by the *Stellvetreter* is not implied. In his theology dissertation, *E latere Christi* (discussed extensively below in Chapter 4), Rahner refers to Christ as the Representative of God and Mediator of God's gifts [*Gottes Stellvertreter und Vermittler der Gaben Gottes*] (*E latere Christi*, 26). Clearly, Jesus is not here envisioned God's "substitute" on earth; rather, as this early text attests, Rahner has maintained a positive, more sacramental usage for *Stellvertretung/ter* from the outset of his theological career.

will discuss below in chapter 5, Rahner asserts that "Jesus Christ, the Mediator, is *the* supreme representative of mankind in his vicarious redemption [der *absolute Repräsentant der Menschheit in seiner stellvertretenden Erlösung*]."[153]

What Is Meant by "Representative"?

Essential to the argument that Rahner's soteriology has a representative component to it is a clear statement of what precisely is meant by Christ being our representative and by representative soteriology. First, it should be clear from the preceding that "representative," as I am using it, is *not* equivalent to "substitute." Just as *"Stellvertretung"* is rather ambiguous, so is "representative," a term used in various ways by theologians, some of whom (especially those within the Reformed tradition) consider representation to be more or less synonymous with substitution.[154]

Although theology in the early twentieth century tended to subsume representative soteriological thought within other categories, the classification began emerging in its own right as the twentieth century went on.[155] William Wolf lists it alongside atonement theories such as the classical "Christus Victor," Anselmian satisfaction, Reformation theories of substitution, and moral influence theories, associating it with twentieth-century thinkers such as Dietrich Bonhoeffer and Dorothee Sölle.[156] (Other recent figures who could be added include Walter Kasper,[157] Karl Barth,[158] Hans Urs von Balthasar,[159] Joseph

---

153. Karl Rahner and Herbert Vorgrimler, "Representation," in *Theological Dictionary* (New York: Herder and Herder, 1965), 404–5. The German above, originally published in 1961, is taken from "Repräsentation," in *Kleines Theologisches Wörterbuch*, 12th ed. (Freiburg: Herder, 1980), 362.

154. For example, see Herman Bavinck's (d. 1921) *Reformed Dogmatics: Sin and Salvation in Christ* (Grand Rapids, MI: Baker Academic, 2006), 3:326, 3:404–5.

155. On the tendency to conflate substitution and representation, as well as the need to distinguish the two ideas, see Dorothee Sölle's *Christ the Representative: An Essay in Theology after the 'Death of God'* (Philadelphia: Fortress, 1967), 19ff and *passim*.

156. "William J. Wolf, "Atonement," in *The Encyclopedia of Religion*, 16 vols., ed. Mircea Eliade (New York: Macmillan, 1987), 1:9–14.

157. Walter Kasper, *Jesus the Christ* (New York: Paulist Press, 1977). More recently, Kasper's writing on the topic has taken on a distinctive Balthasarian flavor which would seem to sit uncomfortably with Rahner and his qualified validation of *Stellvertretung*. After citing 1 Cor 5:21 and Gal 3:13 twice *each* in the preceding chapter, Kasper glosses Paul, writing that "the law's demand is not thereby rescinded; rather, Jesus Christ has discharged the requirement of justice for us and in our place. He has removed from us the requirement of self-justification; he himself has become our righteousness" (*Mercy*, 78). Earlier, however, Kasper writes that the "idea of substitutionary atonement [*Stellvertretungsgedanken*] can be understood only in the context" of a "'corporate' understanding of the human race" (74), and that "Substitutionary atonement is not an action that replaces what we ourselves can and must do" (76).

158. Karl Barth, *Church Dogmatics* (henceforth *CD*), 5 vols. in 31 parts, eds. G.W. Bromiley, T.F. Torrance (London; New York: T&T Clark, 2010). Note Barth's "new Adam" language in *CD* II/2:688–90 and

Ratzinger,[160] Kathryn Tanner,[161] William Placher,[162] Brian Mcdermott,[163] and Clark Pinnock.[164]) This is not to say that this category is one the origins of which is only a century old. On the contrary, recent attention to Christ saving as our "representative" is due to renewal and retrieval of a theme which dominated patristic literature, as we will see below in chapter 3. Irenaeus of Lyons, in particular, will be a figure central to the present study.

In order to describe what is meant by representative soteriology, three characteristics will be offered here. While each or perhaps even all of these characteristics can be found in other theories of atonement, the centrality of these three and the particular way in which they mutually interact account for the distinctness of representative soteriology.[165]

First, representative soteriology is person-centered. One of the refrains repeated tirelessly in soteriological discussions is that the best accounts of atonement unify Christ's "person" and "work." Without slighting the "work" of Christ or rendering his free actions within the world inconsequential to our salvation, a representative soteriology *centers* upon Christ's person. That is to say, at the heart of the process of human salvation is an intimate union with Jesus Christ himself; Christ's free actions and "work" (e.g., gathering disciples, ministry, passion, and death) are at the service of bringing us to himself (e.g., "Follow *me*"[166] and "I, when I am lifted up from the earth, will *draw all people to myself*"[167]). The incarnation was not a means to a super-agent Christ performing a particular salvific task, but the other way around. Christ's tasks are directed toward—they center upon—facilitating our approach

recapitulation themes present in *CD*:III/2 148, 166; *CD* IV/1:48, 58; *CD* IV/2:25, 28, 163, 522. Notably, like Balthasar, Barth often pairs the ideas of "representative" and "substitute" (e.g., *CD* IV/1:230).

159. Hans Urs von Balthasar, *Mysterium Paschale*, especially 20ff.

160. Joseph Ratzinger, *Introduction to Christianity* (New York: Herder and Herder, 1970), 202–5, where he cites Barth and Balthasar extensively, as well as *Jesus of Nazareth: From the Baptism in the Jordan to the Transfiguration* (San Francisco: Ignatius Press, 2008).

161. Kathryn Tanner, "Incarnation, Cross, and Sacrifice: A Feminist-Inspired Reappraisal," *Anglican Theological Review* 86, no. 1 (2004): 35–56, as well as *Christ the Key* (Cambrdige: Cambridge University Press, 2010).

162. William Placher, "How Does Jesus Save? An Alternative View of Atonement," *Christian Century* (June 2, 2009): 23–27.

163. Brian McDermott, *Word Become Flesh*, 246–48.

164. Clark H. Pinnock, *Flame of Love: A Theology of the Holy Spirit* (Downers Grove, Il: InterVarsity Press, 1996), and *A Wideness in God's Mercy: The Finality of Jesus Christ in a World of Religions* (Grand Rapids, MI: Zondervan, 1992).

165. Cf. the three "principles" of Catholicism (namely, sacramentality, mediation, and communion) in McBrien, *Catholicism*, 9–14.

166. Matt 4:19, 8:22, 9:9, 10:38, 16:24, emphasis added.

167. John 12:32, emphasis added.

to and sharing in the locus of the incarnation. Thus, as a person-centered soteriology, representation depends on the notion of incorporation into and participation in Jesus Christ himself.[168]

This point is made articulately by Brian Daley in his article, "He Himself is Our Peace."[169] Taking Anselm's famous question, *Cur Deus homo?*, as his starting point, Daley notes that Western theology has tended to answer that in order to "set things right" after sin, humanity needed a divine Savior who had the means to do so. Daley sets out to provide an alternative, patristic answer which focuses not so much on what Christ *did* as who he *is*. Christ's person, he explains, is for many of the fathers "in itself the realization of salvation," for salvation is ultimately *"achieved in Jesus' identity* rather than *accomplished as his work."*[170] Daley proceeds to review Irenaeus, Origen, Athanasius, Augustine, Gregory of Nyssa, and Cyril of Alexandria, among others. Summarizing and concluding this historical survey, he writes,

> It is the very person of Jesus, for instance, which—for Irenaeus or Athanasius—achieves the full revelation of God's grace and glory in the fallen world, remaking the damaged image (in Athanasius' understanding) or bringing it (as Irenaeus suggests) from simply being an image to being God's full likeness. . . . Jesus has begun in his own person a new humanity, radiant with life and free of the enslaving obligations of the old order. . . . [T]his understanding of Christ as not only the *agent* but also the *locus* of human salvation is articulated in Patristic theology.[171]

Daley has no illusions of these various historical figures sharing a single, monolithic account of atonement. In fact, he emphasizes the distinctive roles that revelation, healing, payment, victory, exchange, and transformation play for different patristic theologians. But what all of them share, he argues, is a central appreciation for how Christ, in his very person and identity rather than in a single restricted act (i.e., his death), brings these things about:

168. "I am the true vine, and my Father is the vine-grower. He removes every branch in me that bears no fruit. Every branch that bears fruit he prunes to make it bear more fruit. You have already been cleansed by the word that I have spoken to you. Abide in me as I abide in you. Just as the branch cannot bear fruit by itself unless it abides in the vine, neither can you unless you abide in me. I am the vine, you are the branches. Those who abide in me and I in them bear much fruit" (John 15:1–5b).
169. Brian Daley, "'He Himself Is Our Peace' (Ephesians 2:14): Early Christian Views of Redemption in Christ," in *The Redemption: An Interdisciplinary Symposium on Christ as Redeemer*, eds. Stephen Davis et al (New York: Oxford Univ. Press, 2004), 149–76.
170. Ibid., 151, emphasis original.
171. Ibid., 166.

for most of the Fathers, redemption or salvation is to be identified not simply as the new relationship between humanity and God that has come into being as the effect of Jesus' sacrifice for us, of his death on our behalf on the cross; rather, it is identified as the union, the living interpenetration, of God and humanity that is first fully realized in his own person. It is in . . . the whole life of Jesus . . . that the "event" of redemption is to be found.[172]

Accordingly, if salvation consists first and foremost in Christ's *person* as the *locus* of salvation, human appropriation and reception of salvation does not consist merely in being "credited" with the fruits of an act, but rather, in entering into an intimate relationship (initiated by God) with Christ himself. That is, in Pauline language, the blessed become "members" of the body of Christ (1 Cor 12), which is the locus of salvation, and thus, in the words of 2 Peter 1:4, participate in the divine nature. The act of appropriating salvation through this participation in and incorporation into Christ constitutes the "subjective" (to use the "self-redemption" and "objective redemption" categories highlighted by Edwards and Wong) element of representative soteriology.

The second and third characteristics of "representative" soteriology serve as complements to one another. The second such marker is that Christ is the presence of God to the world. This marker is, to use Rahnerian language also employed by the ITC above, is descending, focusing upon God's act of incarnation—becoming fully human in Jesus Christ. This incarnational characteristic should not be taken to mean (as some of the fathers have been accused—see the discussion of "physical redemption" in chapters 3 and 4 below) that the moment of Christ's incarnation constitutes the entirety of salvation for a representative soteriology. While the union of God with Christ's humanity is indeed the focus here, the view's person-centered character warns against attributing too much to any single act or moment such as the incarnation. This uniquely intense, intimate, and hypostatic intersection of God and humanity extends rather, over the whole of the Christ-event (and is not without anticipations, as well as echoes, in virtue of God's activity in the Spirit and the Logos). Rather than a saving moment, the incarnation, in a representative soteriology, is a salvific *interval*.

The emphasis on God's presence before us in the person of Jesus Christ is clear in many of the patristic "representative" thinkers men-

tioned above. Augustine, Athanasius, and many others echoed varia-
tions of Irenaeus's claim that Christ "became what we are, so that we
can be what he is."[173] Cyril of Alexandria, as Daley points out, stressed
that God unites himself to our injured flesh in order to bestow life upon
it: "he bore our nature, reshaping it to share his own life. And he is in
us: for surely we have become participants in him, and we have him in
ourselves through the Spirit. For this reason, we have come to be 'partakers in the divine nature' (2 Pet 1:4)."[174] The act of God, through his
Son and eternal Word, coming among us in Christ has rendered God
personally accessible within our world, within time and history—and
the implications are immense. As Athanasius summarized Irenaeus,
"He, indeed, assumed humanity that we might become God."[175] This
result is not some magical outcome of the act of incarnation; rather, it
follows from a proper understanding of *what* salvation is—God's very
presence, which draws us into the divine life, elevating and transforming us.[176] This brings us to the third characteristic.

Of a piece with the second "descending" marker is the third,
"ascending" characteristic of representative soteriology: Christ is the
authentic human before God. This characteristic is often expressed by
the fathers' (with Paul's before them and of Vatican II's after[177]) refer-

173. Specific instances will be considered below in Chapter 3.
174. Cyril of Alexandria, *Commentary on the Gospel of John* 9.1, commenting on John 14:20, qtd. in Daley,
He Himself is Our Peace, 168. Cf. *Commentary on the Gospel According to S. John*, 2 vols., eds. P.E. Pusey
and T. Randell (London: W. Smith, 1885), 320. Also, "For He is Mediator between God and men,
through Himself and in Himself uniting humanity to God. For since He is born of the essence of
God the Father, in that He is the Word, the Effulgence, and the very Image, He is one with the
Father, being wholly in the Father, and having the Father in Himself; while in that He has become
a man like unto us, He is united to all on the earth in everything except in our sin: and so He has
become a sort of border-ground, containing in Himself all that concurs to unity and friendship.
No man therefore will come to the Father, that is, will appear as a partaker of the Divine nature,
save through Christ alone. For if He had not become a Mediator by taking human form, our condition could never have advanced to such a height of blessedness; but now, if any one approach the
Father in a spirit of faith and reverent knowledge, he will do so, by the help of our Saviour Christ
Himself" (ibid., 243).
175. Athanasius, *On the Incarnation* (New York: St. Vladimir's Seminary Press, 2003), 93.
176. "God must work our salvation by becoming one of us . . . because salvation cannot be conceived
simply as a 'work' . . . salvation simply is God's personal presence among us" (Daley, "He Himself
Is Our Peace," 175–76). Cf. Rahner: "Salvation here is to be understood as the strictly supernatural
and direct presence of God in himself afforded by grace" ("The One Christ and the Universality of
Salvation," *TI* 16:200).
177. "Adam, the first man, was a type of him who was to come, Christ the Lord. Christ the new Adam,
in the very revelation of the mystery of the Father and his love, fully reveals humanity to itself
and brings to light its very high calling. It is no wonder, then, that all the truths mentioned so far
should find in him their source and their most perfect embodiment. He who is the 'image of the
invisible God' (Col. 1:15), is himself the perfect man who has restored in the children of Adam that
likeness to God which had been disfigured ever since the first sin. Human nature, by the very fact
that it was assumed, not absorbed, in him, has been raised in us also to a dignity beyond compare.
For, by his incarnation, he, the Son of God, has in a certain way united himself with each individual" (*Gaudium et Spes* (*GS*) n. 22. All translations of documents promulgated by the Second Vatican

ence to Christ as the "New Adam," the fully authentic human person. Early Christian thinking, including that expressed in scripture, relied on typological claims in which Old Testament figures and events precede and point toward counterparts in the New Testament. Adam and Christ serve as one of the most referenced of these pairs: Adam (with Eve) is the progenitor of all earthly life, while Christ (with the church) is the author of renewed spiritual life. Juxtapositions of the two also make up a large part of this typological reflection, with Adam's disobedience being reversed by Christ's perfect obedience, and so on.[178] "New Adam" language serves to articulate the claim that Christ, as *the* perfect human, has changed the entire human situation.[179] In virtue of our relationship to (indeed, incorporation within) this one among us, we participate in the dignity of this one, who has provided a definitive and authentic trajectory for the human race.

This "ascending" component of representative soteriology demonstrates that an essential part of human salvation is our aspiring—in the person of Christ, the New Adam—toward and achieving perfected human existence in union with God. It is not simply a story of God becoming human, but also one of radical human transformation so as to share in the divine life. Christ brought something new to us, but he did so *as a human*, a man among us with whom we can enjoy fellowship, and in whose fellowship we are healed and elevated.

Together with the (descending) incarnational and person-centered markers, this (ascending) divinizing characteristic of representative soteriology allows us to speak of redemption in both its objective and subjective dimensions. The person of Christ, who is both God in our presence as well as the authentic human before God, is the locus of human salvation. *He himself* is "objective redemption," whom we subjectively "appropriate" when we are incorporated into his body. Using Johannine language to make this point, the ITC summarizes the three components succinctly under the banner of "representative headship": "Christ identifies himself with fallen humanity. He is the new Adam, the progenitor of redeemed humanity, the Head or the vine into whom individuals must be incorporated as members or branches. . . . The

---

Council are from *Vatican Council II: The Basic Sixteen Documents*, ed. Austin Flannery (Northport, NY: Costello, 1996), 163–282).

178. Cf. Paul in Rom 5:14ff.

179. "[J]ust as the head has risen from the dead, the rest of the body—the body of every human being found among the living—should also rise, when the time of his condemnation for disobedience is fulfilled, coming together in all its members and joints, and strengthened by the growth of God" (Irenaeus, *AH* III.19.3, qtd. in Daley, "He Himself Is Our Peace," 174).

incarnate Word becomes the gathering point for the constitution of a reconciled and restored humanity."[180]

Rahnerian Representation as a Response to Balthasar

Balthasar's accusation that Karl Rahner's Christ does not really bring about our salvation (which is, for him, already just a *fait accompli*), but rather, testifies to it as a kind of notification to humanity as its prime instance, has garnered a substantial and effective response. In particular, Joseph Wong has compellingly argued that Balthasar's worries about Rahner's soteriology are grounded in a failure to take seriously his category of symbolic-sacramental causality, according to which Christ indeed causes the grace which he preeminently discloses as *das Realsymbol* of God's salvation. In other words, while Christ's life and death do not, for Rahner, bring about God's salvific will in eternity, they do bring it about, in the sacramental mode, with respect to *us*. Accordingly, the originality of my work here lies not in providing a response to an unanswered accusation.

Rather, what I will argue is that Karl Rahner's soteriological thought, which has heretofore been classified virtually unanimously as "sacramental," is a legitimate instance of *representative* soteriology as well. That is, I do not wish to supplant the standard categorization, but wish to expand upon it, arguing that for Rahner, Christ the "representative" is not only a *complement* to Christ the primordial sacrament, but that these two categories imply one another. If this is the case, Wong's answer to Balthasar, the root of whose concern seems to be that Rahner's soteriology is insufficiently christocentric, can be supplemented and strengthened: not only does Christ *cause* our salvation (in a sacramental mode), but for Karl Rahner, Jesus Christ *is himself the very locus* of it.[181] As such, Christ is the unequivocal and indispensable center of human salvation, and concerns that Rahner's Christology and soteriology fail (against Rahner's own claims) to account for the *constitutive* place of Jesus as the *sine qua non* of human salvation can be put to rest, along with the suggestion that Rahner's Christology and soteriology are inimical to Christ representing us.

---

180. *ITC*, "Select Questions on God the Redeemer," Part III nn. 38–39.
181. Cf. *FCF*, 284, 293.

Rationale and Motivation for this Inquiry

The result of my argument, I hope, is a better appreciation for Rahner's nuanced (and, in places, rather opaque) theology. Moreover, by expanding the categories under which Rahner's soteriological thought can be understood, a more robust answer to critics such as Balthasar (and even to advocates who themselves *favor* the sort of reading given by Balthasar) can be made. Such an answer can perhaps advance a rehabilitation of Rahner's thought in contemporary theological conversation, a conversation which has been increasingly dominated by Balthasar's own powerful and creative theology and which has, by extension, adopted or presumed many of Balthasar's (at times vitriolic) criticisms of Rahnerian thought.[182]

But the impetus of the current project has a third dimension as well: with the advent of Rahner's *Sämtliche Werke*, a 32-volume complete works of Rahner begun in 1995 and only now coming to its completion, a renewed attention to Rahner's early writing has come about. Although readers such as Wong have noted Rahner's focus on the church fathers early in his career (a focus which seems, explicitly, at least, to have waned as his career progressed), only recently has the suggestion been made that a profound continuity exists between Rahner's early work in patristics and his later dogmatic essays. In volume three of Rahner's *Sämtliche Werke*, which focuses upon writings concerning patristic spirituality and theology, Karl Neufeld has even suggested that a patristic "substratum" exists within Rahner's later work, even where the fathers are not explicitly cited or even mentioned.[183] Andreas Batlogg has also underlined the importance of traditional historical theology for Rahner, clarifying that Rahner did not see himself as an "innovator," but rather, as mining a tradition which was richer than the confines of the neoscholasticism of his training (which he deeply respected, but to which he did not limit himself).[184]

Rahner's own theological dissertation, *E latere Christi* (published only in the third volume of Rahner's *Sämtliche Werke* in 1999, and still unavailable in translation), will play a significant role in the current

---

182. The movement to relegate Rahner's theology to a (failed) project of a bygone era is exemplified by R.R. Reno, "Rahner the Restorationist: Karl Rahner's time has passed," *First Things* no. 233 (May 2013): 45–51.

183. Karl-Heinz Neufeld, "Editionsbericht," in *SW* 3:xiii–xvi, at xiii.

184. Andreas Batlogg, "Karl Rahners Theologische Dissertation 'E latere Christi': Zur Genese eines patristischen Projeckts (1936)," *Zeitschrift für Katholische Theologie* 126 (2004), 111–30, at 127. This article overlaps significantly with Batlogg's "Editionsbericht: Teil A – E latere Christi," in *SW* 3:xvii–lxvi.

project as evidence that the representative soteriology of the fathers heavily shaped Rahner's own understanding of Christ as Savior during this important, formative time in his career. Sections within Rahner's theology dissertation find clear echoes in his later writings that demonstrate the ongoing continuity and nonexplicit "substratum" noted by Neufeld. Accordingly, a third rationale for this book is to bolster this claim of continuity with specific attention to Rahner's soteriology.

2

Rahner's *Realsymbol*

The Basis for Rahnerian Sacramental Soteriology

That Rahner's soteriology has been primarily classified as sacramental in nature has already been shown, along with a variety of elaborations upon, critiques of, and apologies for his sacramental account of Christ as Savior. However, the theoretical framework that underpins Rahner's suggestion that Christ saves as the *Ursakrament* was left rather undeveloped in the last chapter. This theoretical framework is built upon Rahner's notion of *das Realsymbol*, a concept which is not only the heart of his sacramental thought (and thus indispensable for the predominant classification of his soteriology), but is also, according to his brother Hugo Rahner, the idea which stands as the essence and embodiment (*Inbegriff*) of Karl Rahner's larger theological corpus.[1] In addition to aiding an understanding of the sacramental categorization of Rahner's soteriology, the present exploration of *das Realsymbol* is

---

1. "Another common theological area which immediately applies to the issue of 'God in the world' concerns our efforts . . . on the theological interpretation of the devotion to the Sacred Heart. And what I have written about the theological history of this devotion, you have speculatively underpinned in the essay, which I personally hold to be the essence and embodiment of your foundational, theological direction, 'Theology of the Symbol' (1959)" (Hugo Rahner, "Eucharisticon fraternitatis," in *Gott in Welt. Festgabe für Karl Rahner*, 2 vols., ed. J.B. Metz (Freiburg i.Br.: Herder, 1964), 2:885–99 at 897). Even Karl Rahner himself declared that "no theology can be complete without also being a theology of the *Symbol*" ("The Theology of the Symbol," *TI* 4:221–52, at 235), and "the concept of *Symbol* . . . is an essential key-concept in all theological treatises" (ibid., 245).

a necessary precondition for my claim—with which this chapter will close—that Rahner's sacramental soteriology is compatible with, and, in fact, *implies* a supplementary representative soteriological classification.

The chapter will begin with an overview of Rahner's seminal article on *das Realsymbol*, "The Theology of the Symbol," exploring the concept through a general ontology as well as applications of *das Realsymbol* that Rahner offers as explanatory examples. Second, I will consider the influences, both spiritual and philosophical, which contributed to the development of *das Realsymbol* as a theological concept. Third, I will briefly compare Rahner's *Symbol*[2] category to those of Paul Tillich and Roger Haight. In the fourth section, I will move from the general level to the particular application of interest to the present study: Christ's salvific efficacy. Rahner's writings in which he applies sacramental causality to soteriology will feature prominently; Christ's death on the cross, the *symbolisch* moment in which the Christ-event culminates, will conclude this section. Finally, the chapter will highlight the call for a representative supplement which issues from the sacramental-*symbolisch* world of thought operative here.

"The Theology of the Symbol"

Though the assessment that *das Realsymbol* holds a central place within Rahner's thinking is fairly common,[3] Rahner devoted only one essay of significant length to the topic: "The Theology of the Symbol" (1959). While Rahner certainly speaks of *das Realsymbol* elsewhere in his work,[4] only this article includes a thorough treatment of the concept's general ontology, along with several applications. This being the case, a fairly close reading of this seminal text is warranted in the present chapter.

Rahner opens and closes the article with reference to a particular application of *das Realsymbol*: the theology underlying the devotion to Jesus's Sacred Heart. This fact is not all that surprising; although "The Theology of the Symbol" also appears in the fourth volume of his *Theological Investigations* (*TI*), it was originally written as a contribution to

---

2. Throughout this book, I will use the German "[*Real*]*Symbol*" and "*symbolisch*" when referencing Rahner's concept in order to better distinguish the term from common English usage of "symbol" and "symbolic."

3. In addition to the evaluation of H. Rahner, cf. those of Joseph Wong and Stephen Fields (below).

4. Along with explicitly mentioning "*Realsymbol*," Rahner also signals this concept, as Wong has noted, through his language of "self-expression" (*Selbstausdruck, Selbstaussage*) which appears frequently (especially in his christological writings) (Wong, *Logos-Symbol in the Christology of Karl Rahner* (Rome: LAS, 1984), 39).

a volume on Jesus's Sacred Heart.[5] Rahner's references to the theology of the Sacred Heart (as did the practice of the devotion itself) declined (but never disappeared) over the course of his career, but this connection is important to keep in mind as we try to understand *das Realsymbol* and Rahner's intentions for it.[6]

At the outset of the article, Rahner laments that while the usage of the word *Symbol* is very common—and indeed, even unavoidable in discussions of the Sacred Heart—its meaning is not immediately clear (though it is often presumed otherwise).[7] For instance, Jesus's "physical heart" certainly bears some relation to his redeeming love, but what precisely does it mean to say that Jesus's heart is the *Symbol* of his saving love? By the end of the article, Rahner hopes to have explicated a detailed and specific meaning of *Symbol* which will provide an answer to this question about the Sacred Heart, and hopefully, prove useful in other respects. This explication occurs in two modes, a general ontology of the *Symbol* as well as illustrative examples, which we will consider in that order.

General Ontology

In common parlance, "symbol" is often used almost interchangeably with ideas such as "sign," "emblem," and "metaphor." Rahner, on the contrary, employs the term in a highly specific and technical way. His claims regarding the Sacred Heart, the sacraments, and even the eternal generation of God's Son, all of which appeal to the notion of *Symbol*, would be egregiously misunderstood if *Symbol* were taken in the popular sense. To make this point clear from the outset of the article, Rahner makes a distinction between *Realsymbole* ("symbolic realities") and *Vertretungssymbole* ("symbolic representations").[8] The latter clas-

---

5. Karl Rahner, "Zur Theologie des Symbols," in *Cor Jesu: commentationes in litteras encyclicas Pii PP. XII "Haurietis aquas"*, 2 vols., eds. Augustin Bea et al (Rome: Herder, 1959), 1:461–505.

6. The devotion to Jesus's Sacred Heart as the natural, physical embodiment of Jesus's human and divine love, arose gradually throughout history, having its origins (as we will see below in chapter 4) in the Patristic focus on Christ's pierced side, which was gradually articulated in terms of his heart opened up on the cross. The devotion grew throughout the Middle Ages and received a great increase in public practice after 1673–1675, when St. Margaret Mary Alacoque (1647–1690) received private revelations concerning the devotion. Just before the dawn of the twentieth century, Pope Leo XIII, in his encyclical *Annum Sacrum* (1899) consecrated the entire world to Jesus's Sacred Heart. In the fifty years which followed, which includes Rahner's birth in 1904, the devotion flourished, with further encyclicals being issued in 1928, 1932, and 1956. For further background, see C.J. Moell, "Sacred Heart, Devotion to," in *New Catholic Encyclopedia*, 2nd ed., 15 vols. (Detroit: Gale, 2003), 12:490–92.

7. "The Theology of the Symbol," *TI* 4:221–22.

8. "Symbolic realities" and "symbolic representations" are the English translations provided in *TI* vol. 4. Regarding the former term, other translations of Rahner (e.g., those in *Karl Rahner in Dia-*

sification describes two independent, self-constituted realities which somehow "agree," insofar as the one indicates the other.[9] Since the two already-established realities are only *extrinsically* paired with one another, their relationship to one another can be completely arbitrary. Rahner's interest lies not in these "symbols," but rather, in "the highest and most primordial manner in which one reality can *represent* another [*Weise der* Repräsentanz *einer Wirklichkeit für eine andere*]."[10]

Rahner introduces his idea of *das Realsymbol* by describing entities or beings [*Seiende*] which "necessarily 'express' themselves in order to attain their own nature," and are thus symbolic.[11] If one entity is *das Realsymbol* of another, it is so (unlike *Vertretungssymbole*[12]) in virtue of an intrinsic relation between the two. This intrinsic relation is such that the *Realsymbol* mediates and communicates the very presence of that which it symbolizes: "we call this supreme and primal representation [*Repräsentanz*], in which one reality renders another present (primarily 'for itself' and only secondarily for others), a *Symbol*: the representation [*Repräsentanz*] which allows the other 'to be there' [«*dasein*»]."[13] Thus, self-expression and self-communication through the intrinsically related "other" stand as prominent features of *Realsymbole* that distinguish them from *Vertretungssymbole*.

Another key feature of *das Realsymbol* is the unity of the *Symbol* and "symbolized" achieved in this act of self-expression. In describing this feature, Rahner observes a "unity in plurality" which appears in every

logue: Conversations and Interviews, eds. Paul Imhof and Hubert Biallowons (New York: Crossroad, 1986) and *FCF*) and secondary Rahner literature (e.g., Fields) use "real symbol" or retain the German term (as I have done here). Regarding the latter term *Vertretungssymbole*, it is worth recalling the discussion above in chapter 1 about the ambiguity of the term [*Stelle*]*Vertretung*, which can mean "representation," but also "proxy," "standing-in," or "substitution." The distinction which Rahner makes here between *Realsymbole* (intrinsic relation, participation, self-realization) and *Vertretungssymbole* (extrinsic relation, more or less arbitrary assignment) reinforces his discomfort with language about Christ functioning as our *Vertreter* (cf. his worry is about Christ doing something which I ought to do, but in fact do not). Especially considering the way in which I am using "representative" here, *Vertretungssymbol* is probably better rendered something like "symbolic stand-in" than "symbolic representation."
9. "The Theology of the Symbol," *TI* 4:225.
10. Ibid., 225; *SzT* 4:279, emphases mine. Rahner's choice of the word *Repräsentanz* (rather than *Vertretung*) here is noteworthy.
11. "The Theology of the Symbol," *TI* 4:224. Moreover, Rahner makes the claim that *all* beings are, in fact, symbolic in this way.
12. As Rhodora E. Beaton puts it, "Aware of the many different definition of symbol, Rahner is clear that *Realsymbols* are not arbitrary signs or costumes, which merely share some agreement or similarity with that which they signify" (*Embodied Words, Spoken Signs: Sacramentality and the Word in Rahner and Chauvet* (Minneapolis: Fortress Press, 2014), 117).
13. "The Theology of the Symbol," *TI* 4:225; *SzT* 4:279. Once again, it is important to notice that Rahner's initial introduction to his theory of *Symbol* heavily utilizes "representation" language, especially considering my claim in this book that Rahner's portrayal of the Christ-Redeemer as Sacrament has the implied complement of the Christ-Redeemer as Representative.

instance of being. Noting that all finite beings are plural in virtue of their finitude (and thus, cannot be "absolutely 'simple'") and that even the infinite Triune God is a plurality of persons, Rahner claims that "being is plural in itself."[14] And yet, such plurality is not inimical to unity, but conducive to unity (and, moreover, in the case of the Trinity, to unity in its highest form![15]); after all, the relationship he has in mind is not "the subsequent conjunction of separate elements which once stood only on their own," but a plurality which results from the self-expression of an "original unity." In Rahner's words, "[T]he 'one' develops, the plural stems from an original 'one' . . . 'dis-closing' itself into a plurality in order to find itself precisely there."[16] By "finding itself" in the other through its act of self-expression, the "original one" is brought to perfection and "self-realization."[17] The somewhat paradoxical relationship of unity and plurality which exists between the "original one" and its "other" is apparent in the statement with which Rahner closes his overview of the *Symbol*'s general ontology: "The symbol strictly speaking (*Realsymbol*) is the self-realization of a being in the *other, which is constitutive of its essence.*"[18]

To summarize, *das Realsymbol* describes the phenomenon of an "original one" expressing itself in an "other," in such a way that the other communicates the very presence of the "original." The *Realsymbol* does not arbitrarily "stand for" the symbolized, but exists as *the* expression and self-realization of it, the two forming an ontological unity of the highest kind.[19] Thus, it is incorrect to view the "symbol," as Rahner means it here, as a simple "pointer" to or merely "like" the reality

---

14. "The Theology of the Symbol," *TI* 4:226–27.
15. Rahner claims that "plural" unity is the highest and purest kind of unity, since it "would be theologically a heresy, and therefore ontologically an absurdity, to think that God would be really 'simpler' and hence more perfect, if there were no real distinction of persons in God" (ibid., 227–28).
16. Ibid., 227.
17. Repeating his opening claim that "being is of itself symbolic, because it necessarily 'expresses' itself," he elaborates that this self-expression occurs necessarily precisely "because it must *realize itself* through a plurality in unity" (ibid., 229, emphasis added). "Each being . . . gives itself away from itself to the 'other', and there finds itself in knowledge and love. . . . [B]y constituting the inward 'other' . . . it comes to . . . its self-fulfillment" (ibid., 229–30).
18. Ibid., 234, emphasis added. Cf. The *Symbol* is "the reality, constituted by the thing symbolized as an inner moment of itself, which reveals and proclaims the thing symbolized, and is itself full of the thing symbolized, being its concrete form of existence" (ibid., 251).
19. In a later essay from 1970, Rahner elaborates, "a manifestation of this kind is not merely a subsequent promulgation of something which is in any case present even without such promulgation. Rather, it is something *in which* the reality promulgated brings its own individual history to its fullness and so extends its own real nature in that it integrates within its own individual history more 'material'. In this sense, then, the manifestation is the 'cause' of that which is manifesting" ("Considerations of the Active Role of the Person in the Sacramental Event," *TI* 14:161–84, at 178).

which it symbolizes, though some of his readers have referred to his notion in his way.[20]

Although Rahner's theological applications of *das Realsymbol* will be explored below, his appeal, with which he concludes his section on "general ontology," to the "scholastic philosophical" (i.e., medieval articulations of classical Aristotelian) theory of matter and form for illustrative purposes is worth including within the present overview. Unlike Plato's idea of "form," that is, something existing in a realm entirely separated from (though standing in some relationship of "resemblance" to) matter, Aristotle held that "form" existed as *and only as* the internal, instantiated organizing principle of a material being. To use an example from Aristotle, a bronze statue is not some earthly shadow of a Platonic statue form, but is rather the thing ("substance") constituted by the unity of the form and the thing's matter. The bronze statue is *enformed* bronze; it embodies and expresses the form, which in turn, resides within it as its inner structural principle.[21] Blending this classical account with his own language of *Symbol*, Rahner summarizes,

> the figure-forming essence of a being . . . constitute[s] and perfect[s] itself . . . by really projecting its visible figure outside itself as its – *Symbol*, its appearance. . . . The "form" gives itself away from itself by imparting itself to the material cause. It does not work on it subsequently and "from out-side", by bringing about in it something different from itself and alien to its essence. The "effect" is the "cause" itself.[22]

"Formal causality," a category quite familiar to those (like Rahner) trained in Thomistic philosophy and theology, thus stands as an explanatory touchstone for Rahner's articulations of *das Realsymbol*. Although Rahner's category of *realsymbolisch* causality is broader (cases of *Realsymbole* are not restricted to "substances" instantiating "forms," as will be seen shortly), formal causality is a clear[23] instance of Rahner's

---

20. E.g., Nancy Clasby, "Dancing Sophia: Rahner's Theology of Symbols," *Religion & Literature* 25, no. 1 (1993), 51–65. Clasby gives an accurate treatment of how Rahner, in some ways echoing Heidegger, sees "being in the world" as "expressive" rather than "static" (ibid., 54). However, in places, she offers inferences about (e.g., "the cosmos itself exists as God's symbol, . . . his body," ibid., 57) and summaries ("A symbol discloses its referent indirectly by showing us not what it is, but what it is like," ibid., 58) of Rahner's thought that are certainly not contained explicitly within it, and which, in fact, even seem to depart from it.

21. See Aristotle's *Physics* I.7, in *The Complete Works of Aristotle: The Revised Oxford Translation*, ed. Jonathan Barnes (Princeton: Princeton Univ. Press, 1984).

22. "The Theology of the Symbol," *TI* 4:231–32.

23. Wong actually refers to it as the "best" instance of Rahner's ontology of the *das Realsymbol* (*Logos-Symbol*, 81).

Symbol at work, and one to which he will return in "The Theology of the Symbol."

Explanatory Applications

The second part of Rahner's article consists of theological applications of the general ontology presented in the first part. The article's conclusion also brings this ontology to bear on the matter of Jesus's Sacred Heart, an issue also discussed in the introduction and which thus frames the entirety of Rahner's essay. The order in which he presents these applications is more or less "descending," beginning with God *in se* and moving, via God's sacramental presence in the world, toward anthropological considerations. I will follow Rahner's own ordering here, presenting only broad outlines of the topics he treats.

Rahner begins with what he calls "the supreme form of" the theology of the *Symbol*—namely, the theology of God's Logos.[24] After reiterating that his usage of *Symbol* must be understood in the technical sense just established, Rahner posits that "the Logos is the '*Symbol*' of the Father . . . the inward symbol which remains distinct from what is symbolized [*Symbolisierten*], which is constituted by what is symbolized, where what is symbolized [*Symbolisierte*] expresses itself and possesses itself."[25] That is, the Logos is the "other" into which the "original one" (the Father) self-expresses, forming a perfect unity while maintaining distinction. Rahner thus utilizes *das Realsymbol* to account for the eternal generation of the Second Person of the Trinity.[26]

As Rahner continues, he "nests" the successive *Realsymbole* within one another, constructing a sort of sacramental chain. Having thus established the first "link" in the Son's eternal, *symbolisch* generation from Father, Rahner transitions to the second "link": the *symbolisch* expression of that Son within human history. However, prior to his treatment of the Logos's incarnation, Rahner addresses Augustine's proposal (which Thomas Aquinas follows) that the persons of the Trinity are basically interchangeable when it comes to which person *could* assume Christ's human nature (although, of course, only the Second Person is said to *have in fact* assumed it).[27] For a combination of both

---

24. "The Theology of the Symbol," *TI* 4:235.
25. Ibid., *TI* 4:236; *SzT* 4:292.
26. Cf. "If this God expresses his very own self into the *emptiness* of what is not God, then this expression is the outward expression of his immanent Word, and not something arbitrary which could also be proper to another divine person" (*FCF*, 223).
27. "If, following a theological tradition which began only since St Augustine, one simply takes it for granted that each of the divine persons could set up, each for himself, his own hypostatic rela-

historical and theological reasons, Rahner departs from this Augustinian trajectory, positing instead that God's outward "utterance" *ad extra*
is a continuation of God's own inward self-expression that generates
the Son.[28] In other words, the same Logos which is God's self-expression in eternity in turn self-expresses within history through the incarnation. Rahner elects not to elaborate on the matter here (though he
does elsewhere),[29] but the brief excursus underlines how central the
intrinsic relation of *Symbol* and symbolized is for Rahner.

Turning to his second "link," the incarnation, Rahner voices yet
another concern about theological extrinsicism, raising his perennial
complaint that Christ's humanity is too often understood as a kind of
"uniform" which the Logos dons and uses as a sort of "mouthpiece."[30]
This crypto-Monophysitism, he worries, not only fails to respect
Christ's human will and subjectivity, which end up being construed as
kinds of instruments or puppets operated by God,[31] but it also establishes only a weak (and hardly "intrinsic") union of Christ's natures,
"hypostatic" though it might be.[32] On such an account, Christ's humanity could, at best, function as a kind of "signal" of his divine person.

Rahner's *das Realsymbol* offers a much more satisfying account:
Christ's humanity is not so much something "assumed" as it is the
result of the Logos's act of "exteriorizing" within the world.[33] By positing the human Jesus as "the 'appearance' of the Logos itself, its *Real-*

tionship to a given reality in the world and so could 'appear', then the fact that within the divinity
the Logos is the image of the Father would give the Logos no special character of symbol for the
world, which would be due to him alone on account of his relationship of origin to the Father.
The Father could also reveal himself and 'appear' without reference, so to speak, to the Son. But if
one does not make this pre-supposition with St Augustine, which has no clear roots in the earlier
tradition and still less in Scripture, one need have no difficulty in thinking that the Word's being
symbol of the Father has significance for God's action *ad extra*, in spite of such action being common to all three persons" ("The Theology of the Symbol," *TI* 4:236). Cf. Thomas Aquinas's *Summa
Theologiae* (henceforth *ST*) III q. 3 aa. 5–7 (*Summa Theologica*, trans. Fathers of the English Dominican Province, 5 vols. [New York: Benziger Brothers, 1947]). Thomas does acknowledge that it was
"more fitting" for the Son (rather than the Father or the Spirit) to assume Christ's human nature
(*ST* III q. 3 a. 8).
28. "The Theology of the Symbol," *TI* 4:236–37.
29. *The Trinity* (New York: Crossroad, 1997) [1967], "Remarks on the Dogmatic Treatise *De Trinitate*" (*TI*
4:77–102) [1960], "The Concept of Mystery in Catholic Theology" (*TI* 4:36–73, at 70) [1959].
30. Cf. *FCF*, 224, 287; the complaint is ubiquitous in Rahner's christological writings.
31. It should be noted that "instrument" language, which Rahner frequently criticizes on this topic,
does not automatically entail this "puppet" view of Christ's will. As Rahner certainly would have
been aware, Thomas Aquinas refers to Christ's humanity as the (conjoined) *instrumental* efficient
cause of grace, of which God *in his divinity* is the principal efficient cause (*ST* III q. 62 a. 5). And,
at the same time, Thomas understands Christ's human will, acknowledged to be entirely free (*ST*
III q. 18 a. 4), as part and parcel of its action as an instrument (i.e., Christ's human will: Christ's
humanity:: A saw's sharpness: a saw) (cf. *ST* III q. 62 a.1 ad 2). Rahner's worry here (as it is with
"Anselmian" satisfaction, which vaguely resembles Anselm's doctrine!) seems to be concern a
looser, popular usage of "instrument" language.
32. "The Theology of the Symbol," *TI* 4:237–38.

symbol in the pre-eminent sense," Rahner is able to present Christ's humanity as something intrinsically related to the Logos and genuinely revelatory of God, rather than

> something in itself alien to the Logos and its reality, which is only taken up from outside like an instrument . . . [T]he humanity of Christ is not to be considered as something in which God dresses up and masquerades. . . . [It] is the self-disclosure of the Logos itself, so that when God, expressing himself, exteriorizes himself, that very thing appears which we call the humanity of the Logos.[34]

In addition to rendering Christ's humanity an authentic revelation of the Logos, a *realsymbolisch* incarnation also provides an account of a most intimate union of Christ's natures; for if Christ's humanity is *das Realsymbol* of the divine Logos, the two enjoy the kind of *realsymbolisch* unity which also characterizes the oneness of the eternal divine persons, a unity of which there cannot be any purer kind.[35]

Having established the Father's *Realsymbol* as the Logos, and subsequently, the Logos's *Realsymbol* as the human Christ, it should come as no surprise that Rahner's next "link" is *das Realsymbol* of Christ. This, Rahner says, is the church, which

> is *das Realsymbol* of the presence of Christ . . . [T]his *Symbol* of the grace of God really contains what it signifies; that it is the *Ursakrament* of the grace of God, which does not merely designate but really possesses what was brought definitively into the world by Christ: the irrevocable, eschatological grace of God which conquers triumphantly the guilt of man.[36]

With this move, Rahner openly acknowledges that he is drawing on the work of his contemporaries who have styled the church as the "sacrament" of Christ.[37]

---

33. Cf. especially "On the Theology of the Incarnation" (*TI* 4:105–120), but also "Current Problems in Christology" (*TI* 1:149–213).

34. "The Theology of the Symbol," *TI* 4:238–39. Cf. "Christ's 'humanity' can be seen as that which results when God in his Word literally becomes other to himself in a creature" ("Jesus Christ," in *Theological Dictionary*, 236–41, at 240).

35. "The Theology of the Symbol," *TI* 4:227–28.

36. Ibid. 241. Cf. "the Church is the abiding and ultimate sacrament of the world's salvation . . . [W]herever and however the Church is this ultimate sacrament of salvation for the world, there Christ is present in his Spirit" ("The Presence of the Lord in the Christian Community at Worship," *TI* 10:71–83, at 83).

37. Rahner explicitly cites Otto Semmelroth, *Die Kirche als Urskrament* (Frankfurt: J. Knecht, 1953), as well as the doctoral thesis of Edward Schillebeeckx, *De sacramentele Heilseconomie* (Antwerp: Nelissen, 1952) and Schillebeeckx's later "Sakramente als Organe der Gottbegegnung," in *Fragen der Theologie heute*, ed. Johannes Feiner (Einsiedeln: Benziger 1957), 379–401. Other relevant contemporary works on this theme include Henri de Lubac, *Catholicism: Christ and the Common Destiny of*

Although it is true that by depicting the church as *das Realsymbol,* Rahner follows a larger movement which identified the church as Christ's "sacrament" (a movement which would eventually be enshrined in Vatican II's *Lumen Gentium* in 1964[38]), it is also true that Rahner envisioned the foundations of such a move early on in his career. In the conclusion of his dissertation from 1936, *E latere Christi* (which dealt with patristic exegesis, typology, Christ's wounded side and ecclesiology), Rahner calls for the development of a "general ontology of the presence of the life of Jesus in the life of the Christian."[39] Such an ontology, he envisions, would undergird his dissertation's claim that Christ's pierced side, from which the fathers understood the church to emerge,[40] is a kind of "inward" *Symbol* (as opposed to a *Symbol* given its meaning "from without"),[41] a *Symbol* which stands as "an 'address' to later historical persons," granting Jesus's life a kind of "abiding presence [*Gegenwärtigbleiben*]" to them.[42] In other words, in the mid-1930s, Rahner already envisioned the church and Christ's presence to exist in a *symbolisch* relationship to one another. It is noteworthy that decades later, when he introduces the church as the third "link" of the *realsymbolisch* chain, Rahner repeats this language and theme from his ecclesiological dissertation, speaking of the church bringing about Christ's presence throughout the various eras and locations of history: "the Church is the persisting presence [*Gegenwärtigbleiben*] of the incarnate Word in space and time . . . it continues the symbolic function of the Logos in the world."[43] (I will further address

---

Man (San Francisco: Ignatius, 1988), as well as Schillebeeckx, *Christ, the Sacrament of the Encounter with God* (New York: Sheed and Ward, 1963) (cf. Richard P. McBrien, *The Church: The Evolution of Catholicism* (New York: HarperOne, 2008), 135–37, 399). On the category of "sacramental causality" as it is used in recent Catholic systematic theology, see David N. Power, "Sacraments in General," in *Systematic Theology: Roman Catholic Perspectives,* eds. Francis Schüssler Fiorenza and John P. Galvin (Minneapolis: Fortress, 2011), 461–96, especially "Symbolic Causality," in 481–84.

38. "[T]he Church, in Christ, is a sacrament – a sign and instrument, that is, of communion with God and of the unity of the entire human race" (*Lumen Gentium (LG)* n. 1; cf. *LG* n. 48).

39. *E latere Christi: Der Ursprung der Kirche als zweiter Eva aus der Seite Christi des zweiten Adam, eine Untersuchung über den typologischen Sinn von Joh 19, 34E latere Christi,* in *SW* 3:1–84, at 83.

40. *E latere Christi* centers on the patristic typological idea that the church is the "second Eve" which emerged from the wounded side of the "second Adam" who "slept" on the cross, just as the first Eve was formed from the first Adam while he slept in the Garden.

41. Cf. Rahner's distinction in "Theology of the Symbol" between *Realsymbol* and *Vertretungssymbol.*

42. *E latere Christi,* 82–83.

43. "The Theology of the Symbol," *TI* 4:240. In another essay, Rahner identifies the Holy Spirit as the "medium" of Christ's presence to the church ("The Presence of the Lord in the Christian Community at Worship," *TI* 10:73–74). Lest this inclusion of the Holy Spirit be thought of as an entirely later corrective to his almost exclusive focus on the First and Second Persons of the Trinity in this article, it should be noted that throughout *E latere Christi,* Rahner refers to Christ's pierced side, out of which the church emerges, as the "Source of the Spirit."

how *E latere Christi* anticipates "The Theology of the Symbol" below, especially in chapter 4.)

Although Rahner offers several other applications, his *realsymbolisch* chain ends with his considerations of the sacraments, which he asserts are *Realsymbole* of the church. "The sacraments make concrete and actual, for the life of the individual, the symbolic reality [*Symbolwirklichkeit*] of the Church as the primary sacrament and therefore constitute at once, in keeping with the nature of this Church, a symbolic reality [*Symbolwirklichkeit*]."[44] That is, as Christ's *Realsymbol*, the church mediates his ongoing presence, but the church only achieves this identity through the individual sacraments, which Rahner says elsewhere are "acts in a process of concrete self-fulfilment on the part of the Church."[45] Since they are thus the church's "other" through which the church is mediated and self-realizes, the sacraments themselves are genuine *Realsymbole*. Rahner finds further support for this claim in the classical sacramental axioms which locate the sacraments' efficaciousness precisely in their act of signifying, thus testifying to the intimate, intrinsic relationship between *Symbol* and symbolized.[46]

Before concluding the article, Rahner's attention returns to Thomistic-Aristotelian hylomorphism for one more application of his ontology of the *Symbol*: the human body as *das Realsymbol* of the human soul.[47] Although it is common to hear humans described as the unity of body and soul, Rahner notes that this is a flawed description, both in terms of Thomas's classical anthropology as well as his own *realsymbolisch* version. The "body" cannot exist as such independently and apart from the soul, otherwise there would be not true unity, but only a grouping of two self-constituted realities.[48] This is why Thomas's hylomorphic anthropology speaks of the soul (i.e., the human person's "form") and "prime matter"[49] (which exists purely in *potentiality*, rather than actuality) as constituents of the body, which the human person

---

44. "The Theology of the Symbol," *TI* 4:241.
45. "Considerations of the Active Role," *TI* 14:181.
46. Namely, *Sacramenta efficiunt quod significant et significant quod efficiunt* (Sacraments effect what they signify and signify what they effect), *sacramenta gratiam efficiunt, quatenus eam significant* (sacraments effect grace, insofar as they signify), as well as *sacramenta significant gratiam, quia eam efficiunt* (sacraments signify grace, which they effect). Rahner writes, "If we are to speak of an effectiveness belonging to the sacramental sign, then it . . . is to be envisaged as an effectiveness inherent in the sign precisely *as* such" (ibid., *TI* 14:177).
47. Cf. *FCF*, 182–84.
48. Likewise, the soul "must not be understood – quite unscholastically – as a fragmentary portion of the whole man. It is the one originating source of the whole man" ("The Theology of the Symbol," *TI* 4:248).
49. Philosophers commenting on Aristotle disagree about what he means by "prime matter" and its place within his physics; however, Rahner is here following Thomas's reading.

is. That is, human beings are, like the bronze statue, *enformed* matter, *prima materia* taken up and ordered according to the inner principle of the form/soul.[50] Accordingly, the human body is the expression and full realization—that is, *das Realsymbol*—of the human soul.[51]

"The Theology of the Symbol" closes by returning to the question posed in its introduction: What ought we to make of the statement that Jesus's heart is the *Symbol* of his saving love? Here, Rahner provides some background by describing an ongoing dispute about the proper object of Sacred Heart devotion. For one camp of theologians, the word "heart" is understood in a very broad sense, as indicating one's "entire inner life" (including the bodily heart). A second camp, however, speaks of Jesus's love being adored under the "symbol" of his bodily heart. The former group, Rahner reports, has taken issue with the latter one, arguing that its scheme divides the *single object* of Sacred Heart devotion into a variety of particular devotions.

Such a criticism, as well as the division itself between the two groups, can be dissolved by understanding "symbol" as *das Realsymbol.* Rahner contends that the first group's discomfort with the second presumes that the "symbol" is only "extrinsically ordained" to the "symbolized." However, if "a *Symbol* is not something separate from the symbolized," but is "the reality, constituted by the thing symbolized as an inner moment of moment of itself" and "its concrete form of existence," then devotion to a *Symbol*-Heart is not divided among a variety of objects at all.[52] Indeed, Rahner notes, the first camp can then be included within the second, for Jesus's bodily heart can be adored as the *Symbol* of his "whole," his inner life and saving love.

As in the case of the church, Rahner anticipated this application of *Symbol* to the Sacred Heart nearly 25 years earlier in *E latere Christi*:

Our Sacred Heart devotion today certainly adores the bodily heart of Jesus. This bodily heart has a priority with respect to other parts of Jesus' humanity, which are also worthy of adoration, but it is only the object of a special devotion because it is a *Symbol* to us of the redemptive love of the God-man for us, summing up all of the achievements of this love in a sign.[53]

---

50. "[W]hat we call body is nothing else than the actuality of the soul itself in the 'other' of *material prima*, the 'otherness' produced by the soul itself, and hence its expression and *Symbol* in the very sense which we have given to the term *Realsymbol*" (ibid., 247).

51. "[T]he body is the *Symbol* of the soul . . . it is formed as the self-realization of the soul . . . the soul renders itself present and makes its 'appearance' in the body which is distinct from it" (ibid.).

52. Ibid., 251.

53. *E latere Christi*, 83. He also calls Jesus's Sacred Heart the "*symbolisch* recapitulation of the achievements of God's love" (ibid., 84).

Two paragraphs above this remark about the Sacred Heart in *E latere Christi*, he distinguishes between *Symbole* which have their meaning assigned to them by an observer or only retrospectively, and *Symbole* which have their meaning *intrinsically* and from the outset. That is, Rahner has already made the distinction, which he says dissolves the "first group's" qualms with the second, qualms which are rooted in an "extrinsic" version of "symbol." However, it is only in "The Theology of the Symbol" that he fully develops an ontology which distinguishes the two kinds of *Symbol* and applies this distinction to this debate about "objects" of devotion.

While it remains true that "The Theology of the Symbol" stands as Rahner's only prolonged consideration of *das Realsymbol* within his large body of writing, the judgment of his brother, Hugo, that *Symbol* is the essential center of Rahner's overall theology seems accurate. Not only is it clear that Rahner's thinking on the matter reaches back to at least his theology dissertation in 1936, but the applications of it which he sketches provide the themes and trajectories of topics to which he would return throughout his career. These especially include his adamant rejection of Trinitarian theology in which the divine persons are exchangeable and his insistence that Christ's humanity is not simply a "uniform" donned by the Logos,[54] but also his writing on the sacraments and the idea of "mediated immediacy."[55]

Background and Influences Underlying *das Realsymbol*

Over the course of Rahner's career, he engaged in philosophical as well as theological research and writing. As it is well-known, Rahner's original course of advanced study at the University of Freiberg was in philosophy. However, his dissertation, *Spirit in the World* (which would eventually be published in multiple editions and translations) was deemed unacceptable. Rahner subsequently transitioned to a career in theology, a subject for which he had previously developed a strong interest during his studies at Valkenburg. His theology dissertation, *E latere Christi*, was quickly submitted to, and accepted by, the University of Innsbruck.

---

54. He also briefly mentions the ongoing and perpetual role of Christ's humanity as *Symbol* mediating the beatific vision to us, which stands merely as an assertion in "The Theology of the Symbol" (*TI* 4:244), but which he defends elsewhere (cf. "The Eternal Significance of the Humanity of Jesus for our Relationship with God" (1953), in *TI* 3:35–46).
55. Rahner articulated the eternal significance of Christ's humanity mediating God's presence to us in terms of "mediated immediacy" ("The Theology of the Symbol," *TI* 4:244). Related remarks about "mediated immediacy" occur in "Dogmatic Questions on Easter" (*TI* 4:121–33, at 132) and *FCF*, 83ff.

Rahner's extensive training in both philosophy and theology has led to disagreements over how to interpret his prolific body of work in the latter field. One recent debate[56] which has received significant attention concerns whether Rahner's theology is best interpreted as resting squarely on the "foundation" of his philosophical commitments, a position advanced by Patrick Burke,[57] and which has simply been presumed by many others.[58] Opposed to such a "foundationalist" hermeneutic is Karen Kilby.[59] According to Kilby, no overarching or undergirding philosophy is operative in Rahner's theological corpus; in fact, she contends that several elements in Rahner's mature theology (e.g., the "supernatural existential") are diametrically opposed to his early philosophical claims in *Spirit in the World* and *Hearer of the Word*. His theology, she argues, does not proceed from an underlying and independent philosophy, although it does utilize philosophical ideas (e.g., the *Vorgriff*) at the service of faith seeking understanding.

Interestingly, accounts of the influences behind Rahner's *Realsymbol* also split into two "camps" which offer very different assessments of the importance of philosophy for this concept. Joseph Wong has argued that *das Realsymbol* emerged primarily (though certainly not exclusively) from commitments which Rahner adopted from Ignatian spirituality. Writing after Wong and aware of his account, Stephen Fields has identified the primary factors which shape *das Realsymbol*

---

56. A summative overview of this debate can be found in Robert Masson, "Interpreting Rahner's Metaphoric Logic," *Theological Studies* 71, no. 2 (June 2010), 380–409.

57. See Patrick Burke's *Reinterpreting Rahner: A Critical Study of His Major Themes* (New York: Fordham University Press, 2002). Such a reading has, until recently, been a largely unquestioned default understanding of Rahner (by many of his critics as well as his advocates). Among Rahner's advocates, Gerald McCool refers plainly to "the philosophical foundations of [Rahner's] theology" ("Introduction: Rahner's Philosophical Theology," in *A Rahner Reader*, ed. McCool (New York: The Seabury Press, 1975), xiii–xxviii, at xxvii). Representative of the critical pole of this camp is Robert Barron's *The Priority of Christ: Toward a Postliberal Catholicism* (Grand Rapids, MI: Brazos, 2007), in which Rahner's theology is presented as resting entirely upon (as well as ultimately determined and restrained by) his early philosophical work in *Spirit in the World* and *Hearer of the Word*. For Barron, the fact that Rahner's *FCF* presents anthropology first and Christology second is sufficient confirmation of this foundationalist structure of Rahner's thought, as well as Rahner's reliance upon the "modern" and "liberal" heritage of Kant, Schleiermacher, et al. (32–34). (It is worth noting that the anthropological reflections of Barron's champion, Thomas Aquinas, precede his systematic Christology, the latter of which is reserved for the fourth and final *pars* of the *Summa Theologiae*.)

58. E.g., William Dych: "Rahner delivered a series of fifteen lectures in Salzburg during the summer of 1937 which were to be extremely important in the development of his theology. They were concerned with the philosophy of religion, and he applied the philosophy of knowledge developed in his Freiburg dissertation [i.e., *Spirit in the World*] to the question of knowing God through an historical revelation. They were subsequently published under the title *H?rer des Wortes*, translated into English as *Hearers of the Word* [later, *Hearer of the Word*]. These two books were *the seminal and foundational works* out of which Rahner was to develop his philosophical theology" (*Karl Rahner* (Collegeville, MN: Liturgical, 1992), 7–8; emphasis mine).

59. See Karen Kilby, *Karl Rahner: Theology and Philosophy* (New York: Routledge, 2004).

to be philosophical theses advanced by J. Maréchal, Kant, and Hegel, among others. I do not wish to imply that the differing assessments of Wong and Fields map neatly onto the positions of Kilby and Burke. Nevertheless, the tendency for Rahner's readers to assess and interpret his work primarily from either philosophical or theological starting points (which may say more about the reader than Rahner) is certainly not uncommon.

Ignatian Spirituality

Before directly addressing the "spiritual" bases out of which Wong sees *das Realsymbol* emerging, a few preliminary remarks are in order. First, it should be made clear that Wong acknowledges both spiritual *and* philosophical motivations behind Rahner's understanding of *Symbol*. That said, in his judgment, Rahner's spiritual motivations take priority over his philosophical ones. Accordingly, Wong's "background study" on *das Realsymbol* proceeds in this order: chapter 1 explores the "Religious Origin of Rahner's Symbol Concept," while chapter 2 treats "Rahner's Ontology of 'Realsymbol' and its Philosophical Presuppositions."

Second, Wong's decision to prioritize Rahner's spiritual motivations over his philosophical ones accords with a significant fact, noted above, which Wong himself notes only briefly.[60] While Rahner's seminal article on *das Realsymbol* does address the concept's applicability to Christology, the Trinity, ecclesiology, the sacraments, and even anthropology,[61] "Theology of the Symbol" was originally composed as a contribution to a volume on Jesus's Sacred Heart. The fact that Rahner's most explicit and lengthy treatment of the topic occurs as a prolegomena to devotion to Jesus's Sacred Heart[62] speaks forcefully to the position that *das Realsymbol* emerged primarily from "spiritual" considerations.

Finally, at the service of situating what follows within his overall project, Wong's main thesis is that Rahner's *Realsymbol*, specifically as applied to the Second Person of the Trinity (*Logos-Symbol*), is *the* "key-concept" for understanding and even uniting Rahner's various and disparate christological writings. Rahner himself commented on this project shortly before the end of his life in the volume's foreword.

---

60. Wong, *Logos-Symbol*, 40.
61. It is typically in association with these very topics that Rahner's readers take up interest in *das Realsymbol*.
62. Rahner's own introductory remarks in this article (*TI* 4:221–22) situate it as an attempt to address the question of whether the proper object of devotion to the Sacred Heart is Jesus's physical heart or Jesus's love; by suggesting that the former is *das Realsymbol* of the latter, Rahner is able to provide a most succinct answer to this question: yes.

There, he evaluated Wong's efforts positively, affirming the sort of continuity (even if it was not always consciously operative) posited by Wong and noting that this renewed emphasis on *Symbol*, which Rahner describes as having "developed in the course of writing a theology of devotion to the Sacred Heart," infuses his later "formal" and "abstract" christological work with a richness which was somewhat lacking.[63] To be clear, Rahner offers no evaluation of Wong's thesis about the "priority" of his motivations; however, his reference to Jesus's Sacred Heart when discussing *Symbol* (thus underlining the original context out of which his most explicit writing on the subject emerged) is noteworthy.

Wong begins his "spiritual" account of Rahner's influences by describing Rahner as a "theologian and a philosopher, as well as a mystic."[64] This somewhat startling statement is probably best understood in light of Rahner's famous proposition that "the Christian of the future will be a mystic or he or she will not exist at all," a proposition which he follows by characterizing mysticism not as "singular parapsychological phenomena, but a genuine experience of God emerging from the very heart of our existence."[65] Wong judges that Rahner, as a professional theologian, is more informed by his "mystical" side than his "philosophical" side.[66]

At the center of this mystical side, Wong explains, is the insight that "God is always mediated through created realities, especially through people and events."[67] While this sacramental insight might be more generally described as particularly Catholic, Wong especially credits Ignatius's spirituality, with its emphasis on "finding God in all things," for influencing the Jesuit theologian's sacramental worldview. Moreover, this sacramental worldview is accompanied by a strongly christological vector which directs this widespread mediation of God in the world. Wong describes this vector as a "Christ centered incarnational vision," according to which the human "experience of God is always mediated, explicitly or implicitly, by the humanity of Christ."[68]

---

63. Rahner writes, "considerations essential to my Christology are drawn together here which I had indeed developed in the course of writing a theology of devotion to the Sacred Heart but which I had overlooked in producing my first brief systematic Christology during my years in Muenster. The reassertion of my considerations on devotion to the Sacred Heart, however, enriches and deepens the otherwise somewhat too formal and abstract outline of systematic Christology which resulted in both the work I did in Muenster and in my *Foundations of Christian Faith*" (Wong, *Logos-Symbol*, 6).

64. Ibid., 46.

65. *The Practice of Faith: A Handbook of Contemporary Spirituality* (New York: Crossroad, 1983), 22.

66. Wong, *Logos-Symbol*, 46.

67. Ibid., 47.

68. Ibid.

In fact, along with the call to "find God in all things," Wong identifies "Christ mysticism" as the major factor through which Ignatius of Loyola influenced Rahner's spirituality. "If for [Ignatius] things of the word are 'sacraments,'" Wong explains, "then Christ is the *primordial* sacrament of encounter with God."[69] That is, it is in virtue of the incarnation that other mediations of grace through creation occur, for through God's entering into and uniting with creation, creation itself has been infused with God: "by the fact that the Logos has taken flesh, things of the world are no longer mere 'means' in order to reach God. Rather they are quasi-sacraments mediating the presence of God himself."[70]

Having sketched this "Ignatian" sacramental worldview, according to which the entire created order serves as a sacramental mediation of God's grace dependent upon Christ, Wong offers the Rahnerian deduction that "man's ordinary life is imbued with the grace of Christ," and thus, "one can hardly opt for anything without having to do with God and Christ either by accepting or rejecting them."[71] Anticipating how Rahner may describe this worldview in his technical vocabulary, Wong suggests that "the order of creation is the 'symbol' of the order of grace constituted by it for its own realization and manifestation."[72] To summarize, Rahner's claims (which will be examined below) that all of reality is "symbolic" and that the Logos offers the prime example of *das Realsymbol* are rooted in Ignatius's vision of a sacramental world which is, in turn, dependent upon *the* mediation of grace in Christ.

In company with Ignatius, the devotion to Jesus's Sacred Heart is identified by Wong as central to Rahner's spirituality; importantly, appeals to *Symbol* abound in Rahner's writings on the Sacred Heart. The "basis" of this devotion, as identified by Wong, could easily be described as Ignatian, given the considerations above: all realities mediate God, but "Christ is the one Mediator between God and man."[73] This "basis" is identified as such because in speaking of Jesus's "heart," two layers of *Symbol* are operative. The most basic layer concerns the human being Jesus as the *Ursakrament* of God's grace; the second layer concerns the "heart" which sums up that very human being.

According to Rahner, "heart" is an *Urwort*, a word burgeoning with meaning. "Heart" denotes not only one's "biological heart" or "pulmonary flesh," but also the "heart of the person" in a more profound

69. Ibid., 56.
70. Ibid., 57.
71. Ibid., 57–58.
72. Ibid., 57.
73. Ibid., 63.

sense; in fact, the former is said to be the *Symbol* of the latter.[74] By this, Rahner does not mean that heart is a "conventional sign" or an "arbitrary symbol." Rather, he calls it an *Ursymbol* uniting two intrinsically related realities—the corporal heart and the "heart of the person" are never without each other.[75] Accordingly, talk of Jesus's "heart" concerns both the center of his self-realization as well as the center of his corporal self. Being that both of these realities are, in turn, sacraments which realize God's love within the world, Rahner, combining the two "layers" of *Symbol* mentioned above, ventures to say that "the veneration of the Sacred Heart is, in fact, precisely a devotion to that love of God which has been made present to us in Christ Jesus."[76] Rahner's early and explicit connection of Sacred Heart devotion to his theory of *Symbol* supports Wong's identification of the former and a strong impetus for the latter.

Although Wong's subsequent chapter discusses the philosophical presuppositions underlying *das Realsymbol*, such presuppositions will be, in the interest of space, discussed below through the lens of another of Rahner's readers.

Philosophical Stimuli

In his *Being as Symbol*, Stephen Fields has proposed an alternative principal influence behind *das Realsymbol*—namely, Rahner's philosophical forbearers.[77] Certainly, Fields agrees that Rahner's philosophy—in particular, his metaphysics—is at the service of a larger (theological) project. Nevertheless, he asserts that Rahner's philosophical work is "an original contribution that merits attention in its own right."[78] Without characterizing Rahner's theology as "foundationalist" with respect to his philosophy, Fields endeavors to examine the latter *in se* in *Being*

74. Ibid.
75. Ibid., 65. This statement would, it seems, imbue heart transplants with incredible metaphysical significance.
76. "Unity-Love-Mystery," *TI* 8:229–47, at 235, qtd. in Wong, *Logos-Symbol*, 66. Wong offers his own summary: Jesus's Sacred Heart is a "symbol . . . to be understood in the sense of a *sacramental* sign. It does not merely convey a concept but it actually contains 'in its innermost depths that abundance of grace and power' which it signifies . . . the Sacred Heart is a sacramental symbol which effects by signifying (*significando efficit*). It is the incarnation, or realization in human form, of divine love" (ibid. 67–68).
77. Stephen Fields, *Being as Symbol: On the Origins and Development of Karl Rahner's Metaphysics* (Washington, D.C.: Georgetown Univ., 2000). For more of Fields's work in this area, see his "Symbol," in *Cambridge Dictionary of Christian Theology*, eds. Ian McFarland et al (New York: Cambridge Univ. Press, 2011), 489–90 and *Analogies of Transcendence: An Essay on Nature, Grace, and Modernity* (Washington, D.C.: Catholic Univ. of America Press, 2016), especially "Sacramental Causality" (105–48) and "Appendix: the *Realsymbol* and Selected Modern Symbols" (253–70).
78. Fields, *Being as Symbol*, 1.

as *Symbol*. A significant portion of this work consists of analyzing the influences behind *das Realsymbol*. Explicitly disagreeing with Wong's assessment, Fields "locate[s] the origins of the Realsymbol principally in philosophical theories of the symbol,"[79] summarily stating that "Rahner conceives the Realsymbol by interpreting Thomism in light of the tradition of Kant to Heidegger."[80] In particular, he identifies J. Maréchal and neo-Thomist theories of knowledge, Thomas Aquinas's sacramental thought, and elements common to Goethe and Hegel as influential contributors to Rahner's concept.[81]

Before specifically addressing Fields's account of these philosophical influences, let us situate it within his broader understanding of Rahner's "original contribution" to philosophy. Fields describes this contribution as a "mediation of Thomism through the lens of issues raised in philosophy stretching from Kant to Heidegger," a mediation in which both Thomism and the continental philosophical tradition are each creatively reinterpreted.[82] In Fields's judgment, Rahner's entire metaphysics is developed around *Realsymbole*, that is, beings which "necessarily express themselves in order to constitute their essential nature," beings which are not "inert and static substances, but . . . dynamic self-mediating realities."[83] *Realsymbolisch* "being" is structured according to a process of emanation (signifying itself in a concrete reality) and return (self-perfection).[84] In other words, the *"exitus-reditus"* schema which M.-D. Chenu famously used to describe Thomas Aquinas's organization of the *Summa Theologiae*,[85] an organization which reflected God's Being in the orders of creation and redemption, is applicable to beings on the finite level as well. For the sake of precision, Fields breaks the movement of this schema into three moments of *das Realsymbol:* (i) an "original unity," (ii) a medium/"other," and (iii) a "perfected unity."[86]

---

79. Ibid., 3.
80. Ibid., 20.
81. Peter Fritz has recently expanded on the project undertaken by Fields by examining Rahner's notion of *das Realsymbol* in relation to Friedrich Schelling's philosophy ("Karl Rahner, Friedrich Schelling, and Original Plural Unity," *Theological Studies* 75, no. 2 (2014), 284–307). It should also be noted that Fields engages in a lengthy analysis of the implications which *das Realsymbol* has for a "metaphysics of language," an analysis in which he identifies Kant and Heidegger (in the latter's reflections on artwork) as additional influences to Rahner's theory in this regard. Though certainly worthy of study, the applicability of *das Realsymbol* to these fields is only marginally related to the current project, and will not be further addressed here.
82. Fields, *Being as Symbol*, 2.
83. Ibid.
84. Ibid., 6.
85. Cf. M.-D. Chenu, *Toward Understanding St. Thomas* (Chicago: Henry Regnery Co.,1964), 304, as well as "Le plan de la Somme théologique de saint Thomas," *Révue Thomiste* 45 (1939), 93–107.

Rahner arrived at this theory, according to Fields, through his engagement with Joseph Maréchal, Thomas Aquinas, Goethe, and Hegel. Considering these philosophical influences in this order, let us turn to Fields's account. The thesis of Fields's second chapter is that Rahner's *Realsymbol* can be seen as a development upon Joseph Maréchal's theory of knowledge. Maréchal continued fellow Jesuit Pierre Rousselot's "transcendental Thomist" quest to bring put Kant (with his turn to the subject) and Aquinas (and the *analogia entis*) in conversation with one another. Fields describes Maréchal's particular effort here as an attempt to "overcome Kant's metaphysical agnosticism about the Absolute by justifying how the noumenon penetrates the world of empirical phenomena"; in doing so, Fields suggest, Maréchal "implicitly conceive[s] Being as self-mediational," and is able to bring "symbol and analogy into harmony."[87]

One way in which Fields sees this "implicit symbolism" operative in Maréchal concerns his epistemology. Maréchal, working from Aquinas—and ultimately, Aristotle—recognizes three phases of cognition: (i) *assimilation*, in which the senses collect data from an external object, data which the imagination then synthesizes into a "phantasm"; (ii) *abstraction*, in which the intellect renders the product of assimilation intelligible as a universal, and (iii) *objectivation*, in which one judges the perceived object to exist apart from oneself.[88]

Operative in the act of cognition is an "implicit symbolism," according to Fields. This symbolism is based on a string of "intrinsic mediations" between the various cognitive faculties. Working backward from the three phases just mentioned, Fields explains that "the soul informs the intellect that informs the corporeal powers." That is, the soul's "intrinsic medium" is the intellect, while the intellect's "intrinsic media" are the senses.[89] In short, following the soul's *exitus* through this chain of "intrinsic media" to the perceived "other," "spirit expresses itself immanently in matter," that is, it functions as a "symbol."[90]

The sacramental thought of Thomas Aquinas is the second major

---

86. Fields, *Being as Symbol.*, 6.
87. Ibid., 30.
88. Ibid., 31. The first two of these stages, at least, are at the heart of classical Thomistic-Aristotelian epistemology.
89. Ibid., 32.
90. Wong makes a similar point regarding Rahner's account of human knowledge, in which "knowing is first of all the subject's return to himself" (*Logos-Symbol*, 85); he goes on to claim that the overall ontology operative in Rahner's *Hearer of the Word*, one marked by emanation and return, corresponds with Rahner's ontology of the *Symbol* (ibid., 86).

philosophical influence identified by Fields. Fields suggests that Rahner, at least in part, proposed *das Realsymbol* as an alternative to Thomas's sacramental theory of causality, which Rahner found to be, in some ways, deficient.[91] It should be noted that *das Realsymbol* stands for many of Rahner's readers (and often for Rahner himself) as a functional equivalent for "sacrament."[92]

Fields begins by providing a brief overview of Thomas's treatment of sacraments in the *Summa Theologiae*. There, Thomas defines a sacrament as "a sign of a sacred reality inasmuch as it has the property of sanctifying" human beings,[93] which Fields summarizes as an "efficacious sign" which "causes what it signifies."[94] In accounting for *how* sacraments are efficacious, Aquinas has recourse to the idea of "instrumental causality," a subcategory of "efficient causality."[95] (Thomas likens the instrumental cause to a hatchet used by a carpenter to fashion a bench.[96]) This move by Thomas was a reaction against the sacramental occasionalism or concomitance taught by Peter Lombard, a theory which held that the sacraments are basically signs which present "occasions" on which God always bestows grace.[97] By characterizing sacraments as instrumental efficient causes, Thomas was able to connect their signatory value (e.g., water washing) with what God accomplished *through* them (e.g., cleansing of sins, regeneration). In other words, Thomas wanted the sacraments to operate more like God's hatchet than as a reminder for God to make a bench.

Improvement though they may be, Thomas's efforts did not satisfy Rahner, for two reasons. First, Rahner was unable to see how Thomas's sacraments, as "instrumental efficient causes," establish an "intrinsic" bond with the grace they communicate. Second, Rahner was unable to see how the efficaciousness of Thomas's sacraments is essentially, and not just accidentally, related to the church.[98] Rahner's counterproposal lies in his schema of "nesting" *Realsymbole*. The human Jesus is the *Real-*

---

91. Fields, *Being as Symbol*, 52.
92. Fields does not go so far as to equate the two, though he affirms that the two ideas "intersect." He explains: something is a *Realsymbol* if it "mediates a signified reality intrinsically, dynamically, and reciprocally," while something is a sacrament if it causes or effects what it signifies (*Being as Symbol*, 52–53).
93. *ST* III q. 60 a. 2 co.
94. Fields, *Being as Symbol*, 38–39.
95. Fields seems to indicate that "instrumental causality" is a category taken from Aristotle; however, While "efficient causality" certainly is an Aristotelian category, the subdivisions of *principal* and *instrumental* efficient causes seem to come later. Most likely, Thomas's subdivision here is rooted in John Damascene's language of Christ's humanity as God's instrument (cf. *ST* I–II q. 112 a. 1 ad 1).
96. *ST* III q. 62 a. 1 co.
97. Fields, *Being as Symbol*, 40.
98. Ibid., 46.

symbol of the Logos (i.e., the other into whom the Logos emanates to form a perfect unity), and the church is subsequently the *Realsymbol* of Jesus Christ.[99] Furthermore, the church's sacraments *in turn* function as *its Realsymbole*, "actualiz[ing] the Church: they bring it to self-realization and they consummate its unity."[100] In Fields's judgment, Rahner's development of *das Realsymbol* was at least partially motivated by a desire for an account of sacramental causality which features a strong, "intrinsic" link between the sacraments and the grace they communicate, as well as with the church which bestows them.

Field's final set of influences, which we will examine here, shifts from the previous Thomistic considerations to late-eighteenth and early-nineteenth-century Germany. While the previous influences addressed how *Realsymbol* functions to relate finite and infinite modes of being (Maréchal) and to better account for intrinsically efficacious signs (Thomas), Fields sees in Goethe and Hegel the ingredients for Rahner's claim that *das Realsymbol* brings the "original unity" to *self-perfection* in the "other." More specifically, he argues that Rahner's account of "becoming," which emerges from his engagement with German Idealism, "is an origin of the Realsymbol."[101]

According to Fields, Goethe's description of "reality as self-mediating," which was "systematized" by Hegel, is an important ancestor of Rahner's *Realsymbol*. He explains that for Goethe, the reality which we experience as "manifold" is, in fact, derived from "an underlying unity."[102] As an explanatory example of this multiplicity in unity, he cites Goethe's observation that through reading discrete words or hearing discrete notes, we form singular thoughts and unified phrases or songs.[103] This insight is systematized in Hegel, for whom "reality is a dialectical progression that reconciles duality without suppressing it" into a unity, with its own "opposing other"; applied to rational knowledge, "sublation" reconciles subject and object into a perfected unity.[104]

Fields connects this systemization to Rahner's *das Realsymbol*, through which reality, including God ("Spirit"), mediates itself to the other, and so, achieves a "perfection of unity." For both Rahner and

99. "As a Realsymbol, the Church is both distinct from and identical with its signified reality, the glorified Christ, the effective means of sanctification" (ibid., 47–48).
100. Ibid., 48.
101. Ibid., 55.
102. Ibid., 61.
103. Ibid., 64.
104. Ibid., 65–66.

Hegel, "concrete reality dynamically embodies the perfection of the mediation of its intrinsic opposition."[105] Importantly, Fields notes that Rahner does not wholly adopt Hegel's system, refusing to "reconcile Being's infinite and finite modes into a unity-in-difference that entails the univocity of reality"; for Rahner, the intellect knows sensible things as *finite substances,* rather than as accidents of the Absolute.[106] Rahner's insistence on God's sovereignty and freedom to self-communicate is also an important point of divergence.[107] But in the end, Fields insists that Rahner's reflection on "becoming" and the alterations which he makes to the accounts of German Idealism contribute to the emergence of his *Realsymbol.* Writing over two decades earlier, Gerald McCool states the connection even more boldly, referring to "Rahner's Hegelian metaphysics of the real symbol."[108]

Evaluation: Priority of Spirituality or Philosophy?

Wong and Fields provide detailed analyses of the background out of which *das Realsymbol* develops, although they differ as to whether Rahner's spirituality or his blend of Thomistic and German continental philosophy serves as the principal motivation for constructing the concept. Of course, both sets of influences contributed to *das Realsymbol,* and it is only in accounting for each of these that we obtain a complete picture of the thought world out of which Rahner's concept emerged.[109] Nevertheless, the debate over which set takes priority is not without value. Establishing the primary impetus behind *das Realsymbol* is helpful in understanding how Rahner primarily intended it to be implemented. In light of my own purposes, determining whether Rahner

---

105. Ibid., 73. Cf. McCool, "Rahner's metaphysics contain Hegelian elements. The metaphysics of the Son's relationship to the Father within the Trinity and the metaphysics of the Son's relation to the world in creation and the Incarnation, which are essential to the coherence of Rahner's system, have an unmistakably Hegelian origin. They all follow the Hegelian metaphysics of the spirit which, abiding changelessly 'in itself,' changes 'in the other,' into which it 'goes over' in order to return to itself" ("Introduction: Rahner's philosophical theology," in *A Rahner Reader,* xxii).
106. Fields, *Being as Symbol,* 76.
107. Wong, *Logos-Symbol,* 131, cf. Rahner's insistence on *quasi*-formal causality in "Some Implications of the Scholastic Concept of Uncreated Grace," *TI* 1:319–46, at 330.
108. McCool, "Introduction: Rahner's Philosophical Theology," in *A Rahner Reader,* xxvii.
109. In this respect, Wong and Fields provide almost perfect complements to one another. While Fields does not rule out nonphilosophical influences, such influences are only mentioned in his (almost tangential) remark about disagreeing with Wong's prioritizing spiritual stimuli; Fields's own study is restricted to the philosophical variety. Likewise, although Wong dedicates his second chapter to the "philosophical" presuppositions of *das Realsymbol,* the majority of it is a review of Rahner's *own* writings ("Theology of the Symbol," *Spirit in the World, Hearer of the Word*), and the inclusion of philosophical thinkers occurs only in the process of arguing that Rahner's account of "transcendence" is "Ignatian [*Deus semper major*] rather than Heideggerian" (*Logos-Symbol,* 98).

developed *das Realsymbol* out of spiritual motivations or in efforts to resolve philosophical conundra impacts the likelihood of my claim that Rahner's sacramental soteriology has a complement in representative soteriology. That is, if, as Wong argues, Rahner's concept emerged primarily from a sacramental worldview and reflections on a christocentric devotion to the very center of Jesus's person, a clearer case can be made that a person-centered "representative" account of Christ as Savior is a fitting counterpart to (and indeed, even implication of) a soteriology based upon *das Realsymbol*.

And without any intention of undervaluing Fields's important work, it does seem to me that Wong's prioritization of influences is correct. While Rahner also openly identified himself as a follower of Maréchal, much of Fields's work in this section seems concerned more primarily with Rahner's concept of the *Vorgriff,* rather than *das Realsymbol.* Fields succeeds in showing how Rahner's *Vorgriff* is strongly shaped by Maréchal's considerations, but the *Vorgriff* and *das Realsymbol* are two very different ideas, even if they do both relate "finite and infinite modes of being" to one another. Likewise, Goethe and Hegel certainly shaped the intellectual milieu in which Rahner wrote, and Fields does show compelling similarities between their thought and *das Realsymbol* (and even how *das Realsymbol* makes correctives). Yet, Rahner never self-identified as a "Hegelian," and it is fairly clear (especially from the examples Rahner himself chooses!) that Aristotelian-scholastic accounts of formal causality and hylomorphism provide an even closer analogue to *das Realsymbol* than does Hegelian dialectical thought. Although Fields has certainly shown Maréchal, Goethe, and Hegel to be influences in important respects, he seems to have been most successful in the case of Thomas and the sacraments; but even this "philosophical" influence, centered on the topic of the causal efficacy of the sacraments, is itself situated among "spiritual" concerns which Fields leaves largely unaddressed.[110]

Perhaps the most compelling reason to favor Wong's prioritization is the intimate link in Rahner's writing between the concept of *Symbol* and the devotion of Jesus's Sacred Heart. First of all, it is quite signif-

---

110. In a review of Fields's *Being as Symbol,* Anne Carr observes that Fields "limit[s] his study to the metaphysics of Rahner, a thinker whose primary work was as a theologian and whose use of philosophy was driven by religious, indeed theological concerns. And each of the sources Fields considers had significant theological concerns that he assiduously avoids, preferring to concentrate on philosophy in an effort to separate metaphysics from religious interests" ("Being as symbol: on the origins and development of Karl Rahner's metaphysics," *Journal of Religion* 82, no. 3 (2002): 484–85, at 485).

icant that "The Theology of the Symbol" was originally composed for an anthology about the devotion to Jesus's Sacred Heart. Even so, one may argue, it could be the case that this topic provided a forum for Rahner (who was by now, after all, a theologian by profession) to introduce his (primarily philosophical) concept *via* theological application. But entertaining such an idea of a convenient application is soon halted when one considers that Rahner was speaking of *Symbol*, and even a rough division between *Realsymbol* and *Vertretungssymbol*, in the same breath as "Sacred Heart" in his theology dissertation back in 1936.[111] There, he even issues a sort of call for "The Theology of the Symbol," stating that fully distinguishing these two kinds of *Symbole* would require a "general ontology" which accounts for how a historical reality can be present to a different time, and particularly for how events of Jesus's life (especially being pierced on the cross) can, as *Symbole*, achieve such presence to today's Christians.[112] Thus, it appears, the earliest mention Rahner makes of *das Realsymbol* (even if it has not yet been given the explicit name or the accompanying developed ontology, the latter of which, of course, draws on the philosophical sources which Fields identifies) occurs as Rahner suggests a route for linking the historical person of today with Jesus's own Heart, the Source of the Spirit and recapitulation of his love opened up to us on the cross.

Distinguishing "*Symbol*" in Rahner from Other Usages

In "The Theology of the Symbol," Rahner already distinguished his notion of *Symbol* from that of popular usage. However, "symbol" is likewise employed as a technical term by other theologians and philosophers as well. A lengthy overview of these thinkers cannot be given here, but it is worthwhile to briefly consider two prominent theologians and their own concepts of symbol in order to bring further clarity

---

111. In his dissertation's conclusion, Rahner identifies the patristic fascination with Christ's pierced side (the theme at the center of *E latere Christi*) as an ancient analogue to contemporary devotion to the Sacred Heart: "we can reasonably say that the history of our idea [of the church's origin from Jesus' pierced side] is a piece of the history of Patristic devotion to the Heart of Jesus. . . . When we seek in the Patristic period an analogue or traces of our Sacred Heart devotion, we must not mechanically search for texts in which the Heart of Jesus somehow mentioned. This method leads nowhere. We must instead ask whether the early Christians had a *Symbol* in which everything that they knew of the redeeming love of God was summed up in an object of their devotion. . . . But this was for them the pierced side of Jesus. . . . The difference between the patristic devotion to the wounded side of Christ and the Sacred Heart devotion of today lies not so much in the content and in the *symbolischen* recapitulation of the achievements of God's love, but in a shift of the *Symbol*, whereby attention is directed even more clearly to the love of Christ and the *Symbol* is more easily a special object of devotion" (*E latere Christi*, 83).
112. Ibid., 82–83.

to the distinctiveness of Rahner's idea, and simultaneously to discourage any hasty conflation of these usages of the term. The first of these figures is the influential Protestant theologian writing a generation before Rahner, Paul Tillich. The second is another Jesuit belonging to the generation after Rahner who built upon his insights, Roger Haight.

"Symbol" in the theology of Paul Tillich

As is the case with Rahner's, Paul Tillich's understanding of symbol is a precise one which he makes clear via a distinction between two different groups. On the one hand, there is the mere "sign" (e.g., a street sign or traffic light[113]), which can stand for another reality with which it is paired more or less arbitrarily. On the other hand, the symbol (e.g., a national flag[114]) bears a stronger relationship to the reality which it symbolizes. Tillich writes, "We know that real representative symbols [echte repräsentative Symbole], prevalent in history, art, and religion, cannot be arbitrarily substituted [willkürlich . . . ersetzt] by other symbols. They have come out of a particular encounter with reality and are living only as long as the experience is alive."[115] Thus, the first way in which a symbol distinguishes itself from a sign is by arising "out of a particular encounter with reality"[116]; as Adam Pryor puts it, "by some cultural-historical mechanism, [the symbol] has become the necessary construct for what it symbolizes," and so, is not simply an "arbitrarily assigned . . . placeholder."[117] Part and parcel of this distinguishing factor, as Tillich indicates above, is that when the symbol ceases to be

---

113. "The red sign at the street corner points to the order to stop the movements of cars at certain intervals. A red light and the stopping of cars have essentially no relation to each other, at conventionally they are united as long as the convention lasts. The same is true of letters and numbers and partly even words. They point beyond themselves to sounds and leanings. They are given this special function by convention within a nation or by international conventions, as the mathematical signs. Sometimes such signs are called symbols; but this is unfortunate because it makes the distinction between signs and symbols more difficult" (Paul Tillich, *Dynamics of Faith* (New York: Harper & Row, 1957), 41–42).
114. Ibid., 42.
115. Paul Tillich, "Dimensionen, Schichten und die Einheit des Seins," in *Gesammelte Werke*, 14 vols. (Stuttgart: Evangelisches Verlagswerk, 1959–), vol. 4 (1961), 118–29, at 118–19. Translation taken from Kenan B. Osborne, "Tillich's Understanding of Symbols and Roman Catholic Sacramental Theology," in *Paul Tillich: A New Catholic Assessment*, eds. Raymond F. Bulman and Frederick J. Parrella (Collegeville, MN: Liturgical Press, 1994), 91–111, at 98–99.
116. "Symbols cannot be produced intentionally. . . . They grow out of the individual or collective unconscious and cannot function without being accepted by the unconscious dimension of our being. Symbols which have an especially social function, as political and religious symbols, are created or at least accepted by the collective unconscious of the group in which they appear" (Tillich, *Dynamics of Faith*, 43).
117. Adam Pryor, "Comparing Tillich and Rahner on Symbol: Evidencing the Modernist/Postmodernist Boundary," *Bulletin of the North American Paul Tillich Society* 37, no. 2 (2011), 23–38, at 28.

utilized by the cultural-historical locus which produced it, it "dies." For example, Tillich deems the Virgin Mary a "dead" symbol for most Protestants.[118]

A second distinctive characteristic of Tillich's notion of symbol is its participation in the reality which it symbolizes. To get an idea of what Tillich means by participation, it is instructive to consider his example of a flag:

> [T]he symbol . . . participates in that to which it points: the flag partici-pates in the power and dignity of the nation for which it stands. There-fore, it cannot be replaced except after an historic catastrophe that changes the reality of the nation which it symbolizes. An attack on the flag is felt as an attack on the majesty of the group in which it is acknowl-edged. Such an attack is considered blasphemy.[119]

Since Tillich's symbols share in the power of the reality which they symbolize, Ronald Modras explains, they "can be stirring, elevating and integrating, as in the case of the cross for Christians, or destructive and disintegrating, as in the case of the Nazi swastika."[120]

Finally, Tillich's symbol has the power to convey and communicate the reality symbolized. In the case of an "ultimate" symbol, God's pres-ence is communicated, and in such a way that the symbol "expresses not only the ultimate [i.e., God] but its own lack of ultimacy."[121] Given Tillich's desire to strongly distinguish God from the symbols which convey God's presence, the language of "manifestation"[122] and "aware-ness"[123] is often used to describe such communication.

The similarities between the accounts of Rahner and Tillich are clear. Both distinguish between "thicker" and "thinner" symbolic enti-ties, with Rahner's *Realsymbole* and Tillich's symbols (even "real rep-resentative symbols," as we just saw) standing against "arbitrarily assigned" signals (*Vertretungssymbole* and signs, respectively). More-over, these more robust categories successfully communicate the real-

---

118. Ronald Modras, "Catholic Substance and the Catholic Church Today," in *Tillich: A New Catholic Assessment*, 33–47, at 37.
119. Tillich, *The Dynamics of Faith*, 43.
120. Modras, "Catholic Substance and the Catholic Church Today," 37.
121. Ibid.
122. "The Church 'manifests' the invisible community of grace. . . . It 'represents' the kingdom of God in history" (Ibid., 40).
123. "The symbol provides the concrete locality for the symbolic awareness of being-itself" (Pryor, "Comparing Tillich and Rahner on Symbol," 28). Notably, Tillich defines "sacrament" as "any object or event in which the transcendent infinite is *perceived* as present to the finite" (ibid., emphasis added). Cf. Tillich, *The Protestant Era* (Chicago: Univ. of Chicago Press, 1948), 108, 111.

ities with which they are associated, expressing their presence in their act of symbolizing.

However, there are significant points of divergence between the accounts as well, two of which I will point out here. Although Tillich and his readers are largely content to speak of the symbol's communication of the symbolized in terms of "manifestation," Rahner consistently adds qualifications to any such usage, rendering any such "manifestation" a *signum efficax*:

> a manifestation of this kind is not merely a subsequent promulgation of something which is in any case present even without such promulgation. Rather, it is something *in which* the reality promulgated brings its own individual history to its fullness and so extends its own real nature in that it integrates within its own individual history more "material". In this sense, then, the manifestation is the "cause" of that which is manifesting.[124]

Accordingly, for Rahner, it is more accurate to speak of "self-realization" *via das Realsymbole* than of "manifestation."

The other major point of divergence concerns Tillich's appeal to "participation" as a distinguishing characteristic of the symbol. As Pryor has summarized, for Tillich, the symbol participates in the reality symbolized, while the sign does not.[125] Rahner's bar for distinguishing between *Vertretungssymbol* and *Realsymbol* is set significantly higher. Only the latter is "the self-realization of a being in the other, which is constitutive of its essence"; that is, the *Realsymbol* is distinguished by "the 'intrinsicity' of the relationship between the two realities, 'whether or not the symbol is the expression of the other being,

---

124. "Considerations of the Active Role," *TI* 14:178. Cf. Rahner's qualifications like "effective manifestation" ("The Presence of the Lord in the Christian Community at Worship," *TI* 10:81) and "brought about and made manifest" ("Considerations of the Active Role," *TI* 14:166). Tillich occasionally makes similar qualifications. E.g., "On the other hand, 'becomes manifest' does not mean only 'becomes known.' Manifestations are effective expressions," or "actualizations" (*Systematic Theology*, 3 vols. [Chicago: Univ. of Chicago Press, 1951–1963], 2:175). However, in this case, Tillich promptly turns around and roots this "actualization" in subjective experience of the one who witnesses the manifestation (ibid., 176). Accordingly, while Tillich's "manifestation" may not be reducible to "becomes known," it seems closer to "becomes known" than it does to Rahner's "self-realization."

125. Pryor, "Comparing Tillich and Rahner," 28. Although Pryor opens his analysis of Rahner's *Realsymbol* by noting this difference, he posits that the major point of divergence between Tillich's and Rahner's theories of the symbol is Rahner's concern with a "network" of mutually related symbols, while Tillich is more focused upon individual instances. In my own judgment, Rahner's "The Theology of the Symbol" devotes greater amounts of space to individual instances (e.g., filial generation, incarnation, etc.) than it does to any explicit treatment of a "network" (although the "nesting" character of *Realsymbole* certainly stands out structurally); Rahner's *intrinsic* criterion, of which Pryor indeed makes note, seems to me to be the greatest point of divergence from Tillich.

for that being's self-realization.'"[126] Although a country's flag, indeed arising out of "cultural-historical" factors, "participates" in its country to a degree sufficient for it to be a (even *the prototypical*) Tillichian symbol, it is hardly *intrinsically* related to its country, nor does the country "self-realize" through it. As Wong has commented, the flag would surely be classified by Rahner as a "conventional sign."[127] Similarly, Wong judges Tillich's claim that Christ is a symbol of "Godmanhood" is not "serious," given that Tillich "envisages the possibility of other 'incarnations'" in other times or planets. Such speculation is impossible for Rahner and his *realsymbolisch* human being Jesus, who *simply is* the Logos he symbolizes, "exteriorized" within time and history.[128]

"Symbol" in the theology of Roger Haight

While much of Tillich's symbol theory was being worked out at roughly the same time as Rahner's,[129] the work of Rahner's fellow Jesuit Roger Haight on the subject came decades later. This work is contained in Haight's magnum opus, *Jesus: Symbol of God*.[130] There, Haight offers an attentive and overall accurate account of Rahner's theory in the midst of articulating his own concept of the symbol. Haight classifies Rahner's soteriology as both revelation-based[131] and sacramental, with Jesus acting as the "symbolic or sacramental cause" of God's universal grace[132]; in fact, Christ is, for Rahner, the "constitutive cause of this grace."[133] Focusing on the "mediating" dimension of *das Realsymbol*, Haight explains that

Jesus does not only speak *about* God, nor is here merely a message *about* God. He is the very Logos of God made present. Rahner is insistent upon

126. Ibid., 29.
127. Wong, *Logos-Symbol*, 192.
128. Ibid.
129. Rahner began thinking about and proposing the development of an ontology of *das Symbol* by 1936 (with *E latere Christi*) at the latest (large sections of his dissertation had clearly been prepared before his arrival at Innsbruck).
130. Roger Haight, *Jesus: Symbol of God* (Maryknoll: Orbis, 1999). Although the book was awarded the U.S. Catholic Press Association's top prize in theology in 1999, it received mixed reviews from other Catholic theologians, and also instigated an investigation by the Congregation for the Doctrine of the Faith (CDF). The investigation led to an official notification on the work in 2004, and eventually, in 2009, to Haight's suspension from teaching or writing on theological matters.
131. Ibid., 344ff. Haight offers a perhaps surprising (but perceptive and indeed accurate) pairing by situating both Rahner and Karl Barth within this revelation-based descriptor.
132. Ibid., 350. For Rahner, Haight continues, "the salvation of historical human existence as such requires the actualization of the complete union of God with human existence in an event in history" (ibid.).
133. Ibid., 434.

this even while being resolute about the real humanity of Jesus. All of this makes sense within the context of Rahner's theology of the symbol. . . . As a symbol makes present something other than itself, so Jesus makes present God as Logos, that is, the self-expression of the Father.[134]

Like Wong, Haight recognizes the robust role that Rahner's soteriology envisions for Christ as the indispensable and constitutive sacramental mediation of God's saving grace; such a *symbolisch* Christ is no mere indicator or notification of salvation, but rather, stands the very conduit which brings it about.

The majority of *Jesus: Symbol of God* is devoted to Haight's own usage of "symbol," a concept which differs from Rahner's *Realsymbol* in several important respects. Early on, Haight makes the same basic move made by Tillich and Rahner, distinguishing between two symbolic groups; for Haight, they are the "conceptual or conscious symbol" (e.g., a "metaphor") and a "concrete symbol" (e.g., the "human body" mediating the "human spirit").[135] Elaborating upon the latter, "thicker" category, Haight explains that the "concrete symbol" mediates the presence of another reality. Although Haight's example (the human body) and mediation-criterion match well with *das Realsymbol*, Haight omits any talk of "self-realization" or "exteriorization," as well as any assertion of the symbol and symbolized achieving a "perfected unity." The "intrinsic" factor which is the hallmark of Rahner's *Realsymbol* is thus nowhere to be found. It comes as no surprise, then, that when Haight goes on to apply his concept to Jesus, he opens with a major qualifier and cashes the statement out purely in terms of mediation: "for Christians, Jesus is the concrete symbol of God. . . . People encountered God in Jesus, and they still do . . . in a large variety of ways they experienced God and God's saving presence mediated by him."[136]

In addition to being evident in the language which Haight omits, the contrast between Haight's symbol and Rahner's *das Realsymbol* can be observed in new language which Haight employs quite frequently—namely, that of consciousness and awareness.[137] Consider, for instance, his account of Jesus as God's revelation "from above."[138] As

134. Ibid., 438–39, emphasis original. Of course, Rahner would further add that in addition to being the Logos's "other," Jesus exists in intrinsic and perfected unity with the Logos as its self-realization; indeed, Jesus *is* the Logos "exteriorized."
135. Ibid., 13.
136. Ibid., 14.
137. Whereas *das Realsymbol* is employed by Rahner as predominately metaphysical, ontological concept (i.e., the human Jesus simply *is* the Logos "exteriorized" within the world's history), Haight regularly gives indications that his "concrete symbol" (despite its juxtaposition to "conceptual or conscious symbol") is much more epistemological in nature. Such a character accords with

the "concrete symbol" of God, Jesus "reveals God" and "makes God present" according to "symbolic or sacramental causality."[139] Thus far, the account is thoroughly Rahnerian. However, Haight makes a significant divergence in explaining, "Symbolic or sacramental causality effects by bringing to consciousness and explicit awareness something that is already present within, but latent and not an object of clear attention or focused recognition."[140] Rahner, on the contrary, explicitly dissociates his notion of sacramental causality from any account of simply raising awareness.[141] Moreover, Haight's focus upon symbols functioning so as to bring about consciousness is scattered throughout *Jesus: Symbol of God*, from its opening pages[142] to its statement that

> no empirical causality can amount to salvation; only God causes salvation. . . . Thus the causality of Jesus for human salvation is in the genus of symbolic or sacramental causality. By representing God's action for salvation, Jesus makes conscious and explicit to human beings something that would not have been revealed, known, or conscious in the same way without him.[143]

Given such statements, one might justifiably say that Balthasar's concern about Christ functioning simply as a "prime instance" and notification of human salvation wrought by a "God-who-is-always-reconciled" were perhaps voiced a generation too early.

Another theme which distinguishes Rahner and Haight concerns another Balthasarian worry—namely, the constitutive place of Christ in God's plan of salvation. While Rahner unabashedly affirms such a place,[144] Haight's account of Christ's role in human salvation is better

---

Haight's deliberate effort to write for a postmodern milieu in which universal, metaphysical claims are often regarded with deep suspicion, if not rejected outright.

138. Haight will go on to downplay any "from above" approach as largely irrelevant in the postmodern milieu (ibid., 432).

139. Ibid., 358–59.

140. Ibid., 359.

141. In speaking about the *symbolisch* salvific efficacy of Christ's death, Rahner explains that "in a sacramental sign the saving will of God and grace find historical expression. Sign and signified are essentially one . . . so that the reality signified comes to be in and through the sign, and the sign therefore, in this specific and limited sense, causes the reality signified . . . [T]he cross can and should be understood in this sense as the cause of the salvation signified and *not merely regarded as the cause of our awareness of salvation* in faith" ("The One Christ and the Universality of Salvation," *TI* 16:199–224, at 215, emphasis added).

142. See *Jesus: Symbol of God*, 12–13, in which Haight is actually expositing Rahner (referencing *FCF*, 51–55).

143. Haight, *Jesus: Symbol of God*, 350. On the same page, Haight again employs language of "explicitly conscious encounter" and "consciously effective."

144. Rahner opens his essay, "The One Christ and the Universality of Salvation" with a statement which he considers to be "dogmatically binding" (even if it has not been explicitly defined as

classified as "normative" than "constitutive."[145] According to Haight, Christ remains universally *relevant* since his story is one of authentic salvation; however, Haight stops short of making any "constitutive" claims, and in fact, denies that Christ "causes" salvation in every instance.[146]

Finally, Haight makes an important remark near the end of *Jesus: Symbol of God*, which underlines how he and Rahner differ over the "intrinsic" relation of the symbol and symbolized. Explicitly criticizing Rahner over the matter, Haight entertains the possibility (and even probability) of God's Logos becoming incarnate in many different ways and media, stating that there's "no hard reason" to rule it out. Indeed, even Thomas Aquinas affirmed the *possibility* of the Son (or even the Father and/or the Spirit) assuming other human natures (although Thomas held that only one such union ever *in fact* occurred).[147] But while Haight and Thomas may not have any "hard reason" to rule out multiple incarnations of the Logos, Rahner does—namely, his ontology of *das Realsymbol*. After all, the act of "incarnation," for Rahner, is not one of the Son extrinsically assuming or uniting with any given "way" or "medium" of being. Rather, "when God, expressing himself, exteriorizes himself, that very thing appears which we call the humanity of the Logos."[148] In Rahner's judgment, the intrinsic connection between *Symbol* and symbolized (a connection which is absent in Haight's account) rules out any possibility of multiple incarnations.[149] God has indeed self-exteriorized, and the Christ-event is what occurred.

---

such): "the achievement by any man of his proper and definitive salvation is dependent upon Jesus Christ" (*TI* 16:200).

145. Haight, *Jesus: Symbol of God*, 403–10, cf. part VI of the CDF's notification.

146. "The particular saving action of God in Jesus Christ remains a particular story. . . . It is also a true story, and therefore it carries a universal relevance for all of humankind. . . . But it is not the only story of God saving . . . the event of Jesus reveals the salvation of all in revealing God, but it is not the cause of the salvation of all" (Haight, *Jesus: Symbol of God*, 353). Also, "God alone effects salvation and Jesus' universal mediation is not necessary" (ibid., 405).

147. *ST* III q. 3 a. 7; cf. aa. 5, 6, and 8.

148. "The Theology of the Symbol," *TI* 4:239.

149. In the final years of his life, Rahner was interviewed about his soteriology. Specifically, he considered the issue of whether a "from below" starting point, which identified Christ's as *the* story of authentic human success, entailed the possibility of multiple "incarnations" (which might seem to follow from the possibility of multiple "success stories"). To his traditionalist detractors favoring strictly "from above" soteriological-christological approaches who might level such an objection, Rahner responded, "'Dear scholastic theologian, you who come out of the Middle Ages, you least of all are able to prove that the Incarnation *can* only take place once.' For my part I would say that *it is nonsense to imagine and to think that it could take place several times.* Perhaps *I have even offered better reasons against such an idea* than are ordinarily given" (*Karl Rahner in Dialogue*, 125, emphasis added). This last statement is almost certainly a reference to his theology of *das Realsymbol* (which operates, it should be noted, from above, and to which he still has recourse even in his final years).

Summary: Distinguishing "Symbol" in Rahner from Other Usages

In "The Theology of the Symbol," Rahner himself underlined the importance of distinguishing his usage of Symbol (precisely, das Realsymbol) from popular usage of the term. Such importance emerges from the potential for egregious misunderstanding of what Rahner means by referring to the sacraments, the humanity of Jesus, and even the Second Person of the Trinity as Symbole. The same goes for distinguishing Rahner's usage of the term from that of other prominent theologians, such as Tillich and Haight. While each of them speaks of "symbol" in a specific, technical sense, Rahner diverges from those senses on several counts. While both Tillich and Haight, with Rahner, stress the ability of the symbol to render present the symbolized, they often cash out such statements in terms of "manifestation," effecting "awareness," or bringing something to "explicit consciousness."

For Rahner, Realsymbol's mediatory function occurs by way of the "self-realization" of the symbolized, a process which results in the "perfected unity" of the two. "Self-realization" and "perfected unity" stand as two Rahnerian criteria for das Realsymbol which reflect Rahner's perennial insistence upon "intrinsicity," and which are lacking in the concepts of symbol found in Tillich and Haight. That both Haight and Tillich entertain the idea of supplementary incarnations, an idea at which Rahner bristles, underscores the divergent ways in which Jesus is being identified as the Symbol of God.

Das Realsymbol and Christ's Salvific Efficacy

Having considered Rahner's theory of das Realsymbol in general terms, its influences and origins, and the characteristics which distinguish it from other theologians' conceptions of the symbol, let us finally turn to Rahner's soteriological application. Although the basic moves which Rahner makes in this application have already been sketched in the previous chapter's overview of secondary literature on Rahner, it is important to allow Rahner's own writings to speak for themselves, at least as much as they can through my own (inevitably interpretive) treatment of them here. Although Rahner discusses his soteriology in a number of writings and interviews, the most pertinent articles, upon which the following overview will center, are "The One Christ and the Universality of Salvation" (1975) and "The Christian Understanding of Redemption" (1981). I will proceed by considering once again the importance of sacramental or *realsymbolisch* causality (and its relation to other forms), and subsequently, how this causality is operative for Rahner in both "objective" and "subjective" dimensions of human salvation in Jesus Christ.

By What Kind of "Causality" Does Christ Save?

As we have already seen, Rahner consistently introduces discussions of Christ accomplishing salvation via warnings against a popularized atonement theory which centers upon Christ's death as mollifying God's wrath.[150] According to such a theory, reconciliation with God is something which originates from Christ's death, insofar as that death provokes God's willingness to save (i.e., it "changes God's mind" about humanity). In such a framework, God appears to be either capricious, an object for human manipulation, or intransigently set on getting his "pound of flesh"; in any of these cases, human salvation is something which is brokered by a particular act of appeasement or propitiation.[151]

Christians would do well, Rahner suggests, to turn this framework on its head, so that the salvific Christ-event is primarily understood as a consequence of God's desire for human salvation, rather than vice-versa. Rather than originating from a brokered arrangement, the offer of salvific grace is then seen as flowing from God *through* Christ, and even as something grounded in God's very identity as Love itself;[152] accordingly, Rahner is inclined to speak about Christ's salvific lifetime, including and especially its termination at the cross, as *the result* of God's salvific will, rather than its "cause" (in the sense of "origin").[153]

---

150. "First . . . the saving will of God in our regard is primarily not the result but the cause of the cross of Christ, preceding both the cross and the whole Christ event. He loved us and *therefore* sent his son to us (see John 3:16). The popular conception that presupposes a violently angry God who then in some strange way is reconciled through the cross of Christ, a God who would not himself therefore have been the free and unconditioned cause of redemption, is plain and simple nonsense" (*Karl Rahner in Dialogue*, 128, emphasis original). Cf. "The One Christ and the Universality of Salvation," *TI* 16:207–209; "Jesus Christ in the Non-Christian Religions" *TI* 17:39–50, at 45; *Opportunities for Faith: Elements of a Modern Spirituality* (London: S.P.C.K., 1974), 29; *FCF*, 282.

151. For an examination of the impact such an approach has on notions of mercy and satisfaction, see my "Would a Forgiving God Demand Satisfaction? An Examination of Mercy and Atonement," *Angelicum* 93.4 (December 2016), 875–94.

152. "[O]ne must not lose sight of the fact that the event of the cross is itself the *effect* and ultimately not the cause of an initiative of God himself which is a result of nothing other than God's free love and his unmerited grace, of a God who reconciles because he is the love that forgives and overcomes all guilt" ("Reconciliation and Vicarious Representation," *TI* 21:262).

153. Here, Rahner's language is worth comparing to that of Paul Tillich. In fact, one may legitimately wonder whether Balthasar's evaluation of Rahner's soteriology, particularly when it comes to "He-who-is-always-reconciled" (*TD* 4:276), was in some way shaped by Balthasar's reading of Tillich as well. Tillich denounces "the type of doctrine of the atonement according to which God is the one who must be reconciled . . . [T]he message of Christianity is that God, who is eternally

That said, Rahner is not about to abandon his affirmation of the causal efficacy of Jesus and his death, for "it is part of the Christian confession of faith that the death of Jesus *means something* for the salvation of all men."[154] (Indeed, Hebrews 5:9 refers to Jesus as the αἴτιος ("cause") of our salvation.) Rahner is able to affirm both: (i) salvation's origin in God's unswerving salvific will, and (ii) Jesus as the cause of that salvation in virtue of an important distinction: although Christ does not "cause" God to love us or suddenly to become inclined toward granting us salvation, Christ is indeed the "cause" of salvation *with respect to us*. That is, he is causally constitutive of salvation because it is only given to us through and in virtue of him. In other words, one might adjust Balthasar's portrayal of Rahner's God as "He-who-is-always-reconciled" this way: While God consistently wills that we be reconciled to him (1 Tim 2:4), such reconciliation is only made available to us through the Mediator Jesus Christ (1 Tim 2:5). Rahner's God is thus "He-who-always-desires-reconciliation," a reconciliation which is only possible for us through Jesus Christ, who thus exists as a genuine, constitutive, *sine qua non* cause.

At this point, it should come as no surprise that the kind of causality best fit to account for this kind of causal efficacy is identified by Rahner to be that of *das Realsymbol*.[155] For it is in its *Realsymbol* that something self-realizes definitively and self-communicates; *das Realsymbol* "extends" a reality so as to incorporate its "other" into itself, bringing about an otherwise impossible presence of the most intimate kind.[156]

reconciled, wants us to be reconciled to him. . . . Once more, it must be stressed that it is a basic distortion of the doctrine of atonement if, instead of saying 'becomes manifest,' one says 'becomes possible'" (*Systematic Theology* 2:169–70, 175).

154. "The One Christ and the Universality of Salvation," *TI* 16:212. Elsewhere, Rahner writes that "the crucifixion certainly cannot be regarded (as by some modern Protestant theologians, appealing to 2 Cor 5:18–21) as an attestation (directed to us) of God's forgiving love, which moves *us* to believe in this love; it has to be acknowledged as the *cause* of our salvation . . . [T]he real problem, at least for understanding Christian soteriology in our situation at the present day, is why this original forgiving will of God does not simply effect forgiveness 'vertically from on high' in the same way and directly at all points of space and time, but comes to mankind from a definite historical event, which itself is the 'cause' of forgiveness" ("Salvation," in *Sacramentum Mundi: An Encyclopedia of Theology* (henceforth *SM*), 6 vols. (New York: Herder and Herder, 1968–1970) 5:405–38, at 430; emphasis original).

155. "Of course, I must be able to say that I am redeemed through Christ, although Christ himself is the consequence, the effect and not the cause of the saving will that is (and insofar as it is) referred to me. One would have to develop here a category of causality that would perhaps be clearer than it is in our average soteriology. If and insofar as this history of salvation as supernaturally finalized and rendered dynamic necessarily tends to the Christ event [*notwendigerweise auf das Christusereignis hinzielt*] as its historical and historically irreversible manifestation [*Erscheinung*], then I can also understand such an event as the cause of the history of salvation. . . . The manifestation in which what is being manifested comes to its own fulfillment and definitiveness can rightly be conceived as the cause of what is being manifested. Here one might bring into consideration what I have said about the real symbol" (*Karl Rahner in Dialogue*, 128).

That is, *das Realsymbol* "causes" the reality *precisely in* signifying it. Since this kind of terminology is quite familiar to classical sacramental theology, Rahner uses *realsymbolisch* and sacramental[157] causality as interchangeable terms when proposing proper "causal" language for speaking of Christ's soteriological efficacy:[158]

> The life and death of Jesus taken together, then, are the "cause" of God's salvific will (to the extent that these two things are regarded as different) insofar as this salvific will establishes itself really and irrevocably in this life and death, in other words, insofar as the life and death of Jesus, or the death which recapitulates and culminates his life, possess a causality of a quasi-sacramental and real-symbolic nature. In this causality what is signified, in this case God's salvific will, posits the sign, in this case the death of Jesus along with his resurrection, and in and through the sign it causes what is signified.[159]

Rahner's solution is to posit that Christ and his death cause human salvation, without being its absolute origin, since the Christ-event stands as *das Realsymbol* of God's salvation.[160]

---

156. A "manifestation of this kind is not merely a subsequent promulgation of something which is in any case present even without such promulgation. Rather, it is something *in which* the reality promulgated brings its own individual history to its fullness and so extends its own real nature in that it integrates within its own individual history more 'material'. In this sense, then, the manifestation is the 'cause' of that which is manifesting" ("Considerations of the Active Role," *TI* 14:178).
157. "[I]n a sacramental sign the saving will of God and grace find historical expression. Sign and signified are essentially one . . . so that the reality signified comes to be in and through the sign, and the sign therefore, in this specific and limited sense, causes the reality signified" ("The One Christ and the Universality of Salvation," *TI* 16:215).
158. It should also be noted that Rahner's favored soteriological causality is sometimes identified as "final causality" (e.g., Balthasar in *TD* 4:276, Ogden, *Is There Only One True Religion*, 94–95). It is true that Rahner occasionally speaks in these classical Thomistic-Aristotelian terms ("Since . . . the goal of a movement sustains that movement itself as its secret activating force and does not merely come at the end, we can and must say that God gives himself to the world *because* of this event of the cross" (*Opportunities for Faith*, 30; cf. "Jesus Christ and the Non-Christian Religions," *TI* 17:46; *FCF*, 194–95), and final causality does bear an important relationship to Rahner's *realsymbolisch* category, particularly when it comes to "culmination" language and our orientation toward Christ as the source of grace. Yet, Rahner more consistently utilizes the *Realsymbol*-sacrament concept as his basic explication for soteriological causation; in places, "final cause" even seems to function for Rahner as a locution for *das Realsymbol*—e.g., "intrinsic *causa finalis*" in "Salvation," *SM* 5:431, which, sentences later, Rahner links to "the causality of the sacraments," and even explicitly to *Realsymbol* (ibid., 431–32).
159. *FCF*, 284.
160. If, upon recalling that the human being Jesus Christ is *das Realsymbol* of the Logos (and ultimately of God himself), concerns arise that Rahner may be, so to speak, "double-booking" Christ's standing as *Realsymbol* (Is he *das Realsymbol* of God *via* the Logos or *das Realsymbol* of human salvation?), it is helpful to recall that for Rahner, God himself *is the content* of human salvation: "Salvation here is to be understood as the strictly supernatural and direct presence of God in himself afforded by grace" ("The One Christ and the Universality of Salvation," *TI* 16:200). Cf. Rahner's remarks on "uncreated grace" in "Some Implications of the Scholastic Concept," *TI* 1:319–346 and "Immanent and Transcendent Consummation of the World" *TI* 10:273–89 at 282–84. As Roman Siebenrock summarizes Rahner's thinking on the matter: "Grace is first of all uncreated grace, the person of

Das Realsymbol and Causality: The "Objective" Dimension

Joseph Wong has helpfully structured his analysis of Rahner's soteriology by organizing it into "from above" and "from below" dimensions; that is, Rahner's account of God effecting human salvation has both a descending "humanward" component and an ascending "Godward" component, which converge in the person of Jesus Christ. A second device, common in classifications of various soteriological models is the objective/subjective distinction.[161] Of course, it is an almost universal *desideratum* to claim both objective and subjective components in one's soteriology, and the facile assignment of a particular model entirely to one side or the other is usually more polemical than helpful. Nevertheless, the objective/subjective distinction (which Rahner himself utilizes[162]), paired with the "descending" and "ascending" categories, is useful for exploring Rahner's multifaceted account of human salvation.

Let us begin by considering Rahner's soteriology as both descending and objective, that is, as accounting for a concrete and universal change wrought by God which has made (an otherwise impossible) human salvation available. As we just seen, the way that God causes salvation, according to Rahner, is by way of sacramental or *realsymbolisch* causality. To cash this out in descending and objective terms: since God is himself the content of human salvation, in God's act of self-communicating, human salvation has been made available—in the person of Jesus Christ—via a sacramental mode. Moreover, since this act of *realsymbolisch* self-communication is *free* (rather than the necessitated outcome of a Hegelian emanation), it is the definitive expression of God's salvific will, a sacramental expression which *effects* that desired salvation *precisely in* revealing it. Human salvation, understood as God's gra-

---

Jesus Christ himself" ("Gratia Christi. The Heart of the Theology of Karl Rahner: Ignatian Influences in the Codex De Gratia Christi [1937/38] and Its Significance for the Development of His Work," in *Revista Portuguesa de Filosofia*, 63, no. 4, Os Domínios da Inteligência: Bernard Lonergan e a Filosofia. / The Realism of Insight: Bernard Lonergan and Philosophy [Oct. – Dec., 2007], 1261–72, at 1267).

161. This tendency holds especially in Protestant literature on theories of atonement. The "moral influence" theory (by which Jesus impacts our actions as an exemplar) favored by Liberal Protestants is typically cited as the paradigmatic "subjective" soteriology, while more "traditional" Protestants tend to emphasize Christ's "objective" act of taking on our sins and dying to balance the scales of justice (often articulated in penal substitutionary terms).

162. See "Salvation," where Rahner differentiates "objective redemption" and "subjective redemption" (*SM* 5:426–27, 437), as well as "The One Christ and the Universality of Salvation," where Christ's incarnation, death, and resurrection are said to constitute "redemptio objectiva" (*TI* 16:207).

cious and direct presence to and with humanity, has been objectively accomplished in the Christ-event.[163]

One of the most consistent and frequent ways in which Rahner describes this dimension of his soteriology is his claim that the Christ-event has definitively rendered God's salvific will "irreversible" and "irrevocable" (descriptors often paired with "victorious" and "unsurpassable"). Such language may seem to indicate that the objective accomplishment here amounts to "cornering" a wishy-washy God, so to speak, who might otherwise change his mind.[164] One might ask: If what is significant is that God's salvific will is now irreversible and irrevocable, is it not implied that the alternative reality (now rendered impossible) is precisely God revoking or reversing his desire for salvation? However, this sort of interpretation of Rahner's "irrevocable" language would render this thinker, recognized as highly nuanced by followers and critics alike, downright schizophrenic; after all, such language occurs in virtually the same breath as his (almost tirelessly repeated) condemnation of popular soteriologies which presuppose a capricious God who is "swayed" by Christ's death.

I would suggest that Rahner's "irrevocable" language is instead intended to communicate two ideas. The first is the *freedom* which characterizes God's act of *realsymbolisch* self-communication, evidenced in a passage from "The Theology of the Symbol": "[Jesus Christ] is not merely the presence and revelation of what God is in himself. He is also the expressive presence of what—or rather, who—God wished to be, in free grace, to the world, in such a way that this divine attitude

---

163. "The sacramental salvation-reality of Christ – in the Incarnation and the sacrifice of the Cross – is the one and only truly valid and final saving act of God in the world and therefore the one and only final mediation between God and man. In so far as it is final, that is, in so far as it cannot now be surpassed by any event whether initiated by man or by God, the history of salvation is in principle concluded" ("Priestly Existence," *TI* 3:239–62, at 247).

164. Some of Rahner's formulations about "irrevocability" may, taken in isolation from other statements, seem to imply this line of thought. E.g., "Everything that is finite and subject to a historical process, when considered as such in itself, remains retractable, revocable, always the object of a divine freedom which never establishes itself absolutely through this finite object as such alone, nor is it able to do so. Therefore every revelation in which God objectifies and manifests his will through a finite word or a historical occurrence remains open-ended, capable of revision, provisional. Something that as such is merely finite in itself alone is of its very nature incapable of signifying and mediating to us a divine communication which cannot be superseded. The communication always remains provisional in view of the infinity of God's possibilities and the sovereignty of his freedom. If, however, God communicates to us his self-promise as one that is irrevocable and definitive, then the created reality through which this takes place cannot simply stand at the same distance from God as other created realities. It must be the reality of God himself in such a unique way that God would disown *his very self* if he should supersede it because of its created finiteness" ("Jesus Christ—The Meaning of Life," *TI* 21:218; cf. *FCF*, 202). Notably, this statement puts the lie to Balthasar's claim that Rahner's Christ (i.e., this irrevocable self-communication of God) is not "essentially different" from any other human beings (*TD* 4:277).

[*Haltung*], once so expressed, can never be reversed, but is and remains final and unsurpassable."[165] Rather than locking an erratic God into a static disposition, the emphasis here is on who "God wished to be, *in free* grace, *to the world*." Indeed, the classical notion of the soul's formal-causal relation to the body is Rahner's exemplary instance of *das Realsymbol*; however, he refrains from speaking of God's grace (that is, God's self-gift), particularly in the case of Christ's incarnation, purely in terms of formal causality (instead, appending the prefix *quasi*-formal causality) precisely because doing so would imply a necessary emanation and thus impinge on God's freedom. Accordingly, while "irreversible" provokes thoughts of the possibility of God reversing a course set for human salvation, Rahner's claim here is not about getting a fickle God to settle down. Rather, it's about a steadfast God freely opting to take a definitive step: establishing a maximally intimate relationship with the world by making the world's story his own.

The second idea which Rahner wishes to communicate through "irrevocable" language flows from the first. It is that in the *realsymbolisch* communication of the Logos to the world, God has definitively established a sort of soteriological "anchor," or objective locus at which human salvation is achieved.[166] Rahner writes of the "fact" that "in the human life of Jesus . . . the victory of [the believer's] personal life has irrevocably and definitively been promised him, and that in this . . . the ultimate and definitive, the unsurpassable word of God has been promised him."[167] This sort of claim should not understood so as to reduce Jesus to a "guarantee" that human salvation occurs, as its "most successful instance." Rather, the key part of Rahner's statement here occurs in the beginning: it is "*in* the human life of Jesus" that victory for the believer lies.[168] Jesus does not merely guarantee that "we

165. *TI* 4:237. "God's salvific will is not identical with his metaphysically necessary goodness and holiness, nor something strictly derived from this. It is not a metaphysical attribute of God which can be established everywhere and always, but a divine attitude in the nature of an event, which has to be experienced and proclaimed in history. This free attitude of God, which is directed towards the salvation of every man, has only become a manifest principle, definitively and irrevocably, in Jesus Christ" ("Salvation," *SM* 5:406).
166. Cf. ibid. 431: "Christ and his destiny (the *complete* accomplishment of which appears in the resurrection) are *the* cause of salvation as historically constituting the historically irreversible saving *situation* for *all*" (emphasis original).
167. "Considerations of the Active Role," *TI* 14:168. Cf. "[T]here is a man by reason of whose existence I may dare to believe that God has promised to give himself irrevocably and finally to me; there is a man in whom God's absolute promise to give himself to every spiritual creature, and the acceptance of this promise by the creature, are both proved and rendered credible to me without ambiguity, irreparably and in a manner I can understand" ("Thoughts on the Possibility of Belief Today," *TI* 5:3–22 at 12).
168. Similarly, Rahner writes that "God by his own sovereign efficacious grace has already decided . . . in favour of the salvation of the world in Christ, and in Christ has already promulgated this event"

can make it," but he is, in fact, God's very self-promise.[169] Indeed, Rahner speaks about the person of Jesus as "our reconciliation":

> Christians know full well that God's forgiving and reconciling love that encompasses all guilt has entered the world in such a way that it can never be revoked. This love has revealed itself in the cross of Jesus Christ who has become our reconciliation. . . . God's forgiving love has reached its historically visible culmination in Jesus' death on the cross, because this love has become irrevocable and has found its acceptance in a human being. . . . God has reconciled the world to himself in Jesus the crucified . . . [I]t also becomes reality for its part when human beings accept it.[170]

As a sort of "soteriological anchor," Rahner's Christ does not "objectively" effect salvation simply by acting so as to alter a state of affairs (be those affairs understood in terms of penal justice, honor, etc.); rather, he *is* the objectively wrought state of affairs, the free and "externalized" self-promise of God, the very reconciliation of God and the human family. The excerpt above brings us to consider the next two components of Rahner's soteriology: the (objective) finalization of Jesus as "soteriological anchor" in his death, and the (subjective) realization of this salvation in our acceptance of it in relationship with Christ.

The Place of the Cross: Christ's Death and *das Realsymbol*

The foregoing section considered Rahner's soteriology from a descending and objective perspective. It is important to recognize that for Rahner, these two descriptors are not synonymous, nor inseparable. Indeed, an angle crucial for understanding his soteriology is, at the same time, objective and *ascending*. Included within the objective achievement of salvation in the Christ-event is Christ's own human acceptance of God's grace "from below." In the person of Christ, Rahner explains, God

("Salvation," SM 5:408). Likewise, "This Jesus proclaims that with him God turns to us definitively and irrevocably in a love that is forgiving and that contains the offer of himself; that the 'kingdom of God' has come irrevocably; that on God's part the triumph of God's forgiving love establishes itself in human history in a way that cannot be overcome" ("Jesus Christ—The Meaning of Life," TI 21:216).
169. "Jesus is the consubstantial Son of God. His human reality, notwithstanding its genuine, free, human subjectivity, is the reality of the eternal Logos of God. For Jesus is the irrevocable, unsurpassable, and definitive self-promise of God to us. And he can only be this as the consubstantial Son" (ibid., TI 21:218).
170. "Reconciliation and Vicarious Redemption," TI 21:261.

communicate[s] himself to a man in such a unique manner that this man would [*from above*] become the definitive and irreversible self-gift of God to the world. He would also [*from below*] freely accept the divine self-gift in such a manner that this too would be irreversible, i.e., through his death as the definitive culmination of his free actions in history . . . [T]his historically tangible occurrence must be a sign of the salvation of the whole world in the sense of a "real symbol."[171]

Recall, a constantly reiterated part of Rahner's *realsymbolisch* account of the incarnation is his insistence that Jesus is not simply the Logos donning a human nature, "something in which God dresses up and masquerades."[172] Rather, the human Jesus who results from the "exteriorization" of the Logos is entirely free (anything less would result in a diminished human nature, and thus, a sort of crypto-monophysitism).[173] A central and essential part of the Christ-event is therefore Jesus's exercise of genuine human freedom, which coincides with the reception of God's grace. In fact, Jesus's total openness to God throughout the course of his life constitutes the perfect human "Yes" to God's self-offer in grace. Jesus Christ, considered as an objective soteriological "anchor," stands at once as *the* definitive expression and establishment of God's will for human salvation, as well as *the* definitive human acceptance of it. That is, in the person of Jesus, descending and ascending movements of grace coalesce into a single objective basis for human salvation.[174]

It must be immediately added, however, that any such statement about the person of Jesus and his lifelong "Yes" to God as an ascending, objective basis for Rahner's soteriology is deficient without reference to the cross. It remains true that the entire Christ-event, including

171. "The One Christ and the Universality of Salvation," *TI* 16:214.
172. "The Theology of the Symbol," *TI* 4:239.
173. "In accordance with the fact that the natures are unmixed, basically the active influence of the Logos on the human 'nature' in Jesus in a physical sense may not be understood in any other way except the way this influence is exercised by God on free creatures everywhere. This of course is frequently forgotten in a piety and a theology which are tinged with monophysitism. All too often they understand the humanity of Jesus as a thing and as an 'instrument' which is moved by the subjectivity of the Logos" (*FCF*, 287).
174. "The whole movement of this history of God's self-communication lives by virtue of its moving towards its goal or climax in the event by which it becomes irreversible . . . [T]his saviour, who constitutes the climax of God's self-communication to the world, must be at the same time *both* the absolute promise of God to spiritual creatures as a whole *and* the acceptance of this self-communication by the savior. . . . Only then is there an absolutely irrevocable self-communication on both sides" (*FCF*, 195). Similarly, Rahner writes that the "absolute climax" of God's self-communication "takes place in the incarnation of the Logos because here what is expressed and communicated, namely, God himself, and, secondly, the mode of expression, that is, the human reality of Christ in his life and in his final state, and, thirdly, the recipient Jesus in grace and in the vision of God, all three have become absolutely one" (*FCF*, 174).

Jesus's incarnation, life,[175] death, and resurrection,[176] is redemptive. Nonetheless, the final hours of Jesus's life hold a particular prominence in Rahner's thought. This prominence is grounded in Rahner's theology of death; space permits only a cursory look at key, relevant points of this rich topic here.[177]

A person's death, according to Rahner, is best understood as the finalization of that person's life of freedom.[178] One's actions are not merely functions of an already-established identity, but genuinely shape the person via the freedom of self-disposal.[179] Moreover, the "supernatural existential," an ever-present, transcendental offer of relationship to God, stands as an abiding backdrop to each free act of every human person. Inescapably, and regardless of one's reflexive awareness of the matter, one's free actions correspond with the possibilities of either being "freely given over to God in his grace or [someone] refused to God and thus condemned to [her] own finiteness."[180] This lifetime of decisions for and against God, of "Yes"s and "No"s, culminates in one's death, which is an "event that gathers together the whole personal act of man's life in to the one consummation."[181] In other words, as one's final[182] and culminating act of freedom,[183] a person's death recapitulates and integrates[184] the whole of a person's

175. See Batlogg's dissertation, published as *Die Mysterien des Lebens Jesu bei Karl Rahner: Zugang zum Christusglauben* (Innsbruck: Tyrolia, 2001) on the salvific value of the individual events of Jesus' life.
176. "Because Christ's bodily humanity is a permanent part of one world which has one dynamism the resurrection of Christ is soteriologically and objectively the commencement of the ontologically coherent event which is the glorification of the world; in this commencement the final consummation of the world has been decided in principle and has already begun. The resurrection of Christ is also more than his private destiny because it creates Heaven and is not (together with the Ascension, which basically is an element of the Resurrection) simply an entrance into a pre-existent heaven" ("Resurrection of Christ," in *Theological Dictionary*, 405–8, at 407–8).
177. Rahner's most extensive treatment can be found in *On the Theology of Death*. See also "The Life of the Dead" (*TI* 4:347–54), "Christian Dying" (*TI* 18:226–56).
178. "Following the Crucified," *TI* 18:157–70 at 164.
179. "A Brief Theological Study on Indulgences," *TI* 10:150–65 at 151.
180. "The Comfort of Time," *TI* 3:141–57 at 145.
181. "Christian Dying," *TI* 18:253. As Joseph Wong puts it, "death as the final and total act of freedom exercised by man gives definitive orientation to one's whole life" (*Logos-Symbol*, 161).
182. "Death brings man, as a moral and spiritual person, a kind of finality and consummation which renders his decision for or against God, reached during the time of his bodily life, final and unalterable" (*On the Theology of Death*, 26). Later in his career, Rahner is willing to at least entertain thoughts of relaxing the hardness of this "finality" for the difficult cases of those who die before ever having the chance to exercise freedom at all ("Christian Dying," *TI* 18:237–41; "Purgatory," *TI* 19:181–93).
183. For Rahner, "death", as a theological concept, need not correspond with one's biological demise, though this is often the case (e.g., Jesus's passion) ("Christian Dying," *TI* 18:229).
184. Regarding the "integration" of life, shaped as it is by sinful "No"s to God, to a fundamental "Yes", cf. Rahner's writings on purgatory and indulgences: "Remarks on the Theology of Indulgences" (*TI* 2:175–202), "Problems Concerning Confession" (*TI* 3:190–206), "A Brief Theological Study on Indulgence," and "Purgatory."

life within a single and final "Yes" or "No" to God. Since his death on the cross[185] recapitulates the entire Christ-event (which, viewed from below, is an extended and perfect lifetime of "Yes"s to God), Rahner speaks of the whole and its summary almost interchangeably at times.[186] Accordingly, the cross stands for Rahner as the singular moment which "sums up" the objective, ascending dimension of his soteriology.[187]

Das Realsymbol and Causality: The "Subjective" Dimension

Both God's descending self-communication in grace and the human Jesus's perfect and ascending acceptance of that grace converge in the Christ-event, and so, Rahner is able to say that, objectively, "God has reconciled the world to himself in Jesus the crucified"; but as we noted above, Rahner quickly adds the *subjective* qualification that this reconciliation achieved in the person of Christ "also becomes reality for its part when human beings accept it."[188] It is this subjective appropriation of objective reconciliation in Christ to which we now turn.[189]

A central component of this subjective dimension to Rahner's soteriological thought is a term which has been referenced and only briefly described a number of times already, the "supernatural existential."

185. Rahner consistently articulates Jesus's "Yes" here in his final words in Luke ("into your hands I commend my spirit," 23:46), the radical, fiduciary character of which can in turn only be understood in light of the utter darkness which Jesus experienced simultaneously ("My God, my God, why have you forsaken me?" (Mark 15:34). Cf. "See, What a Man!," in *TI* 7:136–39 at 138–39; "A Basic Theological and Anthropological Understanding of Old Age," *TI* 23:50–60 at 60; *Grace in Freedom* (New York: Herder and Herder, 1969), 124.

186. "The life and death of Jesus taken together, then, are the 'cause' of God's salvific will (to the extent that these two things are regarded as different) insofar as this salvific will establishes itself really and irrevocably in this life and death, in other words, insofar as *the life and death of Jesus, or the death which recapitulates and culminates his life*, possess a causality of a quasi-sacramental and realsymbolic nature. In this causality what is signified, in this case God's salvific will, posits the sign, in this case the death of Jesus along with his resurrection, and in and through the sign it causes what is signified" (*FCF*, 284, emphasis added). Indeed, given Rahner's theology of death, there is a most intimate unity between one's entire lifetime and one's death, for it is in one's death that one's lifetime comes to expression and full realization; one would be justified in saying that there is a *realsymbolisch* quality of Rahnerian death.

187. I classify Jesus's death on the cross as "objective" here with a view to the "saving situation" it establishes for us; of course, from Christ's perspective, his free assent to God is "subjective" insofar as it constitutes his own "self-redemption." As Rahner says, "the 'objective redemption' in Jesus Christ consists precisely in the subjective act of his obedience in death, in which he gave himself totally to God as a member of the human race" ("Salvation," *SM* 5:437).

188. "Reconciliation and Vicarious Representation," *TI* 21:261.

189. Rahner laments that neoscholastic treatments of soteriology neglect this subjective dimension: "The traditional doctrine of the *fides qua* remains very abstract, and soteriology speaks ordinarily only of the 'objective' redemption. The actual subjective structure of this salutary faith, insofar as it bears on the 'objective' redemption . . . , is not sufficiently analysed in itself and in its conditions of possibility in man" ("Salvation," *SM* 5:437).

Like his theology of death, Rahner's notion of the supernatural existential is a rich and nuanced term to which an entire book itself easily could be devoted. Once again, only a brief review of several salient and relevant points is possible here.[190] Though it is woven into the fabric of Rahner's entire theological corpus, the supernatural existential is perhaps best located within his contribution to the nature and grace disputes in the first half of the twentieth century. At the extreme ends of the dispute were two unpalatable alternatives. If, following Cajetan, human nature is understood as a self-sufficient reality without reference to God's supernatural grace (a grace laid as a kind of superstructure upon our "pure" nature), how do we, as human, have anything to do with or find any fulfillment in the supernatural destiny (namely, participation in God's own life) afforded by this grace? On the other hand, if human nature is naturally oriented toward God from the outset, how does one avoid the implication that God, having created us, *owes* the fulfillment of grace (which thus loses its pure gratuity) to his creatures?[191]

Rahner's solution posits that while human beings *could* meaningfully exist according to "pure nature," in actuality, there is no such thing since God has gratuitously infused human nature with an essential and constitutive openness to grace. This openness is at once "supernatural" (freely given by God for a transcendental finality) and an "existential" (a constitutive part of concrete human nature existing prior to any exercise of freedom)[192]; the former element safeguards the gratuity of grace while the latter avoids the extrinsicism of a Cajetanian superstructure framework.

While it is beyond the scope of the current project to address the success of the supernatural existential vis-à-vis the nature and grace disputes, the concept is important since it retains a prominent and abiding place in Rahner's anthropology.[193] In short, the supernatural existential is a gracious invitation to relationship with God that exists

---

190. Rahner's extended treatments of this matter can be found, among other places, in "Concerning the Relationship Between Nature and Grace" (*TI* 1:297–317), "Nature and Grace" (*TI* 4:165–88); cf. *FCF*, 121–28.

191. Henri de Lubac traces this problem from Cajetan on forward in his, *The Mystery of the Supernatural* (New York: Herder & Herder, 1998), 7–9 and following (cf. de Lubac's earlier groundbreaking work, *Surnaturel* (Paris: F. Aubier, 1946). For a contemporary overview of the problem and various solutions (including his own, which draws on both Rahner and Balthasar), see Fields's *Analogies of Transcendence*.

192. See translator's note on *FCF*, 16. Other "existentials" include human conscience, inquisitiveness, and freedom.

193. Fields offers a perceptive and critical treatment of the supernatural existential as jeopardizing nature's theological significance in *Analogies of Transcendence*, 65–72.

in the heart of every person. As such, it is the key for understanding how human beings subjectively appropriate the reconciling grace communicated in the Christ-event. It is important to recall that God's grace is, for Rahner, not simply an abstract self-communication of God, but fundamentally tied to the person of Christ since he is, as *das Realsymbol*, *the* exteriorization of the self-communicating God.[194] Accordingly, Rahner describes the supernatural existential as a person's orientation toward grace *in Christ*.[195]

This connection between every human person and Christ provides the basis for the "anthropological" procedure which Rahner consistently employs, especially in his later work. This procedure moves from the human person's faith, hope, and trust in God's final salvation (or even in her affirmation of her *genuine* humanity, as it is oriented toward this fulfillment[196]) to the affirmation of Jesus Christ, who (objectively) realizes this state of affairs in his own person. In addition to providing Jesus as an answer to the "meaning of life," Rahner sees this "anthropological" methodology as a valid and even preferable approach for conducting contemporary Christology.[197] To be clear, Rahner is not proposing any "deduction" of the Christ-event from foundational anthropological concepts; rather, he is clear that this approach is only possible in light of the Christ-event.[198] Its strength lies

---

194. "Christ is God's will for our salvation made historical, made flesh; *God's personal, loving will does not encounter man in some unattainable, intangible 'inner realm'; since Christ, since the One who became man, all grace is Christ's grace with a body*, grace dependent on the historical event that at one particular space time point in our human history the Word became man and was crucified and rose again" ("The Parish Priest," in *Mission and Grace: Essays in Pastoral Theology*, 3 vols. (London: Sheed and Ward, 1963–1966), 2:35–52, at 39 (emphasis added).

195. Rahner explains that since the "free self-communication of God in Jesus Christ and in his Spirit must be accepted by the spiritual creature in a dialogical partnership that is equally free, it presupposes a permanent human constitution (freely determined by God) . . . one prior to God's self-communication in such a way that man must receive this latter as an event that is free favour, unforeseeable in the light of man's constitution, that is to say not transcendentally implicit in human self-realization, though man is essentially open to this self-disclosure of God (Potentia obedientialis, Supernatural existential) and involves his whole being in calamity if he foregoes it" ("Grace," in *Theological Dictionary*, 192–96, at 193).

196. "Anyone who accepts his humanity fully, and all the more so of course the humanity of others, has accepted the Son of Man because in him God has accepted man" (*FCF*, 228).

197. See the consecutive essays in *TI* 21 "Jesus Christ–The Meaning of Life" (208–19), "Christology Today" (220–27), and "Brief Observations on Systematic Christology Today" (228–38).

198. "Speaking in the most general terms, there is no transcendental theology that would limit itself so exclusively to the realm of the transcendental, the aprioristic, and the speculative that it would omit any attempt to bring in a posteriori experience and to interpret it. Aristotle's logic, for example, is an aprioristic transcendental logic. But even with its a priori character, universal validity, and transcendental validity it is obvious that it exists only because the peasants' wives who sold potatoes in the marketplace engaged in logic. And so I would naturally not claim to have designed a transcendental theology if there had not been the a posteriori experience of Jesus of Nazareth" ("Jesus Christ—The Meaning of Life," *TI* 21:235). Cf. *FCF*, 207, "Thoughts on the Possibility of Belief Today," *TI* 5:12.

not by way of deduction, but by way of presenting Christ as intrinsi-cally related to human persons precisely in their transcendent long-ings and openness to God.

The subjective appropriation of salvation which occurs in positively responding to one's openness and invitation to grace constitutes what Rahner calls "self-redemption." Since God's invitation precedes any acceptance on our part, an acceptance which is itself "also a gift of God's grace,"[199] Rahner uses this term with no Pelagian connotations. Instead, it signifies that the human person does not "merely receive his salvation in a passive manner but rather realises it with total, and not just partial, freedom."[200] Self-redemption accounts for the fact that sal-vation is not something realized entirely externally to the human per-son;[201] the "redemptio objectiva" wrought by the incarnation, death, and resurrection of Christ must be freely accepted by the human sub-ject.[202]

Finally, we must note that Rahner utilizes *das Realsymbol* within this subjective and ascending dimension of his soteriology. First of all, he describes the very process of self-disposal in freedom in such terms, calling one's life a "concrete process of self-fulfilment . . . a 'real sym-bol' under which the individual brings to fruition this basic attitude of his, his *option fondamentale.*"[203] In other words, one can legitimately think of the final "Yes" or No" to God's self-offer which sums up, expresses, and realizes the totality of a person's free acts (i.e., what Rahner terms "death") as *das Realsymbol* of that person's life. A person's *realsymbolisch* "Yes" in death constitutes "the radical and final coming of subjective redemption."[204]

---

199. "The One Christ and the Universality of Salvation," *TI* 16:207.
200. Ibid. Cf. "redemption in the sense of ultimate salvation is impossible without faith, hope, and love, and that this redemption in its ultimate phase is nothing other than the perfection of faith, hope, and love" ("The Christian Understanding of Redemption," *TI* 21:241).
201. "Naturally Jesus' death has a meaning and a dignity that we cannot attribute to our own. It was the once and for all, irrevocable and unrepeatable word of God's power to us, the act of *the* Word of God. As fundamental as this is for Christians, it remains true that his abandonment of self in faith and hope into the incomprehensibility of death in which God dwells is also demanded of us in our death. In us too the redeemed and redeemer must become one; salvation by another and salvation by oneself, when seen in their ultimate significance, do not represent contradictions for a Christian" ("Good Friday: Gratitude for the Cross," in *The Great Church Year: The Best of Karl Rah-ner's Homilies, Meditations, and Sermons* [New York: Crossroad, 1993], 159–63, at 161).
202. "[I]f the cross of Christ (rooted in the incarnation of the Logos and reaching fulfilment in the res-urrection) is made the cause of our salvation as the 'redemptio objectiva', then the causality of the cross must *be* understood in relation to the general and the individual conditions of possibil-ity of self-redemption" ("The One Christ and the Universality of Salvation," *TI* 16:207, emphasis original).
203. "Considerations of the Active Role," *TI* 14:177.
204. "Salvation," *SM* 5:438.

94

Moreover, *das Realsymbol* is not only operative in reference to a person's own history of freedom, for the supernatural existential backdrop against which that freedom operates itself possesses a *realsymbolisch* relationship to the person of Jesus Christ. For Christ himself is the grace (i.e., self-communication) of God, fully exteriorized in its *Realsymbol*, to which every person is open and responds. Rahner thus makes claims like "anyone who seizes upon the grace of God as the radical dimension of his own personal life, as its ultimate and definitive hope, has *ipso facto* posited an assent to *the historical manifestation of the definitive nature* [read '*Realsymbol*'] *of this grace* in Jesus Christ."[205] This *realsymbolisch* connection also enables him to argue for an "intrinsic unity" (rather than just an "extrinsic" or "factual" relationship) between Christ's incarnation and "the self-transcendence of the whole spiritual world into God through God's self-communication."[206] For "although the hypostatic union is a unique event in its own essence, and viewed in itself it is the highest conceivable event, it is nevertheless an intrinsic moment within the whole process by which grace is bestowed upon all spiritual creatures."[207] Far from being a mere "prime instance" of an ongoing activity on the part of God achieved at a high degree, the Christ-event "is already an intrinsic moment and a condition for the universal bestowal of grace."[208]

The concept of *das Realsymbol* pervades the entirety of Rahner's soteriology, considered in all of the dimensions. Viewed objectively and "from above," the act of incarnation is the *realsymbolisch* exteriorization of the Logos. Viewed objectively and "from below," Christ's death on the cross is the summative *Realsymbol* of his entire, lifelong "Yes" to God. Finally, the ascending and subjective act of "self-redemption" is intrinsically bound by *das Realsymbol* to Christ since he *is* the exteriorized realization of the grace to which the human person's freedom responds.

205. "Considerations of the Active Role," *TI* 14:168, emphasis added.
206. *FCF*, 200.
207. *FCF*, 201.
208. *FCF*, 199. "The reality of Christian salvation, being essentially something that is present to us in the word, calls on us for a free, personal assent. It is a reality for us and in us, giving us its blessings, gracing us in our free assent to it, just insofar as we not only undergo it but act it ourselves as well, with God. Christ becomes our life only when we are doing that which is done to us; when that word which blesses us with the tidings of his life, that word by which he himself enters into our life, is spoken by us too, with him, testifying to our faith and our love; when the primary sacramental word of Christianity becomes, simultaneously, the primary word of our co-operative fulfillment of this Christ-reality" ("The Parish Priest," 41–42).

Connecting Points for Representative Thought

In this chapter, I have examined Rahner's seminal article "The Theology of the Symbol," exploring the concept of *das Realsymbol* through its general ontology as well as through several applications made by Rahner. I have also considered the influences, both spiritual and philosophical, which contributed to the formation of this concept, arguing that the former possess a certain primacy of place. I have furthermore distinguished Rahner's *Realsymbol* from the concepts of symbol posited by Paul Tillich and Roger Haight, both of whom argue that the symbol manifests and even *makes present* the reality symbolized, but whose concepts lack the robust intrinsicity which characterized Rahner's version. Finally, I have offered my own summary of Rahner's soteriological application of *das Realsymbol*, considering his account of God's reconciliation with humankind from various permutations of ascending, descending, objective, and subjective perspectives.

All of the above analysis has operated within the standard classification of Rahner's soteriological thought as "sacramental," with Jesus Christ communicating human salvation as the *Ursakrament* of God's grace. As this second chapter comes to a close, I would like to expand the conversation by returning to the previously discussed representative soteriological category, but without exactly leaving the sacramental one. To speak visually, if Rahner's *sacramental* soteriological thought were to be considered a bounded area within a two-dimensional plane, the corresponding *representative* component might be said to develop along an intersecting, perpendicular axis, granting a full, three-dimensional body to his theology of human salvation. Although an extended historical and conceptual analysis of this new "representative axis" will occur in chapters 4 and 5, I want here to briefly demonstrate that there truly is the "intersection" I have just described. That is, I will substantiate my earlier claim that Rahner's sacramental soteriological thinking *implies* a representative counterpart.

The most efficient way to demonstrate this implication is to return to the above exposition of Rahner's sacramental soteriology and indicate its direct correspondence to the three "markers" of representative soteriology (centered on Jesus's person; God's incarnational presence to the world in Christ; humanity's transformation and divinization in the New Adam) described in chapter 1. The second of these markers is the most obviously "sacramental" of the three, and it corresponds with the descending and objective perspective of Rahner's soteriology.

The Logos's exteriorization in its *Realsymbol*—namely, the human being Jesus—obviously constitutes the saving presence of God to humanity. But almost any theology which recognizes some version of the incarnation could claim such a connection. What is especially interesting here is that Rahner's own insistence that salvation itself consists precisely of God's direct presence to humanity[209] matches almost seamlessly with Brian Daley's summary of patristic soteriological thought-patterns[210] (patterns which I am considering as normative for representative soteriology). For both sets of thought, the incarnation (considered as an interval rather than a moment) thus has great salvific significance.

The third marker of representative soteriology, the divinization of humanity through the New Adam, corresponds with Rahner's soteriology viewed objectively and from below. Recall, Christ is not only, for Rahner, *the* culminating presence of God to humanity, but also humanity's own culminating "Yes" to God. Christ is, for Rahner, quite literally the perfect human,[211] a "New Adam" for the human race. Nor is he just the prime example or most successful instance but, as we saw above, his own perfect "Yes" is a "condition for the universal bestowal of grace."[212] This being the case, Rahner calls Christ "the one who is definitively affirmed and accepted by God,"[213] and says that "in him God has accepted man."[214] Considering these claims, as well as the intrinsic connection between any human "Yes" to God and the Christ-event (just treated in the "subjective" considerations above), it is more than fair to say that Rahner's Jesus stands as the head of a new humanity, marked by divinization through God's grace.[215]

Finally, the first characteristic of representative soteriology is its person-centeredness. Rahner undoubtedly has a profound respect for the acts and events of Jesus's life, particularly his passion and death. Nevertheless, as we have seen, Christ's actions are, for Rahner, not car-

---

209. "Salvation here is to be understood as the strictly supernatural and direct presence of God in himself afforded by grace" ("The One Christ and the Universality of Salvation," *TI* 16:200).
210. "God must work our salvation by becoming one of us . . . because salvation cannot be conceived simply as a 'work' . . . salvation simply is God's personal presence among us" (Brian Daley, "'He Himself Is Our Peace' (Ephesians 2:14): Early Christian Views of Redemption in Christ," in *The Redemption: An Interdisciplinary Symposium on Christ as Redeemer*, eds. Stephen Davis et al (New York: Oxford Univ. Press, 2004), 149–76, at 175–76).
211. Cf. Rahner's well-known remark that "Christology may be studied as self-transcending anthropology, and anthropology as deficient Christology" ("Current Problems in Christology," *TI* 1:164).
212. *FCF*, 199.
213. "Jesus Christ—The Meaning of Life," *TI* 21:216.
214. *FCF*, 228.
215. On the Rahner and divinization, see Francis J. Caponi, "Karl Rahner: Divinization in Roman Catholicism." *Partakers of the Divine Nature: The History and Development of Deification in the Christian Tradition* (Madison: Fairleigh Dickinson University Press, 2007), 259–80.

ried out as those a super-agent attempting to alter a judiciary state of affairs or rebalance a system of honor. Rather, the import of Christ's free human actions (especially in his final, summative "Yes" to God on the cross) resides in their establishing *him* as *the* definitive openness to God. Jesus Christ *is himself* the redemptive state of affairs, both "from above" as God's definitive self-communication to the world (the irreversibly established "soteriological anchor") and "from below" as the definitive human acceptance of it. Operating through sacramental or *realsymbolisch* causality, Rahner's Christ does not simply effect our reconciliation with God, but, as seen above, he in fact *is* that very reconciliation.[216]

It thus seems that an analysis of Rahner's sacramental or *realsymbolisch* account of human salvation in Christ (as inevitably selective, yet textually grounded, as that analysis might be) leads to the very building blocks and constitutive markers of a representative soteriology akin to those present in patristic theologies such as that of Irenaeus of Lyons. Moreover, this connection between Rahner's *realsymbolisch* soteriology and a figure such as Irenaeus should not be entirely surprising, despite the fact that Rahner is typically associated with Thomism and transcendental philosophical thought and only rarely considered in connection with patristic theology. After all, the call for the most basic components, and even some applications of his later "The Theology of the Symbol" are already present in the conclusion of his 1936 dissertation, a dissertation which focuses on the patristic typological claim of the church as the New Eve emerging from the pierced side of the New Adam. That the category of *das Realsymbol*, according to which his soteriology is virtually unanimously classified, appears (at least in gestational form) within a meticulous analysis of Migne's Greek and Latin patrologies provides a suggestive historical basis for understanding his soteriology in the manner which I am arguing here.

In the following chapter, I will examine the writings on the topic of human salvation from several figures who stand among the normative exemplars of representative soteriology—namely, Irenaeus and others

---

216. "Christians know full well that God's forgiving and reconciling love that encompasses all guilt has entered the world in such a way that it can never be revoked. This love has revealed itself in the cross of Jesus Christ who has become our reconciliation. . . . God's forgiving love has reached its historically visible culmination in Jesus' death on the cross, because this love has become irrevocable and has found its acceptance in a human being. . . . God has reconciled the world to himself in Jesus the crucified . . . [I]t also becomes reality for its part when human beings accept it" ("Reconciliation and Vicarious Representation," *TI* 21:261).

of the church fathers. A further analysis of the historical connection between Rahner and such patristic figures, including an overview of his dissertation *E latere Christi*, will have to wait until chapter 4. Finally, a more thorough consideration of how Rahner's mature writings align with the constitutive markers of representative soteriology will occur in the fifth and final chapter. But while much more remains to be shown, the present chapter has sought to demonstrate that even if Rahner's theology of salvation can (and should!) be characterized as "sacramental," his is not an account of an abstract operation of *realsymbolisch* causality, but of a person who is *the* Sacrament and *Realsymbol*, and as such *is* our reconciliation with God.

3

———

Representative Soteriology in the
Patristic Period

The conclusion of the previous chapter marked a shift in this project's procedure. The previous two chapters have focused on readings of Rahner's soteriology which are prevalent in the literature on the topic. These readings, both critical and sympathetic alike, largely agree that Rahner's account of Christ as Savior is best understood through the category of sacrament or *Symbol*. However, as I have just argued, the way in which Rahner crafts this category himself entails a supplementary "representative" understanding of Christ. From here on forward, we will direct our attention to this representative category. The fifth and final chapter will analyze arguments and passages from Rahner's mature corpus that attest to representation in his soteriology. Prior to that, chapter 4 will consider Rahner's training and early career, particularly his prolonged engagement with patristic theology, through which he encountered classical articulations of representative soteriology and which formatively shaped his own theological system.

In the present chapter, we will take a hiatus from focusing on Rahner's writings in order to make clearer precisely what is meant by "representative soteriology." This clarification will, first of all, be rooted in this soteriological category's three characteristic markers, which will be revisited momentarily. The bulk of the chapter will consist in a historical survey of early Christian thinkers who utilize the representative category to varying degrees. The scope of this project will restrict this survey to the patristic roots—especially Irenaeus of Lyons (d. 202), in whose thought this category was first fully exemplified)—although it will also make brief references to theologians from recent decades who, along with Rahner, articulated their accounts of salvation in accordance (again, in varying degrees) with representative soteriology.

Overview of Representative Markers

Toward the end of the first chapter, I suggested three characteristic markers which distinguish a representative soteriology from other models for Christian understandings of human salvation. None of these markers is exclusively associated with the category; indeed, one might even argue that all three could be predicated of another classical model. However, the way in which these three makers relate to one another, their particular configuration, is what differentiates this unique soteriological category. Since I will appeal to these categories throughout this third chapter, let us briefly review them.

The first characteristic of our soteriological category is that it considers Christ as God's representative before us. This "descending," human-ward characteristic, which is the centerpiece of a sacramental soteriology, accounts for our salvation. Indeed, salvation is nothing other than the fullest realization human flourishing, which supposes the direct, loving presence of God: Irenaeus's celebrated dictum, *Gloria Dei vivens homo* ("The glory of God is a living human being") is followed with *vita hominis visio Dei* ("human life consists in beholding God").[1] However, Jesus is not God the Father, nor even *simply* God's Word, the divine Logos, among us—rather, he is God's *Representative* in our midst. The idea of representation at work here implies both identity and differentiation. God's presence to us is accomplished through another, through the human being Jesus of Nazareth, whose differentness from God allows him to stand with us and whose sameness with God allows God to self-communicate through him. The incarnate Word, the Representative who "the Father . . . sent forth" (John 20:21), is the descending Mediator of salvation to humankind.

The second characteristic (inversely related to the first) states that

---

1. *Against Heresies* (henceforth *AH*) IV.20.7. Unless otherwise noted and with occasional minor adjustments, quotations from *AH* are taken from *Ante-Nicene Fathers* (henceforth *ANF*), 10 vols., eds. Alexander Roberts, James Donaldson, and A. Cleveland Coxe (Christian Literature Publishing Co., 1885), 1:315–567.

Christ is *our* Representative before God. This category requires looking at the person of Christ "from below," in an ascending, God-ward manner. Again, the idea of "representative" implies both sameness and difference; Jesus is at once fully human but set out from among us in a unique, distinct way. Somewhat ironically, part of this distinctiveness arises from his being fully human, for the rest of us, insofar as we are sinners, fall short of fully realized, authentic humanity. Christ is the "New Adam" among us, whose sinless life of love for God encapsulates what we are called to be. Moreover, as our Representative, Christ is this perfect human "for our sakes" and "on our behalf," different from us, yet communicating us to the God whom he has so perfectly loved. This ascending, God-ward elevation of the human race is classically expressed in terms of divinization or *theosis*, a transformation of humanity unto God. The deification of humanity is possible through God's prior self-communication to us, together with our incorporation into the person of Christ, whose "Yes" to God becomes our own.

Finally, a representative soteriology is characteristically person-centered. Unlike soteriological schemas according to which the human Jesus is fully divine in order to perform a great redemptive task (e.g., making satisfaction, defeating Satan, being penalized in our stead as a substitute), the representative view takes Christ's tasks as oriented toward his person. In this view, salvation is not the extrinsic *result* of the saving agent's action, but rather, salvation finds its very *locus* in the Representative himself. That is to say, our reconciliation with God is realized via our incorporation into Jesus Christ—the nexus point in which God is united fully with creation—as his members. The incarnation, life and ministry, death, and resurrection of Christ are thus not *primarily* about balancing the cosmic scales of justice, vanquishing the "evil one," or restoring divine honor, but more fundamentally aimed at establishing a renewed humanity united with God and rendering it accessible to us in our current state. Our salvation is not only through Christ but *in* Christ. As we saw Brian Daley argue in chapter 1, this sort of soteriological vision provides an answer quite different from the one which Anselm provided to his famous question, *Cur Deus homo?* Moreover, it is an answer which, as Daley attested, is pervasive among the thinking of the fathers.

A reader with a careful eye could detect strands of representative soteriology in writings that span the entirety of the Christian tradition from the NT on forward. However, it was in the post-NT period of the fathers that the idea became the object of prolonged, sustained theo-

logical attention. The watershed moment for representative soteriology was Irenaeus's formulation of "recapitulation," an idea which he
utilized in a variety of ways but which seems primarily ordered toward
accounting for the unity of salvation history over and against dualistic,
"Gnostic"[2] systems of thought. Irenaeus's logic for reading the contents
of scripture as a whole, with Christ as their recapitulating culmination,
proliferated in the patristic theologians who wrote after him.

Since Irenaeus stands as a monumental figure in the development
of representative soteriology, his own theology will be considered at
some length below. And because a detailed consideration of those who
drew from his soteriology is impossible in a single chapter, I will subsequently gesture toward his influence by looking at three theologians
from Northern Africa, where Irenaeus's writings are known to have
spread and taken root even within his own lifetime[3]: Clement of
Alexandria (d. c. 215), Athanasius of Alexandria (d. 373), and Augustine
of Hippo (d. 430).

Irenaeus: Recapitulation as a Kind of Representative Soteriology

More than a single instance of representative soteriology, Irenaeus of
Lyons and his notion of recapitulation constitute the standard for the
category as I have characterized it. Accordingly, significant space will
be dedicated to Irenaeus's articulation of this idea. Below, we will consider the sources which he drew upon, his person-centered theology
of Christ the New Adam, his "descending" connection of the Word's
incarnation with human divinization, and his "ascending" theology of
human maturation throughout history, reaching its apex in the person
of Christ.

Irenaeus's Sources

Before addressing Irenaeus's theology of recapitulation, it is important
to recognize the interlocutors with whom he was engaged and the
source material to which he had frequent recourse. As Matthew Steenberg, an Orthodox patrologist who has published extensively on Irenaeus, has demonstrated, Irenaeus was deeply engaged in dialogue

2. In order to guard against the common and false idea of a singular religious tradition and system
of thought called "Gnosticism," which is, in fact, a loose label used to group a variety of related
movements, I will often put words like "Gnostic" in quotation marks.
3. Matthew C. Steenberg, *Of God and Man: Theology as Anthropology from Irenaeus to Athanasius* (New
York: T&T Clark, 2009), 19.

and dispute with Christian and non-Christian thinkers, figures such as Justin Martyr,[4] Theophilus, Plato, the Stoics, and representatives of several strands of Judaism.[5] But, as it is well known, Irenaeus's most direct and primary conversation partners were a variety of esoteric religious groups which have come to be labeled "Gnostic." In Steenberg's judgment, Irenaeus's main task, especially in his monumental work *Against Heresies* (*Adversus Haereses*), was biblical in character; Irenaeus was keenly aware of the fact that Valentinus and other Gnostics read and utilized scripture, but in doing so, they managed to neglect the heart of the apostolic message.[6]

Thus, the Bible stands as the main source for Irenaeus's theology, including his distinctive notion of recapitulation. In particular, Ephesians can be singled out for containing the terminology which Irenaeus adopted for the concept. The tenth verse of the first chapter speaks of God's plan (*oikonomia*), that is, God's gradually unfolding management of creation. The author elaborates, explaining that the culminating moment of God's "economy," the content of his plan, is to gather up or recapitulate (*anakephalaiosasthai*) all things in Christ.[7] The idea of *anakephalaiosis* used in Ephesians is borrowed from Greek literary terminology and references the summative end of a story. For Irenaeus, taking his cue from the author of Ephesians,[8] "God saves by taking over the human story and appropriating it to himself," reversing points of derailment in that story and fulfilling past promises.[9]

Another significant locus for the idea is Paul's references to Adam and Christ in Romans 5. There, in vv. 12–21, Paul describes how death,

4. Justin merits particular mention here, in light of the fact that Irenaeus specifically cites a (now lost) work of Justin's, Πρὸς Μαρκίωνα ("Against Marcion"), in which Justin mentions the idea of recapitulation: "In his book against Marcion, Justin does well say: 'I would not have believed the Lord Himself, if He had announced any other than He who is our framer, maker, and nourisher. But because the only-begotten Son came to us from the one God, who both made this world and formed us, and contains and administers all things in Himself, my faith towards Him is steadfast, and my love to the Father immoveable, God bestowing both upon us'" (*AH* IV.6.2).

5. Steenberg, *Irenaeus on Creation: The Cosmic Christ and the Saga of Redemption* (Leiden: Brill, 2008), 10.

6. Irenaeus thus set out "to exegete those same scriptures, particularly around the points raised by the groups in question, but to do so after a manner he considers authentic to the reading and exegesis of apostolic heritage" (Steenberg, *Of God and Man*, 20).

7. "[H]e has made known to us the mystery of his will, according to his good pleasure that he set forth in Christ, as a plan (οἰκονομίαν) for the fullness of time, to gather up (ἀνακεφαλαιώσασθαι) all things in him, things in heaven and things on earth" (Eph 1:9–10).

8. Cf. Irenaeus's explicit citation of the Ephesians text in *AH* V.20.2, immediately after which he elaborates, "These things [on earth], therefore, He recapitulated in Himself: by uniting man to the Spirit, and causing the Spirit to dwell in man, He is Himself made the head of the Spirit, and gives the Spirit to be the head of man: for through Him (the Spirit) we see, and hear, and speak."

9. Richard J. Clifford and Khaled Anatolios, "Christian Salvation: Biblical and Theological Perspectives," *Theological Studies* 66, no. 4 (2005): 739–69, 749.

which emerged through sin, spread to all following upon the sin of the one man, Adam. To this description, he adds that God's life-giving grace also proliferates from the one man, Jesus Christ. While Paul here juxtaposes Adam and Christ when it comes to their lives (sin and trespass vs. righteousness) and the subsequent results (death vs. life and justification), Paul's more basic insight here in comparing Adam and Christ concerns their similarity: it is "because of" and "through" the one that the many are affected.[10] Likewise, Irenaeus frequently juxtaposes Adam and Christ within a framework of their similarity.[11]

Irenaeus's use of the Bible as a source for his theology of recapitulation is, however, significantly more wide-ranging. Richard Clifford and Khaled Anatolios have argued that Irenaeus's soteriology ought to be understood as part of a larger model or system which they classify as "prophetic."[12] According to this model—the other two cited examples of which are the Book of Isaiah and Luke-Acts—God effects salvation in a long process within history by means of human instruments.[13]

The Book of Isaiah, which is generally agreed to have been written by several authors over hundreds of years (beginning in the eighth century BCE), is situated within a context of an Ancient Near Eastern worldview. A common part of this worldview, Clifford and Anatolios explain, is the attribution of political change to a shift in power within the pantheon of the gods. Along similar lines, Amos, Hosea, Isaiah, and Micah all interpreted major political events in terms of the (vulnerable) relationship between God and Israel, a relationship damaged by human sin but open to restoration through Israel's repentance. The Book of Isaiah is particularly unique in that its long period of composition and multiple authors allow it to follow this process of sin, exile, and repentance over the course of a 250-year period.[14] It testifies to a drawn out process of Israel's loss and eventual restoration through

---

10. "If, because of the one man's trespass, death exercised dominion through that one, much more surely will those who receive the abundance of grace and the free gift of righteousness exercise dominion in life through the one man, Jesus Christ. Therefore just as one man's trespass led to condemnation for all, so one man's act of righteousness leads to justification and life for all" (Rom 5:17–18).

11. E.g., "He became incarnate, and was made man, He commenced afresh the long line of human beings, and furnished us, in a brief, comprehensive manner, with salvation; so that what we had lost in Adam—namely, to be according to the image and likeness of God—that we might recover in Christ Jesus" (AH III.18.1)

12. Clifford and Anatolios, "Christian Salvation," passim. The other models discussed are the "liturgical" and "sapiential" models.

13. Ibid., 741.

14. Ibid., 742–43.

God's providential care, which brings about Israel's return from exile by way of Cyrus the Great and the Persian conquerors of Babylon.

Though Isaiah is constantly cited in the NT, Luke, in particular, picks up on Isaiah's interpretation of history. The author's continuity with this tradition can be seen in his account of Jesus's inaugural announcement of his public ministry. There, Jesus adopts the theme of the lengthy process of Zion's renewal, explicitly citing Isaiah 61, situating the present day within this process, and identifying his new movement as its fulfillment.[15] In fact, as the Gospel of Luke continues to unfold, it becomes clear that this fulfillment occurs not only in Jesus's ministry, but in his very person.[16]

Irenaeus appropriates this lengthy, historical view of redemption through his careful reading of scripture, including Isaiah and Luke.[17] As will be discussed more below, Irenaeus understands human salvation primarily in terms of God's saving presence within history, a presence which comes about as a part of a lengthy, multistage economy, which utilizes human agency, and which interacts with our own free history.[18] As Steenberg puts it, an interpretive foundation for understanding Irenaeus's theology (particularly of creation) is that God's act of creation is the "initiation of a coherent, unified economy that shall advance to the eschaton,"[19] an economy which hinges on the New Adam who brings it to completion in himself.

Soteriological Pluralism in Irenaeus

Despite the helpful "prophetic soteriology" categorization of Clifford and Anatolios and my own use of the "representative" soteriological," I should make clear that a careful reading of Irenaeus yields a variety of soteriological models. As David Brondos has argued, Irenaeus, who is writing at a time when Christian theology was still remarkably young and undeveloped, relies on several traditions, resulting in "a range of ideas that are often difficult to reconcile with one another."[20] According to Brondos's lights, Irenaeus appeals at various points to a "physi-

---

15. Ibid., 746; Luke 4:16–21.
16. "[T]he Temple and the traditions will be 'destroyed' in that the presence of God and the authoritative word will move from the Temple and Torah to Jesus himself" (Clifford and Anatolios, "Christian Salvation," 747). Cf. Jesus's self-referential statements, "The kingdom of God is among you" (Luke 17:21), and "Today, this scripture has been fulfilled in your hearing" (Luke 4:21).
17. Clifford and Anatolios, "Christian Salvation," 748.
18. Ibid., 747.
19. Steenberg, *Irenaeus on Creation*, 60.
20. David A. Brondos, "The Redemption of 'Man' in the Thought of Irenaeus," in *Fortress Introduction to Salvation and the Cross* (Minneapolis: Fortress Press, 2007), 49–63, at 50.

cal" model of redemption (in which the incarnation infuses humanity with immortality), a "Christus victor" model (in which Christ defeats Satan, rescuing humankind from his possession), and a model of Jesus revealing God to humankind.[21] Some earnest scholars even claim to find the doctrine of penal substitution in Irenaeus.[22] No orderly and tidy synthesis of these (in many ways inconsistent) models can be achieved, Brondos insists, for Irenaeus was, first of all, a polemicist, not a systematic theologian.[23]

It is certainly the case that, like the NT, Irenaeus's works contain a variety of explanations for how precisely Christ restored humanity's relationship with God. Indeed, Irenaeus's primary purpose was to demonstrate how this multifaceted body of sacred texts refuted the ornate "Gnostic" system of thought, and so, it should come as no surprise that such a demonstration itself reflects the NT's variety of soteriological motifs. Nonetheless, key to Irenaeus's constant hermeneutical theme was the unity of salvation history, an idea which has as its cornerstone the notion of Christ, the New Adam, recapitulating the human race within himself. More than simply a model for understanding atonement, recapitulation was a theological idea which allowed Irenaeus to confute the dualistic, "Gnostic" worldview with a theology of a united human history unfolding in a God-ward direction. As such, recapitulation is a central and privileged idea for Irenaeus. Thus, it is with an understanding of recapitulation as a privileged, though not absolute, soteriological concept for Irenaeus that we offer the following exploration of Irenaeus as an instance of representative soteriology.

Person-Centered: Christ the New Adam

Irenaeus's idea of recapitulation is thoroughly person-centered and thus meets one of our three criteria for representative soteriology. It is true that, in places, Irenaeus indeed speaks of recapitulation as Christ's "work"; however, even the context of these comments makes it clear

21. Ibid., 52.
22. See, for instance, Howard Marshall, "The Theology of the Atonement," in *The Atonement Debate*, eds. Tidball, Hilborn, and Thacker (Grand Rapids, MI: Zondervan, 2008), 49–68, at 61–62. Marshall cites Joel Green and Mark Baker (*Recovering the Scandal of the Cross* (Downer's Grove, IL: InterVarsity Press, 2000), 121), who in turn find evidence of Irenaeus's reliance on a doctrine of "propitiation" in *AH* V.17.1 ("in the last times the Lord has restored us into friendship through His incarnation, having become the Mediator between God and men; propitiating indeed for us the Father against whom we had sinned, and cancelling our disobedience by His own obedience; conferring also upon us the gift of communion with, and subjection to, our Maker.").
23. Brondos, 50.

that the notion of recapitulation is not primarily about Christ performing a singular task as an agent, but rather, about Christ bringing about a definitive reconciliation between God and humankind, between heaven and earth, in his person. For instance, immediately before writing that Christ "has therefore, in His *work* of recapitulation, summed up all things,"[24] Irenaeus, reflecting on the "things on earth" spoken of in Ephesians 1:10, writes, "These things, therefore, He recapitulated *in Himself:* by uniting man to the Spirit, and causing the Spirit to dwell in man, He *is Himself* made the head of the Spirit, and gives the Spirit to be the head of man."[25] Irenaeus considers Christ's "work" of recapitulating to consist in *being* the nexus point between God's Spirit and the human person, between "things in heaven and things on earth" (Eph 1:10).

The person-centered character of Christ's recapitulating work is particularly evident in the way that Irenaeus cites the idea of recapitulation in order to counter Docetist Christians who denied the reality of Christ's humanity. He explains that by hermetically sealing God off from human flesh in their christological accounts, Docetists have entirely missed the rationale of Christ's coming among us in the first place. For "if the Lord became incarnate for any other order of things.... He has not then summed up human nature in His own person."[26] Rather, Irenaeus argues, Christ "had Himself, therefore, flesh and blood, recapitulating in Himself not a certain other, but that original handiwork of the Father ... [T]he righteous flesh has reconciled that flesh ... and brought it into friendship with God."[27]

In the background of this person-centered refutation of Docetism is Irenaeus's overarching theology of history, according to which, the One God's original creation is brought to its completion in Jesus. Indeed, perhaps Irenaeus's most important theological contribution is his persistent and careful effort to show how understanding Christ as the New Adam allows for a unified reading of the Bible. This reading consists of a gradually unfolding economy of several covenantal stages.[28] The dramatic occurrence of this economy, recorded in scripture, provides for Irenaeus what William Loewe has described as a kind

---

24. *AH* V.21.1 (emphasis added).
25. *AH* V.20.2 (emphasis added).
26. *AH* V.14.2.
27. Ibid.
28. "Irenaeus adopts this notion in his account of the divine *oikonomia* as comprised of four stages or 'covenants': the covenant with Adam, the covenant with Noah, the covenant with Moses, and the definitive fulfillment—the summing up or 'recapitulation' of God's salvific engagement with humanity in Christ" (Clifford and Anatolios, "Christian Salvation, 750, citing *AH* III.11.8).

of orthodox "countermyth" vis-à-vis the elaborate, dualistic Gnostic narratives.[29] In constructing this overarching narrative, Irenaeus became, to use the words of Jacques Dupuis, "the founder of the theology of history."[30]

According to Dupuis, Irenaeus's overarching history can be divided into three stages, at the center of all of which is God's self-manifestation.[31] The first stage consists of God's act of creation, for creation itself is part of God's self-disclosure. Unlike Marcion, according to whom the Creator was evil, and unlike many "Gnostic" Christians for whom creation was an unintentional mishap, creation according to Irenaeus was the one, good God's act of love. As Steenberg summarizes Irenaeus's logic, "God the creator is good, the creation itself is good, and the creative act is a manifestation of divine beneficence. . . . God will create in order to bring this goodness to another."[32] For Irenaeus, God created human beings particularly with them in mind as the recipients for this self-communication, and the whole of creation contributes to the "ripening" of humankind as it prepares to receive this gift.[33]

The second stage, according to Dupuis, is the "old dispensation," recorded in the OT. God's relationship with Israel ought to be seen in continuity with God's initial creative act, testifying to God's ongoing, intimate involvement with creation.[34] Once again, this continued involvement with creation is particularly geared toward the process of perfecting the human creature,[35] as Irenaeus attests by recounting the series of intensifying covenants, beginning with Adam and contin-

---

29. "Irenaeus' significance lies first of all in the fact that he responded to the challenge of Gnosticism by forging diverse elements of the Christian tradition into a myth comprehensive enough to match the Gnostic version" (William Loewe, "Irenaeus' Soteriology: Transposing the Question," in *Religion and Culture: Essays in Honor of Bernard Lonergan, S.J.* (Albany, NY: SUNY Press, 1987), 167–79, at 168). I.e., "Irenaeus met the Gnostic myth with a Christian countermyth," which included elements of divine economy, recapitulation, and Pauline Christ-Adam typology (ibid.). Loewe's most recently published treatment of these themes, "Irenaeus of Lyons: The Story of Salvation," draws on his essays cited here (*Lex Crucis: Soteriology and the Stages of Meaning* (Minneapolis: Fortress Press, 2016), 15–70.

30. Dupuis, *Toward a Christian Understanding of Religious Pluralism* (Maryknoll: Orbis Books, 1997), 56, 60.

31. Ibid., 60ff. Dupuis draws heavily on *AH* IV.20, discussing God's creation of human beings for full life and the economy of progressive divine manifestations through the Logos.

32. Steenberg, *Irenaeus on Creation*, 22.

33. "All such [things as have been made] have been created for the benefit of the man who is saved, ripening for immortality that which is possessed of its own free will and its own power, preparing and rendering it more adapted for eternal subjection to God. On this account creation is ordered for the benefit of man; for man was not made for its sake, but creation for the sake of man" (*AH* V.29.1, qtd. in Steenberg *Irenaeus on Creation*, 6).

34. As Steenberg writes, the OT attests to God's "consistent engagement of God's salvific design with the material fabric of creation" (ibid., 33).

35. "God's perfection of the human creature is distinct from, but a continuation of, the act of creation proper – both flow from God's goodness" (ibid., 36).

uing with Noah and Moses (and, in the next "stage," Christ).[36] These covenants, as Dupuis has pointed out, are not—for Irenaeus—simply a matter of God the Father being in relationship to human beings; rather, the OT "theophanies" are, in fact, "Logophanies."[37] Irenaeus insists that it is not the case that "the Word began to make the Father manifest only when he was born of Mary; but he is present at every point in time . . . in all things and through all things there is one God and Father, and one Word, his Son, and one Spirit, and one salvation to all who believe in him."[38] Even from the outset of creation, God's involvement with humanity and the whole of creation has been that of the Father, Son, and Spirit, with the second of the three "rehearsing his future coming in the flesh."[39]

It is precisely this "coming in the flesh" which inaugurates the third stage in Irenaeus's economy. And although his entire overarching series is one of continuity, Irenaeus marks this epoch out as the one in which Christ "brought something completely new, for he brought himself, who had been heralded."[40] Although the Word had hitherto been active in creation, in Christ, the Word becomes fully, tangibly visible in human flesh. As Dupuis summarizes, the Christ-event is, for Irenaeus, "a sacramental Logophany."[41] (To use Rahnerian language, one might even call it the *Realsymbol* of that which was previously present only fragmentarily.) And importantly, this "Logophany" is simultaneously the New Adam, the perfect human who recapitulates the "original handiwork of the Father" in himself.

Thus, the two strands winding their way through Irenaeus's overarching economy—namely, the human race which is being gradually prepared for perfection and the self-revealing God who relates to it—intersect in the person of Jesus Christ, who is both the New Adam and the Word Incarnate. Irenaeus himself adeptly summarizes his person-centered, overarching vision:

> There is, therefore, as I have pointed out, one God the Father, and one Christ Jesus, who came by means of the whole dispensational arrangements connected with Him, and gathered together all things in Himself.

36. There "were four principal (καθολικαί) covenants given to the human race: one, prior to the deluge, under Adam; the second, that after the deluge, under Noah; the third, the giving of the law, under Moses; the fourth, that which renovates man, and sums up all things in itself by means of the Gospel, raising and bearing men upon its wings into the heavenly kingdom" (*AH* III.11.8).
37. Dupuis, *Toward a Christian Understanding of Religious Pluralism*, 64.
38. *AH* IV.6.7.
39. Dupuis, *Toward a Christian Understanding of Religious Pluralism*, 64.
40. *AH* IV.34.1, qtd. in Dupuis, *Toward a Christian Understanding of Religious Pluralism*, 65.
41. Ibid., 66.

But in every respect, too, He is man, the formation of God; and He took up man into Himself, the invisible becoming visible, the incomprehensible being made comprehensible, the impassible becoming capable of suffering, and the Word being made man, thus summing up all things in Himself so that as in supercelestial, spiritual, and invisible things, the Word of God is supreme, so also in things visible and corporeal He might possess the supremacy, and, taking to Himself preeminence, as well as constituting Himself Head of the Church, He might draw all things to Himself at the proper time.[42]

For Irenaeus and his concept of recapitulation, Christ's work *is* his person, the New Adam who sums up humanity, thus allowing human beings to reach their fulfillment by being included in him.[43]

Christ, God's Representative Before Us

A major part of Irenaeus's soteriology is God's descending movement in Christ in order to bring about reconciliation with us. As Brian Daley has noted, Irenaeus consistently utilizes "communication" imagery of God's self-revelation through Christ in order to express this saving, descending movement.[44] Christ is the Father's self-expression, "for the Father is the invisible of the Son," and "the Son the visible of the Father."[45] (Such language, I cannot help but note here, bears remarkable similarity to the "exteriorization" language used by Rahner.) God's revelatory advancement toward us in Jesus allows us to see God, and "those who see God are in God, and . . . those . . . who see God, do receive life."[46]

Although Irenaeus discusses the incarnation frequently in terms of revelation, he does not understand the Christ-event's saving value as simply "manifestive."[47] Rather, the revelation which Irenaeus envisions in an *effective* one which entails human union in God, a union

---

42. AH III.16.6.
43. As Trevor Hart writes, "we must affirm that in some sense for Irenaeus the person of Christ is his work, the incarnation is the atonement. The becoming man on the part of the Son is not merely a prerequisite of something else which is his work, but is in itself a redeeming of humanity, a uniting of mankind to God" ("Irenaeus, Recapitulation and Physical Redemption," in *Christ in Our Place: The Humanity of God in Christ for the Reconciliation of the World*, eds. T. Hart and D. Thimell (Exeter: Paternoster Press, 1989), 152–81, at 167). Hart continues, "In the person of the New Man the entire race is 'summed up'. Christ's humanity is not merely reiterative, but also *inclusive*, such that all men are implicated in his actions . . . [He is] the part which represents the whole, and in which the whole is in some sense included" (ibid., 175).
44. Daley, "He Himself is Our Peace," 154–55.
45. AH IV.6.6.
46. AH IV.20.5.
47. Cf. Steenberg, *Of God and Man*, 47–48.

which flows from the person of Christ who "was truly man, and . . . was truly God."[48] He makes this point clear when he writes that the "Word was manifested when the Word of God was made man, assimilating Himself to man, and man to Himself."[49] Irenaeus even goes so far to speak of the Word's descent to us as "the sign of salvation," but an effective sign through which humankind is reborn into life.[50]

Irenaeus is clear throughout his writings that human salvation depends, first and foremost, upon God's initiative and saving disposition toward us. It would be impossible, he argues, for humanity to be joined to God unless God had first joined himself to us:

> For it was incumbent upon the Mediator between God and men, by His relationship to both, to bring both to friendship and concord, and present man to God, while He revealed God to man. For, in what way could we be partaken of the adoption of sons, unless we had received from Him through the Son that fellowship which refers to Himself, unless His Word, having been made flesh, had entered into communion with us?[51]

Perhaps the most famous way in which Irenaeus expressed the saving value of God's descending movement toward us is his pithy dictum that "our Lord Jesus Christ . . . did, through His transcendent love, become what we are, that He might bring us to be even what He is Himself."[52] God's becoming human, his "attaching man to God by his own incarnation,"[53] entails the symmetrical result of humankind's "passing into God"[54] and being "promoted into God."[55] This latter idea of humankind entering into God's own life is termed "deification" or *theosis*. Once again, for Irenaeus, this divinization of humankind is only possible because the Son first assumed that which was to be redeemed, to use Gregory of Nazianzus's later language.[56] As Steenberg summarizes

48. *AH* IV.6.7, translation slightly adjusted.
49. *AH* V.16.2.
50. "How was mankind to escape this birth into death, unless he were born again through faith, by that new birth from the Virgin, the sign of salvation that is God's wonderful and unmistakable gift?" (*AH* IV.33.4).
51. *AH* III.18.7; cf. *AH* IV.20.4.
52. *AH* V.pref.
53. *AH* V.1.1.
54. "How shall man pass into God, unless God has [first] passed into man?" (*AH* IV.33.4).
55. *AH* III.19.1.
56. "He was made an infant for infants, sanctifying infancy; a child among children, sanctifying childhood, and setting an example of filial affection, of righteousness and of obedience; a young man among young men, becoming an example to them, and sanctifying them to the Lord. So also he was a grown man among the older men, that he might be a perfect teacher for all, not merely in respect of revelation of the truth, but also with respect to this stage of life, sanctifying the older men, and becoming an example to them also. And thus he came even to death, that he might be 'the first born form the dead, having the pre-eminence among all, the Author of Life, who goes

the descending element of Ireaneus's recapitulative soteriology, "That which Christ comes to save, he saves by becoming . . . Christ's salvific action is primarily to become human, to exist as human, redeeming what is human by joining it to God."[57]

However, it must be emphasized that Irenaeus does not envision any sort of automatic infusion of salvation into the whole of humankind to follow upon the incarnation. Although those who have categorized Irenaeus as a proponent of physical redemption (a category analyzed later in this chapter) have associated him with such an idea, Irenaeus places a great emphasis on the need for faith and the very real possibility of being separated from God. The "effective" nature of God's incarnation over the course of the Christ-event is best understood as the necessary but not entirely sufficient basis for the salvation of all humankind. To "actualize" this reality, human beings must freely participate in person through whom God has come among us, as we will consider more in the "ascending" dimension of recapitulation.[58]

Christ, our Representative before God

In the last two sections treating the "person-centered" and "descending" dimensions of recapitulation, we have already encountered the idea of Christ as the New Adam who "present[s] man to God,"[59] so the idea of Christ as the Representative of humankind is already on the table. However, there are four elements of Christ's identity as our Representative which merit further discussion—namely, his place in the process of human maturation, his overturning of sin, his role as Teacher, and the place of God's Spirit in the concept of recapitulation. These latter two, especially, concern the need, just mentioned, to freely "actualize" our salvation by being incorporated into the person of Christ.

---

before all and shows the way" (AH II.22.4). Cf. "the Son of God, although He was perfect, passed through the state of infancy in common with the rest of mankind, partaking of it thus not for His own benefit, but for that of the infantile stage of man's existence, in order that man might be able to receive Him" (AH IV.38.2).

57. Steenberg, Of God and Man, 44.

58. Brondos has noted that for Irenaeus heretics and unbelievers remain separate from God, and "the 'man' who has been redeemed set free form bondage, restored to health, and joined to God is neither one particular man alone nor all human beings collectively, since 'he' is distinct from them. . . . While 'man' in general has been saved 'potentially' or 'in principle,' in order for that salvation to become 'actual,' particular men and women must believe and be baptized: only those who do so come to be joined to this redeemed 'man'" (Brondos, "The Redemption of 'Man,'" 54).

59. AH III.18.7.

1. Ascending: Christ and Human Maturation

A widely known part of Irenaeus's theology of history is his account of humanity's ascending development from "infancy" into adulthood and friendship with God. This theme of maturation is best understood in light of a "Gnostic" objection to Christians who insisted on a single God behind all of salvation history: If one good God creates, that God would produce good results; however, the world is clearly flawed in many ways, so there cannot be just a single, good Creator.[60] Irenaeus responds to this argument by agreeing with the rationale that a good God gets good results. However, after affirming the goodness of the world, Irenaeus adds that the world is yet incomplete and still on its way, much like a good infant who nonetheless has to grow and mature before coming into her own.[61] By appealing to the "infantile" state of humanity, Irenaeus is able to account for its flaws without recognizing an evil or rival god.[62]

In his reading of Genesis, Irenaeus describes Adam as "infantile . . . unaccustomed to, and unexercised in, perfect discipline."[63] Irenaeus does not intend such "infant" and "infantile" descriptors pejoratively. Rather, they are meant to point out the cause of human imperfection—for Irenaeus, human "'infancy' is in fact logically antecedent to [human] imperfection."[64] (Moreover, it may be noted, it is likely that in reading Genesis, Irenaeus envisioned Adam and Eve quite literally as children.[65]) Irenaeus's overarching series of covenantal stages from creation onward is at the same time a "coming of age" story for humanity.[66] By these lights, salvation history is not simply a perfection-fall-

---

60. Cf. *AH* IV.38.
61. See Loewe, "Irenaeus' Soteriology: Transposing the Question," 174.
62. Ibid. "[M]an receives increase and advancement towards God" (*AH* IV.11.2, qtd. in Loewe, "Irenaeus' Soteriology: Transposing the Question," 175).
63. *AH* IV.38.1.
64. Andrew P. Klager, "Retaining and Reclaiming the Divine: Identification and the Recapitulation of Peace in St. Irenaeus of Lyon's Atonement Narrative," in *Stricken by God? Nonviolent Identification and the Victory of Christ*, ed. Brad Jersak (Grand Rapids, MI: Eerdmans, 2007), 422–80, at 428.
65. Irenaeus thus understands Adam's and Eve's "unashamedness" in light of their youthfulness: "they had been created only a short time before and possessed no understanding of the procreation of children" (*AH* III.22.4). Steenberg notes that only recently have scholars began taking Irenaeus's "youthful" descriptor at face value, that is, that he wasn't speaking metaphorically, but that he *actually did* envision Adam and Eve as "prepubescents" (Steenberg, *Irenaeus on Creation*, 143).
66. "Salvation, for Irenaeus, is not so much God's unexpected intervention in history to rescue his faithful ones from destruction as it is the end-stage of the process of organic growth which has been creation's 'law' since its beginning. So eschatology, in this apocalyptic sense of the expectation of a wholly new age, is replaced in Irenaeus' theology by a grand, continuous conception of salvation history" (Daley, *The Hope of the Early Church: A Handbook of Patristic Eschatology* (Cambridge: Cambridge Univ. Press, 1991), 29 (qtd. in Brondos, "The Redemption of 'Man,'" 51).

redemption narrative, but rather, one of imperfection, growth, and maturation.[67] And, as Irenaeus indicates from the outset of explicating this idea of maturation in *AH* IV.38.1 by describing Christ's humanity as "milk" for receiving God's Word,[68] it is through Christ the New Adam that this maturation finally occurs.[69] As Steenberg puts it, "Perfected humanity and the person of Christ are theological synonyms."[70]

2. Ascending: Christ Overturning Sin

It is important to note that while Christ's perfect human life anchors human salvation teleologically, it also stands as a *corrective* to Adam's imperfect life.[71] In other words, Christ's saving identity as the New Adam is wrapped up in both the *perfection* of Adam as well as his *purification*.[72] This latter element of Irenaeus's thought, which Trevor Hart stresses,[73] draws heavily upon Paul's own treatment of Adam and Christ

67. Steenberg, *Irenaeus on Creation*, 143, cf. 153. As Steenberg notes, such a reading shares much in common with contemporary scholarship and Jewish readings of Genesis.

68. "If, however, any one say, 'What then? Could not God have exhibited man as perfect from the beginning?' let him know that, inasmuch as God is indeed always the same and unbegotten as respects Himself, all things are possible to Him. But . . . as it certainly is in the power of a mother to give strong food to her infant [but she does not do so], as the child is not yet able to receive more substantial nourishment; so also it was possible for God Himself to have made man perfect from the first, but man could not receive this [perfection], being as yet an infant. And for this cause our Lord, in these last times, when He had summed up all things into Himself, came to us, not as He might have come, but as we were capable of beholding Him. He might easily have come to us in His immortal glory, but in that case we could never have endured the greatness of the glory; and therefore it was that He, who was the perfect bread of the Father, offered Himself to us as milk, [because we were] as infants. He did this when He appeared as man, that we, being nourished, as it were, from the breast of his flesh, and having, by such a course of milk-nourishment, become accustomed to eat and drink the Word of God, may be able also to contain in ourselves the Bread of immortality, which is the Spirit of the Father" (*AH* IV.38.1).

69. "[I]n Christ God . . . brought the human race to maturity" (Loewe, "Irenaeus' Soteriology: Transposing the Question," 176).

70. Steenberg, *Irenaeus on Creation*, 7.

71. Christ "points out the recapitulation that should take place in his own person of the effusion of blood from the beginning, of all the righteous men and of the prophets, and that by means of Himself there should be a requisition of their blood . . . the Lord . . . summed up these things in Himself . . . saving in his own person at the end that which had in the beginning perished in Adam" (*AH* V.14.1).

72. Speaking of the latter, Jeff Vogel writes, "Christ's central role in [Irenaeus's] theology is to be the man who receives from God, undoing the disobedience of Adam and reorienting humanity to God" ("The Haste of Sin, The Slowness of Salvation: An Interpretation of Irenaeus on the Fall and Redemption," *Anglican Theological Review* 89, no. 3 (2007), 443–59, at 451). Irenaeus explains, "as, at the beginning of our formation in Adam, that breath of life which proceed from God, having been united to what had been fashioned, animate the man, and manifested him as a being endowed with reason; so also, in [the times of] the end, the Word of the Father and the Spirit of God, having become united with the ancient substance of Adam's formation, rendered man living and perfect, receptive of the perfect Father, in order that as in the natural [Adam] we all were dead, so in the spiritual we may all be made alive. For never at any time did Adam escape the *hands* of God, to whom the Father speaking said, 'Let Us make man in Our image, after Our likeness.' And for this reason in the last times (*fine*). . . . His hands formed a living man, in order that Adam might be created [again] after the image and likeness of God" (*AH* V.1.2, emphasis original).

in Romans 5, and it demands that our understanding of Irenaeus's theology of history as progressively ascending be nuanced. Although his model is indeed one of steady progression, Irenaeus does take human sin very seriously as presenting a major obstacle to that progression. As Steenberg explains, the "saga of creation" is "drastically altered by sin. The economy will advance still, and its course shall continue to be the perfection of that which was first called forth from the void. Henceforth, however, it shall make this advance in and through the context of the obstacles caused by human transgressions."[74] Thus, while Steenberg deems it more fitting to describe Ireaneus's overall vision of salvation history as one of maturation rather than rescue,[75] he also cautions that "to read Irenaeus as presenting no scheme whatever of an Edenic 'fall' would be to over-estimate the case."[76]

The narrative of progressive human maturation and serious attention to sin need not be seen as competitive with one another. As Jeffrey Vogel has argued, Irenaeus understands Adam's sin (and the very heart of human sinfulness itself) to be a premature "grasping" after something for which we are not yet adequately prepared—namely, sharing in divine life.[77] Rather than something to be too quickly "grabbed," this authentic goal of human life is something to which we must be raised only gradually. And it is Christ, the Word of God himself, refusing to "grasp" equality with God,[78] who brings the process of maturation to its completion through his life of obedience to God. Thus, as Vogel writes, we should not understand the initial *moment* of the Word's incarnation as sufficiently redemptive for Irenaeus, but rather, it is the case that the entire incarnate life of Christ, including his own ascending "consent to the necessity of growth over time," effects our salvation.[79]

---

73. Irenaeus's Christ offers "a radical reversal of the essential direction of man's life before God, from disobedience to obedience, from sin to faith, from apostasy to fellowship, and hence from death to life" (Hart, "Irenaeus, Recapitulation and Physical Redemption," 171). In offering this corrective, however, Hart seems to overemphasize Irenaeus's focus upon human sinfulness. This overemphasis even leads Hart to say things like "Christ assumed flesh and blood in order to suffer and die" (ibid., 173). However, Irenaeus never makes such statements, and Hart himself acknowledges six pages earlier that the "becoming man on the part of the Son is not merely a prerequisite of something else which is his work."

74. Steenberg, *Irenaeus on Creation*, 152.

75. Ibid., 143.

76. Ibid., 168.

77. Vogel, "The Haste of Sin, the Slowness of Salvation," *passim*. Cf. "[H]umanity's proper life is one expressive of and participatory in the life of the triune Father, Son and Spirit" (Steenberg, *Irenaeus on Creation*, 137). Steenberg goes on to explain that Genesis presents a "positive affirmation of the proper limits of human knowing in its present stage of development" (ibid., 154), and states, "Knowledge must not 'exalt' humanity to a state of self-professed grandeur that exceeds 'its own measure'" (ibid., 155).

78. Phil 2:6.

Irenaeus's theology of the cross, on Steenberg's reading, confirms this point: Christ's obedience to God, even in the face of death, "epitomizes" and "actualizes"[80] his summing up of the human story, providing humanity with both a summative *telos* and a corrective.[81]

3. Ascending: Christ the Teacher

The third "ascending" aspect of Irenaeus's theology of recapitulation which will be mentioned here is Christ's identity as Teacher. Irenaeus's frequent references to this teaching role make it easy to recognize, and it is important not to simply attribute these references to Irenaeus's soteriological pluralism. In fact, Christ's role as Teacher is intimately bound up with this theology of recapitulation, particularly in the "ascending" dimension in which he represents humankind before God.[82]

The relationship between Christ's pedagogical activity and his theology of recapitulation is particularly evident at the beginning of *AH*'s fifth book. In its preface, Irenaeus identifies Christ as the "true and steadfast Teacher," directly following this title with the assertion that the Word was made incarnate so that "He might bring us to be even what He is Himself."[83] Here, Irenaeus does not speak as if the incarnation were a *fait accompli* in which humanity is mechanically or automatically "recapitulated" in the person of Christ. Rather, he includes Christ's enabling us to be what he is within the same breath as Christ's

---

79. Vogel, "The Haste of Sin, the Slowness of Salvation," 444. Cf. "Christ's "acts are redemptive inasmuch as he lives out, as man and as *a* man, the perfect relationship of Son to Father, sanctified by the Spirit, obedient unto death" (Steenberg, *Of God and Man*, 51).
80. The marriage of "epitome" and "actuality" once again bears a striking resemblance to Rahner's own *realsymbolisch* theology of salvation discussed in the last chapter.
81. Steenberg, *Of God and Man*, 49.
82. William Loewe understands this teaching role to be at the very heart of Irenaeus's theology of salvation, and he links it to Irenaeus's thoughts on Christ's victory over Satan and the incarnation ("Irenaeus' Soteriology: *Christus Victor* Revisited," *Anglican Theological Review* 67, no. 1 [1985], 1–15). Regarding the former: Although Gustaf Aulén (*Christus Victor: An Historical Study of the Three Main Types of the Idea of Atonement* [New York: Macmillan, 1969], especially chapter 2) interpreted Irenaeus's soteriology primarily according to this idea of the devil's defeat, Loewe reads Irenaeus in such a way that Christ's victory is *itself* pedagogical. That is, for Loewe Christ's defeat of Satan (which is essentially a victory of Christ's will) on the cross is a kind of extension of the earlier temptation episode in the desert (Loewe, "*Christus Victor* Revisited," 7–8). Regarding the latter, Loewe understands Irenaeus's emphasis on Christ the Teacher in relation to emphasis elsewhere on the incarnation: "Knowledge of the Father comes through acting as Christ acts and doing what he bids, and in that activity a relationship of communion with Christ, the eternal Word incarnate, is forged" (Loewe, "*Christus Victor* Revisited," 4).
83. Irenaeus proposes to refute heresies by "following the only true and steadfast Teacher, the Word of God, our Lord Jesus Christ, who did, through His transcendent love, become what we are, that He might bring us to be even what He is Himself" (*AH* V.pref).

role as the "true and steadfast Teacher," indicating that our learning from Christ is closely related to our transformation in him.

Irenaeus immediately confirms this connection in the opening of book five. There, Irenaeus blends together his theme of human maturation, Christ's pedagogical function, and a person-centered soteriology. He explains that our learning occurs in "seeing our Teacher, and hearing His voice with our own ears, that, having become imitators of His works as well as doers of His words, we may have communion with Him, receiving increase from the perfect One."[84] Here, we see that the pedagogical aspect of Irenaeus's Christ-centered soteriology is at the service of grounding *communion with Christ himself*. Christ's pedagogical activity is, at its root, aimed at instructing us so we may exist in communion with him. Thus, Irenaeus speaks elsewhere of discipleship not in terms of following a set of teachings, but as following a person.[85]

Irenaeus's Christ is thus both Teacher and Representative, and identity which can be characterized as "ascending" since our following Christ fulfills a dynamic, God-ward aspect of our humanity.[86] From its infantile outset in Adam, humanity is growing dynamically toward its fullness of life, which is life in God.[87] Christ's teaching, done at the service of bringing about our incorporation into him, helps to bring about this *telos* which God intends for humanity.[88]

4. Ascending: God's Spirit

Central to Irenaeus's vision of human incorporation into the person of Christ is the Holy Spirit. Vogel emphasized this point, explaining that for Irenaeus, the goal of the incarnation is the complete indwelling of the Spirit in Christ's humanity,[89] in virtue of which Christ can give "the Spirit to those who participate in him through faith. As Irenaeus writes, 'The Lord, receiving this as a gift from his Father, does himself also confer it upon those who are partakers of himself, sending the Holy Spirit upon all the earth' [*AH* III.17.2]."[90] It is precisely the Spirit which links

---

84. *AH* V.1.1.
85. "For to follow the Saviour is to be a partaker of salvation, and to follow light is to receive light" (*AH* IV.14.1, qtd. in Loewe, "Irenaeus' Soteriology: Transposing the Question," 172).
86. Cf. Steenberg, *Of God and Man*, 52.
87. "For the glory of man is God" (*AH* III.20.2); cf. Irenaeus's oft-quoted remark that "the glory of God is a living man; and the life of man consists in beholding God" (*AH* IV.20.7).
88. Irenaeus's goes so far as to say, "Man had been created by God that he might have life. If . . . he were not to return to life . . . then God would have been defeated" (*AH* III.23.1).
89. Cf. Steenberg, who explains that "without the Spirit the incarnate Son is not fully redeemer, since he who redeems recapitulatively does so by uniting humanity to the full life of God, which is only and ever the life of 'the Father with his two hands'" (*Of God and Man*, 36–37).

the blessed to Christ, who is the preeminent locus of the Spirit in the world.[91]

As is well known, Irenaeus speaks of the Son and the Spirit as God's two hands,[92] and, as Vogel explains, these two hands work in tandem to recapitulate humanity in the person of Christ:

> The Spirit is the incorporating agent, the hand of the Father that does the gathering up. . . . This is the cooperation between the two hands of God: Christ recapitulates all things in himself (*omnia in semetipsum recapitulans*; III.16.6), restoring to human beings the capacity to grow into the image and likeness of God, and the Spirit gathers creatures into himself (*complectens hominem in semetipsum*; V.8.1), thus realizing in them the potential recovered by Christ.[93]

This reading of Irenaeus's Trinitarian theology is confirmed in the soteriological rich opening of *AH* V, where he says that Christ "has also poured out the Spirit of the Father for the union and communion of God and man, imparting indeed God to men by means of the Spirit, and, on the other hand, attaching man to God by His own incarnation, and bestowing upon us at his coming immortality durably and truly, by means of communion with God."[94] Irenaeus's pneumatology thus presupposes the person-centered soteriology of recapitulation, and likewise, the latter cannot be understood apart from the former.

Conclusion: Irenaeus's Representative Soteriology

In his theology of recapitulation, Irenaeus establishes the standard for that which I have termed representative soteriology. In identifying Christ as the "visible of the Father" whose effective "manifestation" accomplishes salvation in revealing God to us, Irenaeus constructs a robust descending component of his soteriology which holds Christ to be God's Representative unto us. Likewise, he establishes Christ's ascending identity as our Representative before God in numerous

---

90. Vogel, "The Haste of Sin, The Slowness of Salvation," 453. Cf. *AH* III.9.3, qtd. in Steenberg, *Of God and Man*, 36: "So the Spirit of God descended upon him, the Spirit of him who through the prophets had promised that he would anoint him, that we might be saved by receiving from the abundance of his anointing."

91. "According to Irenaeus, Jesus Christ proved a site where the Spirit of God could once more dwell among human beings and work to join them to the Father" (Vogel, "The Haste of Sin, the Slowness of Salvation," 453).

92. E.g., *AH* IV.pref.4, IV.20.1, V.6.1.

93. Vogel, "The Haste of Sin, the Slowness of Salvation," 453, 457.

94. *AH* V.1.1.

ways: Christ is the New Adam who "present[s] man to God," who both perfects and purifies an infantile humanity intended for growth toward divine life; he is both the "true and steadfast Teacher" and the Source of God's Spirit, working to incorporate us into the locus of grace which is his person. This last point brings us back to our third characteristic of representative soteriology, its person-centeredness. Christ saves us by recapitulating the human family within *himself*, allowing us to share in the abundance of grace which he has received as *the* authentic human being with us and among us. "The story of human salvation . . . is an economy of recapitulation in which the ends and the beginnings unite in the person of Christ, through whom the creation of the cosmos and of the child Adam eventually reach perfection in beholding the glory of the Father, Son and Spirit, 'becoming a perfect work of God.'"[95]

Irenaeus's Heirs

In addition to standing as the paradigm case of representative soteriology, Irenaeus's theory of recapitulation had a significant impact on subsequent Christian theology. In fact, in the judgment of J. N. D. Kelly, Irenaeus's theory was woven within the very fabric of patristic soteriological thought:

> Running throughout almost all the patristic attempts to explain the redemption there is one grand theme which, we suggest, provides the clue to the fathers' understanding of the work of Christ. This is none other than the ancient idea of recapitulation which Irenaeus derived from St. Paul, and which envisages Christ as the representative of the entire race. Just as all men were somehow present in Adam, so they are, or can be, present in the second Adam, the man from heaven. . . . Because, very God as He is, He has identified Himself with the human race, Christ has been able to act on its behalf. . . . All the fathers, of whatever school, reproduce this motif.[96]

Clearly, a survey of the fathers sufficient to support Kelly's claim is beyond the scope of this book. Nevertheless, since this chapter does seek to indicate the importance of representative soteriology in the Patristic Period, a few figures will be treated below (though in less detail than Irenaeus received above).

95. Steenberg, *Irenaeus on Creation*, 216.
96. J. N. D. Kelly, *Early Christian Doctrines*. Rev. ed. (San Francisco: Harper & Row, 1978), 376–77.

Irenaeus's *AH* is known to have made its way to Egypt (even within Irenaeus's own lifetime), and so, I have selected several figures from Northern Africa for this brief overview.[97] In addition to drawing on Irenaeus, this group of influential figures drew upon each other as time progressed, leaving a significant impact on both the Western and Eastern Church. While their theologies bear their own distinctive characteristics and exhibit developments (for better or worse)[98] on Irenaeus's thought, I will make a limited attempt to show important ways in which their writings draw on Irenaeus's motifs and rationale described above, relying once again on the three markers of representative soteriology as a touchstone. The following glimpses into the theology of Clement of Alexandria, Athanasius of Alexandria, and Augustine of Hippo are not intended as full explications of their soteriological writings,[99] but rather, as demonstrations of how key components of Irenaeus's theology of recapitulation redounded through the broader patristic heritage.

Clement of Alexandria († c. 215)

Born roughly a generation after Irenaeus in 150 CE and dying around ten or so years after Irenaeus, Clement of Alexandria was roughly a contemporary of the Bishop of Lugdunum (modern-day Lyons, France). Nevertheless, their geographical distance from one another seems not to have prevented Clement from learning from Irenaeus. As stated earlier, the latter's major work had already traveled to Egypt by at least the end of his life (circa 200 CE). Moreover, as Veronika Černušková has recently argued, Clement's use of Irenaeus's terminology, specifically that of recapitulation, indicates that he was both familiar with and borrowing from Irenaeus's theology.[100] Černušková points out that

---

97. Steenberg, *Of God and Man*, 19. Steenberg reports that Irenaeus stood as "kind of principal voice from the late second century," but he was a "voice familiar to few in the third, fourth and beyond," though the themes and overall contours of his thought proliferated (ibid., 18).

98. Brian McDermott detects a monophysite tendency which creeps into the theologies of Alexandrians like Athanasius and Cyril (*Word Become Flesh Dimensions in Christology* (Collegeville, MN: Liturgical Press, 1993), 198–99, 202). Irenaeus's theology, McDermott argues, did not have this feature: "According to this soteriology, the human reality of Christ is intrinsically important as a contributor to our salvation; it is not, as in some other patristic views, simply an instrument of the Logos, who is then regarded as the only truly saving principle" (ibid., 212). McDermott may overstate the monophysite tendency in Athanasius (see the section on Athanasius below).

99. Even the lengthier treatment of Irenaeus above does not stand as an effort to fully explicate his plural and multifaceted soteriological thought, but as an examination of "recapitulation" specifically.

100. "Clement, who probably knew Irenaeus, clearly uses the terminology and concept of *anakephalaiosis*" (Veronika Černušková, "*Stromateis* VII and Clement's Hints at the Theory of *Apokatastasis*," in *The Seventh Book of the* Stromateis, eds. M. Havrda, V. Hušek, and J. Plátová (Leiden: Brill, 2012),

Clement's use of recapitulation language closely mirrors that of Irenaeus in its application to God's gradual self-revelation within creation. For example, Clement speaks of Jesus's crown of thorns as a
"recapitulation" of the burning bush seen by Moses, the latter mark-
ing the beginning of the Logos's self-manifestation through the Law
and the former concluding the Logos's earthly incarnation before "His
departure from this world to the place whence He came."[101] Clement
also writes that Jesus's commandment to love "recapitulates" the
entirety of the Law (cf. Rom 13:9),[102] echoing Irenaeus's overarching
vision of God's gradual self-revelation throughout history, summed up
in the Christ-event.[103]

Like Irenaeus, Clement infuses his theology of history with soteriological and pedagogical motifs. The following passage, worth quoting
at length, is a prime example of this phenomenon:

The Saviour has many tones of voice, and many methods for the salvation
of men; by threatening He admonishes, by upbraiding He converts, by
bewailing He pities, by the voice of song He cheers. He spake by the burning bush, for the men of that day needed signs and wonders. He awed men
by the fire when He made flame to burst from the pillar of cloud—a token
at once of grace and fear: if you obey, there is the light; if you disobey,
there is the fire; but since humanity is nobler than the pillar or the bush,
after them the prophets uttered their voice,—the Lord Himself speaking
in Isaiah, in Elias,—speaking Himself by the mouth of the prophets. But if
thou dost not believe the prophets, but supposest both the men and the
fire a myth, the Lord Himself shall speak to thee, "who, being in the form

239–57, at 246). Černušková is not alone in such a judgment. Otto Reimherr writes, "Other Greek
writers who were near contemporaries, such as Clement of Alexandria and Origen, shared the theological interests of Irenaeus and were familiar with his works" ("Irenaeus Lugdunensis," in Catalogus Translationum et Commentarium: Mediaeval and Renaissance Latin Translations and Commentaries,
9 vols., eds. Virginia Brown et al (Washington, D.C.: Catholic University of America Press, 1960–),
vol. 7 (1992), 13–54, at 16.
101. "For when the Almighty Lord of the universe began to legislate by the Word, and wished His
power to be manifested to Moses, a godlike vision of light that had assumed a shape was shown
him in the burning bush (the bush is a thorny plant); but when the Word ended the giving of the
law and His stay with men, the Lord was again mystically crowned with thorn. On His departure
from this world to the place whence He came, He repeated the beginning of His old descent, in
order that the Word beheld at first in the bush, and afterwards taken up crowned by the thorn,
might show the whole to be the work of one power, He Himself being one, the Son of the Father,
who is truly one, the beginning and the end of time" (The Instructor [Pædagogus], in ANF 2:207–298,
at II.8 [ANF 2:257], cited in Černušková, 246). Černušková judges, "Here, the notion of anakephalaiosis comes close to that of Irenaeus, related to the telos and to the salvific economy" (ibid.).
102. "The commandments, 'You shall not commit adultery; You shall not murder; You shall not steal;
You shall not covet'; and any other commandment, are summed up in this word, 'Love your neighbor as yourself.'"
103. Stromateis IV.3 [10.2–3] (ANF 2:411, which renders anakephalaioutai "comprehended"), VII.16
[105.4–5] (ANF 2:554), cited in Černušková, 247.

of God, thought it not robbery to be equal with God, but humbled Him-self,"—He, the merciful God, exerting Himself to save man. And now the Word Himself clearly speaks to thee, shaming thy unbelief; yea, I say, the Word of God became man, that thou mayest learn from man how man may become God.[104]

Here, a number of Irenaeus's motifs are present: the activity of the Word in the OT, the divine economy of gradually increasing intensity, the pedagogical function of Christ, and finally, the culminating exchange dictum, in which we previously saw Irenaeus combine God's saving descent, humanity's divinizing ascent, and the person of Christ.[105] Although all three characteristics of representative soteriol-ogy are touched upon in this dictum, Clement's thinking here is pre-dominately "from above," testifying to the Word's descending action in which God himself, rather than simply fire or an emissary-prophet, comes among humanity in Christ, his Representative.

The pedagogical function of Christ echoed in the passage above occurs frequently in Clement's writing, sometimes combined with another of Irenaeus's favorite motifs: infancy and maturation. Like Irenaeus,[106] Clement identifies Christ as "milk," milk for us "infants" which comes from "the Father's breasts of love." (Clement also refers to Christ as milk in his "Hymn to Christ the Savior," where he likewise identifies us as "infants," but renders the imagery more complex with references to the church and the Spirit.[107]) He goes on to affirm that the one who regenerates us is also our Creator, the loving Father who con-tinues to nourish with his own Word that which he began. Moreover, the goal of such nourishment is that "In all respects, therefore, and in all things, we are brought into union with Christ," for this "nour-ishment . . . flows from the Word; and into immortality, through his guidance."[108] Here, Clement's theology matches with both "ascending"

104. *Exhortation to the Heathen* ANF 2:171–206, at ch. 1 (*ANF* 2:173–74).
105. This dictum is, once again, found in *AH* V.pref: "our Lord Jesus Christ . . . did, through His tran-scendent love, become what we are, that He might bring us to be even what He is Himself."
106. Cf. *AH* IV.38.1, cited above.
107. "Holy shepherd / of sheep of the logos, / lead, o king, / the unharmed children; / the footprints of Christ, / are the path to heaven. / Ever-flowing word, / unlimited age, / undying light, / source of mercy, / artisan of virtue / of those who praise God / with their holy life. / Christ Jesus, / heav-enly milk / pressed from the sweet breasts / of the bride, / gracious gifts / of your wisdom. / The tiny infants / with tender mouths, / suckled / at the nipple of the logos / and filled / with the dewy Spirit" ("Hymn to Christ the Saviour," in *The Seventh Book of the* Stromateis, eds. Havrda et al (Leiden: Brill, 2012), 319–22, at 320–22). Jane Schatkin Hettrick writes that this hymn is "appended to manuscripts of Clement's *Paedagogus*" ["The Instructor"] and "is considered to be the most ancient hymn (text) of the Christian Church" ("Musical Settings of Clement's 'Hymn to Christ the Saviour,'" in ibid., 323–39, at 323).
108. *The Instructor*, I.6 (*ANF* 2:221–22). The relevant passages in its entirety reads, "[T]o us infants, who

maturation element of Irenaeus's theology of recapitulation, as well as Irenaeus's person-centered concluding point and *telos* of that maturation.

Finally, Clement combines the "ascending" and "person-centered" elements again in *The Stromata*, once again emphasizing the theme of Christ's pedagogical function. "[H]e who listens to the Lord, and follows the prophecy given by Him," Clement writes, "will be formed perfectly in the likeness of the teacher—made a god going about in the flesh."[109] Taken together with his descending and person-centered thinking quoted above, these ascending remarks testify to a representative soteriology present in Clement's theology. For him, Christ is simultaneously the Word of God himself sent among us, the heavenly milk on which infantile humanity grows, the Teacher guiding us toward mature life, and the human being the *union with whom* constitutes our maturation.

Athanasius († 373)

Athanasius was born at the end of the third century, almost 100 years after Irenaeus's death. Like Clement, he was a theologian who spent a good portion of his life in Alexandria; unlike Clement, however, Athanasius became the Archbishop of the region, being elevated to the position shortly after the Council of Nicaea (325 CE). Although his theological writings address a range of issues, Athanasius is best known for his fierce opposition to Arianism, a task which dominates his corpus. Accordingly, important parts of his soteriology are visible through the window of his carefully reasoned rejoinders to Arian theology, which held that Christ was less than divine. For Arius and his followers, Christ was a figure analogous to an Archangel above the rest of creation, but still, in some sense, himself created. (A favorite dictum among Arians was "There was [a time] when he was not.")

Athanasius's arguments against such a position, a large portion of which are exegetical in nature, are too manifold to review here. But

drink the milk of the word of the heavens, Christ Himself is food. Hence seeking is called sucking; for to those babes that seek the Word, the Father's breasts of love supply milk. . . . For if we have been regenerated unto Christ, He who has regenerated us nourishes us with His own milk, the Word; for it is proper that what has procreated should forthwith supply nourishment to that which has been procreated. And as the regeneration was conformably spiritual, so also was the nutriment of man spiritual. In all respects, therefore, and in all things, we are brought into union with Christ, into relationship through His blood, by which we are redeemed; and into sympathy, in consequence of the nourishment which flows from the Word; and into immortality, through His guidance."

109. "The Stromata," in *ANF* 2:299–567, at VII.16 (*ANF* 2:553).

one significant method for undercutting Arius's low Christology is Athanasius's soteriological rationale, a rationale which is thoroughly "representative" in character. Although it is difficult to say whether this rationale was taken directly from Irenaeus, Athanasius was almost certainly familiar with his writings, which—by this point—had impacted both Greek- and Latin-speaking worlds of the Christian church.[110]

Perhaps the most direct point of continuity between the two thinkers is the exchange dictum which encapsulates the three markers of representative soteriology and which we saw Clement also utilize. Athanasius's most explicit use of this dictum, which may be the most oft-cited instance of it, occurs in his *On the Incarnation of the Word*, where he writes that "He was made man that we might be made God."[111] But the logic is operative elsewhere, even if not expressed in so pithy of terms. For instance, in *Against the Arians* (the text on which most of our attention will focus here), Athanasius writes, "for as the Lord, putting on the body, became man, so we men are deified by the Word as being taken to Him through His flesh, and henceforth inherit life 'everlasting.'"[112] This instance, in fact, includes an even more detailed picture of Athanasius's soteriological rationale. The dictum as stated in *On the Incarnation* leaves the *manner* of human divinization understated, appealing only to the Word's becoming human. Here, Athanasius elaborates, grounding human deification in our "being taken to Him through his flesh." Here, an ascending dimension, according to which Christ exists as our Representative, is apparent in Athanasius's thought. Our "becoming God" is grounded in our incorporation into Christ's own body.

This ascending component of Athanasius's soteriology is apparent in other parts of *Against the Arians*. Athanasius argues that Christ's own exaltation as a human among us is on our behalf, that we too may receive such glorification in virtue of our *being in* him: "as a man, He

---

110. Reimherr, "Irenaeus Lugdunensis," 16–19. Specifically, Reimherr writes, "Irenaeus was also known to several later authors either through their personal reading of his writings or through florilegia; among these are Methodius of Olympus (d. 311), Athanasius (d. 373), Cyril of Jerusalem (d. 386), and Basil of Caesarea" (ibid., 16).

111. "On the Incarnation of the Word," in *Nicene and Post-Nicene Fathers: Second Series* (henceforth *NPNF* II), 14 vols., eds. Philip Schaff and Henry Wace (Buffalo: The Christian Literature Publishing Co., 1890–1900), vol. II/4 (1892), 36–67, at 54.2–3 (*NPNF* II/4:65). The exhortation preceding the dictum reads, "marvel that by so ordinary a means things divine have been manifested to us, and that by death immortality has reached to all, and that by the Word becoming man, the universal Providence has been known, and its Giver and Artificer the very Word of God. For He was made man that we might be made God."

112. *Against the Arians*, in *NPNF* II/4:306–447, at Disc. 3 ch. 26 n. 34 (*NPNF* II/4:413).

is said because of us and for us to be highly exalted, that . . . in Christ Himself we might be highly exalted, being raised from the dead, and ascending into heaven."[113] Here, Athanasius describes Christ precisely as our Representative before God, the "from below" component of representative soteriology.

This ascending rationale is employed by Athanasius specifically to counter the Arian suggestion that Christ's title, "Son of God," was a sort of reward bestowed upon him, or a status earned by one who was "man, and then became God."[114] Against this sort of adoptionistic ascending thinking, Athanasius deploys an alternative ascending logic, which in turn, relies upon a *descending* complement: Christ *descended* precisely in order to promote those things which were not yet divinized to his own status, in virtue of his relation to them.[115]

Accordingly, a strong descending component, according to which Christ is God's Representative among us, is inherent in Athanasius's soteriological thought. Put simply, "He was God, and then became man, and that to deify us."[116] Christ's humanity is, for Athanasius, clearly a medium through which God's divinizing grace becomes available to us.[117] And yet (though some places seem to indicate the contrary!),[118] this descending component does not render Christ's humanity a sort of static "tool," effectively effacing (in a sort of pseudo-monophysite way) what would eventually be defined as Christ's full "human nature" at the Council of Chalcedon. For although Athanasius clearly condemns any sort of adoptionist thinking, he does speak of Christ's "exalt[ation] as man," specifically in his death and resurrection. Athanasius blends descending and ascending representative thinking, insisting that Christ both presents humanity to God via exaltation, and simultane-

113. Ibid., Disc. 1, ch. 11, n. 41 (*NPNF* II/4:330).
114. Ibid., Disc. 1, ch. 11, n. 39 (*NPNF* II/4:329).
115. "He had not promotion from His descent, but rather Himself promoted the things which needed promotion; and if He descended to effect their promotion, therefore he did not receive in reward the name Son of God, but rather He Himself has made us sons of the Father, and deified men by becoming Himself man" (ibid., Disc. 1 ch. 11 n. 38 [*NPNF* II/4:329]).
116. Ibid., Disc. 1, ch. 11, n. 39 (*NPNF* II/4:329).
117. McDermott writes, "The eternally begotten Son mediates the Father soteriologically, in the incarnation, by being the full coming of the Father into the world. To the question 'If the Father loved us so much, why didn't he come in person, instead of sending an emissary, the Son?' Athanasius long ago gave the answer: The Son's coming in the Spirit *is* the full and complete arrival of the Father; the incarnate Son is the full *self*-communication of the Father and the only, and complete adequate, way in which the Father comes into the world" (*Word Become Flesh,* 169). This kind of logic closely mirrors Irenaeus's notion of the Son as the "visible of the Father," as well as Rahner's idea of "exteriorization" explored above in Chapter 2.
118. "For the Word was not impaired in receiving a body, that He should seek to receive a grace, but rather He deified that which He put on, and more than that, 'gave' it graciously to the race of man" (*Against the Arians,* Disc. 1 ch. 11 n. 42 [*NPNF* II/4:330]).

ously that, as God from the very outset, Christ presents God to us through the incarnation: "For as Christ died and was exalted as man, so, as man, is He said to take what, as God, He ever had, that even such a grant of grace might reach to us."[119]

Finally, these interwoven ascending and descending soteriological strands of Athanasius's thought coalesce in a person-centered understanding of human salvation. We have already seen how Athanasius's rationale for the exchange dictum relies on our being "taken to Him through His flesh," and our exaltation is understood to occur "in Christ Himself." Rather than an extrinsic effect produced by an agent, divinization for Athanasius is something effected in our union and participation in Christ's very person.

> He sanctifies Himself to the Father for our sakes, not that the Word may become holy, but that He Himself may in Himself sanctify all of us. . . . He himself should be exalted, for He is the highest, but that He may become righteousness for us, and we may be exalted in Him. . . . And if the Son be Righteousness, then He is not exalted as being Himself in need, but it is we who are exalted in that Righteousness, which is He.[120]

Augustine of Hippo († 430)

Although Irenaeus's *AH* were originally composed in Greek, the original work in its entirety has been lost. Along with Greek fragments, the entire work translated into Latin has survived. This Latin translation opened Irenaeus's thought to the church in the West, although major Western theologians such as Tertullian and Jerome seem to have read Irenaeus in the original Greek.[121] The final theologian exhibiting a representative soteriology which will be considered here is Augustine, who is widely regarded as the preeminent theological authority in the West in the centuries which followed those just considered. Augustine certainly relied upon the extant Latin translation of *AH*, quoting it in his *Contra Julianum* (422 CE)[122] and possibly relying upon it for several other works, including some composed relatively early on after his conversion.[123]

119. Ibid.
120. Ibid., Disc. 1, ch. 11, n. 41 (*NPNF* II/4:330).
121. Reimherr, "Irenaeus Lugdunensis," 17–18.
122. *AH* IV.2.7 and V.19.1 are quoted in *Contra Julianum* (*Against Julian*, vol. 16 of "Writings of Saint Augustine" (Washington D.C.: Catholic Univ. of America Press, 1974), I.3.5 and I.7.32, concerning original sin.
123. "When writing *De catechizandis rudibus* in 400, he may have used as a model Irenaeus' *Demonstratio apostolicae praedicationis*, a work which perhaps also influenced his *De doctrina christiana* (largely

As with Athanasius, it is difficult to definitively draw any direct connection between Irenaeus's and Augustine's soteriologies. Like Clement and Athanasius, Augustine had recurrent recourse to a version of Irenaeus's exchange dictum (although it was so ubiquitous by that point that Augustine could have encountered it any number of places). Augustine proclaimed versions of this dictum during his Christmas homilies, asking his congregation "what greater grace could have shone upon us from God, than that having his only-begotten Son he should make him a Son of man, and thus in exchange make the son of man into the Son of God?"[124] and declaring that "in order to make gods of those who were merely human, one who was God made himself human."[125] However, Augustine did not restrict the soteriological logic of exchange and divinization to his preaching on the Christ-event's *inauguration*. As David Vincent Meconi points out,[126] Augustine returned to this theme in his preaching on Easter as well, giving it even greater emphasis.[127]

As with all of the fathers, Augustine's soteriological writings are multifaceted and it is difficult (and likely impossible) to systematize all of them into any singular theory of the atonement. Moreover, in the judgment of J. N. D. Kelly, the exchange logic of deification at work in the homilies above constitutes a "secondary motif" in Augustine's soteriology, the primary focus of which is "redemption as our release from Satan's bondage" (a release which, Kelly goes on to say, is "consequent upon and . . . presuppos[es] our reconciliation" with God).[128]

---

written in 396–397, but completed only in 426" (Reimherr, "Irenaeus Lugdunensis," 18). As his own source of information, Reimherr cites Berthold Altaner, "Augustinus und Irenäus, eine quellenkritische Untersuchung," *Theologische Quartalschrift* 129 (1949), 162–72.

124. "Sermon 185" (Christmas 414), *Sermons (184–229z)* in *The Works of Saint Augustine: A Translation for the 21st Century*, ed. John E. Rotelle (Hyde Park, NY: New City Press, 1990–), vol. III/6 (1993), 185.3, 22.

125. "Sermon 192" (Christmas after 412). Augustine continues, "without forfeiting what he was, he wished to become what he himself had made. He himself made what he would become, because what he did was add man to God, not lose God in man" (*Sermons (184–229z)* in *The Works of Saint Augustine*, ed. Rotelle, vol. III/6, 192.1, 46).

126. David Vincent Meconi, "*O Admirabile Commercium*: The True Christmas Exchange," *Homiletic and Pastoral Review* 111, no. 3 (Dec. 2010), 47–50. Several of the citations in this section from Augustine's corpus have been reproduced from Meconi's short article.

127. "A marvelous exchange! He became flesh, these became spirit. What have we got here? What exquisite courtesy, my brothers and sisters! Lift up your spirits to hoping for and taking hold of the things that really count. . . . For your sakes *the Word became flesh* (Jn 1:14). For your sakes the one who was the Son of God became the Son of man, in order that you who were sons of men might be turned into sons of God. What was he, what did he become? What were you, what have you become? He was the Son of God and he became the Son of man. You were sons of men and you have become sons of God." ("Sermon 121" (Easter 412 or 413) in *Sermons (94a–147a)* in *The Works of Saint Augustine*, ed. Rotelle, vol. III/4 (Hyde Park, NY: New City Press, 1992), 121.5, 236).

128. Kelly, *Early Christian Doctrines*, 391–92.

Nonetheless, Augustine's soteriological writings certainly include sufficient appeals to the "representative" rationale of redemption to include him here. Let us therefore briefly turn our attention to a few instances in Augustine's corpus, specifically his scriptural expositions, which correspond with the three markers of representative soteriology, and then, finally, to one locus in which he integrates all three.

Augustine understands Christ to effect our redemption as God's Representative in our midst, descending in order to bring God among us. As he begins his "Exposition of Psalm 145," Augustine exhorts his listeners to attend to God's word as it is recorded in the Psalms, playing on *verbum* ("word") to transition into a reflection on the Second Person of the Trinity:

> we must be so entirely present to the word of God which sounds here on earth that we are exalted by it, and are no longer held by the earth. God is with us in order that we may be with him; he who came down to us in order to be with us is at work now to draw us up to himself, so that we may be in his company. Until this should be finally accomplished he did not disdain to share our exile, though he who created all things is nowhere an exile himself.[129]

Here, the emphasis is clearly on God's coming to be "with us," the God who "came down" to "share in our exile." Nevertheless, Augustine connects this theme of the presence of God's Word on earth to ascending ("we are exalted," "draw us up") and person-centered ("that we may be with him," "draw us up to himself") themes as well.

Elsewhere, Augustine emphasizes the ascending theme, characterizing Christ saving as our Representative before God. Commenting on Psalm 82:6 ("I say, 'You are gods, children of the Most High, all of you'"), he endeavors to tease out the nuances of deification. The Psalmist calls human beings "gods," Augustine explains, "in the sense that they were deified by [God's] grace, not because they were born of his own substance." The *one who* defies, on the contrary, must be "God of himself," who in deifying us has made us, by adoption, "gods," that is, "children of God." In other words, "Our Lord and Savior Jesus Christ is the unique Son of God; he is God. . . . Others, who become gods, become so by his grace. They are not born of God's very being in such a way that they are what he is; it is through a gracious gift that they have come to him and become with Christ his coheirs."[130] Three major points

---

129. "Exposition of Psalm 145," *Expositions on the Psalms, 121-150* in *The Works of Saint Augustine*, ed. Rotelle, vol. III/20 (Hyde Park, NY: New City Press, 2004), 145.1, 400.

are operative here. First, deification does not somehow render us equal to the persons of the Trinity. Second, we are nonetheless "sons and daughters of God" ("gods" in the Psalmist's language) who participate in the Trinitarian life. Lastly, the first two points are mutually possible only in virtue of Christ, the Mediator and Representative of humankind who by grace allows us to be his co-heirs.

Augustine's soteriology is also representative in that it is centered on the person of Christ (the third marker). Psalm 31 begins with words of fear, "In you, O Lord, I seek refuge; do not let me ever be put to shame." Commenting on these words, Augustine explains how Christ, too, can be said to have "feared," precisely as the "Head" of his "body," the church. As he continues, Augustine spells out the soteriological import of this connection within the person of Christ:

> But in fact he who deigned to assume the form of a slave, and within that form to clothe us with himself, he who did not disdain to take us up into himself, did not disdain either to transfigure us into himself, and to speak in our words, so that we in our turn might speak in his. This is the wonderful exchange, the divine business deal, the transaction effected in this world by the heavenly dealer. . . . Without him, we are nothing, but *in him we too are Christ*.[131]

Here, we hear more from Augustine precisely how we become the co-heirs of Christ, our Representative before God. It is because he has "take[n] us up into himself . . . transfigur[ing] us into himself." Augustine so emphasizes the centrality of Christ's person to our salvation that he declares, "in him we too are Christ."

Finally, the three markers of representative soteriology are woven together with Augustine's characteristic eloquence in his comments upon John 3:13.

---

130. "Exposition of Psalm 49," *Expositions on the Psalms, 33-50* in *The Works of Saint Augustine*, ed. Rotelle, vol. III/16 (Hyde Park, NY: New City Press, 2000), 49.2, 381. The section preceding this quotation reads, "It is quite obvious that God called human beings "gods" in the sense that they were deified by his grace, not because they were born of his own substance. It is proper to God to justify us because his is just of himself and not by derivation from anyone else; and similarly he alone deifies who is God of himself, not by participation in any other. Moreover, he who justifies is the same as he who deifies, because by justifying us he made us sons and daughters of God: *he gave them power to become children of God* (John 1:12). If we have been made children of God, we have been made into gods; but we are such by the grace of him who adopts us, not because we are of the same nature as the one who begets" (ibid.).

131. "Exposition 2 of Psalm 30," *Expositions on the Psalms, 1-32* in *The Works of Saint Augustine*, ed. Rotelle, vol. III/15 (Hyde Park, NY: New City Press, 2000), 30/2.3, 322–23, emphasis added.

And [the Lord] goes on: "And no man hath ascended into heaven, but He that came down from heaven, the Son of man who is in heaven." Behold, He was here, and was also in heaven; was here in His flesh, in heaven by His divinity; yea, everywhere by His divinity. Born of a mother, not quitting the Father. Two nativities of Christ are understood: one divine, the other human: one, that by which we were to be made; the other, that by which we were to be made anew: both marvelous. . . . He had taken a body of Adam,—for Mary was of Adam,—and was about to raise that same body again. . . . God has willed to be the Son of man; and willed men to be sons of God. He came down for our sakes; let us ascend for His sake. For He alone descended and ascended, He who saith, "No man hath ascended into heaven, but He who came down from heaven." Are they not therefore to ascend into heaven whom He makes sons of God? Certainly they are. . . . Then how is it that no man ascends, but He that descended? Because one only descended, only one ascends. What of the rest? What are we to understand, but that they shall be His members, that one may ascend?[132]

Although the explicit word "recapitulation" is absent from these remarks, it pervades Augustine's thoughts here. Not only does the skilled orator movingly blend the ascending and descending movements of human salvation with the idea of our incorporation into Christ's body, but in the midst of doing so, he identifies Christ as Adam exalted, the Son of God through whom we have been made "sons of God." Whatever one judges to be Augustine's primary soteriological emphasis in his voluminous corpus of writings, representative soteriology was clearly within them as a choice theme which appears time and again.

Physical Redemption: Distorting a Theme of Patristic Soteriology

At this point, having reviewed four instances of representative soteriologies in patristic thought, we must address a common soteriological category for the important purpose of distinguishing it from the representative one which we have been considering. This common soteriological category is that of "physical redemption" (alternatively "physical," "natural," even "magical" theory of the atonement, "physicalism," "naturalism"). Distinguishing physical redemption from our representative soteriological category is important here for two main reasons. First, especially over the past century and a half, theologians have

132. *Lectures or Tractates According to the Gospel of St. John*, in *Nicene and Post-Nicene Fathers: First Series* (henceforth *NPNF* I), eds. Schaff & Wace, 14 vols. (Buffalo: The Christian Literature Publishing Co., 1886–1890), vol. I/7:7–452, at 12.8 (*NPNF* I/7:84).

commonly associated physical redemption with Irenaeus, with his idea of recapitulation, and with the related idea of deification which runs through the fabric of the fathers' theologies of human salvation. Second, many of these same theologians, including those who coined the category, have sharply criticized the physical theory for traits (to be explicitly enumerated below) which, I will argue, can only be unfairly predicated of Irenaeus and (at least many of) his heirs; such criticism has resulted in the category and patristic figures which allegedly exemplify it being quickly dismissed and marginalized in many discussions of redemption and atonement. Specifically, physical redemption functions as a kind of straw-man by which the profound category of representative soteriology has been marginalized, especially by Liberal Protestant theologians advocating the thesis of Christianity's Hellenization. Let us consider physical redemption and its origins, followed by some reasons to believe that the category is problematic when attributed to the fathers broadly, and especially to Irenaeus.

Origins in Liberal Protestantism

The idea of physical redemption as a soteriological category seems to have first gained currency among Liberal Protestant theologians around the end of the nineteenth century. Chief among this group was Adolf von Harnack, who refers to the theory throughout his monumental *History of Dogma*.[133] According to Harnack, the theory was roughly approximated by Justin Martyr,[134] nearly (and in places virtually) endorsed by Irenaeus,[135] and came to fully flourish in the theologies of many church fathers who followed.[136] For Harnack, the theory of physical redemption which the fathers came to adopt is a prime example of Christianity's Hellenization, an overarching subject of *History of Dogma*. Irenaeus and his "formula" of recapitulation, in Harnack's view, end up (albeit inadvertently) setting the trajectory toward the Hellenization of soteriology which would come with the full emergence of physical theory.[137]

133. Adolf von Harnack, *History of Dogma*, 7 vols. (New York: Dover Publications, 1961).
134. "Yet we certainly find hints [in Justin] pointing to the notion of a physical and magical redemption accomplished at the moment of the incarnation. See particularly the fragment in Irenæus [*AH* IV.6.2] (already quoted on page 220), which may be thus interpreted, and Apol. I. 66" (Harnack, *History of Dogma*, 2:223).
135. Ibid. 231–34, 241–47, 273–75, 290–93.
136. Harnack lists Gregory of Nyssa, Hilary of Poitiers, Basil of Caesarea, Ephraim, Apollinaris, and Cyril of Alexandria, his "etc." indicating that he believed there to be many more (ibid., 3:301).
137. "The pronounced hellenising of the Gospel, brought about by the Gnostic systems, was averted by Irenæus and the later ecclesiastical teachers by preserving a great portion of the early Christian

Fellow Liberal Protestant Friedrich Loofs defines the physical theory as "the understanding of redemption as the removal of the *phthora* [corruption] from human nature, completed through the union of manhood and Godhead in Christ."[138] As it is typically described, physical redemption concentrates the entirety of human salvation in the moment of Christ's incarnation, when human nature and God's nature were united to one another. Moreover, this unity is thought to have "mechanically" or "magically" transmitted to all humans the immortality which properly belongs to God, doing so solely in virtue of these abstract, Platonic natures (*physeis*) being united in the God-man (hence, "natural" or "physical" redemption). Finally, the full permeation of human nature with immortality which follows upon the hypostatic union logically entails *apokatastasis*, or universal salvation. This theory, Liberal Protestants lamented, smacked of Greek concerns about immortality and ontology, marginalizing the cross and the moral imperative which they read within the gospel's message about salvation.[139]

To Harnack's credit, his careful reading of Irenaeus led him to stop short of pinning him with the "physicalist" label. Harnack recognizes that at least in parts of Irenaeus's theology, salvation is neither completely accomplished in the moment of the incarnation,[140] nor mechanically communicated to the entirety of the human race. Nevertheless, in working out his theory of recapitulation,[141] Irenaeus is said by Har-

---

tradition, partly as regards its letter, partly as regards its spirit, and thus rescuing it for the future. But the price of this preservation was the adoption of a series of 'Gnostic' formulæ. Churchmen, though with hesitation, adopted the adversary's way of looking at things, and necessarily did so, because as they became ever further and further removed from the early-Christian feelings and thoughts, they had always more and more lost every other point of view. The old Catholic Fathers permanently settled a great part of early tradition for Christendom, but at the same time promoted the gradual hellenising of Christianity" (ibid., 2:246–47).

138. Friedrich Loofs *Leitfaden zur Studium der Dogmengeschichte* 4th edn. (Halle: M. Niemeyer, 1906), 203 (translated and quoted in Hart, "Irenaeus, Recapitulation and Physical Redemption," 154).

139. "The point would seem to be that Irenaeus substitutes metaphysical categories for moral ones in his presentation of the Gospel, reflecting an essentially Greek interest in man's ontological standing with regard to the eternal realm (his 'being'), as opposed to a more biblical concern with his moral standing in relation to the categories of sin, judgment, and guilt. . . . Redemption is consequently seen as *complete* in the very joining of manhood to Godhead in the person of Christ, the *acts* of Christ being obscured by a concentration upon his *nature*, and in the incarnation usurping the place of the cross as the focal point of Christian soteriology" (Hart, "Irenaeus, Recapitulation and Physical Redemption," 154–55).

140. "[B]eing in earnest with his idea of Christ as the second Adam, [Irenaeus] was able to contemplate the whole life of Jesus as redemption in so far as he conceived it as a recapitulation" (Harnack, *History of Dogma*, 2:290). See also note 491 in ibid., 241, quoted below.

141. "Now the sole way in which immortality as a physical condition can be obtained is by its possessor uniting himself *realiter* with human nature, in order to deify it 'by adoption' ('*per adoptionem*'), such is the technical term of Irenæus. The deity must become what we are in order that we may become what he is. Accordingly, if Christ is to be the Redeemer, he must himself be God, and all

---

nack to "verge" on "soteriological naturalism,"[142] his historical theology of the first and second Adams possessing "an almost naturalistic shape."[143] Moreover, he reads Irenaeus's soteriology as "dominated" by concern about human immortality[144] and Christ's ontological status.[145] And while Irenaeus understood himself to be simply expositing the NT, in Harnack's estimation, he was, in fact, infusing it with Greek and even Gnostic concepts.[146]

Although Harnack, who also has a profound respect for Irenaeus, expressed serious qualms about the "Greek" flavor of his soteriological writings, his most ardent denunciations of the physical redemption which Hellenized Christian soteriology occur in his treatment of Gregory of Nyssa. Gregory, Harnack explains, pushed Irenaeus's thinking about Adam and Christ "represent[ing] all mankind as their head"[147] to the problematic affirmation that

> the stress must fall upon his birth as man. 'By his birth as man the eternal Word of God guarantees the inheritance of life to those who in their natural birth have inherited death.' But this work of Christ can be conceived as *recapitulatio* because God the Redeemer is identical with God the Creator; and Christ consequently brings about a final condition which existed from the beginning in God's plan, but could not be immediately realised in consequence of the entrance of sin. It is perhaps Irenæus' highest merit, from a historical and ecclesiastical point of view, to have worked out this thought in pregnant fashion and with the simplest means, *i.e.*, without the apparatus of the Gnostics, but rather by the aid of simple and essentially Biblical ideas" (ibid., 241–43).

142. "In working out this thought Irenæus verges here and there on soteriological naturalism. . . . But he does not fall into this for two reasons. In the first place, as regards the history, of Jesus, he has been taught by Paul not to stop at the incarnation, but to view the work of salvation as only completed by the sufferings and death of Christ (See II. 20. 3 . . . ; III. 16. 9: III. 18. 1–7 and many other passages), that is, to regard Christ as having performed a *work*. Secondly, alongside of the deification of Adam's children, viewed as a mechanical result of the incarnation, he placed the other (apologetic) thought, viz., that Christ, as the teacher, imparts complete knowledge, that he has restored, *i.e.*, strengthened the freedom of man, and that redemption (by which he means fellowship with God) therefore takes place only in the case of those children of Adam that acknowledge the truth proclaimed by Christ and imitate the Redeemer in a holy life" (ibid., 241n491).
143. Ibid., 275 (Harnack's treatment of the two Adams in Irenaeus spans from 273–75 of ibid.).
144. "[D]ominating everything, we find [Irenaeus's] firm belief in the bestowal of divine incorruptibility on believers through the work of the God-man" (ibid., 245).
145. "[I]nasmuch as this view represents Christ not as performing a reconciling but a perfecting work, his *acts* are thrust more into the background; his work is contained in his constitution as the God-man" (ibid., 292–93).
146. "[C]ertain interests, which had found expression in the speculations of the so-called Gnostics, were adopted in an increasing degree among all thinking Christians, and also could not but influence the ecclesiastical teachers" (ibid., 231). He continues, "Irenæus uttered most urgent warnings against subtle speculations; but yet, in the naivest way, associated with the faithfully preserved traditional doctrines and fancies of the faith theories which he likewise regarded as tradition and which, in point of form, did not differ from those of the Apologists or Gnostics. The Holy Scriptures of the New Testament were the basis on which Irenæus set forth the most important doctrines of Christianity. . . . Whilst stating and establishing the doctrines of tradition with the help of the New Testament, and revising and fixing them by means of intelligent deduction, the Fathers think they are setting forth the faith itself and nothing else" (ibid., 233–34).
147. Ibid., 274. Johannes Zachhuber has rebutted Harnack's reading of Nyssa in his *Human Nature in Gregory of Nyssa: Philosophical Background and Theological Significance* (Brill, Leiden, 1999). For more on this matter, see Morwenna Ludlow's *Gregory of Nyssa, Ancient and (Post)modern* (Oxford: Oxford Univ. Press, 2007), 100–101.

Christ did not assume the human nature of an individual person, but human nature. Accordingly, all that was human was intertwined with the Deity; the whole of human nature became divine by intermixture with the Divine. Gregory conceives this as a strictly physical process: the leaven of the Deity has pervaded the whole dough of humanity, through and in Christ; for Christ united with himself the whole of human nature with all its characteristics. This conception, which was based on the Platonic universal notion "humanity" ... also led to the doctrine of Apokatastasis (universalism), which Gregory adopted.[148]

Here, Harnack sees full-fledged naturalistic redemption at work. It is entirely "physical" insofar as human nature (*physis*) has been taken *in toto* to God in the incarnation, infusing humankind with immortality in the hypostatic union's inaugural moment and resulting in universal salvation.[149]

Impact of Physical Redemption in Subsequent Theology

By coining the soteriological category of physical redemption, and furthermore, pairing it with the overarching thesis of Christianity's Hellenization in the patristic period, Liberal Protestants such as Harnack had a significant impact on how redemption in the theology of the church fathers has been understood. According to Gustaf Aulén, writing in 1930, physical redemption was the standard category according to which Irenaeus's theology had come to be understood.[150] Aulén even cites Harnack himself as interpreting Irenaeus in this way.[151]

Thus, as Rahner and his contemporaries were undergoing their theological training, the association of the fathers with the category of "physical redemption" would have been fairly strong. For instance,

148. Harnack, *History of Dogma*, 3:297–98.
149. "The way in which this transfusion of humanity with immortality is conceived as having been achieved is vaguely described as 'realistic' or 'physical' ... [T]hrough the physical joining of divine and human natures in the person of the God-man this condition [of divine immortality] is communicated to the human race, being infused into the humanity of Christ, and thereby passing in a 'naturalistic' or 'mechanical' manner to all men by virtue of a 'mystical union' with the Redeemer" (Hart, "Irenaeus, Recapitulation and Physical Redemption," 154–55).
150. "Irenaeus has been commonly interpreted by theologians of the Liberal Protestant school as teaching a 'naturalistic' or 'physical' doctrine of salvation; salvation is the bestowal of 'divinity' – that is, immortality – on human nature, and the idea of deliverance from sin occupies quite a secondary place. The gift of immortality is regarded as dependent on the Incarnation as such; by the entrance of the Divine into humanity, human nature is (as it were) automatically endued with Divine virtue and thereby saved from corruption. This is, then, a theology primarily of the Incarnation, not of the Atonement; the 'work' of Christ holds a secondary place" (Aulén, *Christus Victor*, 18).
151. "So Harnack interprets Irenaeus: 'The work of Christ is contained in the construction of His person as the God-man'" (Aulén, *Christus Victor*, 18, quotation from Harnack, *History of Dogma*, 2:274).

Joseph Ratzinger exhibits a wariness of this category in his commentary on the first chapter of Vatican II's *Dogmatic Constitution on the Church in the Modern World*, making sure to clarify that its concluding article (n. 22, which appeals to incarnational and "final Adam" thinking) is not an instance of it.[152] Rahner himself explicitly (and also disapprovingly) refers to the physical theory a number of times.[153] J. N. D. Kelly utilizes the label,[154] as do more contemporary theologians such as Brian McDermott[155] and David Brondos. McDermott is quite positive in his treatment of the fathers' soteriology, especially that of Irenaeus, so it seems he uses the "physical" label without implying the objectionable characteristics which the Liberal Protestant tradition associated with it.

These associations, however, do seem to have lived on (at least in part), for instance, in Brondos's evaluation of Irenaeus. As Brondos critiques elements of Irenaeus's soteriology, he echoes many Harnackian talking points. "If what actually saves and transforms human beings is the union of the earthly and heavenly in Christ's incarnation," he writes, "then it would appear that Christ's real work of salvation was already completed when he become incarnate as a man to unite the immortal divine nature to the fallen human nature."[156] Brondos elaborates, saying that at points Irenaeus envisions not "merely some type of restored relationship of friendship and communion between God and humanity, but instead conceives of the divine nature as some type of incorruptible and immortal substance that, when brought into contact with the substance of human nature, made it immortal and incorruptible as well."[157] This idea, he judges, "would appear almost magical, as if the union of God to 'man' at the incarnation automatically brings

---

152. Although he does not use the title physical redemption, Ratzinger writes, "A theology of the incarnation situated too much on the level of essence, may be tempted to be satisfied with the ontological phenomenon: God's being and man's have been conjoined. This appears as the real turning-point, and in comparison with it the factual life of Jesus and his death are secondary, as it were the realization of a principle which ultimately adds nothing to the principle itself" ("Introductory Article and Chapter 1: The Dignity of the Human Person," in *Commentary on the Documents of Vatican II*, ed. Herbert Vorgrimler, 5 vols. (New York: Herder and Herder, 1967–1969), vol. 5 (1969), 115–63, at 160). He goes on to clarify that *Gaudium et Spes* (GS) n. 22 does not fall into this "pure essence" thinking; it does not portray Christ as a "general form" and its foundational "theology of the incarnation necessarily leads to a spirituality of the cross" (ibid., 160–61).
153. These will be discussed below, in Chapter 4.
154. Kelly, *Early Christian Doctrines*, 375f.
155. "The type of soteriology formulated by the Fathers of the Church, again particularly in the East, has been called 'natural' or 'physical,' in the sense that the focus falls on the divine nature communicated in Christ and on the Spirit transforming out human nature" (McDermott, *Word Become Flesh*, 215).
156. Brondos, "The Redemption of 'Man,'" 55.
157. Ibid.

about the union and reconciliation of God with all women and men independently of any subjective response on their part."[158]

Responses to Physical Redemption

Despite the associations of Irenaeus (and the theology of the larger patristic period) with physical redemption which flourished in Liberal Protestantism's heyday and beyond, many theologians have recognized the problematic nature of such associations. Several authors have explicitly dissociated Irenaeus from physical redemption. Aulén, after noting this connection between Irenaeus and this theory made by "the Liberal Protestant school," says that it "seriously misinterprets his meaning."[159] J. N. D. Kelly, who continues to use the label, nonetheless distinguishes "physical theory" from Irenaeus's idea of recapitulation, saying that the former is an "elaboration" upon the latter, "parting company with it when, under the influence of Platonic realism, it represents human nature as being automatically deified by the incarnation."[160] Kelly also seems to soften the category itself, clarifying that while it emphasizes the soteriological value of the incarnation, it is usually not done so to the exclusion of the cross.[161] (William Placher, citing Kelly in his call for a return to a "mystical" or "physical" theory of redemption, softens it in the same manner).[162]

Among Irenaeus's most staunch defenders on this count is Trevor Hart. As he notes, any talk of a "mechanical" or "automatic" infusion of immortality into the whole of humanity ignores Irenaeus's insistence of the "need for faith" for salvation,[163] as well as the import of Christ's death for such a communication.[164] Moreover, Hart continues, the mortality which follows upon human sin remains of secondary concern to Irenaeus, who is much more attendant to the *relationship* between God and human beings which is perfected and purified over the whole Christ-event.[165] In fact, Hart argues, the two concerns are intimately

158. Ibid.
159. Aulén, *Christus Victor*, 18–19.
160. Kelly, *Early Christian Doctrines*, 377.
161. "In most forms of the physical theory . . . the emphasis on the incarnation was not intended to exclude the saving value of Christ's death" (ibid., 376).
162. William Placher, "How Does Jesus Save? An Alternative View of Atonement," *Christian Century* (June 2, 2009), 23–27. In advocating for "physical redemption," Placher nonetheless insists that Christ redeems us through the "whole course of his obedience" (ibid., 26).
163. Hart, "Irenaeus, Recapitulation, and Physical Redemption," 155–56.
164. Irenaeus, Hart writes, "often links together the communication of immortality to man and the death of Christ" (ibid., 166).
165. "Sin and disobedience do no result in merely 'physical' consequences . . . but serve to separate man from that fellowship with God for which he was created . . . man's plight is described by Ire-

related in Irenaeus's mind: "Throughout *AH* the language of immortality and incorruptibility is inseparable from the language of atonement and reconciliation. . . . For Irenaeus it would seem to be the case that what man *is* (his essence or nature) is not considered in a static manner, but is bound up with his relationships, and more particularly with his relationship to his Creator."[166]

Likewise, Christ's saving us through *who he is*, as the New Adam, recapitulating humanity in himself, cannot be understood in a static, "physical" way either. The incarnation is, for Irenaeus, itself centrally redemptive, but in reference to *its extension and duration* rather than as accomplished in its first moment.[167] As Loewe puts it, "for Irenaeus, the incarnation embraces the whole earthly career of Jesus."[168] Balthasar goes even farther, declaring that the idea of Greek theology positing a redemption achieved at the moment of the incarnation, with the cross as an "epiphenomenon," is a "widely disseminated myth of the theological textbooks."[169]

Along with Balthasar, other theologians have gone beyond the apologetic task for Irenaeus, questioning the category itself. Romanus Cessario notes the shift in scholarship away from using "physical" as a descriptor for soteriological accounts of Christ's relationship to us, a relationship of mystical membership in Christ's body which is alive and well in the theology of Thomas Aquinas.[170] Admittedly, Cessario says, we can

trace the theory that some kind of ontic communion exists between Christ and his members as far back as Irenaeus of Lyon and his theory of recapitulation. As its root "physis" suggests, "physical" points initially to a union

naeus in relational language as well as that which has been termed 'physical'" (ibid., 157). He continues, explaining that Irenaeus "certainly gives full credence to the *relational* consequences in terms of guilt and condemnation, and to the interpretation of salvation as consisting essentially in an *atonement* of reconciliation between God and man, worked out in the life and death of Jesus Christ. It is untrue, therefore, to suggest that he sees the incarnation in itself as the sum of Christian soteriology, beyond which nothing more needs to be said" (ibid., 158).

166. Ibid., 166 (emphasis original). Cf. "It is in this establishing of man in his proper relationship of communion with God, therefore, that the communication of immortality consists, life itself being defined in terms of this fellowship, and death or non-existence in terms of its absence" (ibid., 169).

167. "[I]t is truer to Irenaeus to see 'nature' as defined not in some absolute or static sense, but rather in terms of man's existence as creature in relation to his Creator and other men, then we may say that for him the union of 'natures' takes place in and through this entire history, from the conception in the virgin's womb, through the ministry and death upon the cross to the resurrection and ascension of Christ" (ibid., 168).

168. Loewe, "Irenaeus' Soteriology: *Christus Victor* Revisited," 11.

169. Hans Urs von Balthasar, *Mysterium Paschale: The Mystery of Easter* (San Francisco: Ignatius Press, 2000), 22.

170. On this connection, see my "Paving the Way? Penalty and Atonement in Thomas Aquinas's Soteriology," *International Journal of Systematic Theology* 15, no. 3 (July 2013), 265–83, at 271–73.

based on common nature, but not, for that reason, an automatic incorporation of all rational creatures into Christ. Rather, the possession of an individual human nature establishes the threshold condition for direct and personal participation in the mystery of Christ.[171]

Cessario puts it well. Our "natural" or "physical" connection to Christ in virtue of the incarnation, far from entailing salvation as a matter of course in virtue of a purely ontological mechanism, is rather a "threshold condition" which needs to be activated, so to speak, by the subjective act of faith.

Moreover, this somewhat potential "physical" connection need not be understood as baptizing a Platonic theory of universal natures into Christian theology. Although several contemporary advocates of retrieving a patristic representative soteriology presume that the fathers rely on this Platonic theory (e.g., McDermott[172] and Walter Kasper,[173] each of whom suggest circumventions for contemporary soteriological appropriations), others have suggested that such a theory is not necessitated. Placher, pointing to Athanasius's story of an entire town being transformed by a great king who enters it,[174] writes "There are many ways, in short, to think of humanity as sufficiently one whole that Christ could transform it,"[175] and Kathryn Tanner insists that the imagery used by the fathers is "not of a technical philosophical sort but rather 'homey' and commonsensical even to modern

---

171. Romanus Cessario, *The Godly Image* (Petersham, MA: St. Bede's Publications, 1990), 174–75.

172. In *Word Become Flesh*, McDermott explains that Gregory Nazianzus understood his idea that "'was not assumed by Christ was not healed because it was not united to God' . . . in terms of a Platonic theory of universals," while contemporary theologians "would anchor Christ's universal inclusion of all humanity in his presence through the Spirit as the Risen One, but the point made remains true for all Christians: in assuming human nature Christ assumed the whole of it and in taking to himself all that is concretely human (as good creation and sinfulness) through his ministry, death, and resurrection, he saved it. Christ assumed fallen human nature and thus healed it" (213).

173. In his *Jesus the Christ*, Kasper notes that the "idea of representation seems strange to the modern way of thinking mainly because the starting-point of modern thought is the autonomy of the person," and suggests, "For the future of faith much will depend on whether the biblical idea of representation and the modern idea of solidarity are successfully combined" (221).

174. "For the solidarity of mankind is such that, by virtue of the Word's indwelling in a single human body, the corruption which goes with death has lost its power over all. You know how it is when some great king enters a large city and dwells in one of its houses; because of his dwelling in that single house, the whole city is honored, and enemies and robbers cease to molest it. Even so is it with the King of all; He has come into our country and dwelt in one body amidst the many, and in consequence the designs of the enemy against mankind have been foiled. . . . For the human race would have perished utterly had not the Lord and Saviour of all, the Son of God, come among us to put an end to death." (*On the Incarnation* [Crestwood, NY: St. Vladimir's Seminary, 2003] 9.3 at 35; cf. *NPNF* II/4:41).

175. Placher, "How Does Jesus Save?," 27.

ears—darkness overcome by being drawn to the light, wood catching fire when put next to a flame."[176]

Distinguishing Representative Soteriology from Physical Redemption

The clarifications which these various theologians have made in order to dissociate the fathers from physical redemption help to show how representative soteriology differs from it as well. In many ways, the physicalist theory coined by Liberal Protestants stands as an exaggeration of elements which are genuinely part of representative soteriology. That is, while important aspects of the physicalist category are reflected in patristic thinkers, these aspects are singled out and overemphasized in a way which ultimately distorts the fathers' thinking. It is likely no coincidence that these isolated and emphasized elements resonate particularly strongly with Hellenistic (especially Platonic philosophical) thought, providing the Liberal Protestant coiners of physical redemption a tool for furthering their thesis of Christianity's early Hellenization, particularly on the soteriological plane. Let us consider a few of this distortions and how they relate to representative soteriology, a category which I have argued better encapsulates much of the fathers' soteriological thought.

Although eternal life is God is part and parcel of salvation, salvation on a representative schema cannot be reduced to ideas such as immortality or incorruptibility. As stated at the beginning of this chapter, salvation consists of the full human flourishing, at the heart of which is the direct, loving presence of God. Hart's apology on behalf of Irenaeus likewise applies here: everlasting life for human beings is wrapped up in our relationship to God, and representative soteriology only attends to the former insofar as it is entailed by the latter.

Moreover, just as Loewe clarifies that, for Irenaeus, the salvific value of the incarnation concerns Jesus's *entire* life, representative soteriology cannot be reduced to a salvific moment. Indeed, the category is *person*-centered, not moment-centered. In fact, a physicalist shifting of

---

176. Kathryn Tanner, "Incarnation, Cross, and Sacrifice: A Feminist-Inspired Reappraisal," *Anglican Theological Review* 86, no. 1 (2004), 35–56, at 45. Tanner continues by comparing this (non-)issue with concerns about other theories of atonement (e.g., penal substitution and satisfaction): "There is nothing particularly objectionable here, compared to modern worries, say, about the justice of putting innocent people to death, and nothing especially time-bound its incomprehensibility to contemporary people, as the feudal code of honor underlying the vicarious satisfaction model might now seem to be" (ibid.).

the emphasis entirely onto the moment Christ became incarnate renders the category just another "act-centered" theory of atonement, the act here occurring at the *beginning* rather than the end of Jesus's life. The person-centered marker of representative soteriology means that we must think of the salvific encounter between God and humankind as having its nexus point in the *interval* of Christ's incarnation rather than its first moment.

Likewise, Christ's identity as our Representative in this person-centered schema does not deprive it of a subjective dimension, a deprivation associated with the "mechanical" transmission of salvation to humanity in physical redemption. As Dorothee Sölle insists repeatedly in her classic *Christ the Representative*, the representative does not *replace* the one represented, for this would amount to substitution.[177] Rather, the representative holds open a place for the one represented, not negating her freedom, but rather, allowing it to fully develop.[178] To be incorporated into Christ himself (and the person-centered marker of representative soteriology depends on this incorporation) means to participate in Christ's own "ascending" and affirmative stance toward God. Moreover, a legitimate subjective dimension to representative soteriology obviates the objection about a *necessarily* entailed universal salvation.

Finally, this idea of incorporation may be explained by appealing to the idea of Platonic universals, but it certainly need not. As Placher and Tanner have explained above, there are many methods and images for describing how one human being, Christ, can stand in an intimate relationship and have a most profound effect upon other human beings. In addition to their explanations, I would like to briefly make reference to two biblical ideas—the Pauline notion of our being "members" of Christ's body (1 Corinthians 12, cf. Ephesians 4-5, Colossians 1-2), as well as the Johannine description of Christ as the Vine and us as the branches (John 15). Although the idea of Christ as "head" and the church as "body" in Ephesians and Colossians sets discrete parts in relation to one another, the Pauline imagery in 1 Corinthians and that

177. "In substitution, what is replaced is treated as unavailable, useless, or dead. Substitution demands permanence, not a merely provisional status. The replacement represents the other person completely and unconditionally. . . . The substitutionary way of thinking, . . . by speaking of man as a replacement turns him into a thing" (Sölle, *Christ the Representative*, 21).
178. "Any act of representation can turn into substitution if the place of the one who is represented is no longer held open, but is seized by the representative for himself." Thus, "Anyone who is represented runs the risk of being replaced" (ibid., 48).

of the Fourth Gospel are radically inclusive: we are the parts, while Christ is *himself the whole*.

It may be tempting to appeal to Platonic universals (or even the troublesome notion of the Word assuming the entirety of human nature rather than a single instance of it) to cash out these images and representative idea of incorporation, especially given the difficulty of accounting for the relationship between this first-century Jewish man and humans far removed in time and space from him. However, the presence of the Spirit, Christ's own mysterious glorified and resurrected status, and Christ's sacramental presence, especially in the Eucharist, stand as important ways for Christians to account for this relationship. The sacraments are particularly essential for understanding this unity and participation in Christ. As Augustine so eloquently attests, the sacraments of initiation shape us into a single "loaf," a loaf which we are and yet which we become upon receiving it.[179]

Conclusion

This chapter has sought to argue that the category of representative soteriology, with its ascending, descending, and person-centered markers, is a central and reoccurring part of patristic theology about human salvation. More specifically, I have sought to show how Irenaeus's idea of recapitulation, in particular, is a paradigm case of representative soteriology which quite likely had significant influence on subsequent theologians in both the Greek- (e.g., Clement of Alexandria, Athanasius) and Latin-speaking (e.g., Augustine) church. But more important than definitively proving any Irenaean soteriological lin-

---

179. From Augustine's "Sermon 227" (Easter 414 or 415): "That bread which you can see on the altar, sanctified by the word of God, is the body of Christ. That cup, or rather what the cup contains, sanctified by the word of God, is the blood of Christ. It was by means of these things that the Lord Christ wished to present us with his body and blood, which he shed for our sake for the forgiveness of sins. If you receive them well, you are yourselves what you receive. You see, the apostle says, *We, being many, are one loaf, one body* (1 Cor 10:17). That's how he explained the sacrament of the Lord's table; one loaf, one body, is what we all are, many though we be. In this loaf of bread you are given clearly to understand how much you should love unity. I mean, was that loaf made from one grain? Weren't there many grains of wheat? But before they came into the loaf they were all separate; they were joined together by means of water after a certain amount of pounding and crushing. Unless wheat is ground, after all, and moistened with water, it can't possibly get into this shape which is called bread. In the same way you too were being ground and pounded, as it were, by the humiliation of fasting and the sacrament of exorcism. Then came baptism, and you were, in a manner of speaking, moistened with water in order to be shaped into bread. But it's not yet bread without fire to bake it. So what does fire represent? That's the chrism, the anointing. Oil, the fire-feeder, you see, is the sacrament of the Holy Spirit" (in *Sermons (184-229z)* in *The Works of Saint Augustine*, ed. Rotelle, III/6:254).

eage is the widespread presence of representative soteriological thinking, whatever the cause.

It is important to distinguish the fathers' theology regarding salvation from the category of physical redemption, a soteriological theory coined by Liberal Protestants which helped advance the thesis of Christianity's Hellenization, but which seriously distorted aspects of patristic thought. The fathers' representative thinking centers not on human immortality and incorruption, but on the relationship with God which entails those qualities; it affirms the value of the incarnation, not as an isolated salvific moment, but as the entirety of the Christ-event, including the cross; it locates the communication of salvation within our incorporation into Christ, but not in any mechanical or automatic way; finally, it insists on the whole being represented in the one, but not in a way which necessitates baptizing Platonic universal forms.

For theologians in the early part of the twentieth century, the association of the fathers with physical redemption would have been well known. However, close readers of patristic theology, especially of Irenaeus,[180] would have been able to identify this association as a false one, as Balthasar (who cited the theory as a "myth of the theological textbooks") proves. Some of these close readers may even have been so affected by the fathers' pervasive representative thinking that it would come to eventually influence their own creative soteriological efforts. As I will argue in the following chapter, Karl Rahner was one such close reader.

---

180. Even Harnack refrained from formally labeling Irenaeus a proponent of the theory, as stated above.

4

———

Rahnerian Ressourcement

A Historical Basis for the Fathers' Influence

The preceding chapters have functioned primarily to set the stage for my thesis that, contra Hans Urs von Balthasar's analysis of it, Karl Rahner's soteriology can be legitimately classified as "representative" in character. This stage-setting includes: (i) specifying what I mean by representative, utilizing the three characteristic markers as well as the contentious term *Stellvertretung*, (ii) demonstrating that Rahner's sacramental or *realsymbolisch* concepts entail representative counterparts when he utilizes them in christological and soteriological writings, and (iii) considering other major proponents of representative soteriology, especially patristic theologians such as Irenaeus of Lyons. The connection on the "conceptual" level between Rahner and representative soteriology, made in a somewhat limited way in chapter 2, will be the focus of the fifth and final chapter below.

My focus now, however, will be upon establishing the *historical* plausibility of identifying Rahner as a representative thinker, a plausibility rooted in his early engagement with and ongoing appreciation for theology and doctrine from the age of the church fathers. I will proceed with some initial biographical considerations, followed by an examination of Rahner's doctoral dissertation on patristic typology, *E latere Christi* ("From the Side of Christ"). This dissertation, to which little attention has been paid, focuses its ecclesiological and soteriological claims upon the idea of Christ as the New Adam, an idea paramount within the theology of the fathers (who receive the lion's share of Rahner's attention in his dissertation). Finally, I will argue that in addition to having a formative impact on Rahner's own creative systematic theology, the theology and dogmatic pronouncements of the early centuries of Christianity remained indispensable for Rahner throughout his career. Although he is known primarily for his efforts to render the gospel intelligible to the contemporary person (efforts which might be accurately summarized by the term *aggiornamento* or "updating," heard frequently in discussions surrounding Vatican II), Rahner made it clear in his final years that he saw himself as a deeply "historical" (or, to once again use conciliar parlance, *ressourcement*) theologian.[1] Rahner's recourse to "the sources" of Christian soteriology, particularly as seen in *E latere Christi*, provide a historical and biographical explanator for my contention that he articulated a representative soteriology in common with patristic thinkers such as Irenaeus.

The Biographical Status Quo

For a well-known and heavily studied figure such as Rahner, short biographies abound.[2] In their treatment of Rahner's early years as a student and, eventually, lecturer, the majority of such biographies devote their attention to his philosophical interests, particularly his reading of various philosophers (e.g., Immanuel Kant, Maurice Blondel, Pierre Rousselot, and especially Joseph Maréchal), his participation in Martin Heidegger's seminars at Freiburg, his philosophy dissertation (*Spirit in the World*), and his subsequent work on anthropology and philosophy of religion, *Hearer of the Word*. Reference to Rahner's interest in the fathers is either made in passing or, more typically, is omitted entirely.[3] It is, of course, true that these philosophical interests and the

---

1. On this thesis, see my "Karl Rahner on Patristic Theology and Spirituality," *Philosophy & Theology* 27, no. 2 (2015), 499–512.
2. E.g., Geffrey B. Kelly (ed.), *Karl Rahner: Theologian of the Graced Search for Meaning* (Minneapolis, MN: Fortress Press, 1992), 1–31; Gerald McCool, "Introduction: Rahner's Philosophical Theology," *A Rahner Reader*, ed. McCool (New York: The Seabury Press, 1975), xiii–xxviii, at xiii–xxviii; Leo O'Donovan, "Preface" *A World of Grace: An Introduction to the Themes and Foundations of Karl Rahner's Theology* (Washington D.C.: Georgetown Univ. Press, 1995), vii–x; Thomas O'Meara: *God in the World: A Guide to Karl Rahner's Theology* (Collegeville, MN: Liturgical Press, 2007), 16–21; Thomas Sheehan, "Introduction," *Karl Rahner: The Philosophical Foundations* (Athens, OH: Ohio University Press, 1987), 1–15; Herbert Vorgrimler, *Karl Rahner: His Life, Thought and Works* (Glen Rock, NJ: Deus Books, 1966), 18ff; William Dych, *Karl Rahner* (Collegeville, MN: Liturgical, 1992), 4ff; Robert Kress, *A Rahner Handbook* (Atlanta: John Knox, 1982), 1–18, etc.
3. While the publications in the previous note more or less exemplify with this tendency, exceptions

corresponding figures significantly shaped Rahner's career as a theologian.[4] Rahner himself cites Maréchal as a major influence[5] and even identifies Heidegger as his "master," the "only *one* whom I can revere as my *teacher.*"[6] Yet, it is important not to overestimate these influences as if Maréchal and Heidegger somehow determined Rahner's theology.[7] In fact, he denies that either figure even had this kind of decisive influence on his *philosophy.*[8] Rahner specifies that Heidegger's effect upon him came by means of "a style of thinking" rather than any "specific doctrines."[9]

Unfortunately, the widespread tendency to portray Rahner's theol-

to it include Neufeld's authoritative work *Die Brüder Rahner: Eine Biographie* (Freiburg i.br.: Herder, 1994); Joseph Wong, *Logos-Symbol in the Christology of Karl Rahner* (Rome: LAS, 1984); Annice Callahan, *Karl Rahner's Spirituality of the Pierced Heart: A Reinterpretation of Devotion to the Sacred Heart* (Lanham, MD: University Press of America, 1985); and Herbert Vorgrimler, *Understanding Karl Rahner: An Introduction to His Life and Thought* (New York: Crossroad, 1986), 64–67.

4. In *Karl Rahner's Theological Aesthetics* (Washington, DC: Catholic University of America Press, 2014), Peter Fritz offers a new and compelling perspective on Rahner's relationship to Heidegger, challenging the frequent suggestion that as a "transcendental Thomist," Rahner exemplifies "modern subjective" thought.

5. *Karl Rahner in Dialogue: Conversations and Interviews*, eds. Paul Imhof and Hubert Biallowons (New York: Crossroad, 1986), 13.

6. "On Martin Heidegger," in Sheehan, *Karl Rahner*, xi (emphasis original). Also, "I have to confess . . . that I would not have done philosophy in a transcendental manner had I not studied the philosophy of Maréchal and of Heidegger" (*Karl Rahner in Dialogue*, 132), and "I owe my most basic, decisive, philosophical direction, insofar as it comes from someone else, more, in fact, to the Belgian philosopher and Jesuit, Joseph Maréchal. His philosophy already moved beyond the traditional neoscholasticism. I brought that direction from Maréchal to my studies with Heidegger and it was not superseded by him" (ibid., 190).

7. "Insofar as it is philosophical, my theology does not really show the systematic and thematic influence of Heidegger. What he communicated was the desire to think, the ability to think. . . . I would say that Martin Heidegger was the only teacher for whom I developed the respect that a disciple has for a great master. That had little to do with individual questions or individual formulations of my theology. I would say that Heidegger had little influence on my philosophy or even my theology, although I am really extremely grateful to him" (ibid., 257).

8. "Certainly, while Maréchal influenced me, it cannot be said that my philosophical ideas were completely and adequately determined by him. There were many other profound influences that help elaborate and at times transform what Maréchal said" (ibid., 13–14).

9. "One may perhaps say that it is not specific doctrines that I have taken from Heidegger, but rather a style of thinking and of investigating which has proved most valuable. This may be described as a method or approach by which one does not examine dogmatic truths *merely* as evidence derived from the positive sources, but one seeks to construct a synthesis. One takes the various dogmatic propositions and reduces them to certain fundamental principles. In that way an internal, coherent body of dogmatic truth is established. The modern person is thus able to perceive the order and harmony in the mysterious truth of the Church and Christianity. The modern person no longer is satisfied with taking a collection of the truths and various opinions that are proven in Denzinger and thinking no more about it. Rather, he or she looks for some synthetic idea, even though it might be quite simple, to organize the immense material of Christian dogma. Once this is achieved, other specific truths are able to be understood as obvious and necessary consequences of the principle idea" (ibid., 13). Elsewhere, Rahner writes that "surely [Heidegger] has taught us *one thing*: that everywhere and in everything we can and must seek out that *unutterable mystery* which *disposes* over us, even though we can hardly name it with words. And this we must do even if, in his own work and in a way which would be strange for a theologian, Heidegger himself abstains from *speech* about this mystery, speech which the theologian must *utter*" (in Sheehan, *Karl Rahner*, xi–xii, emphasis original).

ogy as emerging from the crucible of modern continental philosophy has led many of his readers, both enthusiasts and critics alike, to operate within an excessively narrow scope when considering the influences on his theological career. Two years prior to his death, Rahner declared to an interviewer, "I refuse to be condemned as a theologian to being subject exclusively to a completely determined philosophical system."[10] A full appreciation of Rahner's thought requires giving serious (rather than mere passing) attention to other early, formative factors which shaped his theology.

Especially beginning in the 1980s, such attention began to appear in writings on the significance of Rahner's Ignatian spirituality. Joseph Wong,[11] Annice Callahan,[12] and Herbert Vorgrimler[13] offered somewhat brief but important forays into the manner in which Rahner's Jesuit training, specifically Ignatius's *Spiritual Exercises*, heavily shaped his projects.[14] In more recent years, increasing attention has been rightfully called to this topic.[15]

With the exception of Neufeld and Batlogg (whose relevant work is only available in German), the efforts to examine Rahner's early non-philosophical influences have focused almost entirely on prayer and spirituality. And, as with that on Rahner's philosophical influences, such a focus is warranted and valuable. However, Rahner's writings (including his theology dissertation) which concern the church fathers have received sparse attention, especially in the English-speaking

---

10. *Karl Rahner in Dialogue*, 311.
11. Wong, *Logos-Symbol*, 46–70.
12. Callahan, *Karl Rahner's Spirituality of the Pierced Heart*, 79–80, 86–90.
13. Vorgrimler, *Understanding Karl Rahner*, 33–39.
14. It should be noted that only four months before his death in March of 1984, Rahner expressed approval of Wong's emphasis on Rahner's devotional life, particularly to the Sacred Heart, impacting his theology: "above all, considerations essential to my Christology are drawn together here which I had indeed developed in the course of writing a theology of devotion to the Sacred Heart but which I had overlooked in producing my first brief systematic Christology during my years in Münster. The reassertion of my considerations on devotion of the Sacred Heart, however, enriches and deepens an otherwise somewhat too formal and abstract outline of systematic Christology which resulted both in the work I did in Münster and in my *Foundations of Christian Faith*" ("Foreword," in Wong, *Logos-Symbol*, 7).
15. See especially Philip Endean, *Karl Rahner and Ignatian Spirituality* (Oxford: Oxford Univ. Press, 2001). Also cf. Roman A. Siebenrock's "Christology," in *The Cambridge Companion to Karl Rahner*, eds. Declan Marmion and Mary Hines (Cambridge: Cambridge Univ. Press, 2005), 112–27, as well as his "Gratia Christi. The Heart of the Theology of Karl Rahner Ignatian Influences in the Codex De Gratia Christi (1937/38) and Its Significance for the Development of His Work," in *Revista Portuguesa de Filosofia* 63, no. 4, Os Domínios da Inteligência: Bernard Lonergan e a Filosofia. / The Realism of Insight: Bernard Longeran and Philosophy (Oct.–Dec., 2007), 1261–72; Arno Zahlauer *Karl Rahner und sein "productives Vorbild" Ignatius von Loyola* (Innsbruck: Tyrolia, 1996); Neufeld, *Die Brüder Rahner*; Andreas Batlogg *Die Mysterien des Lebens Jesu bei Karl Rahner: Zugang zum Christusglauben* (Innsbruck: Tyrolia, 2001); Harvey Egan, "Karl Rahner: Theologian of the 'Spiritual Exercises'," *Thought* 67 (1992), 257–70.

world.[16] Accordingly, the short biography which I will offer below is not intended to be at all comprehensive nor balanced in its attention to the variety of sources which influenced Rahner. Rather, it is intended to fill in lacunae concerning historical theology which exist in many biographical summaries of Karl Rahner, situating these lacunae within the more widely reported timeline of Rahner's early years.[17]

A Biographical Corrective: Rahner's Early Years

Rahner entered the Jesuit novitiate in Feldkirch, Austria during April 1922, having turned 18 about a month earlier. Within two years, Rahner penned his first publication, on "Why we need to pray."[18] During this time, his brother Hugo, who preceded Karl into the novitiate, reports that the two of them undertook "timid, early attempts at collaborative work . . . to sense and present in the field of scholarship the presence of God to the world."[19] Karl Rahner studied philosophy at Feldkirch in 1925 and then continued his philosophical studies in Pullach through 1927. Following the convention of his Order, Rahner spent some time doing "practical" work between his philosophical and theological studies, returning to Feldkirch as a Latin instructor. During this period, he also studied Greek at Innsbruck (1928). In the fall of 1929, Rahner set out for Holland to begin his theological studies in Valkenburg, where he would stay until 1933.[20]

Although Rahner's Jesuit Provincial had, by this time, decided that his future lay in teaching philosophy for the Order, Rahner immersed himself in these theological studies. Although the theology taught to him at Valkenberg was markedly neo-Scholastic in its approach, Rahner reportedly "enjoyed" it; he would even go on to say that he would *prefer* it to the theology being taught by the German theological faculties in his final years.[21] That said, Rahner certainly recognized the shortcomings of neo-Scholasticism, which tended to reverently treat

---

16. This dissertation, *E latere Christi*, was only published relatively recently (1999) in vol. 3 his collected works, *SW*. It remains unavailable in an English translation.
17. This biographical summary draws extensively on the "Editionsbericht" of Neufeld and that of Batlogg in *SW* vol. 3. Cf. also Batlogg's "Karl Rahner in Innsbruck: Aus der Wissenschaftsbiographie eines Jesuitengelehrten-zugleich ein Stück Fakultätsgeschichte," in *Zeitschrift für Katholische Theologie* 129 (2007), 397–422.
18. K. Rahner, "Warum uns das Beten nottut," *Leuchtturm: Monatsschrift der neudeutschen Jugend* 18 (1924–25), 310–11. Available in *Frühe spirituelle Texte und Studien: Grundlagen im Orden*, eds. Karl Lehmann and Albert Raffelt, vol. 1 (2014) of *SW*, 3–4.
19. H. Rahner, "Eucharisticon fraternitatis," 896.
20. During this period, Rahner was ordained a priest in Munich on July 26, 1932.
21. K. Rahner, *Faith in a Wintry Season: Conversations and Interviews with Karl Rahner in the Last Years of His Life* (New York: Crossroad, 1990), 42.

the works of Thomas Aquinas as a sort of "second Scripture" to be commented upon; this theological approach which dominated Valkenburg was, in large part, a matter of "mere decoration. I certainly didn't have a living and inspirational contact with Thomas then."[22]

Rahner's enthusiasm for his theological studies seems to have been rooted in additional historical reading which he took up during this period. In fact, Rahner maintained a reading list for self-guided study, a list which Karl Neufeld has described as a "probably quite exhaustive" record of Rahner's reading beyond his courses' neo-Scholastic textbooks.[23] Neufeld has described in detail a section, entitled "Valkenburg 1929/30," of this record:

> First, a group of patristic texts catches one's eye. Named are: the letters of Ignatius [of Antioch]; *Shepherd of Hermas*; Polycarp; the *Apologies* of Justin Martyr, as well as his *Dialogue with Trypho*; Pseudo-Justin and his "Oratio ad Graecos"; *Epistle of Barnabas*; *Acta* of the second-century martyrs; the "Muratorian Fragment"; Irenaeus and his *Adversus Haereses* as well as his *Demonstratio apostolicae Praedicationes*; the complete works of Tertullian; the complete works of Clement of Alexandria. Further added are Chrysostom's *De sacerdotis*; Gregory of Nyssa's *On Prayer*; Augustine's *De praedstinatione SS.* And *De dono perseverantiae*; also, Aponius's commentary on the Song of Songs.[24]

Astoundingly, this extensive program of additional readings concerned only Rahner's first two (of eight total) semesters at Valkenburg.

As Heinrich Bacht has noted, Rahner's spare time during this period was, as the program above would indicate, consumed with patristic studies.[25] Bacht reports that during the course of his four years at Valkenburg, Rahner's relentless reading of the church fathers so dominated his time that his peers were moved to designate him accordingly: "With unfailing persistence Karl Rahner worked his way through the tomes of Greek and Latin patrology by Abbé Migne. . . . When he sat behind his tomes, he was not easily distracted. It is no wonder that on account of his stubborn doggedness, he was nicknamed 'the wood-head.'"[26] (Any reservations one might have about possible exaggeration on this count are quickly put to rest when looking at the

---

22. Ibid., 42, 45.
23. Neufeld, *Die Brüder Rahner*, 98.
24. Ibid., 99.
25. Heinrich Bacht, "Theologie in Valkenburg (1929–1933)", in *Karl Rahner - Bilder eines Lebens*, eds. P. Imhof and H. Biallowons (Zürich: Herder, 1985), 22–23, at 23.
26. Ibid.

staggering number of citations of Jacques Paul Migne's patrologies[27] in Rahner's dissertation, *E latere Christi*.) Given his rigorous program of self-directed study in his spare time, it is hardly surprising that Hermann Lange, the dean of the theology faculty at Valkenburg, praised Rahner for his "exceptional independent work."[28] This extracurricular program of study at Valkenburg led to several published articles during his final years there (discussed below) and would directly contribute to his theology dissertation at Innsbruck; Batlogg has further referred to this program as "the fund and pool from which [Rahner] could draw throughout his entire life."[29]

Rahner's (predominately patristic) program of reading cultivated an "extensive and intensive engagement with the issues of penance and conversion."[30] Specifically, Rahner's reading of secondary literature on these topics at Valkenburg centered on Augustine's treatment of them.[31] This fascination, which Rahner maintained throughout his theological career,[32] led him to produce an article on the topic which would be published in 1934, shortly after he completed his theological studies at Valkenburg in 1933.

Rahner's Provincial, deeming him "'destined' to become a professor of the history of philosophy," assigned him to Freiburg in 1934 to attain his degree.[33] Rahner enrolled as a doctoral candidate under Martin Honecker, a Catholic, neo-Scholastic professor of philosophy; he also participated in Heidegger's seminars over the next two years. Rahner chose to write his dissertation on a Thomistic metaphysics of knowledge. Honecker, who read the completed dissertation in the early summer of 1936, protested that Rahner imported a modern "subjective" focus into Thomas's thought. Vorgrimler, and even Rahner himself, has suggested that Honecker detected Heidegger's influence in the dissertation and, judging this influence to be excessive for a dissertation

---

27. There are 161 volumes of the Greek *Patrologiae Cursus Completus* (PG), 221 of the Latin (PL). It should also be noted that several volumes have multiple codices, and each volume typically exceeds 1000 pages. (*Patrologiae Cursus Completus: Omnium SS. Patrum, Doctorum Scriptorumque Ecclesiasticorum Sive Latinorum, Sive Graecorum*. Paris, 1844).

28. See the letter, dated 2 November 1934, transcribed in Batlogg's "Editionsbericht," in *SW* 3:xxxi (KRA III, C, Konvolut 2, Viertes Blatt).

29. Batlogg, "Editionsbericht: Teil A," xxxiv.

30. Neufeld, *Die Brüder Rahner*, 99.

31. This secondary literature is listed in ibid., 99.

32. Cf. vol. 15 of *TI*, devoted to the topic. Penance and the related topic of indulgences also contributed to Rahner's treatment of purgatory, a topic with which he continually grappled into even his later years.

33. Vorgrimler, *Understanding Karl Rahner*, 58. This period has been written on extensively; only basic information will be included.

purportedly on Thomas Aquinas, failed the project.[34] Rahner exmatriculated from Freiburg on June 25, 1936.[35]

Within days, Rahner arrived back at Innsbruck,[36] where his Provincial now intended for him both to receive a doctorate in and teach theology. When asked about this transition and Honecker's rejection, Rahner has reported that he was not disappointed over the matter. In addition to providing an opportunity for further collaboration with his brother Hugo, it allowed Rahner to reengage with the material into which he had poured himself at Valkenburg. Perhaps obliquely referencing the dissertation he would write at Innsbruck (on Christ's pierced side), Rahner said of this transition, "to be frank, I myself had no great inner attraction to the history of philosophy: Certainly I would have been a quite respectable historian of philosophy, but my heart didn't bleed."[37]

Incredibly, it only took Rahner about two weeks from his arrival at Innsbruck to submit his completed theology dissertation, *E latere Christi*.[38] As Arno Zahlauer has noted, "Even for a man with the talent of Karl Rahner, two weeks would have been too short of a time to write a dissertation."[39] Clearly, Rahner had done significant work on this project prior to his arrival at Innsbruck.

This work began more than five years earlier in collaboration with his older brother, Hugo, whose own dissertation (entitled *Fons vitae* [Fount of Life][40]) already nodded in its foreword to the patristic insight upon which Karl's own dissertation would focus: The early church, Hugo Rahner writes, saw in Christ the Source of life, "in that miraculous stream of blood and water, which flowed from the pierced side of the Lord. In this Source of life, the church, the *Domina*-Mother of the living, was born."[41] The themes upon which the Rahner brothers worked in their doctoral dissertations[42]—namely, devotion to the per-

---

34. Ibid., 62; cf. *I Remember: An Autobiographical Interview with Meinold Krauss* (New York: Crossroad, 1985), 42f.

35. Rahner has stated that the move had less to do with Honecker's rejection at Freiburg than with the need for theology professors at Innsbruck after the departure of Johann Stufler and Joseph Müller (*Faith in a Wintry Season*, 44).

36. The first official record of Rahner's presence at Innsbruck is June 29, 1936.

37. *Faith in a Wintry Season*, 44.

38. Batlogg notes that the dissertation appears to be "hurriedly typed" ("Editionsbericht: Teil A," xxiv).

39. Zahlauer, *Karl Rahner und sein "produktives Vorbild,"* 175f, note 424.

40. *Fons Vitae: Eine Untersuchung zur Geschichte der Christusfrömmigkeit in der Urkirche. 1.-3. Jahrhundert* ["Fount of Life: A Study of the History of Devotion to Christ in the Early Church (1st to 3rd Centuries")]. Hugo completed this dissertation in Feb. 1930 and received his doctorate at Innsbruck on 2 May 1931.

41. Qtd. in Neufeld, *Die Brüder Rahner*, 91.

son of Christ and the church's origin from Christ's pierced side (and heart)—overlapped significantly, and Karl has himself acknowledged that Hugo influenced his selection of topic.[43] Moreover, there is an extant letter to Hugo dated 13 June 1930 in which Karl, writing from Valkenburg, requests sources and materials related to Hugo's recently completed dissertation, and specifically to "the *Ecclesia ex latere Christi.*"[44]

Thus, it was clear that Karl Rahner was already collecting materials for *E latere Christi* in the summer after his first year of theological studies at Valkenburg, six years before he would formally complete it at Innbruck. Batlogg has recorded several undated preparation materials from within this six-year interim period. One such artifact is a compilation of excerpted patristic writings, "excerpts of Tertullian, Justin, Clement, Athenagoras, Irenaeus and other authors – a kind of card-catalogue, as it were."[45] Together with this "card-catalogue" is a 34-page (double-sided A5) manuscript in Rahner's own handwriting.[46] From its lack of Heideggerian terminology, Batlogg estimates that this draft predates Rahner's time at Freiberg.[47] Thus, Rahner's independent research in his years at Valkenburg basically amounted to dissertation research for a degree which, during 1934–1936, it looked like he would never receive. Although it was undoubtedly influenced by his brother, *E latere Christi* was a labor driven by Karl Rahner's own sheer fascination with this patristic *topos*. As Neufeld has noted, "Rahner developed and freely chose this point of emphasis of his work; no one invited or compelled him."[48]

Rahner had more success with the evaluation of this second dissertation, which was approved by Paul Gächter (professor of New Testament studies), in mid-September 1936. Gächter, in an official statement

<hr/>

42. Hugo Rahner has suggested that his and Rahner's work on these topics influenced Pius XII's 1956 encyclical *Haurietis Aquas*. See H. Rahner, *Symbole der Kirche: Zur Ekklesiologie der Väter* (Salzburg: O. Müller, 1964), 177. See also Walter Kasper, *Mercy*, 113, where Kasper makes note of the same connection between John 7:38 and 19:34 studied by the Rahner brothers in their early careers.
43. Batlogg, "Editionsbericht: Teil A," xxxvii. Batlogg further notes that the Rahner brothers would frequently edit each other's writings, especially during the 1930s (ibid., xxxvi).
44. "If you could send from Innsbruck all of the material that you are finished with, i.e. everything in any way related to the *Ecclesia ex latere Christi* or to the *Fons vitae*, I would be very happy" (qtd. in ibid., xviii).
45. Ibid., xxxi–xxxii.
46. This manuscript and the "card catalogue" are located in the Karl Rahner Archives (KRA I, B, 3). There is also an 80-page typescript covered with Rahner's handwritten marginalia; this copy, unlike the (certainly older) manuscript and like the finalized copy, contains a final section on the significance of the events of Christ's life (KRA I, B, 4). The unbound and official copy of his dissertation filed in the Office of the Dean at Innsbruck is (KRA I, B, 6).
47. Batlogg, "Editionsbericht: Teil A," xxxii.
48. Neufeld, "Editionsbericht," xiii.

cosigned by Franz Mitzka (professor of dogmatics), declared that *E latere Christi* "is not only suitable as a doctoral dissertation according to present applicable standards of the local theological faculty, but it far exceeds typical instances of such work and is, also, by all means ready for publication."[49] At this point, Rahner began preparing for doctoral examinations, which occurred between mid-October and mid-December. On December 19, 1936, the Leopold-Franzens University of Innsbruck awarded Rahner his doctorate of theology.

Before Rahner could begin teaching theology at Innsbruck, he had to satisfy the qualifications, including the completion of a *Habilitationsschrift*, which typically amounts to a second dissertation. However, Rahner's established presence in academic publications (more on this below) sufficed to fulfill this requirement.[50] During the following summer in 1937, during which he began a series of 15 lectures in Salzburg which would later coalesce into *Hearer of the Word*,[51] Rahner was appointed a *Privatdozent* to the Innsbruck faculty. This same summer, Rahner was instructed by his Order to conclude his philosophical studies at Freiburg. Although he continued to take classes there and at Innsbruck, this desired conclusion never came to pass.[52]

Beginning that winter semester, Rahner taught a course on the doctrine of grace, for which he customized his own textbook which emphasized the centrality of Christ. Neufeld has noted that while the theme of Rahner's *Hearer of the Word* lectures in Salzburg was predetermined for him when he was invited to deliver them, Rahner's course on grace had "no such requirements. . . . In other words, here Rahner decided entirely according to his own discretion."[53]

Rahner's customized textbook on grace was not the only such text he worked on in 1937. That same year, he received permission from

---

49. Cf. Imhof and Biallowons (eds.), *Karl Rahner - Bilder eines Lebens*, 34. Despite Gächter's final remark, *E latere Christi* remained unpublished until its inclusion in vol. 3 of the *SW* of Karl Rahner in 1999.

50. What precisely qualified as Rahner's *Habilitationsschrift* is somewhat unclear. Rahner's semi-official bibliography ("Bibliographie des Schrifttums von Karl Rahner," updated September 2016, http://www.ub.uni-freiburg.de/fileadmin/ub/referate/04/rahner/rahnersc.pdf) lists a single article as the *Habilitationsschrift* accepted by Innsbruck in 1936 ("Sünde als Gnadenverlust in der frühkirchlichen Literatur," *Zeitschrift für katholische Theologie* 60 (1936), 471–510; a revised version of this article was included as "Sin as Loss of Grace in the Early Church," in *TI* 15:23–53). Vorgrimler, on the contrary, lists several: "According to the laws which used to apply throughout Austria [teaching qualification] was not difficult if one had already published academic studies. So the five articles on the spiritual theology of Origen, Evagrius Ponticus and Bonaventure, which had been published between 1932 and 1934, were enough. On 1 July 1937 he completed the postdoctoral work (*Habilitation*) required for university teaching" (*Understanding Karl Rahner*, 63).

51. The lectures, which were completed by the winter semester of 1937, were entitled "On the Basis of a Philosophy of Religion." Four years later, they were published as *Hörer des Wortes* (1941).

52. Batlogg, "Editionsbericht: Teil A," xxii, xv.

53. Ibid., xvi.

Marcel Viller to undertake a translation and expansion of his *La spiritualité des premiers siècles chrétiens*,[54] which Rahner would publish as *Aszese
und Mystik in der Väterzeit* ("Asceticism and Mysticism in the Patristic
Period"), a textbook on the church fathers which Rahner intended to
serve as a complement to the theological manuals of the day.[55] Rahner's
own additions to the text resulted in nearly doubling its length. Hugo
Rahner has testified to his brother's "love for the church fathers," a
love which bore "a final, even ripe fruit" in *Aszese und Mystik*, which was
completed in the summer of 1938 (its foreword is dated June) and published the following spring.[56]

The summer of 1938 marks an end to this first, formative period
of Rahner's theological development. Although Rahner continued to
engage patristic sources and do historical theology, his own more
properly "constructive" work began to command an increasingly
greater portion of his (considerable) output. Part of this may be attributed to a divergence between Karl and Hugo,[57] the latter of whom
engaged in a movement called "kerygmatic" theology around this
time.[58] Karl worried that this approach was dangerously satisfied with
statements and formulae of the past, which, in the contemporary setting, were kinds of relics; one could not simply construct a "preach-
able" theology subsequent to and alongside a repetition of theologies
from the past, whether those theologies be scholastic or patristic.
Rather, constantly addressing new questions and situations in a *constructive* retrieval of the church's heritage, Karl ventured in a remark
critiquing his brother's movement, "is itself in the long run the most
kerygmatic."[59] In addition to standing as a sort of intellectual caesura
for Rahner, the summer of 1938 was a professional one as well. After
having marched into Austria months earlier, the Nazis disbanded Innsbruck's theological faculty that July. Rahner's subsequent teaching at
the Jesuit college Sillgasse lasted only around a year before it too was
shut down, and Rahner retreated into work on the diocesan admin-
istrative staff in Vienna for most of the war, though he continued to
travel, teach, lecture, and publish.

54. Marcel Viller, *La spiritualité des premiers siècles chrétiens* (Paris: Bloud & Gay, 1930).
55. Neufeld, "Editionsbericht," xiv.
56. H. Rahner, "Eucharisticon fraternitatis," 896.
57. Hugo himself judges, "From 1938 onwards our theological paths parted ways" (ibid., 896).
58. See H. Rahner's *Eine Theologie der Verkündigung* (Freiberg: Herder, 1939); ET *A Theology of Proclamation* (New York: Herder & Herder, 1968).
59. "The Prospects for Dogmatic Theology," in *TI* 1:1–18, at 7, first published in 1954; cf. Vorgrimler,
Understanding Karl Rahner, 66.

Bibliographical Remarks

Rahner's most genuine and ardently pursued interests during this early and formative period are recorded in the publications and teaching which he undertook completely on his own initiative, activities which had no particular restrictions established externally for him. As we have just seen, these interests include prayer and spirituality, the theology of the fathers, the person of Christ, and grace. Having established the overarching timeline of this formative period from Rahner's time as a student through his initial course as a professor of theology, let us turn to Rahner's early publications. I will explore this portion of his bibliography in three "periods"; the second will consist entirely of Rahner's completed theological dissertation at Innsbruck (which will be considered in detail), and the other two will be divided chronologically around it. No book reviews will be explicitly considered. The first section will be exhaustive,[60] while the third "professional" period, which includes hundreds of entries, will selectively arranged to indicate some continuity with Rahner's earlier writings. This third period will come to a close with the 1940s, after which Rahner (at this point, a well-known figure) began including his writings in his *Theological Investigations* series.[61]

Student Essays and Publications

Rahner began writing and submitting publications early on. His first publication, at the age of 20 in 1924, concerned the theme of prayer and spirituality. This brief, two-page piece addressed "Why we need to pray" and was published in a monthly journal for German youth.[62] Rahner's next publication occurred eight years later, toward the end of his theological studies at Valkenburg. However, Rahner was actively writing in the interim period.

In 1928, on the occasion of their father's sixtieth birthday, the aspiring academics Hugo and Karl presented their father with the lone copy of a typewritten *Festschrift* prepared in his honor. Included within it are five essays by Karl, which Hugo describes and excerpts in his con-

---

60. That is, exhaustive with respect to works Rahner published. I will also consider some (though not all) of the unpublished works which he completed during this period and which have very recently been made available in *SW*.
61. As will be seen below, Rahner did end up retrieving and revising some of his very early articles for inclusion in later volumes of *TI*.
62. "Warum uns das Beten nottut," in *SW* 1:3–4.

tribution to a *Festschrift* for Karl on the latter's *own* sixtieth birthday.[63] Several of Karl's essays, completed by 1928, are direct forerunners to papers which he would eventually publish, as will be noted below. Others, which we will presently consider, appear not to have been developed any further.

The first essay in the 1928 *Festschrift* is entitled "History and Historical Knowledge in the Spirit of Thomistic Metaphysics."[64] At this point, Rahner had just completed his three years of philosophical studies at Feldkirch and Pullach, and it seems he had already immersed himself in the issue of knowledge in Thomas's metaphysics, on which he would eventually write his (both ill-fated and wildly successful) philosophy dissertation at Freiburg. In fact, Hugo refers to this 1928 piece as "a veritable prelude to the work which would follow, *Spirit in the World.*"[65] The essay emphasized the historical situatedness of the human person's spiritual life in what he would later call the "categorical" world, and also attested to the restless (indeed "transcendental") longing of that person for "the restful clarity" which is God himself.[66] Notably, this early expression of the self-transcending person coming to realization in the categorical world is expressed in undeniably Augustinian terms of a "restless heart" finding its rest in God.[67] This theme of longing for the clarity of God's self-revelation recurs in the second essay of the 1928 *Festschrift*, entitled "The Doctrine of Happiness in Aristotle and Thomas."[68]

The fourth essay, which brings Augustine explicitly into Rahner's

---

63. Hugo addresses Karl, "Perhaps you do not remember yourself any longer in the face of this first-born of your mind. May I therefore show it to you to prove, that even the later metaphysically-clarified beliefs of sixty-year-old scholars have their history and their youth? God always comes into this world only slowly and timidly" ("Eucharisticon Fraternitatis," 897).
64. "Geschichte und Geschichtserkenntnis im Geiste thomistischer Metaphysik" (ibid., 897–98). Included in *SW* 1:245–54.
65. Ibid., 898.
66. The excerpt cited by Hugo reads, "So the spiritual life of the human person 'occurs' in time. It 'is' slowly in the vicissitudes of the ages. An always-striving effort is possible for the human, a daily self-conversion, with all the hope and all the fear that such a word contains. She can die and become. So also is humanity interwoven into the eternal, restless changes of nature, until all *Geist* is received into the blessed unchangeableness of God, into the restful clarity of the eternal Spirit" (ibid.).
67. Cf. Augustine's famous prayer in the opening of his *Confessions*, trans. F.J. Sheed (Indianapolis: Hackett, 1993).
68. "Die Lehre von der Glückseligkeit bei Aristoteles und Thomas." Hugo includes an excerpt concerning Thomas's conception of the beatific vision: "In any case, this teaching shows how high St. Thomas's ideal of intellectual bliss is, and how stupid it would be to confuse with ideal with the pleasure of professors and philosophers. The Thomist *visio* contains much more than the *theoria* of Aristotle, all the personal, the near, the unique as it only can be in the blessed communion of Spirit with the beloved God. The human person longingly awaits his revelation: I pray that it be that which I so desire" ("Eucharisticon Fraternitatis," 898). Included in *SW* 1:255–73.

writings, is entitled "St. Augustine's Theory of Illumination."[69] As Hugo notes, this essay concerns "both the theology of the fathers as well as . . . metaphysical speculation" about human knowledge. In this essay, Karl Rahner writes that Augustine's understanding of illumination "leads him into the depths of his own soul, and to the one who he sought and found, whom we also seek. For it is eternally true, what constitutes the most profound meaning of St. Augustine's theory of illumination: Cognition means participation in the eternal Logos."[70] It is clear from the excerpts provided by Hugo that by 1928, Karl Rahner had developed interests in the church fathers and the metaphysics of human knowledge, interests which intersect with his ongoing themes of spirituality and the person of Christ.

Karl Rahner's publishing activity resumed in 1932 in his final years of studying theology at Valkenburg. Given the intense, independent schedule of patristic readings which Karl undertook at the outset of these studies, it is no surprise that these early publications demonstrate a commitment to the church fathers' world of thought, a commitment which his brother has said begat a genuine "love" for patristic theology.[71] Such an interest was by no means unique to Rahner. Indeed, the *nouvelle théologie* movement was gaining momentum in France as a reaction to the neo-Scholastic approach (increasingly viewed as stultifying) regnant in Catholic theology and was gaining followers in other parts of Europe. As Vorgrimler has noted, Hugo Rahner embraced this movement and "made important contacts in Louvain, Brussels and Paris" in connection with studies at the University of Bonn, which began in 1931 and were completed with a second thesis in 1934; these connections, Vorgrimler writes, "were very helpful for his brother Karl."[72]

Rahner's one publication from 1932 is in French, appearing in *Revue d' Ascétique et de Mystique* (RAM). This article, entitled "The Debut of a Doctrine of the Five Spiritual Senses in Origen," was included in shortened form in a later volume of Rahner's *Theological Investigations*.[73]

---

69. "Die Illuminationstheorie des heiligen Augustinus," in *SW* 1:277–304.
70. "Eucharisticon Fraternitatis," 898.
71. Reflecting on their later methodological parting of ways, Hugo writes, "At the beginning, from 1932 on, as the first entries of your bibliography prove, it looked as if you wanted to commit yourself to the wisdom of the fathers, and a final, even ripe fruit of this love of the church fathers is the reworking of M. Viller, *Aszese und Mystik in the Väterzeit* (1939)" ("Eucharisticon Fraternitatis," 896).
72. Vorgrimler, *Understanding Karl Rahner*, 65.
73. "Le début d'une doctrine des cinq sens spirituels chez Origène," *Revue d'Ascétique et de Mystique* 13 (1932), 113–145. An abridged version, "The 'Spiritual Senses' according to Origen," can be found in *TI* 16:81–103. The unabridged original can be found in *SW* 1:16–65.

However, it has a *predecessor* as well in the 1928 *Festschrift*, in a piece called "The Sources of the Doctrine of the Five Spiritual Senses."[74] In addition to generating the 1932 piece on Origen, this predecessor also provided the basis for another publication in *RAM* the very next year, entitled "The Doctrine of the 'Spiritual Senses' in the Middle Ages: Especially in St. Bonaventure."[75] Rahner's one other publication in 1933 is yet another piece on historical (in particular, patristic) Christian spirituality, "The Spiritual Doctrine of Evagrius Ponticus: Its Basic Structures."[76] This piece was not in *Revue d' Ascétique et de Mystique*, but in the similarly titled journal *Zeitschrift für Aszese und Mystik (ZAM)* out of Innsbruck, in which Rahner would also begin publishing frequently.[77]

As Rahner began his philosophical studies at Freiburg in 1934, he continued to publish historical studies on Christian spirituality. The first, "The Concept of 'Ecstasis' in Bonaventure" (published in *ZAM*) is largely excerpted (though now in German) from the previous year's piece on Bonaventure in *RAM*.[78] Another 1934 piece in *ZAM* is "The Meaning of Frequent Confessions in Devotion," which situates frequent confession within the more general sacramental movement of God within the world and identifies it as a means for developing one's spiritual life.[79] Rahner maintained a keen interest in the topic of frequent confession, which recurred as a theme in the very last entry of *Theological Investigations*.[80] Another minor publication from 1934 on sacramental thought is "On the Sacrament of Charity," which occurred in two brief pieces.[81] Rahner also published a short piece in *RAM* this year, entitled "Jesus' Sacred Heart in Origen?"[82] According to Hugo, this arti-

---

74. "Die Quellen der Lehre von den fünf geistlichen Sinnen," in *SW* 1:305–335. Hugo writes of this piece, "it grapples immediately the problem of God and the world with evidence that the highest and most spiritual, the divine and its action on the soul, can be best expressed only with the images of immediate sense-knowledge: 'Mystical experience is always described with images of immediate sense-perception'" ("Eucharisticon Fraternitatis," 898–99).

75. "La doctrine des 'sens spirituels' au Moyen-Age: En particulier chez St-Bonaventure," *Revue d'Ascétique et de Mystique* 14 (1933), 263–99, published in *SW* 1:82–147. An abridged version, "The Doctrine of the 'Spiritual Senses' in the Middle Ages," can be found in *TI* 16:104–34.

76. "Die geistliche Lehre des Evagrius Ponticus. In ihren Grundzügen dargestellt," *Zeitschrift für Aszese und Mystik* 8 (1933), 21–38. This material was revisited in M. Viller, *Aszese und Mystik in der Väterzeit*, ed. and trans. K. Rahner (Freiburg i.Br.: Herder, 1939). The article itself can be found in *SW* 1:66–81.

77. This journal would eventually be renamed *Geist und Leben*.

78. "Der Begriff der ecstasis bei Bonaventura," *Zeitschrift für Aszese und Mystik* 9 (1934), 1–19, published in *SW* 1:148–63.

79. "Vom Sinn der häufigen Andachtsbeicht," *Zeitschrift für Aszese und Mystik* 9 (1934), 323–36. Included as "The Meaning of Frequent Confessions of Devotion," in *TI* 3:177–89.

80. "The Status of the Sacrament of Reconciliation," in *TI* 23:205–18, especially 209–13, 216–18.

81. "Vom Sakrament der Nächstenliebe," in *Kirchenanzeiger St. Michael* (Munich) 5, no. 37 (9–15 Sept. 1934), 151f and 5, no. 38 (16–23 Sept. 1934), 154f. Also published in *SW* 1:170–73.

cle is an expanded version of Karl's third essay in the 1928 *Festschrift* for his father.[83] Rahner would return to the relationship between Origen and the Sacred Heart in his dissertation, the basis of which was likely written by or being written at the time of this publication.[84] Indeed, the conclusion of this brief article and that of his dissertation bear remarkable similarities.[85]

Hugo and Karl Rahner teamed up in 1935 to co-author an article on Jesuit devotional theology, entitled "On the Grace of Prayer in the Society of Jesus, According to Jerónimo Nadal, S.J."[86] Although explicit co-authorship between the two brothers was very infrequent,[87] Hugo has described this period as marked by regular collaborative work between them. He and Karl had a "shared concern to engage the problem of 'God in the world' as realized in the theology of the holy father Ignatius," and this publication stands as a "first fruit of this effort."[88]

Aside from a review, Rahner's other publications from 1935 consist of three homiletic articles published consecutively within the span of

82. "'Coeur de Jésus' chez Origene?," *Révue d'Ascetique et de Mystique* 15 (1934), 171–74. The German version is available in *SW* 1:165–69.
83. "Your third essay argues that Origen does not come as a witness for the question of thought pertaining to the Sacred Heart, and it then appeared in expanded form in a 1934 essay, as your bibliography demonstrates" ("Eucharisticon Fraternitatis," 898).
84. *E latere Christi*, 32: "Now, what is the symbolic meaning which John saw in the outstreaming of blood and water from the pierced side of Christ? Following the early Origen, the answer is not too difficult. The Messiah is indeed according to his own words the Source of living water. From his 'heart,' his interior flows the stream of the Spirit. The source of the Spirit, however, can only be the Messiah lifted onto the cross, the 'glorified' Messiah. He is source of the water and the spirit only in the blood. That was why blood and water streams from the pierced heart of the crucified Redeemer." Cf. 47, 54–55, and Rahner's concluding remarks on 83: "So when we seek in the patristic period an analogue or traces of a of our Sacred Heart devotion, we must not mechanically search for texts in which the Heart of Jesus somehow mentioned. This method leads nowhere. We must instead ask whether the early Christians had a *Symbol* in which everything that they knew of the redeeming love of God was summed up in an object of their devotion (whether this *Symbol* was already the object of a special adoration is another question). But this was for them the pierced side of Jesus."
85. Compare the conclusion of *E latere Christi* (cited in the previous note) to this article's concluding remarks: "But if, in our text, Origen does not employ the same word 'Sacred Heart of Jesus', it remains true, however, that the passage in question reflects corresponding patristic ideas which are, in some manner, ideas underlying our modern devotion to Jesus' Sacred Heart. For the fathers, Jesus Christ was always the flowing spring of the water of grace. It is from his pierced side that these rivers of grace flow, in which humans draw the sacraments, and from there the emergence of the holy church, our virgin mother, the second Eve, issues from the side of the second Adam. And it is from this side that John, the prophet, drew the mysteries of his sublime doctrine. Thus, for the fathers, the pierced side of Christ was a lively symbol of the Savior's redeeming love for his spouse, whom he sanctifies by the blood and water which sprung forth from the wound of his heart" ("Coeur de Jésus' chez Origene?", 173–74).
86. "Über die Gnade des Gebetes in der Gesellschaft Jesu. Nach P.Hieronymus Nadal S.J.," *Mitteilungen aus den deutschen Provinzen [der Gesellschaft Jesu] (Eupen)* 13 (1935), 399–411.
87. The next item of Rahner's bibliography co-authored with Hugo, *Prayers for Meditation* (New York: Herder and Herder, 1962), occurs more than 20 years later (*Gebete der Einkehr* (Salzburg: Otto Müller), 1958).
88. "Eucharisticon Fraternitatis," 896.

about a month that fall. The first is "On the Feast of the Lord's Transfiguration."[89] The only figure quoted in this homiletic piece is Augustine. In it, Rahner discusses the transfiguration in terms of Jesus fully revealing himself as the locus of human "union with God."[90] Continuing, he makes several remarks which anticipate (or, at this point, perhaps echo) themes in his dissertation about Jesus as "Source of the Spirit," which is poured out from his pierced side upon believers, sanctifying them.[91]

Three weeks later, a second homiletic piece from Rahner, on "The Feast of St. Augustine," was published.[92] The essay focuses on two main Augustinian ideas. The first is the notion of the human "restless heart," which, recall, Rahner wrote on in his first entry in the 1928 *Festschrift*, an entry Hugo called a "veritable prelude" to *Spirit in the World*. The second is Augustine's directive to "put on the Lord Jesus Christ." An excerpt from this article is worth quoting at length:

We only discover God in Christ, for no one comes to the Father except through him. Only he knows the way, the truth, and the life, because he is these things himself. . . . We approach God, the rest of our restless hearts, only through God become man. Only if we believe him and in him, love him with our whole heart, are joined to him by grace, are made living members of his mysterious body, the church, healed and divinized by the life of the Head that streams down upon us, his body, in the sacraments, only then are we in the truth and in God. So Augustine lived and taught: Draw near to the Lord Jesus Christ.[93]

This excerpt, and the article as a whole, brings together themes (namely, restless hearts and the mystical body of Christ) at the heart of Rahner's two dissertations from the following year, *Spirit in the World* and *E latere Christi*. In it, we witness Rahner appropriate several Augustinian (and, more generally, patristic) ideas as his own: Christ as *in*

89. "Zum Fest der Verklärung des Herrn (6. August)," *Kirchen-Anzeiger St. Michael* (Munich) 6, no. 32 (4–11 Aug. 1935), 130–33. Included as "The Transfiguration of the Lord (6 August)," in *The Great Church Year: The Best of Karl Rahner's Homilies, Meditations, and Sermons* (New York: Crossroad, 1993), 340–42.
90. "Union with God, which Jesus otherwise holds hidden in the ultimate depths of his soul, now fills up all the chambers of his soul, it embraces his body, drawing it, too, into the blessedness of God's light and God's unity" ("The Transfiguration of the Lord," *The Great Church Year*, 342).
91. "[Jesus] is the wellspring and the plentitude of every Spirit at work in the prophets and presently to be poured forth upon all who believe in him . . . [A]ll redemption and all Holy Spirit takes its departure from the cross" (ibid.).
92. "28. August (Fest des hl. Augustinus)," *Kirchen-Anzeiger St. Michael* (Munich) 6, no. 35 (25 Aug. – 1 Sept. 1935), 142–43. Included as "Feast of St. Augustine (28 August)," in *The Great Church Year*, 353–55.
93. "Feast of St. Augustine," *The Great Church Year*, 354.

his person salvation (the Way, Truth, and Life), incarnational soteriology, divinization, and participation in the body and person of Christ by being joined to it as "members."

Rahner's third essay, which appeared in publication the following week and which I will not discuss here, is "On the Angels."[94] I will also pass over Rahner's Freiburg dissertation, *Spirit in the World*, at this point due to the scope of this biographical/bibliographical overview discussed above. Examinations and summaries of this important work, which has received abundant attention, are already widely available in Rahner literature in English.[95]

In this overview of Rahner's writings prior to his theology dissertation, we have seen Rahner's fascination with and dedication to (especially Jesuit) spirituality, a commitment which has rightly generated a renewed appreciation in recent years for how this spirituality shapes the whole of his theology from the beginning. These years also show Rahner's genuine philosophical interests, especially concerning the metaphysics of knowledge, well before his time at Freiburg. But together with these widely recognized interests is that of the theology of the church fathers, particularly Origen and St. Augustine. In the topic of the Jesus's Sacred Heart, Rahner's interests in spirituality and historical theology clearly overlap, as devotion concerning Jesus's person intersects with patristic soteriological thought regarding that person as salvation itself, to whom we are joined to realize union with God. This intersection comes to a height in Rahner's dissertation at Innsbruck, which we will now consider at length.

E latere Christi [From the Side of Christ]:
The Origin of the Church as Second Eve
from the Side of Christ the Second Adam.
A Study of the Typological Meaning of Jn 19:34

Most references to "Rahner's dissertation" which one encounters in theological conversation concern his philosophical work at Freiburg; as it was mentioned at the outset of the chapter, many biographical

94. "Von den Engeln," *Kirchen-Anzeiger St. Michael* (Munich) 6, no. 36 (1–8 Sept 1935), 146–47. Included as "The Angels (2 October)," in *The Great Church Year*, 356–58.
95. Among the many short summaries of *Spirit in the World* are Vorgrimler, *Understanding Karl Rahner*, 59–62; McCool (ed.), *A Rahner Reader*, xvi–xviii. A more extended treatment can be found in Louis Roberts, "Philosophical Prolegomenon," in *The Achievement of Karl Rahner* (New York: Herder and Herder, 1967), 7–51, Sheehan's *Karl Rahner: The Philosophical Foundations* (especially 135–317), and the first two chapters of Fritz's *Karl Rahner's Theological Aesthetics*.

accounts of Rahner's life omit any mention of *E latere Christi* at all. Even Rahner himself has downplayed the value of the work, calling it "a small, miserable, but by former standards sufficient theological dissertation."[96] On the one hand, Rahner, who has also claimed not to have any significant impact on the Second Vatican Council, has a tendency to understate the value of his own work.[97] As it has been noted above, the Innsbruck faculty assessed Rahner's dissertation in terms quite different from "small, miserable, but by former standards sufficient," calling the project "not only suitable as a doctoral dissertation according to the present applicable standards . . . , but it goes far beyond the norm for such work and is . . . ready for publication."[98] On the other hand, his later lack of enthusiasm may be rooted in more than just modesty.

Rahner's reservations about the value of *E latere Christi* later on in life might be, at least in part, attributed to a pair of factors. The first has to do with the dissertation's central, typological idea that the church (styled as the "Second Eve") originated from the pierced side of ("sleeping") Jesus (the "Second Adam"). At this point in his career, Rahner seems to have been fascinated with Johannine thought, and indeed, the birth of the church roughly around this time of Christ's death makes considerable sense within a Johannine framework, in which Christ's death, resurrection, ascension, and giving of the Spirit are largely collapsed into a singular event of glorification.[99] However, later in his career, Rahner seemed more inclined to relate his "dogmatic" theological reflections to contemporary biblical scholarship of the time[100] and less to particular frameworks like that of John. Most his-

96. In an interview during the mid-1970s, Rahner said of his transition from Freiburg to Innsbruck in 1936, "A spectacular transition from philosophy into theology did not occur, not on that account, since I myself even during my religious studies in Valkenburg was really interested in theological questions, over all in spiritual theology and religious history, in patristic mysticism and also Bonaventure, and also produced a small, miserable, but by former standards sufficient theological dissertation" ("Gnade also Mitte menschlicher Existenz. Ein Gespräch mit und über Karl Rahner aus Anlaß seines 70. Geburtstages," in *Herder-Korrespondenz* 28 [1974], 77–92, at 79f.).

97. "I must say that I did not exercise any great influence at the [Second Vatican] Council. To say anything else is just not true. There were so many *periti* and collaborators at the Council that no one, except the pope himself and the moderators, could be said to influence the Council in any significant way. It is true that I attended almost all of the meetings of the Theological Commission and that I collaborated with the other theologians. As you know the most important schemata of this commission were on the Church and revelation. I was a member of certain subcommissions that worked on these, but my contribution was not great" (*Karl Rahner in Dialogue*, 20). For more on Rahner's understatement regarding his contribution to Vatican II (a phenomenon impacted by more than just humility), see Wassilowsky, *Universales Heilssakrament Kirche*, 102.

98. Batlogg, "Editionsbericht: Teil A," xx.

99. "The death-resurrection-ascension of Jesus is his glorification (7:39; 12:16, 23; 13:31)" (George Eldon Ladd, *A Theology of the New Testament*, Rev. Ed. [Grand Rapids: Eerdmans, 1993], 311).

100. See Peter Schineller et al, "A Changing Ecclesiology in a Changing Church: A Symposium on Development in the Ecclesiology of Karl Rahner," in *Theological Studies* 38, no. 4 (1977), 736–62, at 745.

torical critical scholars, Rahner writes in *Foundations of Christian Faith*, recognize that "something like the constitution of the church is found soon after *Easter*."[101] Even more than this particular issue of the about the time of the church's origin, Rahner's manner of utilizing the Bible in these early years may have tempered his enthusiasm for the dissertation.

A second factor may be a later hesitancy about his bold historical undertaking in *E latere Christi* to demonstrate that this particular typological idea about the emergence of the church from Christ's pierced side can be traced back to the preaching of the apostles themselves. This claim, which occurs in multiple, prominent places in the dissertation, about the very words of the apostles, is a difficult one to substantiate. Moreover, undertaking such a task may reflect the influence of a kind of Catholic dogmatic positivism (i.e., anything authoritative said by the church and not explicitly in the Bible came directly from the apostles, if not from the mouth of Christ himself!) which abounded during this largely "anti-modernist" period. While Rahner was certainly no warrior against "modernism," he did receive a very traditional, neo-Scholastic theological training that impacted his method for doing theology, and this environment may, at least in part, help to explain Rahner's attempt to make this historical claim. Although such an endeavor may have been relatively routine in the 1930s, it sounds somewhat bizarre to the later Catholic ear, including, quite likely, that of Rahner. Whatever they may be, Rahner's reasons for later belittling of *E latere Christi* seem to go beyond just modesty. Even ten years before Rahner's remarks in the mid-1970s cited above, his brother Hugo referred to their dissertations, "to this day buried in the faculty archive," as "probably belong[ing] to the writings about which we smile and count among the 'prehistory' of our scholarship."[102]

Nevertheless, even if the Rahner brothers considered *E latere Christi* to be a "prehistorical" effort which preceded Karl's more developed theology, it still holds great value for understanding his thought. After all, the theme of "God in the world" which might best summarize the whole of Rahner's scholarly corpus was, as Hugo reports, already a central interest of Karl's back in 1922.[103] If the formative beginnings of Rahner's intellectual trajectories are detectable some 14 years prior to the completion of *E latere Christi*, this early project, "pre-historic" as

---

101. *FCF*, 327, emphasis added.
102. Hugo Rahner, "Eucharisticon Fraternitatis," 896.
103. Ibid.

one may consider it to be, certainly deserves attention as a formative moment itself. Its importance is even more evident when one considers the length of time Rahner was involved in this project; recall, Karl was soliciting bibliographical material on "the Ecclesia ex latere Christi" from Hugo six years earlier in June 1930. In addition, *E latere Christi* was undertaken for entirely independent reasons while Rahner was completing numerous actual requirements during his formal theological and philosophical training. Even taking into account what come across later on as minor embarrassments, the sheer energy which Rahner spontaneously invested into this project attests to the value it harbors for understanding the history and even early foundation of his thinking.

And yet, relative to the enormous body of secondary literature on Karl Rahner, very sparse attention has been dedicated to *E latere Christi*, which seems typically to have been regarded (inasmuch as it is regarded at all) simply as a degree requirement.[104] A testimony to this dearth of interest is the fact that *E latere Christi* was only published in 1999 (and even then not as a standalone publication, but within Rahner's "Collected Works" series). In the introductory remarks to volume three of these collected works, Andreas Batlogg explicitly laments that *E latere Christi* has generally been ignored, dismissed as randomly chosen, and only marginally related to his later work.[105] Karl Neufeld shares Batlogg's complaint, asserting that Rahner's interests motivating *E latere Christi*, a work which was "more than just a ticket of admission into academia," serve as a "substratum" underlying parts of his later work, even if Rahner did not openly identify them as such.[106]

---

104. The modest attention it *has* received focuses heavily on the work's brief conclusion, which lays a (fascinating) agenda for Rahner's future work. Joseph Wong's short analysis (*Logos-Symbol*, 40–45) and the even briefer remarks of James Buckley ("On Being a Symbol: An Appraisal of Karl Rahner" *Theological Studies* 40, no. 3 (1979), 453–73, at 458–59) and Bernd Jochen Hilberath and Bernhard Nitsche ("Das Symbol also vermittelnde Kategorie zwischen Transzendentalität und Geschichte in der transzendentalen Theologie Karl Rahners," in *Erfahrung-Geschichte-Identität: Schnittpunkt von Philosophie und Theologie*, ed. M. Laarmann (Freiburg i.Br.: Herder, 1997), 239–60, at 242, 258) consider Rahner's early references to *Symbol* in *E latere Christi*. A. Callahan's treatment is oriented toward Rahner's interest in devotion to Jesus' Sacred Heart (*Karl Rahner's Spirituality of the Pierced Heart*, 2–9). A. Batlogg's interest, at least for his own (now published) dissertation, lies in the soteriological import of the events occurring over the course of Jesus' earthly life (*Die Mysterien des Lebens Jesu bei Karl Rahner*, 288–99). Rahner's intense engagement with historical theology, especially that of the fathers, which comprises the majority of the dissertation, has elicited little interest.

105. Batlogg, "Editionsbericht: Teil A," xxxii.

106. *E latere Christi*, Neufeld writes, "represents more than just a ticket of admission into the academic arena. Rahner has developed and freely chosen this point of emphasis of his work; no one invited or compelled him. The free choice of the theme of the theological dissertation and hence the further interest in the thinking of the church fathers up through *Aszese und Mystik* allows a deeper bond to come to light, which was long ago established to the end even without explicit references

E latere Christi: Introduction

On the lookout for themes in continuity with Rahner's later soteriology, let us turn to E latere Christi itself.[107] The central idea (I will refer
to this idea as "Rahner's theme") around which the dissertation is constructed is a typological one: Just as Eve was formed from the side of
sleeping Adam, so the church (the "Second Eve") originated from the
pierced side of Christ (the "Second Adam") "sleeping" on the cross.
Adam and Eve are thus "types" [Vorbilder] of Christ and the church
(antitypes).[108] Although E latere Christi, with its focus on the church as
the Second Eve, may very well be described as an "ecclesiology" dissertation, it could also be accurately described as a dissertation on
typology, on biblical exegesis, on the development of preaching and
doctrine, and also on soteriology and the person on Christ (the Second Adam), with some brief forays into pneumatology as well. The dissertation's ecclesiology is not focused so much on the church in se as
a phenomenon, but upon the relationship of the body of Christians to
the person of Christ through the Holy Spirit, as expressed in biblical
terms.[109]

In his introduction, which spans just two and a half pages, Rahner
explains that when he uses the words "type" or "typology," especially
concerning the event of Christ's pierced side, he intends to convey a
twofold meaning. The first facet is that a typological moment like the
piercing is deeply symbolisch, insofar as this moment demonstrates an
intimate, symbolisch interrelationship between Christ (the Source), the
Spirit (the Renewer), the church (the renewed); the second facet is the
more temporal type/fulfillment relationship between Adam and Eve in
the OT and Christ and the church in the NT.[110] Although Rahner does

and citations – established as a substratum in places, where they are not explicitly and themati-
cally named" (Neufeld, "Editionsbericht," xiv).
107. Hilberath and Nitsche explicitly note the soteriological import of E latere Christi: "Rahner's theological dissertation analyzes the interpretation of John 19:34, presenting the image of Christ's
wounded side in the theology of the fathers. This theology read the outflow of water and blood as
the birth of the church, which is completed anew in the sacraments of the baptism (water) and the
Eucharist (blood). Simultaneously, the theology of the early church understood the emergence of
the Church typologically, placing it parallel to the emergence of Eve from the side of Adam. Just
as Eve, the mother of the living, was formed from the rib of Adam, so the church is born from the
opened side of the 'New Adam,' raised on the cross. Rahner is interested in this moment first with
respect to the anticipatory function of the Symbol, and secondly in its soteriological relevance"
("Das Symbol als vermittelnde Kategorie," 241–42).
108. E latere Christi, 9.
109. In one of the dissertation's opening sentences, Rahner writes, "From the pierced side of the Crucified flows the living stream of the Spirit, which creates humanity anew, able to be born again to
the church. For all who are born again in the waters of baptism, have one life, they form a mysterious unity, a body, the church" (ibid.).

not elaborate here on the first facet (the second is fairly standard), he returns to the idea of *Symbol* throughout the dissertation, especially in its conclusion.

As Rahner closes his introduction, he asserts that although his theme is not articulated explicitly in the NT, it is "biblical" insofar as it can be traced back to apostolic preaching; it is present in the NT in the mode of an idea of which John is "reminding" his readers in John 19:34.[111] In order to better understand this theme, Rahner will turn to the early church and its exegesis of John 19:34. These patristic theologians, he argues, remained within the (Johannine) world of thought which produced John 19:34, so we ought to read *it* in light of *them*; the fathers do not only build upon it, but also provide a window back to it.[112]

E latere Christi: Chapter 1—Biblical Foundations

Although the Bible itself does not explicitly contain Rahner's theme, it does contain what Rahner identifies as the "essential elements" of which the theme is composed. Rahner identifies these elements by exploring Pauline and Johannine writings in the NT, in that order. Paul's use of "types" is well known,[113] especially his appeal to Christ as the "New Adam" (Rom 5:13, 1 Cor 15:45–47).[114] Echoing his introduction, Rahner insists that "type," as Paul uses it, indicates a robust theological (even *symbolisch*) correspondence between two realities.[115] This is especially true of the Adam/Christ typology, which centers on the way in which the one relates to the many or to all. As Rahner exegetes Romans 5, "One man stands against the rest of humanity in a way that the destiny of all humankind hangs on his conduct"; he continues, "the fact that one particular individual can have such a significant influence on all other people, must somehow be rooted in the nature of this individual, in a deeper-lying relationship of this individual to the rest of

---

110. "'Typological' is meant in a double sense: [1.] the act by which the blood and water emerged from the side of Christ is a *Symbol*, that the church as founded in the Holy Spirit draws its origin from the Crucified, insofar as he as such (blood) is the Source of the Spirit (water). And insofar as the emergence of blood and water is the *Symbol* of the emergence of the church, the second Eve, it is [2.] the fulfillment of that type (*typos*) which was included in the formation of Eve from the side of Adam" (ibid., 10).

111. Ibid. John 19:34 states, "one of the soldiers pierced his side with a spear, and at once blood and water came out."

112. *E latere Christi*, 10–11.

113. Rahner mentions Gal 4:21, 24; 1 Cor 5:7, 10:1–6, 11; 2 Cor 3:13–18.

114. *E latere Christi*, 12.

115. Ibid., 13–14.

humanity."[116] Such a "nature," according to which the one truly represents the many, is that of the first and second Adams.

Rahner's attention to strands of representative Christology in Paul becomes even sharper when he shifts to explicitly soteriological considerations. Rahner underlines that Christ's restoration of humanity is not just the result of his actions, but is rooted in the Christ-event itself, in Christ's *being* the incarnate Word of God. Still reflecting on Romans 5, he writes, "Christ is ancestor and head of all the spiritually living and not only through his redemptive activity, but rather by his very nature as the God-man, and as such he shares, as new life-source, the supernatural life with all people, so that this life can only be found in him."[117] Christ constitutes the very *locus* of supernatural life (i.e., salvation), which is realized in our incorporation into his body (i.e., the church). Paul's preferred way of speaking about the church is always in terms which are intimately related to Christ himself, either as his body[118] or in conjugal imagery as his bride.[119] While Paul does not go so far as to name the church the "Second Eve," Rahner writes, the idea is latent in his theology, which knows the church to be the bride of the Second Adam.[120] The place of Christ's wounded side, however is entirely absent from Paul.[121]

Unlike in Paul, typology is not an object of explicit reflection in Johannine theology.[122] Nevertheless, Rahner argues, typological thinking is operative (e.g., the brazen serpent, bread of life and manna, the Passover lamb, etc.). Again echoing his introduction, Rahner insists that Johannine types do not simply relate past (OT) and newer (NT) events, but have a symbolic, soteriological significance: "According to John, the individual events of the Jesus' life themselves have a *symbolischen* sense, are expressions of the fundamental relationships in the Reign of God and redemption."[123] The events described by John which fulfill OT types also effect human salvation in a particularly sym-

116. Ibid., 14–15.
117. Ibid., 15. Rahner evaluates 1 Corinthians 15 similarly, saying of v. 22 that "Both, Adam and Christ, stand to determine the fates of all" (ibid.), and of vv. 48–49: "the two Adams bequeath their essential properties, which arise out of their origin (1 Cor 15:47), to the people. . . . The first Adam is thus the ancestor of the 'physical/natural' being of humankind, while Christ, the final Adam, is the origin of the 'spiritual' mode of human being. . . . Both transmit to all of their descendents the life that they themselves possess" (ibid., 16).
118. Ibid.
119. Ibid., 16–21.
120. Ibid., 18, 21.
121. Ibid., 21.
122. Rahner considers the Fourth Gospel, Johannine epistles, and Revelation under this "Johannine" category.
123. *E latere Christi*, 22.

bolic mode. Rahner explains, "Jesus' miracles are for John clearly not seen merely as 'signs' [σημια] in the general sense, as 'notifications' [Anzeigen] of his messianic mission in general, but rather they are also Symbole for certain aspects of the messianic efficacy of Jesus in particular."[124] (For our purposes, Rahner's early distinction here between "signs" and Symbole, only the former of which stand as "notifications," is particularly important, insofar as it anticipates the distinction between Vertretungssymbole and Realsymbole in "Theology of the Symbol" two decades later and also militates against reading his soteriological role for Christ as God's "Notifier."[125])

The majority of Rahner's treatment of the Fourth Gospel centers around two loci, 7:35-37 and 19:34-35. The first of these loci concerns the idea of Christ as the "Source of the Spirit" or the "Fount of Life" (fons vitae).[126] Rahner argues that John's account of Christ's piercing in chapter 19, which depicts water flowing forth from his side, is directly foreshadowed earlier in chapter 7. The interconnection of water, the Spirit, and Jesus Christ permeate the Gospel of John.[127] Christ promises to give the gift of God himself in outpouring water (John 4:10, 14),[128] Christ invites those who thirst to come to him (John 7:37),[129] for his water is the Holy Spirit (John 7:39).[130]

In this regard, John 7:38 is especially important: "Let the one who believes in me drink. As the Scripture has said, 'Out of his heart shall flow rivers of living water.'[131]" As Rahner notes, the "his" (αυτου) is ambiguous, although it is usually understood to refer to "the one who believes in me."[132] Rahner, however, vigorously argues that John intended for it to refer to Christ.[133] He reasons, "When Jesus says . . .

124. Ibid., 22–23.
125. See Chapter 2 and Chapter 1 above for these (respective) points.
126. Notably, this second descriptor was the title of Hugo Rahner's own dissertation at Innsbruck. The interplay of the two brothers' research is readily apparent in this section of E latere Christi.
127. "Since the gift of the Spirit, which is the means of salvation (Acts 2:16, 33, 38), appears as a gift of water, thus the Messiah must give this water, he must give this living water to all to drink, he must himself be the Source of the living Spirit-water" (E latere Christi, 25, emphasis original).
128. "Jesus answered her, 'If you knew the gift of God, and who it is that is saying to you, "Give me a drink", you would have asked him, and he would have given you living water. . . . [T]hose who drink of the water that I will give them will never be thirsty. The water that I will give will become in them a spring of water gushing up to eternal life.'"
129. "On the last day of the festival, the great day, while Jesus was standing there, he cried out, 'Let anyone who is thirsty come to me.'"
130. "Now he said this about the Spirit, which believers in him were to receive; for as yet there was no Spirit, because Jesus was not yet glorified."
131. " . . . Ποταμοι εκ της κοιλιας αυτου ρευσουσιν.'"
132. I.e., "Out of the believer's heart shall flow rivers of living water." (This is the NRSV translation.)
133. I.e., "Out of Christ's heart shall flow rivers of living water." Cf. the "Rivers of Living Water" icon by Mickey McGrath, which appears on the cover of this book.

that one should come to him in order to drink, he describes himself as the Source of the living water (7:37). If now Scripture,[134] which leads Jesus to affirm this idea, explains the *faithful* as the Source of the living water, it would generate an unlikely leap in thought, and it would introduce a thought which would be entirely external to the previous thinking of his listeners and Jesus' words."[135] Since *God himself* is the source of the Spirit and thus human salvation, Rahner concludes, "Jesus can rightly claim, as Scripture says, that rivers of living water will emanate from the interior of the *Messiah* (as the Representative [*Stellvertreter*] of God and the Mediator of God's gifts)."[136]

Rahner links this claim in John 7 about Christ as the Source of the Spirit (*fons vitae*) to the piercing episode in chapter 19, during which water and blood flow from the wounded side of the Crucified, via Christ's "heart" [κοιλιας], out of which the living water to said to flow (John 7:38). The likely Hebrew ancestors of this words, as well as their Greek, German, and English counterparts, "have, in addition in addition to their physiological meaning of 'belly,' 'womb,' and 'bowels,' a common, distinct spiritual sense: the 'inside' of a person, the 'heart' as the seat of the soul and of private spiritual stirrings."[137] This double sense of "heart" ought to shape our understandings of both John 7:38 and 19:34, in which case "the 'heart of the Messiah is the source of the stream of living water. From his heart pours out the water of salvation, from which we should draw in joy (cf. Isa 12:3)."[138] In Rahner's understanding, Jesus's words about his heart as the source of living water in John 7:37 are brought to fulfillment in the piercing of his side, out of which John reports water to have flowed (19:34).[139]

---

134. Rahner states that the "Scripture" to which Jesus alludes most likely refers to *God* pouring out the gift of water: Prov 10:11 ("The mouth of the righteous is a fountain of life, but the mouth of the wicked conceals violence."), Prov 18:4 ("The words of the mouth are deep waters; the fountain of wisdom is a gushing stream."), and Sir 21:13 ("The knowledge of the wise will increase like a flood, and their counsel like a life-giving spring.").

135. *E latere Christi*, 26.

136. Ibid. It is clear here that Rahner's (clearly favorable) use of the term *Stellvertreter* does not connote the idea of a proxy or substitute, but rather one who participates intimately in *and in fact is* the represented "other." This usage, which demonstrates how intimately linked the ideas of *das Realsymbol* and (authentic) representation are for Rahner even early on, accords with his qualified approval of the term in his mature years (see chapter 1 above).

137. Ibid., 29.

138. Ibid.

139. Like "typology," Rahner's idea of "fulfillment" is not simply a past-future correspondence, but a profound *symbolisch* relationship. "The outflowing of blood and water from the side of Jesus is thus a symbolic [*symbolische*] fulfillment of the prophecy which Jesus gave in Jn 7:38, according to which from his 'heart' the stream of living water will flow, that, as John notes the same, only from the glorified Messiah on the cross could be *realized*" (ibid., 33, emphasis added). That is, Christ's identity as the *Fons Vitae* in fact comes to pass fully precisely in the piercing of his side.

Rahner also links the flow of blood in 19:34 to Jesus's earlier words. In John 7:39,[140] Jesus explains that the gift of the Spirit (i.e., water from the heart of the Messiah) can only occur subsequent to Christ's glorification (i.e., his being 'lifted up' on the cross). Christ's bloody glorification/crucifixion is bound up inextricably with the *symbolisch* fulfillment of his being the cleansing Source of the Spirit, both in John 7:38–39 ("rivers", "glorified") and John 19:34 ("water", "blood"). Rahner estimates that John strongly married the "blood" and "water" components of his *fons vitae* thinking in order to ward off a restrictive focus on Christ's baptism (to the exclusion of his crucifixion) as soteriological noteworthy, a focus advocated by some Gnostic groups.[141] Thus, the water from Jesus's side ought not to be understood exclusively or even principally in terms of baptism, but even more fundamentally as the Holy Spirit, as grace itself.[142]

Rahner concludes the chapter by noting that the *fons vitae* thinking of John 7:37–39 and 19:34–35 stands as a central component of his typological theme about the Second Eve emerging from the side of the Second Adam. John's *fons vitae Symbol*-typology, together with Paul's typology of Christ as the New Adam and his bride, together provide all of the "elements" of which Rahner's theme is composed. However, explicit articulation of the theme itself only occurs in the fathers. Did the fathers then, Rahner asks, build upon these Johannine and Pauline elements to construct the theme for the first time, or were they rather restating an idea which, John particularly, presumed his readers to know? In his subsequent chapters, Rahner sets out to argue for the latter.

E latere Christi: Chapter 2—
The Patristic Literature Up to the Mid-Third Century

There is about a century-long gap, Rahner estimates, between the Fourth Gospel (c. 90 CE) and an extant record of the first full-fledged articulation of Rahner's theme by Tertullian (*De Anima* c. 200 CE). In

---

140. "Now [Jesus] said this about the Spirit, which believers in him were to receive; for as yet there was no Spirit, because Jesus was not yet glorified."

141. *E latere Christi*, 34. Rahner, almost certainly relying on Irenaeus (cf. *AH* III.11.1) specifically posits John to have been countering the thought of a Gnostic by the name of Cerinthus. Rahner sees the effort to combat this thinking in other Johannine literature as well, e.g., 1 John 5:6, 1:7b, and 2:2).

142. "From the wounded side of the Messiah flows, with the blood, the sign of the redemptive suffering, also the water, the *Symbol* of the outpouring of the Spirit. . . . So we need to think about water from the wounded side of Jesus not exclusively in terms of baptism, but rather as the 'Holy Spirit,' as grace in general" (*E latere Christi*, 35).

his second chapter, Rahner seeks to show how the biblical "elements" for his theme were transmitted and developed during this intervening period. Rahner's emphasis, once again, is on the transmission of these elements, which he believes to already have formed a completed version of his theme during the time of apostolic preaching, a version which was repeated within a broad, typological oral tradition.[143] Elements which Rahner seems to think are apostolic in origin, but only recorded during this intervening period, include the idea of Adam as a prophet[144] as well as the theme's "sleeping" motif (Eve emerges while Adam sleeps in the garden; the church emerges as Christ "sleeps" on the cross).[145]

Although the "element" of Christ as the Second Adam is quite clear during this intervening period, Rahner struggles to demonstrate the element of the church as the Second Eve, which is much more inchoate in this early patristic literature. Rahner cites language about the church as bride, virgin, wife and mother in a host of these writers,[146] but the actual descriptor "Second Eve" remains rather implicit, entailed by (but not specified within) their works.[147] Irenaeus presents an especially interesting challenge, as he appears to identify Mary, rather than the church, as the "New Eve" in AH III.22.4.[148] In fact, Rahner does not mention this passage, but focuses rather on Irenaeus's writings about the church as Christ's bride,[149] and in a footnote, argues that other Irenaean passages about "rebirth" and a "virgin" better correspond to the church than to Mary.[150] The inchoate nature of the

143. Rahner ventures that "the NT types are not only the foundation of the patristic doctrine of types, but rather only scattered testimony to a much richer, typology of oral tradition existing from the beginning, so that one could speak of types without the use of the NT." Rahner continues, citing examples: "where Adam appears as a type, immediately equality–relations between Adam and Christ are worked out which are missing in Paul. So, for Irenaeus (AH III.21.10; Epid. 32) Adam, in his creation, is a prototype of the virgin birth of Jesus, since he was formed from the untilled, virgin earth. The same thinking guides Tertullian (De res. carn. 6; Adv. Jud. 13)" (E latere Christi, 37).
144. Clement, Tertullian, and Origen regard Adam as a prophet insofar as he spoke about Eve not primarily in terms of marriage but in looking forward to Christ and the church (ibid., 37–38).
145. Rahner cites this sleeping motif in Justin Martyr, the Sibylline Oracles, Irenaeus of Lyons, Clement of Alexandria, Hippolytus, Tertullian, and Cyprian of Carthage (ibid., 38).
146. These writers include Ignatius of Antioch, Clement of Rome, Shepherd of Hermas, Eusebius of Caesarea, Odes of Solomon, Sibylline Oracles, Clement of Alexandria, Tertullian, Hippolytus, Novatian, Cyprian (ibid., 39–41).
147. "Insofar as [the church] becomes one flesh, one body with Christ, which communicates new life (particularly in peoples' baptism), she is the true mother of the living. Insofar as she herself carries all of these features which were possessed by Eve in paradise, she is the second Eve" (ibid., 38).
148. E.g., "For what the virgin Eve had bound fast through unbelief, this did the virgin Mary set free through faith."
149. Namely, AH IV.20.12 and III.24.1 (E latere Christi, 39).
150. Note 52 on ibid. These passages state that our rebirth is a "rebirth of a virgin through faith" (AH

"church as Second Eve" element during this period seems to be a weak point in Rahner's argument for the apostolic origin of his full-fledged theme.

Rahner is able to garner patristic witnesses for a much more robust demonstration of another element—namely, Christ's wounded side as source of the Spirit.[151] Rahner offers an impressive and wide-ranging survey of early Christian attestation to this idea, citing the *Gospel of Hebrews*, *Epistle of Barnabas*, Ignatius, *Odes of Solomon*,[152] Justin,[153] *Sibylline Oracles*, *Apocalypse of Baruch*, *Letter from Vienna and Lyons*,[154] Apollinaris Claudius of Hierapolis,[155] the Gnostic *Pistis Sophia*,[156] and Clement of Alexandria.[157] But longer than his treatment of any of these figures is his treatment of Irenaeus and his attestation to the Spirit issuing forth from Christ's side, establishing the church.[158]

Rahner cites a veritable catalogue of pneumatological and ecclesiological excerpts from Irenaeus's *Adversus Haereses* concerning the Spirit in various respects: within the faithful (*AH* V.18.2), as the living water promised by Christ in John 4:11–14 (*AH* III.17.2), as the dew (*AH* III.17.3), as the water that "binds us as one dough lump, one bread, to become one Church (III.17.2)," and as the a stream which "irrigates the chosen people of God (IV.33.17; *Epid.* 89)."[159] However, Rahner notes in a section worth citing at length, for Irenaeus, the Holy Spirit only so permeates the church on account of the person of Christ:

> all of this water of the Spirit flows to the church from Christ. The Spirit first arose in descending on him, "becoming accustomed in fellowship with Him to dwell in the human race, to rest with human beings" (III.17.1).

IV.33.4). Christ has, as "pure, and in pureness opened a pure womb, that same womb which gives us a new birth into God, which womb he himself made pure" (*AH* IV.33.11).

151. Specific loci for explicit claims made by the fathers to this effect include "water as *Symbol* of the Spirit; the Messiah as Source of life, Christ as the split, water-giving rock; the springing-forth of Spirit-Water on the Cross; the profound meaning of the piercing of Jesus' side and the flowing forth of blood and water; baptism and the cross hanging together" (*E latere Christi*, 41).

152. "The origin of the living, speaking, immortal water is, according to Ode 30, 'from the heart of the Lord,' from the heart of the Messiah" (ibid., 43).

153. Rahner (ibid., 44) cites *Dial.* 138, which is infused with recapitulation theology: "Christ, being the first-born of every creature, became again the chief of another race regenerated by Himself through water, and faith, and wood, containing the mystery of the cross."

154. "It is one unique example which shows that the Asia-minor Johannine tradition of Polycarp and the other *presbyteroi* was transplanted into Gaul. John's thought did not live on in the thought of Irenaeus alone" (*E latere Christi*, 44).

155. "Blood and water are for Apollinaris certainly a *Symbol*, are purifying and expiatory streams of salvation" (ibid., 46).

156. "Water and blood from the side of Christ are thus a *Symbol* of his redemptive operation" (ibid.).

157. Ibid., 42–47.

158. Rahner's treatment of Irenaeus spans 44–46 of ibid.

159. Ibid., 44–45.

So Christ is as the rock, from which the water streamed, already announced in the OT (IV.14.3, 27.3; *Epid.* 46 . . . ; *Frag.* 3). This gift (the drink, which swells unto eternal life, the Spirit), which the Lord received from his Father, he gives also to those, *who have a share in him,* in whom the Holy Spirit is sent to the whole earth (III.17.2). III.24.1 says: "where the church is, there is the Spirit of God; and where the Spirit of God is, there is the church, and every kind of grace; but the Spirit is truth. Those, therefore, who do not *partake of Him,* are neither nourished into life from the mother's breasts, nor do they enjoy that most limpid fountain which issues from the body of Christ."[160]

In the theology of Irenaeus, Rahner is able to connect the ideas of Spirit, water, the church, Christ, and even the *fons vitae* of Christ's body to form a considerable portion of his dissertation's theme. Moreover, and important to my own book here, Rahner is operating in thoroughly person-centered, representative categories. Christ is *himself* the fount of the Spirit, granting salvation to the faithful. It is through "hav[ing] a share in him," by "partak[ing]" of the God-man that we receive "every kind of grace."

Turning to Irenaeus's more explicit reflections on Christ's pierced side, Rahner further underlines Irenaeus's representative soteriology, expressed in the concept of recapitulation. In doing so, Rahner provides one of the most important passages for my argument about his own genuinely representative soteriology. Rahner writes,

> Irenaeus speaks frequently of the opening of Jesus' side and the outpour-ing of blood and water. It is for him a *"symbolon* of the flesh, which had been derived from the earth, which He had recapitulated in Himself, bear-ing salvation to his own handiwork" (III.22.2). For him this blood and water is first of all a sign of the true humanity of Christ, against all Gnostic Docetism. However with and in this truth of the true humanity of Christ, he defends the whole order of salvation, *because Christ is the acceptance of true humanity, the "flesh" which "recapitulated" all flesh.* Since for Irenaeus the incarnation and redemption hang together so tightly, so each sign of Christ's true humanity is precisely a *"Symbol"* of that "flesh which he reca-pitulated in himself."[161]

That Rahner (accurately) describes Irenaeus in person-centered, "rep-resentative" terms is hardly a surprise. But this passage is genuinely remarkable in two respects. First, Rahner explains Irenaeus's repre-

160. Ibid., 45, emphasis added.
161. Ibid., 45–46, emphasis added.

sentative soteriological thought in terms of *Symbol*. According to Irenaeus, Christ saves humanity by recapitulating humanity in himself, the True Human. Moreover, every part of Christ's true human life stands as a *Symbol* directly linking him to the humanity which he saves via recapitulation. In other words, as a doctoral student, Rahner already understands our "subjective" redemption as occurring according to *symbolisch* terms,[162] terms which he expressly links to our participation and partaking in the saving person of Christ. Rahner here provides an explicit connection between patristic, representative soteriological thought and the category of *Symbol*, which figures prominently in his own mature soteriology.

Second, this connection is further underlined as Rahner cashes out the ideas of recapitulation and Christ's "true humanity". He writes, "with and in this truth of the true humanity of Christ, [Irenaeus] defends the whole order of salvation, because Christ is the acceptance of true humanity, the 'flesh' which 'recapitulated' all flesh." In this sentence, Rahner identifies the idea of Christic recapitulation (i.e., the "flesh" which "recapitulated" all flesh) with that of Christ being "the acceptance of true humanity." While these ideas are certainly conceptually close to one another, Rahner's identification here is incredibly significant in light of his own later soteriological language. As we saw in chapter 2, in considering the descending and ascending objective aspects of his mature soteriology, the later Rahner speaks in incredibly similar terms: "God's forgiving love has reached its historically visible culmination in Jesus' death on the cross, because this love has become irrevocable and has found its acceptance in a human being,"[163] Christ is "the one who is definitively affirmed and accepted by God,"[164] "in him God has accepted man,"[165] and Christ is "God's . . . acceptance of the world into God himself in person and as a person . . . the unsurpassable and final event."[166] In Rahner's mature thought, the Christ-event stands as the moment in which the most genuine human, fully open to his transcendent orientation, accepts God and is accepted by God; and at the outset of his career as a theologian, he had more or less equated a basic version of this idea with Irenaean recapitulation.

162. See the section on "Subjective Redemption" above in chapter 2.
163. "Reconciliation and Vicarious Representation," *TI* 21:255–69, at 261.
164. "Jesus Christ—The Meaning of Life," *TI* 21:208–19, at 216.
165. *FCF*, 228.
166. "Thoughts on the Possibility of Belief Today," *TI* 5:3–22, at 14.

E latere Christi: Chapter 3—
The First Explicit Testimony in the Third Century

Three third-century sources are the first to explicitly contain Rahner's typological theme. The earliest of these is Tertullian's *De anima*, particularly a section of the *De amina* having to do with philosophical debates over the phenomenon of sleep. Tertullian argues against philosophers who hold sleep to be "unnatural" and "morbid," appealing to Adam's act of sleeping in the paradisal garden. Within this discussion, Tertullian remarks, "For as Adam was a figure of Christ, Adam's sleep shadowed out the death of Christ, who was to sleep a mortal slumber, that from the wound inflicted on His side might, in like manner [as Eve was formed], be typified in the Church, the true mother of the living."[167]

Rahner makes two observations about this passage. First, it occurs as a kind of "aside," a marginal remark within a discussion over philosophical account of human physiology. Such a context would hardly be the case to propose a novel typological reading. Second, he notes that Tertullian's reference to this typological theme does not even include explicit reference to Eve. Such an omission seems to indicate that Tertullian presumed his audience would "fill in" this part of the type. Both of these observations, Rahner convincingly argues, indicate that the type not only predates Tertullian, but that it was fairly established and widely known.[168]

Rahner's next move, however, stands on more tenuous ground. After establishing that the theme is older than Tertullian, Rahner muses about how easily a text such as *De Anima* might have been lost, in which case, many might presume that Tertullian too, in his other writings, had only the "conditions" for or "elements" of the type but had not yet assembled them in other to invent the full-fledged theme. Such a presumption would obviously be faulty. Rahner ventures, "Then, however, tracing it backwards, no certain *terminus a quo* can any longer be determined, for these 'conditions' were always the same, alive. The church from the side of Christ is good to the earliest Christian tradition."[169] While there is something to be said for dating the type prior to Ter-

---

167. Tertullian, *De Anima* ch. 43, qtd. *E latere Christi*, 48. Translation taken from "A Treatise on the Soul," in *ANF* 3:181–235, at 222.
168. As Rahner puts it, "Tertullian does not discover this idea here for the first time, but rather he casually mentions a long-known thought which is common to him, and also without having to spell out all of its details and conditions, as he can presume they are understandable and known to his readers" (*E latere Christi*, 49).
169. Ibid., 50.

tullian, in placing it within "the earliest Christian tradition," Rahner seems to overstate his case.

The next text, De [duobos] montibus Sina et Sion, originates in early/ mid-second century Africa and its author is unknown. This text too explicitly contains Rahner's theme,[170] and like Tertullian's, it contains no explicit reference to Eve; again, Rahner cites this omission as evidence for the audience's familiarity with the theme. Rahner also discusses Methodius's allusion to the theme,[171] followed by a treatment of other authors from this time period[172] whose writings contain the theme's "conditions" or "elements."

Rahner then returns to his argument about the type's (apostolic) antiquity, doubling down on his previous reasoning rooted in counterfactual thought experiments about lost manuscripts.[173] Again, Rahner succeeds in arguing that Tertullian almost certainly stands as an arbitrary "beginning" point, and so, the doctrine ought not to be thought of as originating with him. Nonetheless, Rahner's bold conclusion about the apostolicity of the typological theme[174] seems to rest on a rather vague rationale: "following it backwards, an earliest terminus ad quo cannot be specified."[175]

Following up on his earlier remark that the fathers do not only develop apostolic themes but also transmit them, Rahner returns to Irenaeus to spell out what precisely he believes John (the apostle to whom

---

170. "Pierced in the side: out of his side streamed a profuse mixture of blood and water, and so he formed for himself the holy church, in which he consecrated the Law in his passion, saying: Let anyone who is thirsty come to me, and let the one who believes in me drink. For out of him streams living water" (qtd. in ibid., 51).

171. Methodius writes, "the Church is formed out of His bones and flesh; and it was for this cause that the Word, leaving his Father in heaven, came down to be 'joined to his wife;' and slept in the trance of His passion, and willingly suffered death for her, that he might present the Church to Himself glorious and blameless, having cleansed her by the laver. . . . For he may fitly be called the rib of the Word, even the sevenfold Spirit of truth, according to the prophet; of whom God taking, in the trance of Christ, that is, after His incarnation and passion, prepares a help-meet for Him – I mean the souls which are betrothed and given in marriage to Him. For it is frequently the case that the Scriptures thus call the assembly and mass of believers by the name of the Church" (Symposium III.8, qtd. in E latere Christi, 52; translation from The Banquet of the Ten Virgins; or, Concerning Chastity, in ANF 6:309–55 at 319–20).

172. Namely, Hippolytus, Cyprian, and Origen (E latere Christi, 53–56).

173. "If Tertullian's De Anima and De Montiubs Sina et Sion would have been lost, which for such writings really easily could have been possible, we would not know of a single direct testimony to the teaching in the third century. Without the background-tradition provided by Tertullian and De montiubus Sina et Sion, then Methodius's testimony, in its ambiguity, also loses much of its worth. The first clear witness would then be Hilary of Poitiers: 150 years later than Tertullian" (ibid., 57–58).

174. "If we bring together all of these individual considerations, then one may well say with some certainty that the doctrine of the generation of the church from Christ's side as antitype of the formation of Eve from the side of Adam goes back to the apostolic age" (ibid., 57).

175. Ibid., 60.

the theme can be supposedly traced back) had in mind in teaching the typological doctrine of the church's origin. In doing so, he again draws on two concepts from his previous chapter: *Symbol* and soteriology. The piercing of Christ's side is a *symbolisch* event[176] of great soteriological significance, even for the apostle John, Rahner asserts.[177] It is a *Symbol*, he explains, of "the soteriological significance of the true human nature of Christ," more than "merely a defense [against the Gnostics] of the true human nature of Jesus as such, but rather its truth, insofar as through it the salvation of humanity is actually given. This connection is explicitly declared by [Irenaeus]."[178]

Christ is for John (as Irenaeus attests) the *True Human*, that is, the New Adam, *in whom* humanity itself is recapitulated and thus *through whom* human salvation is "actually given." This giving of salvation is expressed "symbolically"[179] in the soteriologically crucial event of the piercing, in which the Spirit is poured forth and the New Adam's "Bride" comes to be—a "Bride" which consists of the "body" of the church, the members of which are the baptized faithful.[180] By returning to Irenaeus and the concepts of *Symbol* and salvation, Rahner is able to show how the logic of *fons vitae* thinking about Jesus, something undeniably contained in John, comes to full expression in the typological theme of the church as Second Eve. This Irenaean conclusion of the third chapter thus seems to make an appeal on the *conceptual, theological* level to the doctrine's antiquity and apostolicity, an appeal which supplements his early arguments, which were more historical and textual in character.

For our purposes, Rahner's return to Irenaeus at this point, in a chapter on the century subsequent to Irenaeus himself, shows just how central a thinker the bishop of Lyons and his person-centered soteriology are to Rahner's argument. As Rahner thinks about human salvation, a reality achieved and given in the human Jesus himself, Irenaeus and his doctrine of recapitulation stand as a kind of central axis and reference point around which Rahner constructs both his historical

---

176. "If for Irenaeus Christ is the water-giving rock and the Source of the living water of the Spirit, then Jn 19:34 must have significance as '*Symbol* of the recapitulated flesh' for him, significance which goes beyond that from which his path of anti-docetic polemic initially takes off" (ibid., 59).
177. Ibid., 60.
178. Ibid., 59.
179. Recall, Rahner intends this word to mean more than "sign." (See above, as well as his return to this distinction in *E latere Christi*'s conclusion.)
180. "That the totality of the redeemed is, for John, a unified whole, is in any case clear, since he speaks of her as his woman, the bride, etc. This church as the Reign of God is now established through the water and the Spirit, for through this the individual (and so also the whole) is reborn into the 'Reign of God' therein (Jn 3:5)" (*E latere Christi*, 60).

arguments about his typological theme, as well as his own soterio-logical reflections about the event of the piercing and the concept of *Symbol*, which receives fuller explanation in the conclusion of *E latere Christi*.

E latere Christi: Chapter 4—
The Heyday of Patristic Literature Up to the
End of the Patristic Period

Having already reviewed the earliest complete and explicit references to his typological theme, Rahner sets out in his fourth chapter to track repetitions of this theme from the "heyday" of patristic literature up through the end of this Patristic Age in the eighth century. The chapter is rather short compared to the others, but nevertheless contains a host references to patristic theologians and demonstrates Rahner's extensive reading of texts from this period.

Rahner begins by addressing writings from the height of patristic theology around the beginning of the fifth century, dividing them into Latin, Greek, and Syriac language groups. The Latin group is the largest; it begins in the mid-fourth century, with Hilary of Poitiers and includes the articulations of the theme by Zeno of Verona, Ambrose of Milan, Jerome, and Augustine of Hippo. Augustine, Rahner reports, repeats the typological theme of the Second Eve more than any other of the fathers,[181] and his particular take on this theme is unique in its emphasis on the sacraments.[182]

Augustine's counterpart as the theological giant of the East is John Chrysostom, who also mentions the theme. "Just as his wife was formed while Adam slept," Chrysostom writes, "so, when Christ died, the church was formed from His side."[183] The other Greek figure which

---

181. Ibid., 66. Rahner includes two full quotations from Augustine's *Tractates on John*: "Adam sleeps, that Eve may be formed; Christ dies, that the church may be formed. When Adam sleeps, Eve is formed from his side; when Christ is dead, the spear pierces His side, that the mysteries may flow forth whereby the church is formed" (9.10) and "This second Adam bowed His head and fell asleep on the cross, that a spouse might be formed for Him from that which flowed from the sleeper's side" (120.2) (translations from *NPNF* I/7:66–67, 435). Rahner also cites several other places in which Augustine mentions the theme: *On Genesis: A Refutation of the Manichees* II.24.37; *Reply to Faustus the Manichaean* II.7.8; *Expositions on the Psalms*, 40n10, Ps., 56n11, Ps., 103; *Sermon*, 4n6; Ps., 128n2; *Sermon*, 5n3, *Sermon*, 336 5.5; *City of God* XXII.17.
182. Rahner writes that "the sacraments flow forth from the pierced side of Christ, sacraments by which the church is formed. None of the fathers implemented more clearly than Augustine the idea that the sacraments flow from Jesus' side, as a constructive agent, in order to clarify how the church could result from Jesus' side. The sacraments arise from Christ's side, sacraments which in turn give rise to the church, and so the church is from the side of Christ. This construction is then the norm during the Middle Ages" (*E latere Christi*, 66–67).

Rahner treats from this period is Philo Carpasius; two other theologians writing in Syriac mentioned by Rahner are St. Ephrem and Jacob of Serugh.[184]

Rahner then turns to the later Patristic Age. Although Rahner is able to cite a host of figures referencing the theme, most of them, he notes, simply repeat the doctrine as articulated by either Augustine[185] or Chrysostom.[186] The idea, he judges, becomes "frozen," handed on more or less "formulaically."[187] Even so, he says as he concludes the chapter, the doctrine is so ubiquitous that it ought to be regarded as having the authority of a "common opinion of the holy fathers" (*communis sententia sanctorum Patrum*).[188] The fathers, Rahner judges, held "this Eve-church parallel as a genuine 'type' in the theological sense," and moreover, they "considered this idea as an integral part of the faith tradition."[189]

E latere Christi: Chapter 5—
The Middle Ages and Modern Times

Rahner's stated goal for his fifth chapter is like the fourth chapter in its modesty: to trace the typological theme in a rapid survey of the last twelve centuries in order to show that it "did not disappear . . . to follow the survival of this Johannine thinking."[190] Usage of the doctrine in the early Middle Ages basically consisted of preserving its articulation by patristic thinkers in excerpts, most often in work of scriptural exegesis (but also the occasional sermon). Once, again, Rahner provides citations from a host of theologians leading up the High Middle Ages.[191]

183. Chrysostom, *De Laude Maximi et Quales Ducendae Sint Uxores* 3 (PG 51.225–42, at 229). Translation from *Baptismal Instructions*, ed. and trans. Paul W. Harkins, no. 31 of *Ancient Christian Writers* series (Westminster, MD: Newman Press, 1963), 237.
184. *E latere Christi*, 67–68.
185. Latin authors subsequent to Augustine in whose writing Rahner finds the theme are Quadvultdeus of Carthage, Prosper of Aquitaine, Eugippius, Fulgentius of Ruspe, Leo the Great, Maximus of Turin, Avitus of Vienne, Pseudo-Ambrose, Gregory of Tours, Gregory the Great, Isidore of Seville, and Ildephonsus of Toledo (ibid., 69–70).
186. Nilus of Sinai, Anastasius of Sinai, John Damascene (*Sacred Parallels*) and Theophylakt of Ohrid are cited by Rahner as late Greek patristic figures leaning on Chrysostom to various extents (ibid., 68).
187. Ibid.
188. Ibid., 70.
189. Ibid., 71.
190. Ibid.
191. Rahner cites specific references to the typological theme in the works of the Venerable Bede, Theodulf of Orleans, Berengaud of Ferrières, Wigbold (first appearance of the doctrine in scholastic question about why God created Eve from Adam's side), Alcuin, Rahanus Maurus, Angelomus Luxoviensis, Remigius of Auxerre, Peter Damian, Lanfranc of Canterbury, St. Bruno of Cologne, Ivo of Chartres, Bruno of Segni, Lietbertus of St. Ruf, and Rupert of Deutz.

Beginning in the twelfth century, references to Rahner's theme increasingly occur "in speculative theology, and migrates from this time even further to specific points in the *Summae* and commentaries on Lombard's *Sentences*."[192] Anselm of Laon and Hugh of St. Victor include the doctrine within systematic treatments of humanity's creation, and once it found a place in Lombard's *Sentences*, it "found its place in medieval theology ... in the theological textbook of the Middle Ages and so could no longer be forgotten."[193] Thomas Aquinas and Bonaventure have recourse to the theme in both their "speculative" and "exegetical" writings, Rahner notes.[194] But by this point, Rahner laments, the doctrine had largely been transformed into "a piece of learned knowledge from the academy. For that reason, this thought could be thought no longer to be living as it was in the Patristic Period, since all of 'fount of life' thinking was no longer clear and alive in the theological depth which the fathers knew."[195]

Nevertheless, Rahner points out that the doctrine did manage to survive on a more popular level through hymns,[196] sermons,[197] occasional appearances in Christian artwork. One such piece of art mentioned by Rahner is a thirteenth-century miniature (Figure 2) described by Karl Künstle as follows: "At the feet of the Crucified, God creates Eve from the side of Adam; and from the side of the dying Savior, the church emerges as crowned, naked figure with a chalice in hand, in which she collects the blood of Christ. Immediately beneath her rises the catechumens' baptismal font."[198] Rahner also notes that several Bibles depict images from the life of Christ flanked by other "typologically" related scenes from the Bible. One such common grouping (e.g., Figure 3, which also dates to the thirteenth century and which Rahner cites) is the piercing of Christ's side, flanked by images of the creation of Eve and of Moses striking the rock for water in the desert.

192. Ibid., 72.
193. Ibid., 73.
194. Ibid.
195. Ibid., 74.
196. Rahner specifically cites Peter Abelard (ibid., 76).
197. E.g., those of Bonaventure, Bernardine of Siena, Lorenzo Giustiniani, Thomas à Kempis, Ludolph of Saxony and Hendrik Herp (ibid.).
198. Karl Künstle, *Ikonographie der christlichen Kunst*, 2 vols. (Freiberg i.Br.: Herder, 1926–28), 1:276–77.

Bild 110. Eva und Kirche.
Miniatur der Handschrift „Emblemata biblica"
in der Nationalbibliothek zu Paris.

Figure 2: Thirteenth-century miniature, "Eva und Kirche." Reproduced from Karl Künstle, *Ikonographie der christlichen Kunst*, 1:276–77, labeled as "Bild 110."

In both academic and more popular reference to the theme in the Middle Ages, Rahner sees a significant departure from its context and moorings in the early church. In medieval times, Rahner explains, the "great fundamental truths of faith" are more central to religious life than is *their content*, which capacitates human beings to elevated life; such content was immediately apparent in the Patristic Age and its "fount of life" thinking.[199] Divorced from the larger "fount of life" thinking of which it was a part, medieval reflection on the piercing of Christ's side differed significantly from its patristic forbearer. For the fathers, the piercing of Christ's side was a *symbolisch* event in which Christ was revealed and realized as "Source of the Spirit," the Spirit in

---

199. *E latere Christi*, 75. Rahner continues, "This inner transformation – or organization, if you will – in the piece of the patristic period to the Middle Ages makes itself palpable in the 'fount of life' thinking. It is as if the old patristic formulas, filled with the most profound dogmatic content, from the closing of the patristic period and the early days of the Middle Ages would gradually be depleted, as if one has forgotten their profound content gradually or at least unlearned to find it behind these formulas."

which Christians are born anew in baptism as part of the "body" of the New Eve.[200] But subsequently, the event was dealt with either in speculative, academic terms or in devotional terms, which were much more individualized. The pierced side became increasingly associated with Christ's suffering and his pierced heart as a source of "comfort" (rather than the grace of the Holy Spirit), which Jesus personally offers Christians.[201]

Figure 3: Thirteenth-century Bible illustration. Image reproduced from Karl Atz and Stephen D. Beissel, *De kirchliche Kunst in Wort und Bild* (Regensburg: Manz, 1915), 72, labeled as "Abb. 134." For better use of space, I have rearranged the panels to proceed from left to right (horizontally) rather than from top to bottom (vertically).

200. "For the fathers the pierced side of Christ, from which blood and water streamed forth, was a *Symbol* indicating that the Messiah is the Source of the Spirit, which the Christian receives in baptism and makes him to be born anew; thus the church is constructed" (ibid.).
201. "In the Middle Ages there is also an observation, attributed to William of St-Thierry: 'out of the side of Christ flow the sacraments of redemption,' however the wounded side of Christ is for William even more the portal through which the believer enters, in order to rest in the Heart of Jesus. . . . And if the side of Jesus is the Source of 'grace,' then 'grace' is to be understood in the sense of 'comfort.' During the Middle Ages, the soul sees in the wounded side, in the pierced heart a tender *Symbol*, deep love, with which Jesus, the crucified beloved of the soul, loves in a wholly personal way. The side of Christ is no longer so much the source for the waters of the Holy Spirit, but rather the 'Heavenly source full of all sweetness', as described in a Rhenish mystical manuscript . . . and a *Symbol* of the bitter suffering of Jesus. So, the words in the Patristic and Middle Ages may often seem to be similar, but the spirit is different in the words of the medieval mystics than that of the church fathers" (ibid.).

Rahner's sweeping historical survey concludes by considering the Council of Vienne (1312) and a string of figures leading up to the time of his writing. The Council of Vienne makes mention of the typological doctrine in condemning the idea (associated with Peter Olivi) that Christ had not yet died when his side was pierced. However, Rahner judges after carefully analyzing its statement, the council is best understood as not authoritatively *defining* the typological doctrine itself.[202] Additionally, Rahner demonstrates that the theme was discussed as a possible addition to a draft Vatican I's *De Ecclesia Christi*, an addition which never came to pass.[203] His overview of theologians mentioning the theme in the intervening period includes figures such as Francisco Suárez (d. 1617), Robert Bellarmine (d. 1621), and Leo XIII (in his 1897 encyclical *Divinum illud*).[204]

Chapter 5 thus largely consists of Rahner cataloguing a host of historical figures who have written on his theme. As with the previous chapters, this cataloguing is of interest for my own project here insofar as his intense historical research testifies to just how seriously Rahner takes the history of theology and the faith's tradition. However, Rahner's brief transition from historical accounting into his more "speculative" observation about the theological nature of medieval devotion vis-à-vis that of the fathers is even more valuable for our purposes. By lamenting the shift away from *fons vitae* thinking about the person of Jesus, Rahner tips his own hand when it comes to his preferred Christology, ecclesiology, and soteriology. Remarks like this make it clear that *E latere Christi* is more than a foray into purely historical scholarship, but is, in fact, the basis for an effort of retrieval, that is, *ressourcement*.

202. Ibid., 77–79.
203. Ibid., 80.
204. Around thirty years *after* Rahner's *E Latere Christi*, Joseph Ratzinger would explicitly make use of this typological theme in his *Introduction to Christianity* (1968) as an expression of his own very person-centered soteriology: Jesus is "the man in whom humanity comes into contact with its future and in the highest extent itself becomes its future, because through him it makes contact with God himself, shares in him, and thus realizes its most intrinsic potential. From here onward faith in Christ will see the beginning of a movement in which dismembered humanity is gathered together more and more into the being of one single Adam, one single 'body' – the man to come" ((New York: Herder, 1970), 239). Ratzinger follows with an analysis of John 19:34, explaining, "For John, the picture of the pierced side forms the climax not only of the crucifixion scene but of the whole story of Jesus. Now . . . he is truly no longer a single individual, but 'Adam', from whose side Eve, a new mankind, is formed. . . . The open side of the new Adam repeats the mystery of the 'open side' of man at creation" (ibid., 240–41).

E latere Christi: Conclusion

Whereas the foregoing material in *E latere Christi* offered only brief indications that Rahner saw the work as a basis for a project of "retrieval" which could renew contemporary "speculative" theology, his conclusion intently focuses upon this point. Accordingly, this conclusion likely contains the material which would be deemed most interesting for today's readers of Rahner. Rahner begins it with a more historical claim: since his typological theme "is a common teaching of the fathers," it ought to be deemed a genuine, theological "type" along with those mentioned completely and explicitly in the Bible.[205] But genuine *types*, he reminds us, are imbued with profoundly *symbolisch* meaning.

Elaborating upon the suggestion that the piercing has *symbolisch* meaning, Rahner says that this particular event (as do other events) of Jesus life has great soteriological import.[206] This event, he suggests, is part of a soteriology which cannot be confined within terms of vicarious merit or exemplarism:

> the life of Jesus stands, in the life of the Christian, as soteriological not just entirely though the grace merited on the cross and as moral through the individual mysteries in their exemplarity, but rather that also the individual mysteries as individual (even if, of course, they are thereby parts of a salvific life of Christ) work their way into the life of the Christian as a saving power beyond their moral exemplarity.[207]

This soteriology, which Rahner has argued emerges out of a patristic and indeed apostolic *fons vitae* world of thought, has its basis primarily in the Christian's direct encounter with Jesus himself—the events of his life, which are salvific *in se*, "work their way into" the lives of Christians scattered throughout the ages.

Providing more theoretical underpinnings for this kind of soteriology, Rahner suggests, would require pursuing two paths. The first concerns the "philosophy of history": one must "work out a general ontology of the presence of a human historical process to a 'later' time."[208] Second, one must then "apply such an ontology to considerations of the necessary theological moments of the presence of the

205. Ibid., 81.
206. For more on the soteriological import of the events of Jesus's life to which Rahner attests throughout his career, see Batlogg's *Die Mysterien des Lebens Jesu bei Karl Rahner*.
207. *E latere Christi*, 82.
208. Ibid.

events in the life of Jesus in the life of the Christian."[209] The key for doing this lies in Rahner's insight that the events of Jesus's life are *Symbole*. Rahner explains that the events' "typological character indicates, indeed precisely, that these events are not merely retrospectively considered by their contemporary observer as *Symbole* of the timeless work of the redeeming Logos in the life of the Christian, but rather that they through their setting in historical, spiritual person *are* such '*Symbole*' from the outset."[210] That is, an event like Jesus's piercing is not salvific insofar as we project soteriological meaning upon it, but insofar as it has that meaning *for us* in virtue *of itself.*

If such talk about a *Symbol* does not already point blatantly toward his concerns about "intrinsicity" more than twenty years later in "The Theology of the Symbol," the remark which follows it does. "But then the question arises, by what and how a *Symbol* in the first sense [i.e., retrospectively considered as such] inwardly distinguishes itself from *Symbol* in the second sense [*being* "*Symbole*" from the outset]." This question, which echoes the call he just issued for the development of a "general ontology," is the question of what distinguishes a *Vertretungssymbol* from *das Realsymbol*, to use his later language. This much is clear as Rahner continues, applying the distinction to the "abiding presence [*Gegenwärtigbleibens*]" of the life of Jesus, saying that "if an event of Jesus' life has this *Symbol*-character from the outset," it stands "internally and from the outset . . . [as] an 'address' to the later person."[211]

It thus appears that by 1936 (and perhaps earlier), Rahner already envisioned a project which shares the structure of and even distinctions within "The Theology of the Symbol." Saying, "This cannot all be carried out here,"[212] Rahner uses the conclusion of his dissertation to issue the call for a "general ontology" which would undergird specific, theological applications to account for the presence of Christ and his life to Christians and theirs. And the initial theoretical move, it seems, is the distinction between extrinsic "signs" and intrinsic *Symbole*. Likewise, "The Theology of the Symbol" is structured so as to begin with "The Ontology of the *Symbolwirklichkeit* in General," and subsequently, treat the "Theology of *Symbolwirklichkeit*." Moreover, the former section commences with the distinction between extrinsic *Vertretungssym-*

209. Ibid.
210. Ibid.
211. Ibid., 82–83.
212. Ibid., 83.

bole and intrinsic *Realsymbole*, and while the latter applicative section is by no means devoted exclusively to considerations of Christ's "abiding presence" to the Christian, his treatment of the church therein indeed discusses this issue (among many others), having recourse to the church's *symbolisch* nature to explain the phenomenon.[213]

Finally, the conclusion of *E latere Christi* ends on the same topic which frames the entirety of "The Theology of the Symbol"—namely, Jesus's Sacred Heart. Recall, the conclusion of "The Theology of the Symbol" sought to resolve debates about the object of Sacred Heart devotion (i.e., physical heart or saving love) by positing Jesus's physical heart as *das Realsymbol* of God's saving love. As *E latere Christi* attests, Rahner had formulated such an idea decades earlier.[214] Rahner's purpose for identifying the Sacred Heart as a *Symbol* of God's redeeming love is not here, however, at the service of resolving disputes about the devotion. Rather, it is to posit that as such a *Symbol*, Jesus's Sacred Heart has an earlier, patristic analogue in Christ's pierced side, which is also such a *Symbol*,[215] "the sign of their redemption, Source of the Spirit, all grace and power unto martyrdom. It was for them the Source of Life which flowed to them through baptism," by which they are "united with Christ."[216] The fathers understood this unity in accordance with what I have called a person-centered soteriology, for in their baptism, they understood that "the Spirit flowed to them from the body of the Messiah. When they drank the blood of Christ in the Eucharist and were thus filled with the love of Christ, then they thought that this blood also flowed from Jesus' side."[217] In other words, for the fathers, the sacraments are indeed about participating in the person of Christ

---

213. "[T]he Church is the persisting presence [*Gegenwärtigbleiben*] of the incarnate Word in space and time . . . it continues the symbolic function of the Logos in the world" ("The Theology of the Symbol," *TI* 4:221–52, at 240). Rahner supplements this idea in a later essay by identifying the Spirit as the "medium" of Christ's presence to the Church ("The Presence of the Lord in the Christian Community at Worship," *TI* 10:71–83, at 73–74), thus repeating another of his themes from *E latere Christi*.
214. "Our Sacred Heart devotion today certainly adores the physical heart of Jesus. This physical heart has a priority to other parts of Jesus' humanity, which are also worthy of adoration, but it is only the object of a special devotion because it is a *Symbol* to us of the redemptive love of the God-man for us, summing up all of the achievements of this love in a sign" (*E latere Christi*, 83).
215. "So when we seek in the patristic period an analogue or traces of a of our Sacred Heart devotion, we must not mechanically search for texts in which the Heart of Jesus somehow mentioned. This method leads nowhere. We must instead ask whether the early Christians had a *Symbol* in which everything that they knew of the redeeming love of God was summed up in an object of their devotion (Whether this *Symbol* was already the object of a special adoration is another question)" (ibid.). Recall, Rahner made this suggestion two years earlier in the conclusion of "'Coeur de Jésus' chez Origene?"
216. *E latere Christi*, 83.
217. Ibid.

and the "abiding presence" of the event in which he literally poured himself out to us on the cross.

Ending the dissertation, Rahner notes that the contemporary thinking about the Sacred Heart, while analogous to the pierced side for the fathers, perhaps sharpens the *Symbol* insofar as it presents a more easily identifiable "special object of devotion." Yet, he asks, "can't today's Sacred Heart devotion also learn something from the early church?"[218]

> When the devout Christian in the heart of the Savior in turn sees the sign that this heart entirely, personally loved her and has given itself for her, when this heart is a reminder to her to consecrate her most inner and personal love in gratitude and penance to this heart, then she should also, in the Spirit of the early church, not forget that the love of this heart encompassed an entire world, redeemed a humanity, and also that she only loves in the love with which the Word become human encompassed the church, the holy virgin, his bride and our mother.[219]

Behind this concluding remark is Rahner's earlier observation about the "individualization" which occurred in the medieval West in reflections about Christ's pierced side. *E latere Christi* ends with Rahner's call for contemporary Christians to infuse their devotion to the Sacred Heart with a *fons vitae* Christology, according to which, Jesus encompassed and thus redeemed the entire world in the very center of his being, and that our love is that of the Savior to whom we have been conjugally united. That is, Rahner's dissertation seems to call for the retrieval of a patristic mindset, a major part of which is a person-centered, representative soteriology.

Early Publications After E latere Christi

After the completion of his theology dissertation, Rahner's publications began to proliferate. In particularly, Rahner composed a host of reviews on contemporary literature in patristic studies.[220] Rather than offer a full accounting of his work at this point, the following section will serve to highlight Rahner's continued interest in historical (especially patristic) theology and identify some publications which help us to trace the development of his understanding of Christ as Savior.

In the same year that he submitted *E latere Christi* (1936), Rahner

---

218. Ibid., 84.
219. Ibid.
220. These reviews can be found *SW* 3:393–420.

published five articles, four of which were eventually included in his *Theological Investigations*. The topics included laity and Christian life,[221] the Eucharist and human suffering,[222] Ignatian mysticism,[223] Protestant Christology,[224] and the early church's understanding of sin, grace, and penance.[225] The penultimate article picks up on a theme directly related to *E latere Christi*, considering how various Protestant Christologies account for the "presence" of Christ. The final entry is of special import, for two reasons. First, according to Rahner's bibliography,[226] the 40-page "Sünde als Gnadenverlust in der frühkirchlichen Literatur" was recognized by Innsbruck as Rahner's *Habilitationsschrift*, thus permitting him to teach very soon after he received his doctorate in theology in December 1936. Second, this essay on penance, which traces up to the third century the idea of sin as forfeiting the sanctifying grace received in baptism, once again confirms Rahner's dedication to early Christian theology at this time. Within this article, *Shepherd of Hermas*, "Gnosticism," Tertullian, Origen, Cyprian, and Irenaeus of Lyons all receive attention.

The following year in 1937, Rahner continued to publish works on spirituality[227] and early Christianity, the latter in essays on Clement of Alexandria and the "supernatural"[228] and on baptism and Messalianism (a fourth-century heretical movement).[229] In addition to these essays, Rahner constructed a manuscript, *De Gratia Christi*, for the private use of his students at Innsbruck for his first course, devoted to the subject

---

221. "Weihe des Laien zur Seelsorge," *Zeitschrift für Aszese und Mystik* 11 (1936), 21–34. Included as "The Consecration of the Layman to the Care of Souls," in *TI* 3:263–76.
222. "Eucharistie und Leiden," *Zeitschrift für Aszese und Mystik* 11 (1936), 224–34. Included as "The Eucharist and Suffering," in *TI* 3:161–70.
223. "Die ignatianische Mystik der Weltfreudigkeit," *Zeitschrift für Aszese und Mystik* 12 (1936), 121–37. Included as "The Ignatian Mysticism of Joy in the World," in *TI* 3:277–93.
224. "Die deutsche protestantische Christologie der Gegenwart," *Theologie der Zeit* 1 (1936), 189–202. Available in *SW* 4:299–312.
225. "Sünde als Gnadenverlust in der frühkirchlichen Literatur." *Zeitschrift für katholische Theologie* 60 (1936), 471–510. A revised version was included as "Sin as Loss of Grace in the Early Church," in *TI* 15:23–53.
226. Available at http://www.ub.uni-freiburg.de/fileadmin/ub/referate/04/rahner/rahnersc.pdf.
227. "Gott meines Lebens", "Gott meiner Sendung", "Gott meiner Gebete", "Gott meines Alltags", "Gott unseres Herrn Jesus Christus", "Gott der Gesetze", "Gott der Erkenntnis", "Gott der Lebendigen", "Gott meiner Brüder", "Gott, der da kommen soll." *Korrespondenz des Priestergebetsvereines Associatio Perseverantiae Sacerdotalis* (Vienna) 58 (1937). Also in *Encounters with Silence* (Westminster, MD: Newman Press, 1960) and *Prayers for a Lifetime* (New York: Crossroad, 1984). A similar publication from August is "Freunde Gottes," *Katholische Kirchenzeitung* (Salzburg) 77, no. 35 (26 Aug. 1937), 274, included in *SW* 4:294–95.
228. "De termino aliquo in theologia Clementis Alexandrini, qui aequivalet nostro conceptui entis 'supernaturalis'," *Gregorianum* 18 (1937), 426–31. Included in *De Gratia Christi: Studien zur Gnadenlehre*, eds. Roman Siebenrock, Albert Raffelt, and Theodor Schneider, vol. 5/1 (2015) of *SW*, 3–13.
229. "Ein messalianisches Fragment über die Taufe," *Zeitschrift für katholische Theologie* 61 (1937), 258–71. Included in *SW* 3:87–104.

of grace.[230] Roman Siebenrock has written about this manuscript in his "Gratia Christi. The Heart of the Theology of Karl Rahner," though his own purposes for doing so concern Rahner's Ignatian spirituality more than Rahner's patristic interests. Nevertheless, Siebenrock's general summary of the text from Rahner's first course shows a work which resonates deeply with the person-centered, *fons vitae* thinking which Rahner mined from early theologians such as Irenaeus and dwelt upon in *E latere Christi*:

> Grace is first of all uncreated grace, the person of Jesus Christ himself. In the Holy Spirit this grace touches the whole of humankind in Jesus Christ, as the head of redeemed humanity, and wishes to transform it by redemption into the life of God. Therefore, the world exists that Christ can be. The hypostatic union is the goal (finis) of creation. Because in Christ, as the new Adam, this goal of creation has been realised in history, the completion of the life and love of Christ becomes the distinguishing sign of ("supernatural") salvation: "Our supernatural life is the prolongation and explication of the life of Christ."[231]

The presence of New-Adam, representative soteriology in Rahner's *De Gratia* course confirms that Rahner was not only fascinated with it, but he furthermore saw it as a soteriological basis for teaching about God's grace. Christ is himself, as "the head of renewed humanity," the "finality of grace," in union with whom humankind encounters the immediacy of God and his universal salvific will.[232]

Rahner continued to attend to the themes of spirituality and patristic theology in his writings from 1938. Rahner wrote on the love of God[233] and also composed a collection of prayers and meditations for the Vienna Seminary, which were published as his first autonomous book (translated as *Encounters with Silence*).[234] Furthermore, he wrote an article on Augustine and semi-Pelagianism[235] and that summer, he completed *Aszese und Mystik in der Väterzeit*, his expansion and transla-

---

230. *De Gratia Christi: Summa Praelectionum in usum privatum auditorum ordinata* (Oeniponte 1937–38, republished or reprinted in 1950–51, 1955, and 1959). The first nine of Rahner's 33 theses (amounting to two of nine total chapters) of this lecture are included in SW 5/1:239–494; the remainder are scheduled to be published in SW 5/2 in 2017.
231. Summary of *De Gratia Christi* in Siebenrock, "Gratia Christi. The Heart of the Theology of Karl Rahner," 1267. The latter quote is directly from page 1 of Rahner's *De Gratia Christi*.
232. Siebenrock, "Gratia Christi. The Heart of the Theology of Karl Rahner," 1268.
233. "Die Liebe zu Gott," *Korrespondenz des Priester-Gebetsvereines "Associatio perseverantiae sacerdotalis"* (Vienna) 59, no. 6 (1938), 74–80. Included in *On Prayer* (Collegeville, MN: Liturgical Press, 1993).
234. *Worte ins Schweigen* (Innsbruck: Rauch, 1938). Translated as *Encounters with Silence* and included in *Prayers for a Lifetime*.
235. "Augustin und der Semipelagianismus," *Zeitschrift für katholische Theologie* 62 (1938), 171–96.

tion of Viller's work discussed above. This monumental work in patristics, which Rahner had nearly doubled in size with his additions, was published the next year in 1939. This year also saw the publication of an essay on lay holiness in the age of the fathers,[236] as well as a work in which Rahner's historical and more "speculative" interests coalesced, "Some Implications on the Scholastic Concept of Uncreated Grace."[237] This same year also saw the publication of his now famous *Spirit in the World*.

We have thus brought our bibliographical overview up to date with the biographical section above, as many of these 1939 publications were being composed while Rahner wrote and taught at Innsbruck before its theology faculty was disbanded by the Nazis mid-1938. Looking over Rahner's writings and publications from this period reveal that he had fervent and often intersecting interests in both Christian spirituality and patristic theology. As I have already said, only the former has received widespread attention in contemporary literature on Rahner, especially in the English-speaking world. But, as a matter of fact, Rahner devoted enormous time and energy into working with patristic theology in these formative years as a seminarian, doctoral student, and young professor. As Neufeld has remarked, "The number and scope of his articles reveal that he felt at home in this area and that one cannot speak of this first phase of independent academic work as a side-interest."[238] Indeed, patristic theology was a primary interest, and it was within this crucible that we observe Rahner generating fundamental insights about and programs for developing theology about the Sacred Heart, *Symbol*, Christ's presence and the church, penance, the "supernatural," uncreated grace, and human salvation. All of these concepts would play significant, if not major, roles in the mature theology for which he is so well-known.

In the next section, I will argue that rather than being a "phase" which Rahner eventually abandoned, this early period marked by interest in the theology of the fathers had an ongoing impact on Karl Rahner's theology. However, I would like to close the present bibliographical considerations by drawing attention to one particular passage from 1943, in the midst of a kind of "interim" period between Rahner's "early" years (which we have just considered) and his more

236. "Laienheiligkeit im christlichen Altertum," *Stimmen der Zeit* 135 (1939), 234–51. Included in Viller, *Aszese und Mystik in der Väterzeit*. Available in *SW* 3:105–22.
237. "Zur scholastischen Begrifflichkeit der ungeschaffenen Gnade," *Zeitschrift für katholische Theologie* 63 (1939), 137–56. Included as "Some Implications of the Scholastic Concept," in *TI* 1:319–46.
238. Neufeld, "Editionsbericht," xv.

well-known theology from the 1950s onward. In this passage, worth quoting at length, Rahner offers yet another articulation of a christocentric world of grace and its corresponding person-centered, representative soteriology. Moreover, he appeals to Gregory Nazianzen's famous patristic dictum about the "assumed" and "redeemed" to do so:

> the saving reality of Christ is the consecration, in principle, of the whole creation. If anything was not assumed, neither was it redeemed; but whatever has been united with God has also been saved, says Gregory Nazianzen. But everything has been assumed, for Christ is true man, true son of Adam, truly lived a human life in all its breadth and height and depth, has truly become a star of this cosmos in which everything depends on everything else, a flower of this earth which we love. And hence everything, without confusion and without separation, is to enter into eternal life; there is to be not only a new heaven but a new earth. Nothing, unless it be eternally damned, can remain outside the blessing, the protection, the transfiguration of this divinization of the world which, beginning in Christ, aims at drawing everything that exists into the life of God himself, precisely in order that it may thus have eternal validity conferred upon it. This is the reality of Christ, which constitutes Christianity; the incarnate life of God in our place and our time. A reality to which belongs the word; a reality in which all human reality is called to God and blessed.[239]

Ongoing Impact of Rahner's Early Interests

Like many scholars, Rahner can, and has, been (correctly) understood to have grown through various "periods" in his thought. As noted above, Joseph Wong has noted Rahner's shift in emphasis from a "descending" to an "ascending" christological approach as his career progressed.[240] Moreover, Vorgrimler has noted that Karl Rahner consciously broke with his brother Hugo's heavily historical and "kerygmatic" movement in the late 1930s in favor of a more integrative

---

239. "The Parish Priest," in *Mission and Grace: Essays in Pastoral Theology*, 3 vols. (London: Sheed and Ward, 1963–1966), 2:35–52, at 42. The same recapitulation-based "Nazianzen" logic is operative in another essay from 1959 on prison ministry where Rahner writes "It is with such sinners that this love has, in strict reality, identified itself. For otherwise they would not be redeemed. Otherwise, only what is sound in itself would have been saved (whereas no such thing exists, though it often seems to us; so that we think that this thing, basically good in itself, has been accepted by God because it is good, instead of believing that what was truly lost has been accepted in order that it should be made good). . . . He is, in all truth, in them; because the primary mystery of that love which creates and makes one, which *is* God himself, is not understood, and hence the essence of Christianity is radically misunderstood, unless this improbable, paradoxical truth, with its radical reversal of all our shortsighted experience, is unconditionally accepted in faith" ("The Prison Pastorate," in *Mission and Grace*, 74–97, at 80–81 [originally "Besinnung für Gefangenenhausseelsorger,"] *Der Seelsorger* [Wien] 29 [1959], 460–69).
240. Wong, *Logos-Symbol*, 35–36.

approach to contemporary re-expression of the church's faith.[241] Legitimate as such shifts indeed are, Rahner's intense interest in patristic theology and spirituality was not simply a phase beyond which he moved in his more "speculative" career after World War II. Rather, this period was a formative one which continued to exercise influence in his later, mature writings; many basic and central theological insights which continued to guide Rahner's theology surfaced during this period, and although Rahner consciously decided to craft his theology in a more "contemporary" than strictly "historical" mode of expression, he was also conscious of the indispensable role that the church's tradition and history of dogma played in shaping that expression.

The ongoing impact of this early period has yet to be appreciated by Rahner scholars writing for the English-speaking world, although Batlogg and Neufeld have already presented such a thesis in German publications. Acknowledging the lack of explicit references to patristic theology in Rahner's mature work, Neufeld nonetheless asserts that there are deep resonances between this work and that of Rahner's early period:

> The free choice of the theme of the theological dissertation and hence the further interest in the thinking of the church fathers up through *Aszese und Mystik* allows a deeper bond to come to light, which was long ago established to the end even without explicit references and citations – established as a substratum in places, where they are not explicitly and thematically named.[242]

More particularly, Batlogg argues that *E latere Christi* sets the stage for Rahner's later work. He rightly testifies to the fact that the conclusion to *E latere Christi* stands "as a kind of prelude, indeed an outline with programmatic elements, which Rahner will take up in the following period over and over again."[243] Terms such as mystery-presence [*Mysteriengegenwart*], ontology of presence [*Gegenwärtigkeit*] (of the life of Jesus), and symbol-character [*Symbolcharakter*], among others, Batlogg observes, make meaningful appearances in Rahner's "De gratia Christi" (1937–1938), *Hearer of the Word* (1937/1941) and "Current Problems in Christology" (1954).

Batlogg's point here can be expressed even more strongly: as I noted earlier in chapter 2 and a few pages above, this "prelude" in the con-

---

241. *Understanding Karl Rahner*, 65–66.
242. Neufeld, "Editionsbericht," xiii.
243. Batlogg, "Editionsbericht: Teil A," xxxii.

clusion of *E latere Christi* even stands as a call for, and sketch with the most basic parts of, Rahner's later "Theology of the Symbol" (1959).[244] Underdeveloped as this "sketch" was in 1936, the central place of *das Realsymbol* within Rahner's overall theology illustrates how significantly his early interests impacted his mature theology. The concept of *Symbol* is one instance of a major component of Rahner's theology, the full expression of which results from his attempts to work out the implications of insights made during the course of his early, patristic work. Another such instance is Christ's (not unrelated) role as Savior, the full expression of which will be considered in the next and final chapter.

Yet another instance of Rahner's early interests living on is the topic of Jesus's Sacred Heart, which receives ongoing attention over the course of Rahner's career.[245] A sample of Rahner's writings on this theme include a homiletic reflection from 1938,[246] spiritual essays from 1947[247] and 1958,[248] and more technical treatment also in 1958,[249] a 1966 address to seminarians at Innsbruck,[250] and essay from 1982 which begins by noting the sharp decline in the devotion and which argues for its continued relevance and import.[251] Part of this argument concerns the importance of the church's historical patrimony. Rahner writes that the "Church always brings her history with her into the present and in this way carries it on."[252]

Such statements about the church's history were not mere lip service for Rahner, and Rahner, in particular, is well-positioned to rebut

244. Batlogg makes a similar observation elsewhere, though he once again may understate the connection: "The beginnings of 1936 could be read as enlightening for the background of this later article from 1959" (*Die Mysterien des Lebens Jesu bei Karl Rahner*, 304).
245. For more on this topic, see Annice Callahan, *Karl Rahner's Spirituality of the Sacred Heart*, as well as M.J. Walsh, *The Heart of Christ in the Writings of Karl Rahner: An Investigation of its Christological Foundation as an Example of the Relationship between Theology and Spirituality* (Rome: Gregorian Univ. Press, 1977).
246. In Neufeld, "Karl Rahner: Predigten zur Verkündigungstheologie 1938," *Zeitschrift für Katholische Theologie* 129 (2007), 183–206, at 195.
247. "Geheimnis des Herzens," *Geist und Leben* 20 (1947), 161–65. Included as "The Mystery of the Heart," in *The Great Church Year*, 239–44.
248. "Christus: Das Herz der Welt," *Tag des Herrn: Katholisches Kirchenblatt* (Leipzig) 8, nos. 15/16 (19.04.1958), 57; ET "Easter: A Faith that Loves the Earth," in *The Great Church Year*, 192–97.
249. "Der theologische Sinn der Verehrung des Herzens Jesu," in *Festschrift zur Hundertjahrfeier des Theologischen Konviktes Innsbruck 1858-1958* (Innsbruck: Collegium Canasianum, 1958), 102–9. Included as "The Theological Meaning of the Veneration of the Sacred Heart," in *TI* 8:217–28.
250. 1966 talk to seminarians at Innsbruck, "Der Mensch mit dem durchbohrten Herzen: Festvortrag vom 17. Juni 1966 im Canisianum," *Korrespondenzblatt des Priestergebetsvereines im Canisianum zu Innsbruck* 101 (1966), 19–27. Included as "The Man with the Pierced Heart," in *Karl Rahner: Spiritual Writings*, ed. Philip Endean (Maryknoll: Orbis, 2004), 120–31.
251. "Herz-Jesu-Verehrung heute," *Korrespondenzblatt des Canisianums* 116 (1/1982/83), 2–8. Included as "Devotion to the Sacred Heart Today," in *TI* 23:117–28.
252. "Devotion to the Sacred Heart Today," *TI* 23:121.

any claims to the contrary. Included among Rahner's various editing duties was an intense stint editing Denzinger's *Enchiridion Symbolorum*, a compilation of magisterial statements spanning the church's history, which was among the most commonly cited texts of Catholic dogmatic theology in the first part of the twentieth century.[253] Rahner himself was in charge of producing the twenty-eighth through thirty-first editions of this text. Thus, paired with his intense concern for giving Catholic theology contemporary purchase was an avid interest in particular, historically established doctrines which provided bounds within which that theology could operate. In fact, as Harvey Egan has noted, Rahner was, at times, criticized by "progressive" theologians of the generations which followed him for the privileged place which he gave such statements.[254]

With respect to the particularly important place *patristic* theology held throughout Rahner's career, I will briefly note two items. First, as John McDade has observed,[255] Rahner once made a remarkable statement about the center of his theology: the most "fundamental and basic conception of Christianity," according to Rahner, is "the divinization of the world through the Spirit of God."[256] Rahner continues by adding that "the Incarnation and soteriology arise as an inner moment" out of God's basic, divinizing act within creation. The idea of divinization or deification, commonly cited with reference to 2 Peter 1:4,[257] is commonly expressed in Western theology in terms of God's "elevation" of human nature to share in God's life,[258] but is most frequently associated with Eastern, Greek theology, particularly that of the fathers. The overall worldview out of which the concept of divinization emerges is strongly Irenaean: human beings exist with the divine intention of gradually maturing, through the gift of God's grace,

---

253. *The Sources of Catholic Dogma*, eds. Heinrich Denzinger and K. Rahner (Fitzwilliam, NH: Loreto Publications, 2007). Translated from *Enchiridion Symbolorum*, 13th ed. (Freiburg i.Br.: Herder, 1954). Updated as *Enchiridion Symbolorum*, eds. Denzinger and Schönmetzer (*DS*).

254. "It is one of the ironies of Karl Rahner's life that many of his critics have accused him of neglecting the historical, the cultural, the particular, the finite, the 'categorical.' These critics assert that Rahner focuses almost exclusively on the human spirit's drive beyond the finite, that is, the spirit's 'transcendence.' . . . However, other critics chide Rahner for allegedly being too traditional, for being a 'Denziger [*sic*] theologian,' for defending seemingly outdated church thinking and living, for taking too quickly the church's actual living faith as the starting point for his theology" ("Foreword," in Callahan, *Karl Rahner's Spirituality of the Pierced Heart*, iv–viii, at iv).

255. John McDade, "Catholic Theology in the Post-Conciliar Period," in *Modern Catholicism*, ed. Adrian Hastings (New York: Oxford Univ. Press, 1991), 422–43, at 424).

256. *Karl Rahner in Dialogue*, 126.

257. God "has given us . . . his precious and very great promises, so that through them you may escape from the corruption that is in the world because of lust, and may become participants in the divine nature."

258. Cf. Thomas Aquinas's *ST* I–II q. 109 a. 2; I–II q. 110 a. 3.

into their fullest calling, which consists of participating in God's triune love, and even nature. Francis Caponi has recently demonstrated how central the idea of divinization is to Karl Rahner's metaphysics, anthropology, and theology of the incarnation.[259]

The second item concerns Rahner's short *Theological Dictionary*, published with Herbert Vorgrimler first in 1961 and which was reissued in multiple editions through the 1970s. Two entries, "Anacephalaeosis"[260] [i.e., recapitulation] and "Redemption"[261] are particularly noteworthy. The former is sufficiently brief to cite in its entirety:

> Literally a summary or recapitulation (Gr. αναχεφαλαίωσις); its theological usage, relating to saving history, derives from Ephesians 1:10 and was employed notably by St Irenaeus. It denotes that the whole of creation is referred to the Incarnation of God in such a way that creation as such must be understood as a preparation for collaboration with God made Man. In the present economy, therefore, Christ is not only the goal of creation and the apogee of Adam's race, but having borne our sins and risen as the first-born from the dead, his radical acceptance of every phase of human history has redeemed and "re"-constituted that creation which up until his coming had been subjected to vanity.[262]

Of particular note here is the two-pronged treatment of recapitulation offered by Rahner. The first aspect concerns Christ's person is strictly ontological terms: Christ, in his *being*, precisely *is* "the goal of creation and the apogee of Adam's race." The second concerns the "acceptance" language, which, as we noted above, characterizes both Rahner's treatment of Irenaeus in *E latere Christi* as well as his own mature soteriology. Here, he writes, Christ's "radical acceptance of every phase of human history has redeemed and 're'-constituted . . . creation." While this second aspect concerns Christ's act of "acceptance," it too concerns his *being*—is saving "act" isn't a singular, one-off feat of a super-agent, but is the ongoing act of radically accepting "every phase of human history." In other words, Christ's saving "act" is the person-centered and *symbolisch* act of "truly liv[ing] a human life in all its breadth and height and depth," as Rahner put it nearly two decades earlier.[263]

Rahner's (significantly longer) entry on "Redemption" bears this

---

259. Francis Caponi, "Karl Rahner: Divinization in Roman Catholicism."
260. *Theological Dictionary*, 17.
261. Ibid., 395–97.
262. Ibid., 17.
263. "The Parish Priest," 42.

same, two-pronged structure. He begins by noting human guilt before God and the need for God's forgiveness, which comes in the form of redemption. Rahner then distinguishes between the content of redemption (i.e., "divine life given with the remission of sin") and our appropriating this content in freedom, both of which are depend entirely on God's gratuity. Next, Rahner explains that the phenomenon of redemption is "wholly bound up with the historical Person and work of Jesus," in whom God, rather than "simply setting aside and the provisional character of the whole man in need of redemption," "giv[es] his redemptive grace . . . historical tangibility, presence and power in a world that is to be preserved." Rahner continues, "Jesus' being (as the union of God's life and human existence) and activity (as the acceptance, in loving obedience, of human existence characterized by sin . . .) taken together *are* the historically real, eschatologically victorious bestowal on the world of God's self-communication despite, and in, the world's sinfulness."[264] Elaborating further, he says that "in Jesus God has definitively accepted the one world and humanity, as a whole, in spite of sin and precisely in their culpable destiny,"[265] and that "God willed the human life of his Son to be a total surrender of loving obedience."[266]

Once again, Jesus's person and act are distinguished as the two-pronged origin of our salvation. The first aspect is described in highly ontological terms—"Jesus' being" is described as the saving "union of God's life and human existence." The second aspect pertains to Jesus's act, but once again, concerns his *being* as well. The activity is precisely that of "acceptance, in loving obedience, of human existence characterized by sin." As with the second aspect of "Anacephalaeosis," this second "activity" aspect of Christ's redemption consists of Christ's "acceptance," and not simply the acceptance of the cross and death, but of his human existence in its entirety.

These remarkably parallel entries in Rahner's *Theological Dictionary* offer a valuable testimony to how Rahner's own favored account of redemption in Christ draws heavily upon (his understanding of) patristic, particularly Irenaean theology. While the genre of the majority of his writings (i.e., somewhat lengthy ad hoc essays on challenges faced by contemporary Christians) do not easily lend themselves to demonstrating the historical influences behind his theology,[267] the genre of

264. *Theological Dictionary*, 396, emphasis original.
265. Ibid.
266. Ibid., 397.

short, pithy dictionary entries do. Although Rahner does not here elect to elaborate "redemption" in explicitly patristic terms, the parallels of his account with that of "recapitulation" are striking. It is precisely this sort of influence—as an unidentified yet formatively operative "substratum," to borrow Neufeld's formulation—that the fathers' theology has on Rahner's soteriology.

Factors Contributing to Rahner's Decrease in Explicit Engagement with the Fathers

One may, perhaps, object to my (as well as Batlogg's and Neufeld's) contention that Rahner's early fascination with and use of patristic theology continued to operate as a "substratum" underlying his later theology by appealing to his lack of explicit reference to the fathers and their theological categories. Does not this absence, one might retort, indicate that Rahner abandoned his earlier "historical" mode of doing theology (in favor of a more contemporary, speculative, and "transcendental" approach), and perhaps that Rahner even wanted to dissociate himself from these figures?

First, it should be noted, the perceived "absence" of patristic references in Rahner's later theology is an exaggerated perception. As Karl Neufeld has noted, Rahner *does* make such references and even focuses on particularly patristic issues (especially concerning penance) throughout the course of his career:

> Rahner himself has gradually tried different approaches, depending on which task faced him and what means seemed appropriate. He was not indifferent to the "catchy" problems and the day's methods of handling them. However, if he could determine on his own what he wanted to handle in what way, then with astonishing regularity – e.g. concerning the question of penance – he had recourse to the world of the church fathers.[268]

That said, the language and categories utilized most often in Rahner's writings seem to be Thomistic and transcendental. Even if the use of fathers later in his career is not totally absent, it is relatively sparse (especially in comparison to some of Rahner's contemporaries, whose

---

267. Nonetheless, I will attempt to identify and analyze several portions of such texts in order to demonstrate how Rahner's mature theology indeed conforms to the characteristic markers of a representative soteriology in the next chapter.
268. Neufeld "Editionsbereicht," xiv.

theology has also been identified as having patristic influences and substrata[269]. The question remains: might the relative scarcity of such references reflect a conscious move on Rahner's part to dissociate himself from the historical, particularly patristic, theology which shaped his early career?

Here, I would like to respond to this sort of reaction by positing two explanators for the sparse patristic references in Rahner's soteriological writings after the 1930s. These two explanators, I would contend, stand together as an alternative to a theory according to which Rahner deserted historical approaches to theology and wished to distance himself from patristic soteriology. According to my suggested alternative, Rahner sought: (i) to dissociate himself not from the fathers' soteriological insights, but from the distorted category of physical redemption (discussed above in chapter 3) which, thanks in large part to Adolf von Harnack, had come to be almost synonymous with "patristic soteriology" in the minds of many (especially German) theologians, and (ii) to *infuse*, rather than replace (or even supplement), a historically grounded approach to theology with contemporary concerns, categories, and terminology.

The Fathers and "Physical Redemption"

The first likely explanator for Rahner's reluctance to explicitly articulate and/or categorize his own soteriology in patristic terms is the widespread association of patristic soteriology with the troubled notion of "physical redemption." This theory of atonement, attributed by many Liberal Protestants and others to Greek fathers such as Irenaeus but which is most likely somewhat of a strawman,[270] posits that human salvation is accomplished at the first moment of the Incarnation, at which point, the abstract natures of humanity and divinity coalesce somewhere in the Platonic heavens. This Hellenized, pseudophilosophical myth, it is said, renders the cross devoid of any soteriological meaning, entails a kind of mechanical and universal salvation, and depletes soteriology of any moral imperative.

---

269. E.g., Hans Urs von Balthasar (cf. Kevin Mongrain, *The Systematic Thought of Hans Urs von Balthasar: An Irenaean Retrieval* [New York: Crossroad, 2002], Werner Löser, *Im Geist des Origenes: Hans Urs von Balthasar als Interpret der Theologie der Kirchenväter* [Frankfurt: Knecht, 1976], as well as "Divine Predecessors: the Fathers of the Church," in Aidan Nichols, *Divine Fruitfulness: A Guide Through Balthasar's Theology Beyond the Trilogy* [London: T&T Clark, 2007], 23–56).

270. See Trevor Hart, "Irenaeus, Recapitulation and Physical Redemption," in *Christ in Our Place: The Humanity of God in Christ for the Reconciliation of the World*, eds. T. Hart and D. Thimell (Exeter: Paternoster Press, 1989), 152–81, as well as Chapter 3 above.

Although Gustaf Aulén's famous *Christus Victor*[271] had countered this Liberal Protestant association on a prominent stage by 1930, it was still held in the minds of many, as Rahner was well aware. Let us consider three places in which Rahner explicitly mentions the connection. In "The One Christ and the Universality of Salvation," Rahner begins a section on "Jesus and All Men" by asserting that "the death and resurrection of Jesus, taken together, *do possess* soteriological significance."[272] He then adds that "Jesus possesses *that* relationship to every man which connects all men together," and "history and humanity . . . do not merely consist in a sum of individual human beings and isolated biographies."[273] This "soteriological connection between Jesus and the whole of humanity," he explains, "plays a role in the doctrine of redemption found among the Greek fathers, in that in their view humanity has a form of existence which enables the eternal Logos to enter into communion with the single race of mankind."[274] Thus far, his explicit reference to the fathers is made approvingly, at least insofar as Jesus's relationship to the whole of humankind, a fundamental axiom for Rahner's soteriology, "plays a role" in that of the fathers as well.

Rahner then goes on to discuss the problems entailed by "say[ing] that the redemption was achieved through the incarnation alone," first among which is that such a view deprives Christ's death and resurrection of any soteriological significance.[275] Accordingly, "all forms of causality of a physical . . . type fail."[276] The quick succession Rahner's references to the "doctrine of redemption found among the Greek fathers," "redemption . . . achieved through the incarnation alone," and "forms of causality of a physical . . . type" illustrate Rahner's acute awareness of the Liberal Protestant category of "physical redemption" and the problems entailed with it. However, Rahner does not directly attribute the view to the fathers themselves.

Writing one year later, Rahner mentions physical redemption again in *Foundations of Christian Faith*. In a brief treatment of "classical" soteriology, Rahner makes only a brief allusion to "a 'doctrine of physical

---

271. See "Irenaeus," in Gustaf Aulén, *Christus Victor: An Historical Study of the Three Main Types of the Idea of Atonement* (New York: Macmillan, 1969), 16–35 at 18–19.
272. "The One Christ and the Universality of Salvation," *TI* 16:199–224, at 210 (emphasis original).
273. Ibid. (emphasis original).
274. Ibid., *TI* 16:210–11.
275. "The death and resurrection of Jesus must possess universal importance in themselves for salvation and cannot merely be regarded as isolated events, of no significance in themselves, in a life which only has universal relevance for salvation in being the life of the eternal Logos" (ibid., *TI* 16:211).
276. Ibid., *TI* 16:210.

redemption' which is found in the Greek fathers [*einer in der griechischen Patristik gegebenen 'physischen Erlösungslehre'*], and according to which the world appears as saved because it is physically and inseparably united to the Godhead in the humanity of Jesus," opting "to prescind" [*absehen*] from even examining the theory.[277] Here, the association of physical redemption, of which Rahner clearly disapproves, with the fathers seems to come from the lips of Rahner himself. The English translation could be refined a bit so it would (more literally) read, "a 'doctrine of physical redemption' given in Greek patristics," attributing the category directly to *the study* of the fathers rather than to the fathers themselves. But the passage raises an important question: Did Rahner, after his early years, eventually come to believe that the fathers themselves held a deficient soteriological theory like "physical redemption"? Such a possibility would support a narrative in which Rahner would indeed want to dissociate his own theology from that of the fathers.

However, a third locus in which Rahner writes on the topic suggests that this possibility is, in fact, not the case. In his entry on "Salvation" in *Sacramentum Mundi*, he once again warns of the dangers of physical redemption, and while he does not employ the term itself, it is clear (especially in light of the other two entries just considered) that he has the theory in mind:

> If in an incarnational doctrine of redemption it is emphasized too one-sidedly that mankind was redeemed by the fact of the divine Logos assuming a human nature as member of the one mankind ("quod assumptum est, redemptum est"), then redemption is one-sidedly envisioned only under cosmic and objective aspects and Scripture is not taken seriously when it sees the redemptive event in Jesus' love and obedience even to the Cross.[278]

One might take the reference to Gregory Nazianzen's famous dictum ("quod assumptum est, redemptum est") to signal Rahner's attribution of "physical redemption" to the soteriology of the fathers. However, it is important to recognize that Rahner is here denouncing an excessively "one-sided" emphasis upon the salvific role of the incarnation, a salvific role which he articulates using Nazianzen's dictum and which, properly related to the cross, he openly affirms.[279] The "one-sided" dis-

---

277. *FCF*, 288, cf. *Grundkurs des Glaubens*, 282.
278. "Salvation," *SM* 5:405–38, at 427–28.
279. "The incarnation itself is a divine movement which is fully deployed only in the death and res-

tortion of this truth appears when the mere "fact" of assumption, operating on a "cosmic" scale, suffices for salvation, to the exclusion of Christ's death and resurrection.

The key remark which Rahner makes, however, comes a page later as Rahner undertakes a historical overview of historical contributions to soteriology. There, he writes, "In the Fathers what is most important (over and above the transmission of biblical doctrine) is Irenaeus's recapitulation theory (mystical-incarnational theory of redemption) which, without denying the Pauline theory of ransom and atonement by the Cross, teaches on the basis of Eph 1:10 the reunion of mankind with God in Christ as the all-embracing head."[280] Here, Rahner does not saddle Irenaeus with the "physical" category, but describes his soteriology instead as "mystical-incarnational," and with the familiar term "recapitulation." Moreover, Rahner makes sure to explicitly head-off any association of Irenaeus with his criticism on the previous page, noting that the recapitulation theory does not exclude "atonement by the Cross." This passage makes it quite clear that, at least in the case of Irenaeus, "physical redemption" is not at issue. It is also worth noting that while Rahner offers criticisms of every other soteriological category in this historical overview,[281] Irenaeus and recapitulation receive no such critique.

Taken together, these three treatments of physical redemption from relatively late in Rahner's career do not show an antipathy toward the theology of the fathers on account of this category, but rather, an acute awareness of their widespread association with it (an awareness which led to Rahner's conscious effort to dissociate at least Irenaeus from the "physicalist" framework). Cognizant of this strong association, and perhaps not wanting to invest time into a lengthy historical project disproving it (notwithstanding the brief apologetic assertion on behalf of Irenaeus), it seems plausible that Rahner refrained from articulating his own soteriology in explicitly patristic terms for fear of guilt (or at least confusion) by association.

---

urrection of Jesus Christ (cf. Jn 3:17; 1 Tim 11:15; D 86: the *descensus* is itself *propter nos homines et propter nostram salutem*)" (ibid., 428).

280. Ibid., 429.

281. *Christus victor*, attributed by Rahner to Origen, is described as "strongly mythological" (ibid.); Anselm's satisfaction theory is "situated in the categories of Germanic law," can obscure the fact that the salvific initiative originates with *God*, and is only extrinsically connected to the resurrection of the body and transfiguration of the world (ibid., 430); Liberal Protestant exemplarists cannot sufficiently acknowledge God's forgiving love "as the *cause* of our salvation" (ibid., emphasis original); and theories according to which *God* is changed by the Christ-event and the cross "fall into primitive anthropomorphism" (ibid.).

Contemporary Terms for the Contemporary Person

The second explanator for Rahner's omission of explicit references to the fathers while articulating his own soteriology is perhaps even more likely than the first, as well as less particular to the field of soteriology: especially after 1940, Rahner made a conscious effort to do his theology in contemporary terms for the contemporary person. As stated above, the late 1930s saw an adjustment to Rahner's method, which until that point had been shared largely with his brother Hugo. As Hugo began pursuing the "kerygmatic" theology movement, Rahner consciously diverged, wary of what he saw as a theology which simply proclaimed anew the New Testament and church fathers while adapting a contemporary message alongside them. What was needed, Rahner judged, was a retrieval of these sources in such a way that the retrieval itself rendered their insights intelligible today.[282]

Rahner expressed his desire for such an infusion of contemporary intelligibility and relevance into the theology of the church's tradition not only in his more explicit theological reflections on method,[283] but also in his preaching. In an admonition to newly ordained priests in 1955, Rahner urged,

> Preserve the Church's heritage of truth and experience while reaching out boldly to take hold of the future, which belongs to God precisely in the same way as the past. . . . When you defend the heritage of the past, it must not be out of lazy-mindedness or a false craving for security, but out of loyalty to the truth of God, ever ancient and ever new, to which you are bound. When you are striving for anything that is new, let it be done in humility and with serene courage.[284]

A year earlier, in an essay called "The Student of Theology," Rahner expressed the important truth "that every age . . . has to have *its own theology* (and has had it, from the time of the Fathers to that of the post-Tridentine Baroque)."[285] The theology particular to a given age,

---

282. See Vorgrimler, *Understanding Karl Rahner*, 65–66.
283. E.g., "The Prospects for Dogmatic Theology," *TI* 1:7.
284. "First Mass," in *Mission and Grace* 3:211–20, at 214.
285. Rahner continues by exorting his reader, "try to gauge the gap between the general intellectual situation in the world of today and the situation which it has replaced—approximately, the Baroque world; then measure the gap between a late Baroque treatment of dogmatic theology and a modern one. . . . It seems to me that if anyone does not admit that the second gap is too small in relation to the first, that, in fact, despite all its learning, the modern period has not done the job in theology for its own age that earlier theologies did for their age, then that person is past helping" ("The Student of Theology," in *Mission and Grace* 2:146–81, at 163–64).

he goes on to say, cannot be an "encyclopedic" learning of the brain, but rather, a "living possession."[286] "Obviously," he admits, "no-one is opposed to this ideal in theory. But it is time to face the fact that the gap between ideal and reality has grown so great that there is need for a new, conscious attempt at closing it."[287]

Although a host of examples for Rahner's implementation of this effort could be cited, Rahner's insistence on developing an "ascending" Christology true to Chalcedon is a prominent one to which he returned repeatedly in the last thirty years of his life. In his famous 1954 essay from the first volume of *Theological Investigations*, "Current Problems in Christology," Rahner insists that the doctrine of Chalcedon should be viewed as a beginning, not an end.[288] The fruit which Rahner envisioned this "beginning" producing in our time is expressed ardently in a personal letter sent during the Second Vatican Council, in which he longs for an ascending Christology that expresses the church's faith regarding the person of Jesus but without the "mythological" overtones which the modern ear detects in descending approaches[289]—even the "progressive" theologians at the Council, he lamented, did not appreciate how important this matter was.[290] Still in 1980, Rahner was insisting that theologians strive to rescue Chalcedonian Christology from contemporary "suspicion of being mythological" by reflecting and restating the church's traditional doctrine "with all fidelity, all respect, all deference to the past, with all the normative force established by traditional Chalcedonian Christology."[291]

If Rahner's primary objective with his own later Christology was to express the church's doctrine in contemporary (rather than mythological) terms, it would be no surprise that his insights (shaped though they might have been by his early reading of the fathers) were not couched in patristic terms (especially considering the mythological stigma associated, however unfairly, with them).[292] "Contemporary

286. Ibid., 180.
287. Ibid.
288. *TI* 1:149–200. See Robert Krieg, "A Fortieth-Anniversary Reappraisal of 'Chalcedon: End or Beginning?'," *Philosophy and Theology* 9 (1995), 77–116.
289. Cf. Rahner's December 1971 lecture, "Two Basic Types of Christology," in *TI* 13:213–23.
290. "I also notice here that I'm not yet all that old, even when I sit at a table with Daniélou, Congar, Ratzinger, Schillebeeckx and so on. I find that these still do not realize clearly enough how little, e.g., a christology 'from above', which simply begins with the declaration that God has become man, can be understood today. And the same is true in so many other instances. Of course one can hardly expect that another way of thinking will already make a mark on the schemata of the Council, but I do not find it explicitly enough among the progressive theologians themselves" (Vorgrimler, *Understanding Karl Rahner*, 158).
291. "Brief Observations on Systematic Christology Today," *TI* 21:228–38, at 230.
292. In his classic *Christus Victor*, Gustaf Aulén argues that the earliest, patristic model of Christian sote-

terms for contemporary people" seems to be the answer to a related question, namely, why did Rahner omit his many patristic "history of dogma" essays when he began publishing *Theological Investigations* in the mid-1950s? Such an answer is implicit in the rationale which he offers in the series' preface, which occurs immediately after he calls attention to the absence of these historical essays:

> we have attempted here to disinter a few essays from periodicals, leaving out work concerned purely with the history of dogma. . . . The presumptuous intention of this modest collection of theological studies will be achieved if they help just a little (before they are finally forgotten) to confirm young theologians in the conviction that Catholic theology has no reason to rest on its laurels, fine though those may be; that on the contrary it can and must advance, and in such a way that it remains true to its own laws and its tradition.[293]

The theology which Rahner wanted to influence the next generation was one which *advanced* the church's doctrinal heritage in a way suitable for reception in his day. If such a program was on the forefront of his mind, allowing the fathers and their theology to operate at the level of "substratum" would make a great deal of sense. As we close this consideration of a second likely "explanatory," it is important to note that even if contemporary relevance was on the forefront of Rahner's mind later in his career, he never lost sight of Catholic theology's need to "remain true to its own laws and its traditions," maintaining "all fidelity, all respect, all deference to the past."

Traditional and Contemporary, Historical and Speculative

In this chapter, I have offered an overview of Karl Rahner's early life and writings in order to demonstrate that his early career was marked by an intense and prolonged engagement with patristic theology, particularly that of Irenaeus of Lyons. More specifically, Rahner's theology dissertation *E latere Christi*, which takes as its starting point the idea

---

riology was not "physical redemption," but one according to which Jesus definitively defeat Satan, redeeming those who had fallen in to the latter's possession. One objection against this "Christus victor" theory of atonement, an objection which Aulén himself anticipated, concerns its "mythological dress" (*Christus Victor*, 47). As William Placher succinctly puts it, the theory's "interpreters need to specify whether its battle imagery refers to a metaphorical, spiritual battle (in which case Christus Victor theory turns into something like moral influence theory) or an honest-to-goodness swordfight battle (in which case the questions about mythological imagery become very pressing indeed)" ("How Does Jesus Save? An Alternative View of Atonement," *Christian Century* [June 2, 2009], 23–27, at 24).

293. *TI* 1:xxi–xxii.

of Christ as the New Adam, testifies to Rahner's early fascination with representative soteriology. In exegeting Paul, Rahner dwells on the idea that Christ, like Adam, is the one whose very nature allows him to represent the many: "Christ is ancestor and head of all the spiritually living and not just through his redemptive activity, but already by his very nature as the God-man, and as such he shares, as new life-source, the supernatural life with all people, so that this life can only be found in him."[294] The redemptive character of Christ's person, the very locus of supernatural life, is one of the salient markers of representative Christology; it is also a theme in Rahner's early christological reflections that continued into the 1940s[295] and, we will see in the subsequent chapter, late into his theological career.

Furthermore, I have argued that this early portion of Rahner's career was not simply an abandoned phase or project which he scuttled in a methodological about-face. Jesus's Sacred Heart, *das Realsymbol*, Christian spirituality,[296] penance, God's gracious self-communication, and salvation in Christ the True Human all stand as major streams of continuity linking his later thought to this early period. Finally, I have argued that it is plausible that Rahner allowed patristic soteriological categories to operate at the level of "implicit substratum" in his later writings on human salvation in order to circumvent association with the wrongheaded category of "physical redemption," as well as to aid his project of promoting contemporary relevance.

Before closing this chapter and its foray into Rahner's early patristic interests, it is worth reiterating that even with his concern for contemporary relevance, it is clear that Rahner *did* (even and especially late in his career) want to be considered a historical as well as a speculative theologian. After consciously electing to omit his earlier "history of dogma" essays when inaugurating his *Theological Investigations* volumes, Rahner eventually began integrating these older writings into the series, even devoting the entire fifteenth volume to the topic of

---

294. *E latere Christi*, 15.
295. "the saving reality of Christ is the consecration, in principle, of the whole creation. If anything was not assumed, neither was it redeemed; but whatever has been united with God has also been saved, says Gregory Nazianzen. But everything has been assumed, for Christ is true man, true son of Adam, truly lived a human life in all its breadth and height and depth" ("The Parish Priest," 42).
296. "We also need to ask afresh how we can do still more than has been done to bring into closer relationship theology and the spiritual life, theological instruction and the personal formation of the student's character. . . . It is not that lectures should be sermons and the lecture-hall turn into a chapel. But of all sciences, theology . . . simply is the one to which, as a science, existential acceptance is most indispensable. But it is the case that among theologians, young and old alike, theology is often very undevotional . . . , while piety (in the seminaries) is very untheological" ("The Student of Theology," 176–77).

penance and the early church. In the preface to this volume, Rahner explains that he did so in an attempt to reverse the perception that he is a purely "speculative" theologian:

I am suspected by many people of being only a speculative theologian who works without reference to history and who, in some circumstances, attempts to dispel difficulties which arise in understanding statements of the Church's magisterium by the merely speculative interpretation of such statements. I am absolutely convinced that genuine Catholic theology must always proceed on the basis both of exegesis and of the history of dogmas and theology, even if it must be the free choice of the individual theologian whether, in a study of a particular point, he wishes to work "speculatively" or "historically". It is possible, therefore, that the present volume will dispel the suspicion that I have no appreciation of historical theology.[297]

The later Rahner, too, proclaimed the indispensable role of history for systematic theology.

It is for precisely this reason that, in the closing years of his life, Rahner began to lament the current state of systematic theology.[298] In addition to chiding systematic theologians for a "weariness" which had settled upon the discipline,[299] he suggested that neo-Scholastic manual theology, problematic as it was, fared significantly better than its successors when it came to conceptual precision and attention to the magisterium's body of teachings.[300] Moreover, he explained that his own theology was grounded in this Thomistic foundation, the bounds of which he nonetheless sought to advance beyond.[301] Such a historical, particularly Thomistic basis, Rahner worried, was lacking in the generation of theologians emerging during his final years: "If young the-

---

297. *TI* 15:viii.
298. In "The Present Situation of Catholic Theology" (1979), Rahner judges, "All things taken into consideration I really do feel that Catholic theology today by and large does not rate a higher mark than Grade C" (*TI* 21:70–77, at 75).
299. "Today a certain weariness and resignation seems to have settled on systematic theology. This is certainly not due to the Council, which supplied theologians with many half-forgotten questions" ("Forgotten Initiatives of the Second Vatican Council" [1982] *TI* 22:97–105, at 105). Rahner also wrote that "signs of fatigue can be detected in the theology of the last ten years: an escape into pastoral studies and religious educational theory or to a false anthropocentrism which closes man up in himself" ("The Abiding Significance of the Second Vatican Council" [1979] *TI* 20:90–102, at 95).
300. "[O]ne could wish that students of theology even today were a little more aware of the conceptual exactitude of neoscholasticism and of its orientation to the declarations of the magisterium" (ibid., *TI* 20:94).
301. "I tried to ferret out the inner power and dynamism which is hidden within scholastic theology. Scholastic theology offers so many problems and is so dynamic that it can develop within itself, and then by means of a certain qualitative leap, can surpass itself" (*Faith in a Wintry Season*, 17).

ologians can no longer begin with this Thomistic heritage, that's a bad sign – not for Thomas, but for present-day theologians."[302]

Rahner made clear elsewhere that this "beginning point" extended beyond Thomas Aquinas to the whole of the church's historical and doctrinal patrimony, particularly the christological doctrines of the early centuries and their foundational loci in scripture. In the final years of his career, Rahner began emphasizing the former part of his celebrated dictum that Chalcedon *was a beginning*, not an end. Taking this point to the pages of *Concilium*, he wrote,

> when we come to deal with Christology, we cannot move beyond the traditional formulation of the dogma to the point where we can do without it. . . . We theologians of today . . . have to be people not only who think that they have learned something from the history of faith but also who are still willing to learn from it. If we really do have this willingness, how could we possibly entertain the desire simply to abandon the old christological formulations in favor of new formulations of our own? . . . I have no patience with Catholic exegetes whose work manifests no awareness whatsoever of the Council of Chalcedon. There must be an authentic integration of the past if Christology is to have any future. . . . I can accept the words of the Johannine prologue with a faith so steadfast that I am ready to die for it. These words will always be accepted as a real and vital foundation of my own theology.[303]

Rahner insisted on a robust historical basis for systematic theology, an insistence which received particular emphasis toward the end of his career when, with the demise of neo-Scholastic manual theology, the balance of "historical" and "speculative" seemed to him to have undergone an overcorrection in favor of the latter.

For as many legitimate developments and shifts can be rightly attributed to Rahner as his career advanced, his overall appreciation for and dependence upon historical theology was a hallmark of that career its entirety, from his patristic-steeped beginnings to the some-

302. Ibid., 48.
303. "Christology Today," in *TI* 21:220–27, at 220, 222 (first published in *Concilium* 18 [1982], 212–16). Cf. Rahner's statement two years earlier, "Young theologians who study theology today without learning in Christology what the Council of Chalcedon says, what person, nature, hypostatic union, and communication of properties mean, would be deprived of the obvious and requisite tools of Catholic Christology. It goes without saying that things like these are indispensable even today. If we show just a little respect for two millennia of the history of thought, if we still regard Plato, Aristotle, Augustine, Kant, Descartes, and others as our masters and can still learn something new from them even though we philosophers of today are of an entirely different breed, then the same obviously holds true in the case of the Church's traditional two-thousand-year Christology. Far from being embarrassed, we ought to feel obliged to dig deeper into this christological tradition" ("Brief Observations on Systematic Christology Today," *TI* 21:228).

times grumpy complaints voiced in his final years. Rahner's exhortation in his twilight that today's theologians "have to be people not only who think that they have learned something from the history of faith but also who are still willing to learn from it" echoes the words in his dissertation's conclusion that we "can learn something from the early church."[304] Words from the preface of his 1939 compendium of patristic spirituality may well be said of his entire career: "A spiritual science, especially a theological one, can never dispense with the knowledge of the history of its own life. Only in the lasting engagement with its own past does it gain its ultimate object vis-à-vis its breadth and openness, which enables it to judge appropriately and find its way into the future."[305]

304. *E latere Christi*, 84.
305. *Aszese und Mystik in der Väterzeit*, v.

5

Representative Soteriology in Rahner's Mature Work

In 1965, Rahner was asked whether "the primary end of theology is the contemplation of truth." He responded sharply, "No. The salvation of man is the primary end. . . . Here on earth all reflective knowledge of God's truth that we call theology must be directed toward the salvation of human beings and nothing else."[1] Since the whole of theology is oriented toward human salvation as its foremost *telos*, the subfield of soteriology, the explicit study of that salvation and how it comes about, is paramount within Rahner's thought.

When considering the "what" of Rahner's soteriology, that is, the *content* of salvation, the answer is quite clear and succinct: Salvation is the "supernatural and direct presence of God in himself afforded by grace."[2] The "how" question—namely, the way in which Rahner understands God's gracious presence to humanity to be brought about—is a trickier matter.

Summarizing our previous findings, we could say that Rahner's answer to this "how" question appears as a twofold picture, with God's

1. *Karl Rahner in Dialogue: Conversations and Interviews*, eds. Paul Imhof and Hubert Biallowons (New York: Crossroad, 1986), 17–18.
2. "The One Christ and the Universality of Salvation," *TI* 16:199–224, at 200.

grace as its subject. On the one hand, salvation comes about on account of God's universally operative grace, (i) to which every free human act responds as a "Yes" or a "No," and (ii) which fully self-expresses and self-realizes in the person of Christ, its *Realsymbol*. As demonstrated in the first two chapters, this rationale is at the center of most secondary accounts of Rahner's soteriology, and it is indeed clear that Rahner understands Christ's salvific efficacy largely in terms of a sacramental or *realsymbolisch* conceptual framework. On the other hand, it would tell only part of Rahner's story to attribute human salvation to an abstract idea such as "grace," speaking only of its relation to Christ by way of manifestation ("effective" as such a sacramental manifestation might be). For Rahner, such salvific grace occurs only in union with and incorporation into Christ, the Representative who stands not just as a notification about or even victorious agent accomplishing our salvation, but as the *locus* of such salvation itself. This dimension of Rahner's thought, which has received far less attention than its sacramental counterpart, is readily apparent in his (also largely neglected) early work, especially *E latere Christi*.[3]

In this final chapter, I contend that this second representative dimension to Rahner's soteriology is an important part of his later (and more well-known) writings on Christ and salvation. While this dimension is not articulated during these later years in explicit connection to patristic figures (as was often the case in his earlier writings), it is nevertheless present. Moreover, this dimension occupies such an important place in Rahner's thought that a failure to appreciate it (a failure into which both Rahner's critics and sympathizers have often fallen) can lead to significant misunderstandings of Rahner's theology (e.g., Balthasar's contentions, explored in chapter 1, that the salvific efficacy of Rahner's Christ amounts, in large part, to a notification to the world that God is "already reconciled," and that Rahner's thought is inimical to the idea of Christ as our "representative"). Below, I will identify places in which this representative dimension is operative in works from the second half of Rahner's career, such as essays included in his *Theological Investigations* series, *Foundations of Christian Faith*, entries in

3. In claiming that this dimension has received less attention, I am of course aware that the so-called anthropocentric (i.e., "ascending" or "from below") approach is a dominant and well-recognized theme within Rahner's entire theology. And indeed, even within the sacramental framework, many Rahnerians (especially J. Wong, cf. chapters 1 and 2 above) have pointed out the bidirectional (ascending and descending) character of Rahner's soteriology. However, I do propose that insufficient attention has been paid to how Rahner understands this "ascending" movement as something Christ brings about for us and as our Representative; *in his person*, we may thus share in the movement's completion.

Sacramentum Mundi and *Lexikon für Theologie und Kirche*, and a very late set of essays (which, though not billed as such, stand as a consciously made rejoinder to Balthasar's aforementioned assessment) called *The Love of Jesus and the Love of Neighbor*. The treatment of these loci will be organized according to the threefold markers of representative soteriology which have been used throughout this book: Christ as our representative before God, Christ as God's presence to us, and salvation as something achieved finally and primarily *in* (rather than *by*) Christ's person.

Sacrament and Representative: A Symbiotic Relationship

Prior to delving into the task of analyzing representative elements within Rahner's later work, it must be reiterated that for Rahner, the ideas of Christ as Sacrament and as Representative are necessary complements to one another. As stated above in the conclusion of chapter 2, the two are, for Rahner, intrinsically related as two sides of the same conceptual coin—a coin which, too often in Rahner scholarship, has been analyzed as it lies face up on the ground, without being handled and examined in its totality.

As the primordial Sacrament, the *Realsymbol* of God's salvation for humanity, Christ certainly is oriented toward us as the universal instrument of God's self-communicating bestowal of grace. But, as Rahner makes clear, the Christ-Sacrament cannot be understood in a simple unidirectional sort of manner. In fact, as he states in the essay "One Mediator and Many Mediations,"[4] it is, in many ways, preferable to think of Christ as the universal Mediator not "from above" as the source of descending grace (dispensed through further subordinate mediations), but as the "eschatologically perfect" culmination of human life in relation to God—"the highest, the unique 'case' of intercommunication before God."[5]

It is understandable how such "case" language may provoke concern in Rahner's reader that he may render Christ a sort of supreme instance who functions more or less as an exemplar. Anticipating such a concern, Rahner himself makes clear that his answer must account for Christ's genuine salvific *efficacy*.[6] And, as do his followers and apol-

---

4. Contained in *TI* 9:169–84, this is a revised 1966 lecture at Mainz presented to the Institute of European History, "Der eine Mittler und die Vielfalt der Vermittlungen."
5. Ibid., *TI* 9:173–74.
6. "How can Jesus do more than give us courage to believe in the forgiving love of God, which *exists* but is not effected by him?" (ibid., *TI* 9:175).

ogists (reviewed in chapter 2 above), Rahner accounts for such efficacy in *realsymbolisch* terms—Christ, the *Ursakrament*, stands as a kind of final cause which sustains all other instances of graced humanity, in virtue of its being the highest of such instances.[7] However, Rahner's explanation here does not consist simply of an appeal to a confluence of *realsymbolisch* and final causality. Jesus is "the Mediator of God's self-communication," "the eschaton of the history of this self-communication," and in the Christ-event, Rahner claims, that very history *"is* as it happens throughout its *whole* course, and it takes place in reference to its fulness and its victorious end"—Jesus is the "eschaton" upon which all of "history hangs."[8] In other words, the entire economy of God's grace is summed up or recapitulated in Jesus Christ, its ontological anchor in the world. As such, Christ the recapitulator is not only *"the God-given apogee of this history"* and *"one goal"*[9]—not only a metaphysical-soteriological principle—but a "concrete, historical" *person* "capable of being loved."[10]

It is precisely at this point that the oft-overlooked representative dimension of Rahner's soteriology emerges as a necessary complement to his sacramental framework. The culminating, sacramental cause of our salvation is at once a person to whom we are lovingly directed through grace and who recapitulates (and enables) our own "Yes" to God in himself. One might summarize the symbiotic relationship between sacramental and representative soteriologies in Rahner as follows: Salvation is expressed fully and sacramentally in the world in order to serve as a soteriological "anchor"; at the same time, the blessed are oriented toward and incorporated into Christ precisely *because* his is the fullness of grace in the world.

---

7. "[I]n so far as the highest and ultimate factor in any action must always be called its 'reason' . . .", the "highest and ultimate factor . . . determines and sustains everything else" (ibid., *TI* 9:180). Such a principle in operative throughout the thought Thomas Aquinas (e.g., *ST* I q. 2 a. 3, *ST* I–II q. 90a. 2; cf. Aristotle's *Metaphysics* 993b24–26), including Thomas's explanation for how Christ causes grace in us ("capital" grace) in virtue of his own preeminent "personal" grace (see especially *ST* III q. 8 a.5).
8. "One Mediator and Many Mediations," *TI* 9:179, emphasis original.
9. Ibid., *TI* 9:181–82, emphasis original.
10. Roger Haight begins to address this connection by claiming that in their revelation-based soteriological schema, both Rahner and Karl Barth are laying the groundwork for an understanding of human salvation which centers on our *encounter* with God. "Jesus saves because Jesus is God's being for human beings, God's turning in freedom to be with human beings. . . . Jesus Christ is God with us and this is salvation" (*Jesus: Symbol of God* [Maryknoll: Orbis, 1999], 345).

Christ: Our Representative Before God

Let us now turn to the main task of this final chapter, namely, an overview and analysis of representative soteriology contained in Rahner's mature theological writings. To be clear, the representative dimension, while intrinsically linked to his sacramental articulations of Christ's salvific efficacy, is not simply a conceptual complement implicitly present within Rahner's mature work. Rather, Rahner's later theological writings include considerations which directly pertain to what I have called representative soteriology. These considerations will be presented under the three markers of representative soteriology, beginning with Christ representing the human family before God.

Salvation History Summed up in Christ-event

The notion that all instances of God's self-communication in grace to the world are, in some way, directed toward the Christ-event is a widely recognized aspect of Rahner's thought.[11] But Rahner's soteriological vision for Christ as the *telos* of salvation history consists of much more than Christ being a "meaning-giving end." For Rahner, the persons who are oriented to that end are themselves *participants* in it; the Christ-event draws all of history into itself, not simply as a conceptual parallel to or even highest instance of other events like it, but as *the* event which ontologically supports the others. Indeed, the best way to describe this dimension of Rahner's thought is to say that Jesus Christ sums up or recapitulates the entirety of salvation history in his own person.

While this patristic, specifically Irenaean language of recapitulation is not used frequently by the mature Rahner (possible reasons for which were explored in the previous chapter), he does make use of it on occasion. One such instance occurs as Rahner proposes an alternative entry point for understanding the christological dogma of Chalcedon. Making a point that he would repeat frequently during his theological career, Rahner proposes that the Christology of Chalcedon need not be approached by *beginning* with the standard terms of one divine *hypostatsis* possessing both divine and human *physes*,[12] but can be

11. E.g., Haight acknowledges that for Rahner, "all fragmentary historical realizations of communion between God and human beings, for example, in other religions, are oriented toward this hypostatic union as toward their meaning-giving end" (ibid., 434).
12. To be clear, Rahner had no illusions of discarding such language; his suggestion here is about dis-

accessed through the perspective of salvation history reaching its all-encompassing "entelechy" in Christ. It is in suggesting this latter point that Rahner has recourse to Irenaeus's language:

> [I]f we take at all seriously the unity of this history as centered upon Christ, it follows that Christ has always been involved in the whole of history as its prospective entelechy. . . . Is it not possible so to conceive of Time and History *theologically* (not merely in terms of the philosophy of history) that one has conceptually stated the Christ of Chalcedon when one has said of him that he is the fullness of times, who as their Head definitively comprehends and recapitulates the aions [*der die Äonen endgültig als Haupt zusammenfaßt, rekapituliert*] and brings them to their end?[13]

According to Rahner, Christ is the most authentic human, the one whose "Yes" to God stands without parallel, and Christ is simultaneously (and without contradiction, since human freedom and grace are *directly* rather than *inversely* proportional)[14] the definitive instance of God's self-communication. This "vertical" christological axis (God's definitive self-offer and the definitive, human acceptance of that offer) intersects with a "horizontal" axis, consisting of Christ's relationship to the rest of humanity. From this point of intersection, which consists of his own life, Christ extends the "entelechy" (which he himself is) as a possibility for all with whom it exists in solidarity. Thus, Rahner frequently couples his christological articulations (i.e., the Chalcedonian, "vertical" axis) with a soteriological consideration of the human Christ's "horizontal" relationship with God's creation. For instance, he writes, "Here is a human being who lives in an attitude of matchless nearness to God – someone who lives in pure obedience to God and at the same time in unconditional solidarity with beings, regardless of how the latter may behave toward him."[15] Once again, Rahner does not simply posit Christ as an abstract final-*realsymbolisch* cause, but one whose life of "matchless nearness to God" is *inclusive*—precisely in virtue of his intimate cohesion with the human family, which he recapitulates in himself.

A pithy summary of this soteriological action can be found in Rahner's essay "Thoughts on the Possibility of Belief Today" (1962). There,

---

covering an alternative point of *access* to people who may find the ancient terminology and concepts to be a(n unnecessarily) difficult point of departure for understanding the doctrine.

13. "Current Problems in Christology," *TI* 1:149–200, at 167.
14. Cf. *FCF*, 75–80, especially 79.
15. *The Love of Jesus and Love of Neighbor* (New York: Crossroad, 1983), 58.

Rahner calls Jesus "God's pledge to the world and the acceptance of the world into God himself in person and as a person ... the unsurpassable and final event" of the world's history.[16] He continues: "the end of this history—which is supported by the Godman and is bound together in him, the absolute Mediator—is the absolute nearness to God of all those spiritual creatures who are saved, and their final, and utter immediacy to God, in the same way as this immediacy constitutes of its nature the inner divinization of the Godman in his human reality"; the Godman is the "basis" for all spiritual creatures' closeness to God.[17] Once again, Christ is not simply a conceptual *telos* impacting history *via* final causality from afar, but *as a person* mediates—in fact, "is"—the absolute nearness of the blessed to God. He divinizes us through his *own* (as fully human) *divinization*, for we find salvation precisely *in* him, our Representative.

The idea of Christ saving us as our Representative can be found in one of Rahner's most famous mature work, *Foundations of Christian Faith.* There, Rahner suggests that the "late" soteriology of the New Testament, which understood Jesus's death as a salvific expiatory sacrifice (an understanding which, Rahner states, is "legitimate" when "understood correctly"), was preceded by a more fundamental soteriological rationale, which Rahner refers to as "the original experience of this salvific significance, which is simply this: we are saved because this man who is one of us has been saved by God, and God has thereby made his salvific will present in the world historically, really and irrevocably."[18] Here, Rahner couples his frequently used soteriological language of "irrevocability" (see chapter 2) with what he understands to be a primordial soteriological insight: we are saved because Jesus is saved.[19] The causal element in this claim is not that Christ has performed a great expiatory act by which we are saved—such a suggestion, to which Rahner is not opposed, is a "secondary and derivative expression" of Jesus's saving significance, a "possible but not absolutely indispensable interpretation" of a more basic idea: our salvation hangs on that of Jesus, precisely because it is *in Jesus* that God's definitive gift

---

16. "Thoughts on the Possibility of Belief Today," *TI* 5:3–22, at 14.
17. Ibid., *TI* 5:15.
18. *FCF*, 284.
19. Such an insight is thoroughly Thomistic on character. See *ST* III. q. 7 a. 5, where Thomas specifies that Jesus's *personal* grace is identical to his "capital" grace as Head of the church: "[F]rom this pre-eminence of grace which [Jesus] received, it is from Him that this grace is bestowed on others--and this belongs to the nature of head. Hence the personal grace, whereby the soul of Christ is justified, is essentially the same as His grace, as He is the Head of the Church, and justifies others."

to us (which constitutes salvation) occurs. In other words, particularly those being used in this book, Jesus effects salvation as our Representative: "the actual redeemer is not mankind as a whole, but mankind—as a whole, however—is redeemed by one man."[20]

Revisiting Stellvertretung: "Reconciliation and Vicarious Representation"

At this juncture, we must return a previously considered topic and a corresponding question, namely: if the idea of Christ as Representative is a component both important and lasting for Rahner's soteriology, did he ever offer any rejoinder to Balthasar's rather sharp criticism (noted in chapter 1) that his theology is completely inimical to the suggestion that Christ "represents" us? Although it seems that Rahner was somewhat hesitant to name Balthasar and engage in an explicit debate over this matter (or any of several others),[21] it is also clear that Rahner took this criticism quite seriously and offered equally serious responses.[22] The most concentrated of such responses[23] is an essay called "Reconciliation and Vicarious Representation" ("Versöh-

20. "[I]n addition to history in general there is also a *history* of salvation and not merely a situation in relation to salvation which remains the same for all at all times), and . . . the actual redeemer is not mankind as a whole, but mankind—as a whole, however—is redeemed by one man" ("Salvation," *SM* 5:405–438, at 421). Cf. "Soteriology should not merely discuss the opening up of salvation to all, as the sum of individuals. It must be the soteriology of the one whole race of man as such" (ibid., 437).

21. In this sense, Rahner was a relatively irenic figure when it came to his public interaction with his fellow theologians. (A rare instance in which, during an interview, he discusses an explicit "counterattack" directed at his critics is treated below.) Given his general reluctance to engage in public spats with his colleagues (despite multiple, and sometimes acerbic, *de facto* invitations to do so), it is a sad irony of history that Rahner is often used today as a sort of polemical lightning rod *with* or *against* whom various theological factions often line up. For more on Rahner's relationship to post-conciliar divisions within the Catholic Church, see my "Critical Voices: The Reactions of Rahner and Ratzinger to Schema XIII (*Gaudium et Spes*)" in *Modern Theology* 31, no. 1 (January 2015), 1–26.

22. Rahner was, beyond doubt, painfully aware of the critique. Rahner's longtime friend and colleague Herbert Vorgrimler, citing Balthasar's "Excursus" on Rahner's soteriology, reports that "Rahner suffered very much under the attacks of Balthasar, especially as von Balthasar later also accused him of specifically heretical errors" (Vorgrimler, *Understanding Karl Rahner: An Introduction to His Life and Thought* (New York: Crossroad, 1986), 125). In an interview from February of 1982, Rahner explicitly references the "Excursus," but does not directly respond to it: "When Hans Urs von Balthasar criticizes my theology of redemption in his book or others perhaps find my theology of the Trinity not quite correct, then naturally questions are raised that must be reconsidered. What seems to be correct now? Has something been overlooked? Can anything be done differently? Or after such criticism and after detached examination can we still remain set in our opinion?" (*Karl Rahner in Dialogue*, 335). Though it would be anachronistic to call it a "response," Rahner touches on his ongoing soteriological disagreement with Balthasar in a 1974 interview which can be found in ibid., 126–27.

23. Another such response, which can be found within his *The Love of Jesus and the Love of Neighbor*, will be addressed later in this chapter.

nung und Stellvertretung"),[24] a lecture given two years after the publication of Balthasar's "Excursus" on Rahner's soteriology in *Theo-Drama*.[25] Once again, a term at the center of Balthasar's critique and Rahner's response is the word *Stellvertretung*, which can mean representative, vicar, proxy, stand-in, or any number of designations for taking the place (*Stelle*) of another. As he does elsewhere (cf. chapter 1), Rahner expresses a profound wariness of this term, a wariness which emerges from his respect for human freedom. Indeed, Balthasar's critique is that Rahner so values the inviolability of human freedom and "self-redemption" that his theology is inimical to any idea of *Stellvertretung*.[26]

First, what does Rahner understand *Stellvertretung* to mean? He makes it clear that purely juridical concepts such as "one person acting on another's behalf" (*Setzung*), as in the case of contracting a marriage by proxy (*Prokurator*), cannot adequately capture the idea[27]; likewise, the papal title *Vicarius Christi* (Germ. *Stellvertreter Christi*; Eng. "Vicar of Christ") is too juridical to directly coincide with the term's soteriological usage. Rather, the meaning which Rahner has in mind suggests that "it is conceivable that another person can relieve me of a moral debt before God which, in fact, I myself owe to God," a suggestion which leads Rahner to question: "Can another person really relieve me of a task, or an attitude or a deed before God and oriented to him, of demands which are in fact imposed on me, but which I am not capable of meeting?"[28]

Before answering this question, Rahner considers whether scripture itself makes use of this concept, particularly with its (especially Pauline) language about Christ dying "for us." Although Balthasar interprets the New Testament's *pro nobis* terminology as an attestation to a soteriology of Christ as our *Stellvertreter*,[29] Rahner says that such a connection is spurious—rather, he suggests, this formula can just as well mean "for the sake of," rather than "in the place of."[30]

---

24. This essay was originally a November 1982 lecture in Stuttgart to the Academy of the Diocese of Rottenburg-Stuttgart, presented as, *Maximilian Kolbe und die Kraft der Versöhnung*. It was first published in *Geist und Leben* 56 (1982), 98–110; it can also be found in *TI* 21:255–69.
25. *Theo-Drama* (*TD*), 5 vols.(San Francisco: Ignatius, 1988–1998). Originally published as *Theodramatik*, 4 vols. (Einsiedeln: Johannes, 1973–1983).*Theodramatik* 3 (the English translation is numbered *TD* 4) was published in 1980.
26. *TD* 4:274–77, see chapter 1 above.
27. "Reconciliation and Vicarious Representation," *TI* 21:264.
28. Ibid., *TI* 21:264–65.
29. *TD* 4:274.
30. "One cannot appeal to the New Testament term *hyper hemōn* to justify this notion of vicarious representation [*Stellvertretung*]. It is certain that *hyper* is used in a great number of passages to mean 'for the benefit of,' and in none of these passages is it necessary to understand it in a different sense" ("Reconciliation and Vicarious Representation," *TI* 21:265; cf. *SzT* 15:261).

To be clear, Rahner insists that our redemption is something accomplished only in virtue of the Word incarnate, crucified and risen (i.e., Christ is "constitutive" of our salvation). However, does this dependency necessarily entail that Christ perform some act on our behalf which God expects of us and which we fail to perform ourselves? Against such a suggestion, Rahner makes two interrelated claims. First, no person can be culpable for not doing something which he or she is incapable of doing; second, God does indeed expect each individual to do what he or she *can*.[31] When one's freedom, directed toward the self-communicating God, assents to God fully and definitively, the second of these claims is positively actualized—i.e., "self-redemption" occurs. Rahner's suggestion, however, is that this very actualization, self-redemption, is entirely dependent on Jesus Christ and the grace he definitively establishes within the world. In other words, "self-redemption and redemption from outside are not two mutually exclusive concepts."[32] Rahner elaborates:

> "Redemption from outside" by Jesus Christ does not mean that human beings would be exempted from doing something that they are obliged to do by means of their own freedom or that something would be conceded to them that they cannot do themselves and which would nevertheless be demanded of them. It means that God by his grace, in view of Jesus Christ and his cross, grants and offers people the possibility, in the most radical self-surrender of their existence through faith, hope, and love, of constituting their own ultimate validity in the order of salvation.[33]

The idea of Christ "taking our place" indeed safeguards the indispensable and constitutive place that the Paschal Mystery has in the accomplishment of human redemption. Nevertheless, Rahner maintains, *Stellvertretung* as it is widely used seems to presuppose an interrelationship between human agency and grace which amounts to a zero-sum game, whereas in fact, they increase in direct (rather than inverse) proportion to one another. "To put it another way, redemption from outside is the gratuitous bestowal of our own self-redemption."[34] Thus, Rahner concludes, "it seems to me that the concept of vicarious representation [*Stellvertretung*], when used in the area pertaining to the realization of

31. "Reconciliation and Vicarious Representation," *TI* 21:266.
32. Ibid.
33. Ibid.
34. Ibid.

salvation, is at the very least a concept that leads to misunderstand-ings, and it would do no harm if we avoided it."[35]

Suspicious as Rahner is of the soteriology of Christ "taking our place," he nevertheless acknowledges that there "are the true and valid elements that are evidently envisaged in this problematical notion of vicarious representation [*Stellvertretung*]."[36] It is as Rahner teases out these authentic soteriological elements that we begin to see how he can positively evaluate the claim that Christ "represents" us. He begins his explanation by noting that human beings do not exist as solitary, self-determining monads, but rather, as mutually-related and mutu-ally-conditioned parts of an entire network. Thus, there is "a solidarity of human beings with one another and with the God-man."[37] That said, Rahner emphatically clarifies, the influence of Christ as constitutive of our salvation cannot be exhausted by Christ's membership within a broad network of solidarity.[38] In other words, Christ's soteriological efficacy is *not* reducible to the idea that Christ is part of this web of interconnectedness, even a *very important* part of it (though he is that!). Rather, the *entire network itself* has its foundation in the God-man:

> this single field of unlimited solidarity is ultimately constituted [*konstitu-iert*], or, if you will, consolidated [*verdichtet*] by the deed [*Tat*][39] of the one Jesus Christ who in love freely given remained steadfast in his predestined solidarity with human beings and did not renounce it even when it meant for him the cross and the death of one forsaken by God.[40]

---

35. Ibid., cf. *SzT* 15:262.
36. Ibid., *TI* 21:267, cf. *SzT* 15:262.
37. "[T]he sum total of everything that happens and the deeds that other people do are the biological and social elements which are always at work determining us, and there is no escaping them" ("Reconciliation and Vicarious Representation," *TI* 21:267).
38. It should be noted that Balthasar's "Excursus" on Rahner's soteriology occurs within a subsection on modern soteriologies of "solidarity," and Balthasar himself strongly voices his assessment of "solidarity" as an insufficient concept when it comes to accounting for Christ's salvific efficacy (*TD* 4:266–84, 297).
39. "Each one of us determines by our own free actions what we will ultimately be in eternity, and this ultimate validity is our own and it cannot be transferred to someone else" ("Reconciliation and Vicarious Representation," *TI* 21:267). This act, of course, is the self-determinative recapitulation of who Jesus *is*. Since Rahner sees *who* the human is as ultimately a determination of grace-driven freedom, such a statement does not contravene my thesis of a "person-centered" soteriology for Rahner (though it would contravene an "act-exclusive" or purely-ontological soteriology, cf. considerations of "physical" redemption in Chapter 4).
40. "Reconciliation and Vicarious Representation," *TI* 21:268, cf. *SzT* 15:263. In a course I took with John P. Meier in the Spring 2008 on the Gospel of John, Meier emphatically noted that in the fif-teenth chapter, Jesus does *not* say that he is the "trunk" or the "stem," but that he is the entire vine (αμπελος)—*including* the branches! A similar Johannine dynamic appears to be operative here in Rahner's thought.

The "deed" which Rahner mentions here, Jesus's act of total submission to God on the cross, is the act which "recapitulated" his entire life; indeed, it stands as *das Realsymbol* in which Jesus expresses and actualizes *who he is*, his very person.[41] The proper and authentic idea of "representation" which Rahner has in mind consists not of Christ functioning as a super-agent performing tasks unattainable for others, nor of Christ simply standing as an important member among others in the "field of solidarity," but of the fact that his person "constitutes" *the very field* by summing the whole of it up in himself (a self which was, in turn, definitively summed up in his death). To return to the language of scripture and the fathers, one could say that Christ's *pro nobis* salvific efficacy consists in his identity as the New Adam who recapitulates the whole human family in himself.

Rahner on "Repräsentation"

Without doubt, Rahner (especially in his mature years) remained very suspicious of Christologies and soteriologies built upon the notion of *Stellvertretung*. Nevertheless, rather than fully repudiating the notion in all respects, he admits that it coincides with elements of truth, and, as we have just seen, describes Christ's saving significance in alternative terms of solidarity. This alternative description, which includes Christ "constituting" the whole network of solidarity "in himself," coincides with the concept of "representation" as I am using it in this book. Given Rahner's allergy to the term *Stellvertretung* but his openness toward (and even advocacy of) soteriologies of Christ as our Representative, it is not surprising that in several places, Rahner positively discusses Christ's *pro nobis* salvific efficacy in yet another alternative term—namely, *Repräsentation*.

Theological Dictionary (1961)

Rahner's *Theological Dictionary* provides a unique pathway into his thinking. Although its short entries lack the detail and rigor of his preferred form, the article-length essay,[42] the *Dictionary* allows us to see what Rahner makes of particular theological terms and the concepts associated with them, something which is of great advantage

---

41. *FCF*, 284.
42. Indeed, Rahner almost invariably begins his shorter essays (often intended as hour-long talks) with caveats about their nonexhaustive nature, their inevitably limited scope, and/or the "randomness" of the few (out of many) themes or examples he chooses to treat.

for considering the representative dimension of his soteriology. Rahner's entry, "*Repräsentation*," is sufficiently brief and rich to quote in its entirety:

> The objective unity of the world, which one God has created for one purpose and destiny and which reveals itself in the comprehensive unity of man's intellectual horizon, must also obtain in the personal sphere, though in a special manner. Hence there can be no absolute individualism where supernatural salvation is concerned, though this salvation is the fruit of a free decision which is unique and which one must take for oneself. Even here we are in part sustained by the decisions of others and their consequences. Now when such a decision by an individual has *special* significance for the salvation of others (or everyone), because of the nature of the agent or of his decision, one can speak of representation, in the theological sense: then this one man really stands for all [*dieser eine steht dann wirklich für viele oder alle*], "represents" [*repräsentiert*] them, without, of course, depriving them of their own free decision, for they must at least decide whether they will accept for themselves the meaning and effect of the other man's representative decision [*repräsentativen Entscheidung des anderen*]. Thus Jesus Christ, the *Mediator, is *the* supreme representative of mankind in his vicarious redemption [der *absolute Repräsentant der Menschheit in seiner stellvertretenden Erlösung*]."[43]

Rahner begins this entry the same way he begins his distillation (above) of the "true and valid" elements in *Stellvertretung*—namely, with a discussion of the individual and the whole body of humanity. In both instances, Rahner explains that although human persons are genuinely free and make real decisions about themselves, their salvation is not compatible with robustly individualistic anthropologies. Instead, we are all mutually shaped and co-determined, realizing our ultimate destinies in light of the consequences of an entire network of free actions.

As with his previously considered treatment of the matter, Rahner explains in this entry that Jesus uniquely impacts this network of relations both in his "nature" and in his "decision" (which, we have seen, definitively establishes *who* he is). This one Jesus "stands for" the many or even the entirety, not in a way that deprives them of their freedom, but gives their freedom an available object toward which it can be directed and *in* which they self-realize—namely, himself, the most authentic human who is simultaneously God-in-the-world. As such,

---

43. *Theological Dictionary* (New York: Herder and Herder, 1965), 404–5.

Jesus is the *absolute Repräsentant*, he is *the definitive* Representative of humanity. Given this context for understanding *Repräsentation*, Rahner even goes so far as to here describe the redemption effected by Jesus as *stellvertretenden* ("representative"). Thus, one might say that while Rahner finds the predominant usage of *Stellvertretung* problematic, such usage is, in fact, a distortion of an authentic, even essential Christian idea, which Rahner here reclaims under the term *Repräsentation*. The centrality of this concept to Rahner's understanding of Christianity is apparent in another entry in his *Theological Dictionary*—namely, "Participation." There, Rahner connects the ideas of representation, intrinsic *realsymbolisch* causality, grace, and the Christ-event, assessing the overarching idea of "participation" as paramount for Christians: "it is clear that the concept of participation – very mysterious in itself (two beings remain two and yet are one by participation in each other) – must be of key importance in theology."[44]

Lexikon für Theologie und Kirche (LfTK) (1963)

Two years earlier, Rahner wrote an entry on "Repräsentation" which is both lengthier and more technical than the one just seen in his *Kleines Theologisches Wörterbuch*.[45] In *LfTK*, he writes that "Repräsentation," which has not yet achieved the status of a *terminus technicus* in theology, describes an "existing relationship between two realities which rules between the creature and God and between the created realities among themselves." He continues, "The concept of representation is biblically grounded through expressions such as mediator, *huper*, and through the idea that the action of an individual affects all."[46]

Rahner then addresses the breadth of the term, noting that its mean-

---

44. Ibid., 337. The entry in its entirety reads: "A general term signifying the various ways in which the nature of one being may affect that of another. Every efficient cause which produces something different from itself inevitably gives the thing caused some likeness to itself, and thus a 'participation' in itself. But in addition, the one may grant the other a participation in itself through self-communication, and this in turn may happen at the most various levels and in the most various ways. The soul gives the body a participation in its own life by actual ontic 'information' (one of the kinds of 'intrinsic' *causality). In mutual personal *communication two spiritual personal beings may each give the other a participation in itself. This kind of participation reaches its summit in Gods [sic] communication of himself (*Self-communication of God). If everything has a single origin and thus participates in God, and if God's exinanition which is love, perfects itself in grace and glory as divine self–communication, it is clear that the concept of participation – very mysterious in itself (two beings remain two and yet are one by participation in each other) – must be of key importance in theology" (336–37).
45. *Lexikon für Theologie und Kirche* (henceforth *LfTK*), 10 vols., eds. M. Buchberger et al (Freiburg i.Br.: Herder, 1957–1965), 8:1244–45. Also in *SW* 17/1:389–90).
46. Ibid., 1244.

ing can range from that of a "cause" to a "standing-for some other" (the other being incapable of acting or of being present), and even up to "the bringing about of full presence and efficacy by something through something," though, Rahner adds, "ultimately in every representation a certain presence [*Gegenwart*] of the represented is necessarily implied."[47] Introducing the idea of the network of relations discussed above, Rahner explains that the "possibility of representation ultimately rests on the continuous connection of being, effect, and meaning between God and finite beings and between the latter among themselves."[48]

Thus, God's presence to us and our presence to each other occur through this network of relations. Moreover, the "nature and intensity of representation depends on the essence of the one representing and the character of its connection with the one represented and the third party [toward whom the representation is directed]. . . . The bearer of representation can be a person (office and authority as representative of God, mediator, *Stellvertretung*) or a cause (sacrament, *Symbol*, sign)."[49] And in the case of Christ, the person and *Ursakrament*, we have one whose essence and connection with those represented bring about the most intense of representations. Rahner closes by noting the applications of this concept, which includes (in addition to Christ's mediating activity) "why and how Adam could act in the history of salvation for the whole of humanity (original sin . . .)," the priesthood and offices in the church, the authority of administering the sacraments, mariological titles such as "co-redemptrix," and the principle of solidarity.[50]

Conclusion: Christ the "Representative"

Even within Rahner's mature writings, the idea of Christ "summing up" the human race within himself and representing us before God persists in important ways. Christ *is* the "absolute nearness" of the human family to God, and our salvation hinges on the fact that Jesus *himself* is saved. On occasion, the mature Rahner even explicitly employs "recapitulation" language to express this idea, though such cases are exceptional. The idea also surfaces in Rahner's critical treatments of the term *Stellvertretung*, which Rahner understands to be adulterated by a distorted framework for understanding God's grace and human freedom

47. Ibid.
48. Ibid.
49. Ibid.
50. Ibid., 1244–45.

(which, in fact, increase proportionally to one another). Despite the term's shortcomings, Rahner perceives in it a kernel of truth, which he describes in terms of a network of human solidarity (in which everyone's freedom is mutually conditioned) which is itself "consolidated" in and "constituted" by person of Christ in his summative death. Elsewhere, Rahner gives his own alternative term to this very kernel of truth dwelling within the problematic idea of *Stellvertretung*—namely, "*Repräsentation.*"

Christ: God's Presence to and Encounter with Us

The second marker of representative soteriology which we will now consider concerns Christ as God's Representative before us, the one who brings about God's presence to the blessed definitively and intimately. Of course, the notion of Christ as Sacrament and *das Realsymbol* of God's salvation, a notion which is already widely associated with Rahner's soteriology, is itself an instance of this marker. However, the following observations will not simply be a reiteration of chapter 2, but rather, a look at how Rahner's understanding of Christ's identity as God's Mediator is articulated in ways which draw upon the other two markers as well. Once again, it is not simply the markers themselves which make representative soteriology a unique category for understanding human redemption, but their particular configuration and mutual dependency. Two particular theological themes illustrate this mutual dependency within Rahner's thought, namely, the eternal significance of Christ's humanity for our salvation and the personal inbreaking of God's *basileia* in the Christ-event.

Christ's Ongoing, Eternal Mediation

Perhaps one of the strongest indications of a representative understanding of Christ's mediatory salvific efficacy comes in a 1953 article, "The Eternal Significance of the Humanity of Jesus for Our Relationship with God."[51] The motivating concern underlying this article (especially in its first half) is the danger of contemporary Christian spirituality collapsing all beatified created realities (e.g., saints, angels, Jesus's Sacred Heart) into God's own divine essence, or at least using these divinized realities as circumlocutions for God in Christian thought, and espe-

---

51. "Die ewige Bedeutung der Menschheit Jesu für unser Gottesverhältnis," *Geist und Leben* 26 (1953), 279–88; *ET* in *TI* 3:35–46.

cially, prayer. Out of this concern emerges a thesis, summarized by the title, which directly pertains to Rahner's soteriological framework currently under consideration: the human Christ is not simply someone who once performed a great task and has since vanished into his Godhead—or at least faded in soteriological importance—but rather, Christ's humanity continues to exercise an ongoing role, mediating God to humanity and vice-versa. Heaven is not, Rahner insists, simply a matter of the saints enjoying the beatific vision, but of God being made available to the blessed *continually* through their Savior. Having thus summarized Rahner's thesis, let us consider the article itself in a bit more detail.

As in his writings on *das Realsymbol* and Christ, Rahner begins the article by considering "the sacred heart devotion in theology," particularly reflecting on whether Christ's Sacred Heart, which "is the original source of all our Lord's saving actions," belongs essentially to "the world" or to "God."[52] Although Rahner is quick to answer that, "objectively speaking," the Sacred Heart (along with the saints, angels, etc.) are created by God and thus belong to the world, he notes that when it comes to religious experience of contemporary Christians, these realities are at least treated as if they belong to God. While the average Christian would not set out to explicitly conflate, say, Michael the Archangel with a person of the Trinity, most Christians tend to pray as if Michael were indeed part of God, rather than the world. "[W]ho among us has ever really and genuinely realized in the *Confiteor* that he is confessing his sinfulness to Blessed Michael the Archangel, and that this really is not just a rhetorical amplification of a confession to God?"[53]

The reason behind such a conflation seems to be an insufficient way of understanding the eternal union of creaturely realities with God. The day's predominate understanding, as reflected in theology of the manuals, allows the greatness of God to almost entirely overcome the identity of creatures *as creatures*, including the human nature (and Sacred Heart) of Jesus. Rahner explains,

> Let us take a look at an average theological treatise on the Last Things, on eternal happiness. Does such a treatise mention even a single word about the Lord become man? Is not rather everything swallowed up by the *visio beatifica*, the beatific vision, the direct relationship to the very essence of

---

52. "The Eternal Significance of the Humanity of Jesus," *TI* 3:35–36.
53. Ibid., *TI* 3:37.

God which is indeed determined historical by a past event – namely, the event of Christ – but which is not *now* mediated by Jesus Christ?[54]

A good starting point for addressing this tendency toward conflation, Rahner proposes, is the humanity of Jesus, his Sacred Heart in particular. "This heart – if it is not turned into just another, more colourful word for God and for the incomprehensibility of his unbounded love – is a *human* heart. It must not be extolled merely in the actions which at one time flowed from it."[55] Rather, Rahner will argue, it should be "honoured, adored, and loved"[56] in an *ongoing* manner, not as a circumlocution for "God" but as a created reality which nonetheless *continually* impacts the status of the blessed in heaven.

To set up this conclusion, Rahner returns once again to an anthropological and soteriological theme seen earlier in this chapter—namely, that God's grace and human freedom grow in direct (rather than inverse) proportion to one another. Against a tendency to think that the greatness of God would somehow occlude or supplant the creaturely reality's status as such, Rahner argues, "The nearer one comes to [God], the more real one becomes; the more [God] grows in and before one, the more independent one becomes oneself."[57] God's love for and proximity to his creature does not rob it of its identity, but rather, augments it.[58] A proper devotion to Christ's humanity (including his Heart) requires recognizing: (i) this mutual growth of grace and freedom, in which the former does not undermine the latter, and (ii) Jesus's own relationship to such mutual growth as a wider phenomenon.

the fact that God himself is man is both the unique summit and the ultimate basis of God's relationship to his creation, in which he and his creation grow in direct (and not converse) proportion. This positive nature of creation, not merely measured in relation to nothingness but also in relation to God, reaches its qualitatively unique climax, therefore, in Christ.[59]

The advent of the God-man is not only the unique "summit" and "cli-

54. Ibid., *TI* 3:37–38, emphasis original.
55. Ibid., *TI* 3:38–39, emphasis original.
56. Ibid., *TI* 3:39.
57. Ibid., *TI* 3:40.
58. "When we come thus in a religious way to this God of the truly serious and unconditional love of created reality, however, then we must love him as he is, then we must not maliciously try to turn him in our religious act into someone he precisely is *not*, viz. into a God without a world. . . . We today are in danger of honouring God (or at least trying to honour him) and of letting the world itself be God-less. The Christian attitude, however, would be to honour the world as something willed and loved by God" (ibid., *TI* 3:41–42).
59. Ibid., *TI* 3:43.

max" of a general relationship (of direct proportionality) between God and creation, but Rahner claims here that Jesus also stands as the "ultimate basis" of that general relationship. "For, according to the testimony of the faith, this created human nature is the indispensable and permanent gateway through which everything created must pass if it is to find the perfection of its eternal validity before God. He is the gate and the door, the Alpha and Omega, the all-embracing in whom, as the one who has become man, creation finds its stability."[60]

At this point, Rahner's thesis for the eternal significance of Jesus's humanity for our salvation emerges in full force. Though Rahner, using Johannine language, calls Christ the "gate and the door," Christ is not simply a soteriological portal through which one passes and then leaves. Again, he is the "all-embracing" One, "*in whom*" we find our salvation. Rahner continues, "Jesus, the Man, not merely *was* at one time of decisive importance for our salvation, i.e., for the real finding of the absolute God, by his historical and now past acts of the Cross, etc. but – as the one who became man and has remained a creature – he is *now* and for all eternity the *permanent openness* of our finite being to the living God of infinite, eternal life."[61] On a conceptual level, Rahner admits, many Christians may realize Christ's humanity in heaven can, "alongside" the beatific vision, be occasion for some "accidental" joy to the blessed. Still, Rahner presses,

> where is the clear knowledge, expressed in ontological terms, of the fact that it remains eternally true to say that no one knows the Father except the Son and those to whom he wishes to reveal it: he who sees him, sees the Father? Where is the clear consciousness that, here and now and always, my salvation, my grace, my knowledge of God, rests on the Word in our flesh? . . . Every theologian should allow himself to be asked: have you a theology in which the Word – by the fact that he is man and in so far as he is this – is the necessary and permanent mediator of all salvation, not merely at some time in the past but now and for all eternity?[62]

60. Ibid.
61. Ibid., *TI* 3:44.
62. Ibid., *TI* 3:44–45. Rahner's talk of Christ here as an providing eternal mediation may seem at odds with the words of Pope Benedict XII (in *Benedictus Deus* [1336]), who declared that the blessed in heaven "have seen and do see the divine essence with an intuitive vision, and even face to face, without the mediation of any creature" (*DS* 1000, cf. *CCC* 1023). However, it should also be noted that even Thomas Aquinas, while affirming an "immediate" vision of God, nonetheless acknowledges a "created medium" "by which God is seen; and such a medium does not take away the immediate vision of God" (*ST* I q. 12 a. 5 ad 2). Rahner discusses this matter in company with the Council of Vienne and the notion of "mediated immediacy" in "Dogmatic Questions on Easter" (*TI* 4:121–33, at 132).

BEING SALVATION

At this point, Rahner concludes his essay by returning to the topic with which he opened it—Jesus's Sacred Heart. This Heart "really means the human heart," which is, at the same time, "the original centre of the human reality of the Son of God." That is, as Rahner says elsewhere, Jesus's Sacred Heart is *das Realsymbol* of his whole human reality. This reality, and the Heart which sums it up, are not simply of past interest as, at a point in history long ago, having brought about a new state of affairs, in which human salvation is possible. Rather, Jesus's

> heart itself, taken both as object and as goal, or better, as mediating cen-
> tre, [is] the centre of mediation, through which all our movement must
> pass if it is really to arrive at God. *Ut apertum core . . . piis esset requies et
> poenitentibus pateret salutis refugium . . . .* (so that opened heart . . . might be
> a resting place for the pious and be open to the penitent as a refuge of sal-
> vation . . .). Such words are not just vague pious phrases and sentimental-
> ities; they form an absolutely exact statement which academic theology
> has not yet been able to surpass.[63]

Although Rahner does not endeavor to tease out all of its implications, he does "postulate" a very clear thesis for academic theologians to work on: "The heart is not only the original centre of our Lord's human being, but even within this it is the centre of mediation, without which there can be no approach to God . . . one can never leave this entrance behind as a thing of the past. Rather, one arrives continually by passing through this mediating centre of Christ's humanity."[64]

This article provides perhaps the best evidence of how Rahner's "sacramental" soteriology is one which is both representative and per-son-centered. Here, Rahner touches on the important elements of his soteriology as it is typically understood—Christ is the unique climax of the God's self-communication in history and of the human response to that self-communication. And as such, he is also the *Ursakrament*, the Mediator, and *Realsymbol* of that grace throughout the world. But here, Rahner adds several crucial pieces to his soteriological picture. Christ's role as Mediator is not that of an agent accomplishing a one-off feat. Nor is he a dispenser of grace which, once his grace is received, is ren-dered of mere historical interest and importance. Rather, echoing Paul (1 Corinthians 12) and Irenaeus, Rahner speaks of salvation as some-thing that occurs "in" Christ's person, and subsequently, of Christ's heart as a "refuge" of salvation. Such talk, he stresses, is not vague

63. "The Eternal Significance of the Humanity of Jesus," *TI* 3:46.
64. Ibid.

or pious, but expresses a fundamental truth which theologians must address: salvation is something that occurs not simply *because* of Christ, but has its locus precisely *in* Christ. Accordingly, the divinized, human Christ is of the utmost and ongoing importance for the rest of humanity.

Support for this person-centered and representative view of Christ as Mediator can be found both in Rahner's academic and pastoral writings. In a 1975 essay of the latter type,[65] Rahner underlines how God's self-communication in Christ is conceptually coupled with our salvation being realized in our unity, even *identity* with him. He writes that our gratitude for the cross is

> rooted in the experience that in Jesus God appeared and that through God's act the redeemer and the redeemed are one and the same. To carry this reflection a step further, this unity of redeemer and redeemed is intended, through the grace of God which comes to us from the cross of Jesus and which leads on to the universal triumph of his resurrection, to become a reality in us. What is characteristic of our gratitude for the cross consists precisely in our identity with the crucified one.[66]

One could very well sum-up Rahner here in patristic language by stating that God became human in order to become one with us, and that we, in turn, are called to become one with God in and through the Word made flesh.[67]

This same line of thought is present in a series of three radio addresses from 1966, revised and published as the essay "Hidden Victory."[68] Daniel Pekarske summarizes this essay, which is, at points, quite Balthasarian,[69] as follows: "There is no depth to which death can drag us that has not already been experienced and redeemed by Christ's victory over death."[70] Focusing on what the Paschal Mystery means, in particular, for those who suffer greatly, Rahner writes that "in death [Christ] has overcome and redeemed for ever the very heart and centre of all earthly being. . . . Christ is already at the heart and

65. "Dank zum Kreuz," in *Herausforderung des Christen: Meditationen, Reflexionen, Interviews* (Freiburg i.Br.: Herder, 1975), 42–46; ET "Good Friday: Gratitude for the Cross," in *The Great Church Year: The Best of Karl Rahner's Homilies, Meditations, and Sermons* (New York: Crossroad, 1993), 159–63.
66. Ibid., 160.
67. Rahner continues, "In us too the redeemed and the redeemer must become one; salvation by another and salvation by oneself, when seen in their ultimately significance, do not represent contradictions for a Christian" (ibid., 161).
68. "Hidden Victory," *TI* 7:151–58.
69. Cf. Balthasar's *Mysterium Paschale* and *TD* vols. 4 and 5.
70. Daniel Pekarske, *Abstracts of Karl Rahner's Theological Investigations 1–23* (Milwaukee: Marquette University Press, 2002), 219.

centre of all the poor things of this earth, which we cannot do without because the earth is our mother. He is present in the blind hope of all creatures who, without knowing it, are striving to participate in the glorification of his body."[71] This essay, as did the last, underlines the unity of Christ and the blessed, and it further supports Rahner's earlier thesis regarding the eternal significance of Christ's humanity by accounting for human salvation in terms of "participat[ing] in the glorification of [Christ's] body." Once again, Rahner's particular account of Christ mediating grace to the blessed presupposes a person-centered understanding of that mediation. Our glorification consists of Christ's own glorification, since the blessed are participants in him, or in Pauline terms, his body's members.

The final piece reaffirming Rahner's "eternal significance" thesis which we will consider is Rahner's entry on "Resurrection" in *Sacramentum Mundi*.[72] Here, Rahner critiques those theologians, perhaps even of the dominant opinion in the age of manual theology, who slight the soteriological magnitude of Christ's resurrection since, unlike his crucifixion, it is not a "morally meritorious cause of the redemption."[73] Such a theological position, Rahner protests, unduly separates Christ's death and resurrection. Christ's resurrection, Rahner insists, has great soteriological import, which Rahner articulates in a quite remarkable way. Augmenting his vision articulated in "Eternal Significance," Rahner makes the startling claim that the event of Christ's resurrection, in fact, *created* heaven, rather than enabling entry into a "heaven" which was already extant: "[T]he occurrence of [Jesus'] resurrection created 'heaven' (to the extent that this implies more than a purely spiritual process) and taken together with the ascension (which fundamentally is an element in the resurrection), is not merely an entry into an already existing heaven."[74] It is difficult to imagine a more person-centered account of human salvation than one which posits that heaven's *very existence* has its advent in Christ's resurrection and ascension—such a claim, radical as it indeed sounds, it perfectly sensible, given Rahner's insistence upon the enduring importance of Christ's humanity as the locus of salvation.

Through his academic articles ("Eternal Significance," "Resurrection" in *SM*) and more pastoral pieces ("Hidden Victory," "Gratitude for

---

71. "Hidden Victory," *TI* 7:157.
72. "Resurrection," *SM* 5:323–42.
73. Ibid., 332.
74. Ibid., 333.

the Cross"), Rahner offers a portrait of how Christ mediates God's presence to us in a way which is both person-centered and representative. Christ is not an agent who enables our salvation through a redemptive act and then steps onto the sideline, but is, rather, in his *very person* of abiding significance. This is because, as members of his body, the blessed are glorified as he is glorified, for the redeemed and the Redeemer are "one and the same." Moreover, the "heaven" to which the saved attain is not a pre-existing place or even state, but a reality which comes into being with Christ's own resurrection, for *he is himself* salvation's content, God made present to creation. Christ is, for Rahner, not only the Sacrament of salvation, but he is its very locus.

Christ-Event as the In-breaking of God's Reign in a Person

One other important way in which Rahner discusses Jesus as God's presence to and encounter with us is Rahner's christological account of God's Reign or Kingdom (*basileia*). As with his discussion of the eternal significance of Christ's humanity and Christ's resurrection "creating" heaven, Rahner's account of God's Kingdom breaking into history via the Christ-event gives his sacramental soteriology a heavily person-centered dimension. Let us consider his discussion of God's Reign in two works from late in his career, *Foundations of Christian Faith* (1976) and *Was heißt Jesus lieben?* (1982).[75] Mark Fischer summarizes Rahner's thesis well, writing that Jesus meant in his preaching "to proclaim a historical event. The event was the breaking-in of God's kingdom. It had been achieved in his person."[76]

For as fascinated as Rahner was with the Gospel of John in his early career, he makes it quite clear in *FCF* that during Jesus's earthly ministry, it is almost certain that the explicit centerpiece of Jesus's preaching was God's Reign rather than himself.[77] However, this is not to say

---

75. *Was heißt Jesus lieben?* (Freiburg i.Br.: Herder, 1982). Translated, along with *Wer ist dein Bruder?* (Freiburg i.B.: Herder, 1981), in *The Love of Jesus and the Love of Neighbor. Was heißt Jesus lieben?* is itself a revised collection of two earlier essays, "Über die Liebe zu Jesus" (in *Entschluss: Zeitschrift für Praxis und Theologie* 36, nos. 7/8 (1981), 3–18, 23–24) and "Jesus Christ – The Meaning of Life" (discussed below).

76. Mark F. Fischer, *The Foundations of Karl Rahner: A Paraphrase of the Foundations of Christian Faith, with Introductions and Indices* (New York: Crossroad, 2005), 120. Analysis of Jesus as "the Kingdom of God in person" is not at all unique to Rahner, though it fits well with his representative soteriology. Cf. Walter Kasper's *Jesus the Christ* (New York: Paulist Press, 1977), 101 and Benedict XVI's treatment in *Jesus of Nazareth: From the Baptism in the Jordan to the Transfiguration* (San Francisco: Ignatius Press, 2008), 49, 60ff.

77. "It is true and need not be glossed over that Jesus proclaimed the kingdom of God and not himself. This man Jesus is the perfect man in an absolute sense precisely because he forgot himself for the sake of God and his fellow man who was in need of salvation" (*FCF*, 250–51). Many of Jesus's

Jesus was not himself an integral part of inaugurating the Reign that he proclaimed.[78] In fact, Rahner understands Jesus, in his words, deeds, and overall ministry, to have initiated God's *basileia* within the world in a new, transformative, and irrevocable way, so that the *basileia* is "inseparably" bound to his person.[79] Rahner writes of "an inseparable connection between the closeness of God's kingdom preached by Jesus as *new* and his 'person' . . . the pre-resurrection Jesus thought that this new closeness of the kingdom came to be *in and through* the totality of what he said and what he did."[80]

Rahner's articulation of the Christ-*basileia* connection in *FCF* draws, though not explicitly, upon his sacramental soteriology and its ontology of the *Symbol*. As we saw in Chapter 2, Rahner (unlike, say, R. Haight) allows for only a single occurrence of the Christ-event, for Jesus of Nazareth simply *is* what occurs when God's Word self-exteriorizes within time and space—there can be no other event in which God's presence to the world is surpassed or even paralleled. Likewise, Rahner writes of Christ in *FCF* that he "is the final call of God, and after him no other follows or *can* follow because of the radical nature in which God, no longer represented [*vertreten*] by something else, promises himself."[81] With this *realsymbolisch* framework showing occasionally in the background, Rahner further emphasizes how Jesus's inauguration of God's *basileia* is, as Fischer summarized, something achieved in his *person*. Jesus

> experienced his new and unique "relationship of sonship" with the "Father" as significant for all men by the fact that in this relationship God's closeness to all men has now come to be in a new and irrevocable way. In his unique and yet for us exemplary relationship to God, the pre-resurrection Jesus can experience the new coming of God's kingdom as grounded in his person. . . . He is already before the resurrection the one sent, the one who inaugurates the kingdom of God through what he says and what he does in a way that it did not exist before, but now does exist *through* him and *in* him.[82]

exchanges and discourses in the Fourth Gospel—many of which culminate in the various "I am" statements—take Jesus himself as their main subject.
78. "Hence a statement of Jesus about himself . . . is conceivable to begin with only *if* and because it appears as an unavoidable element in *that* closeness of God's kingdom which Jesus proclaims as taking place now for the first time. The 'function' of Jesus reveals his 'essence'" (*FCF*, 251).
79. "The closeness of God's kingdom . . . is for the pre-resurrection Jesus already inseparably connected with his person" (*FCF*, 251–52).
80. *FCF*, 252 (emphasis original).
81. *FCF*, 253 (emphasis original).
82. *FCF*, 254 (emphasis original).

Once again, since Rahner understands Christ's actions—his self-surrendering death, in particular—to be a free self-determination in grace on Jesus's part, *what* Jesus says and does is closely bound to "his person," allowing Rahner to say that God's *basileia* has been established both *"through* him and *in* him." "Person-centered" redemption cannot be reduced to "natural" or "physical" caricature.

Rahner elaborates on the Christ-*basileia* relationship a few years later in *Was heißt Jesus lieben?* There, he specifies that the one who inaugurates the *basileia* in this unique, definitive, and irrevocable way is the "Messiah."

> Jesus understands himself as the Messiah. He is convinced that with himself the definitive, unsurpassable Kingdom of God has arrived—that in him God shares himself and communicates his own glory and excellence, consoling a sinful world with his irrevocable pardon, speaking his last, definitive Word, after which there shall be no other—and that this Word is indeed God himself, in his own excellence.[83]

This final point—that "this Word is indeed God himself"—is another important indicator (in Johannine language) of Rahner's *realsymbolisch* framework operating in the background. Recall, *das Realsymbol* is the *self*-expression of an original unity, making that original present fully to another. As the Messiah—here understood as the one who inaugurates and mediates the *basilieia* in his *person*—Jesus is God's presence to and encounter with us. Indeed, even *the* basileia, according to Rahner, is nothing other than *God*: "in every case the Messiah is the person with and through whom the definitive Kingdom of God has come. And ultimately, if we may be permitted something of a metaphysical observation here, this Kingdom of God is simply God himself, and not something distinct from him."[84] One could fairly say that Rahner here envisions Christ as *das Realsymbol* of the *basileia*. To this *realsymbolisch* articulation of God's Reign, Rahner marries his consistent usage of "person" language, clarifying that the arrival of this Kingdom is not *simply* an event that achieved through an agent-Jesus, but through the

---

83. *The Love of Jesus and the Love of Neighbor*, 27. Rahner goes on to argue that "Messiah," as he uses the term here, and later christological terms like "Incarnate Word" and "Son of God" are "entirely identifiable with each other, provided we clearly understand that 'Messiah' means substantially more than just any sort of prophet sent by God – that 'Messiah' means the vehicle and bearer of a definitive message that can basically no longer be transcended, a message in which God definitively 'commits himself'" (ibid., 28).
84. Ibid., 27.

One who abides as Messiah. One of Rahner's more pastoral pieces from the late 1960s provides an accessible look at this very point:

> Jesus teaches in the desert but the word which he preaches and wishes to preach is really his revelation of himself as the kingdom of God's mercy come upon the earth. Thus this word of Jesus tends directly to the end that what he reveals – namely, himself as the grace of God made flesh – enters really into the being of the human person, not just in thought but in all truth, in his spirit, in his grace, and in their historical manifestation, the sacraments and the sacrament.[85]

Conclusion: Christ, God's Presence to Us

Rahner's sacramental articulations of Christ's saving work are well known in the secondary literature, and thus, the second marker of representative soteriology (Christ as God's presence to and encounter with us) is, in one sense, the easiest to establish. Yet, the ways in which Rahner's "sacramental" Christology from later in his career draw upon the other two markers is underappreciated.

As we have seen, Rahner insists in "Eternal Significance" that Christ's humanity (his Sacred Heart in particular) does not have the soteriological importance of an instrumental agent with a one-off task of making the grace of salvation available. Rather, Rahner understands Christ's Heart as an enduring "refuge" of human salvation, the locus through which the blessed continually pass in their eternal knowledge of God in heaven. Thus, Rahner openly speaks about the unity, even *identity* of the Redeemer and the redeemed, going so far as to say that heaven itself was not a pre-existing reality to which Jesus grants access, but rather, that with his resurrection and ascension, Jesus *creates* heaven in his own *person*, in whom the blessed participate.

The person-centered character of his sacramental Christology is also evident in his writings on God's Reign. This *basileia*, according to Rahner, is not something established simply through a program or particular efforts undertaken by Jesus, but is inaugurated in "his person." His death of self-surrender on the cross definitively establishes God's Reign, for it simultaneously establishes (by recapitulating the "Yes" of his entire life) *who* Jesus is. For Rahner, Jesus is the Messiah, and the

---

85. "Das Ewige Wort des Vater als Tischgenosse," in *Meditationen zum Kirchenjahre* (Leipzig: Benno, 1967), 330–34; ET "The Eternal Word of God is Our Companion at Table," in *The Great Church Year*, 248–50, at 250.

Messiah is precisely the One who brings about the Kingdom (which is, ultimately, God himself) with his own person as its basis.

Salvation in Christ's Person

Let us now turn to the final marker of representative soteriol-ogy—namely, its person-centered character. The foregoing treatment on Christ as God's presence to us has already engaged this marker, for the way Rahner understands Christ, God's *Ursakrament*, to communi-cate grace to us centers upon Christ's identity (rather than on any par-ticular act he undertook). In addition to the person-centered elements of Rahner's theology which we have already explored in this regard, there are a number of other instances in which Rahner's soteriology shows itself to be strongly person-centered. These instances can be divided up into two main groups, the first of which concerns our salva-tion as bound up in our *relating* to the person of Jesus Chris, the second of which explicitly concerns the import of Christ's *being* (rather than simply *doing*) our salvation.

Rahner's Person-centered Soteriology: Relating to Christ

To underline the importance of having a relationship with Jesus is a commonplace in Christian spirituality. But for a soteriology which is robustly person-centered, relating to the person of Christ takes on spe-cial theological weight. For in this case, one does not relate to Christ in order to simply share the fruits of his saving work as a partner, but one's salvation hangs on relating to Christ since he is *its very locus*. Below, we will consider several manners in which Rahner's soteriology, precisely as person-centered, gives special theological weight to this relationship.

Christ as Constitutive of Our Salvation

In chapter 1, we encountered the distinction between constitutive and normative theories of Christ's role in salvation. To briefly summarize, those who endorse normative christologies would affirm that human salvation has Jesus Christ as its ultimate paradigm, the prototype pro-vided by God to which all other instances conform; in this model, salvation is indeed possible apart from Christ (though he would still stand, at the very least, in a relationship of resemblance to other occurrences). In comparison, constitutive christologies go farther and claim that Christ uniquely inaugurates human salvation and is indispensable to its realization. In other words, if it were not for Christ, there would be no human salvation—there cannot be any human salvation without him. A variety of different atonement models can legitimately claim to grant Christ a constitutive role. Whether the model is Christus victor, satisfaction theory, penal substitution, a person-centered soteriology of representation, or some other, the crucial factor is that Christ genuinely *effects* salvation.

Rahner (contra some of his readers)[86] understands Christ as constitutive of human salvation, and when he discusses the matter, the particularly person-centered character of his soteriology is apparent. In a 1980 lecture, "Jesus Christ–The Meaning of Life,"[87] Rahner addresses a group of Austrian physicians, explaining at one point how Christ can be understood to bring about our redemption. He begins, "Jesus of Nazareth as a human being with a concrete human history, as one who has died and risen, has a constitutive significance (let us attempt to formulate the question in this way) for the total meaning of our lives."[88] He then turns to Scripture and Christian tradition to give examples of *how* this significance can be understood.

First, Rahner states, "In the incarnation of the eternal Logos in Jesus of Nazareth God has accepted the whole of humanity and in this, since he has the same nature as we do, he has become one with the whole of humanity."[89] Here, the emphasis lies on *who* Jesus is, the one who shares our nature, *in* whom God has accepted the human race, and who is "one with the whole of humanity." He then turns to a classical *act*-centered explanation, focusing on Jesus satisfying God's justice in his death. But even here, as in the foregoing one, Rahner ends the explanation by appealing to the logic of Christ's unity with the whole of humanity. "By the obedience of his passion Jesus, as the loving immaculate one who was utterly guiltless, has opened to us sinners the way to the Father. For he has been totally one with us."[90]

In his brief survey of classical ways for understanding Christ's constitutive role in salvation, it is clear that Rahner has the soteriological distinction between Christ's being and Christ's actions in mind. Not

86. Recall, both S. Ogden and J.T. Farmer have characterized Rahner's Christ as having a *normative* role in human salvation; J. Wong has convincingly demonstrated the contrary.
87. Originally published as "Jesus Christus–Sinn des Lebens," *Geist und Leben* 53 (1980): 406–16.
88. "Jesus Christ—The Meaning of Life," *TI* 21:212.
89. Ibid.
90. Ibid., *TI* 21:213.

only does the passage just described indicate this, but Rahner also includes a footnote about "prescinding" from further discussion about the division between "ontical" statements (which understand Christ's *being* as already salvific) and those statements (about sacrifice, blood, obedience, etc.) which understand his being "as a preposition of salvation" (which occurs "in its proper sense" with his act of dying).[91] Of course, like others, Rahner is unsatisfied with simply "taking sides" in such a bifurcation.[92] Instead, Rahner proceeds by presenting *both* the "ontical" and act-centered classical statements as turning on Christ's unity with the whole of humanity. While he may "prescind" from a lengthy discussion of the matter, it is apparent that he sees a singular logic behind both strands: Christ is constitutive of our salvation, "For he has been totally one with us." He is thus able to color not only the "ontical" statements, but also more act-focused ones in scripture and the tradition, as having an ultimately person-centered rationale.

Christology of the Quest

Although, as discussed in chapter 2, Rahner continued to affirm elements of both "ascending" and "descending" christologies throughout his career, his middle and later years were focused predominately on the former, "from-below" methodology. Driven by his perennial concern that the "from-above" approach (while doctrinally unobjectionable) strikes the modern ear as rather mythological, Rahner pushed the theologians of his day to (re-)introduce Christ to contemporary people by beginning with things in their lives with which they were already familiar.[93] One way in which Rahner attempted to do this in his own theology is with an idea he called a "searching Christology," or a "Christology of the Quest." This widely-known idea also attests to the person-centered nature of Rahner's late Christology, for it depicts the human person as inexterminably (even if nonexplicitly) directed toward Jesus, who can be personally present to the mass of humanity

---

91. Ibid., n. 1.
92. Cf. Joseph Ratzinger's treatment of the distinction between the "theology of the Incarnation" and the "theology of the Cross" in *Introduction to Christianity* (New York: Herder, 1970), 228ff.
93. In a letter sent from Rome during the first session of the Second Vatican Council (1962), Rahner wrote, "I also notice here that I'm not yet all that old, even when I sit at a table with Daniélou, Congar, Ratzinger, Schillebeeckx and so on. I find that these still do not realize clearly enough how little, e.g., a christology 'from above', which simply begins with the declaration that God has become man, can be understood today. And the same is true in so many other instances. Of course one can hardly expect that another way of thinking will already make a mark on the schemata of the Council, but I do not find it explicitly enough among the progressive theologians themselves" (Vorgrimler, *Understanding Karl Rahner*, 158).

despite its large spatio-temporal diversity. In other words, the center-piece and teleological apogee of Rahner's anthropology, as attested by his searching Christology, is a genuine relationship with Jesus Christ.

Rahner gives a concise overview of his Christology of the Quest in the 1975 essay, "The One Christ and the Universality of Salvation" (pre-viously considered in chapters 2 and 4). Leading up to this section, Rahner has been discussing those who are not explicit Christians but nonetheless possess the grace of salvation—that is, "anonymous Chris-tians." Rahner is quite clear that such individuals do not simply receive their salvation through a general, nondescript God, but that each such individual stands in an intimate association with Christ: "the heathen in his polytheism, the atheist in good faith, the theist outside the rev-elation of the Old and New Testaments, all possess not only a relation-ship of faith to God's self-revelation, but also a genuine relationship to Jesus Christ and his saving action."[94]

What is not immediately clear, Rahner goes on to say, is *how* these (explicitly, at least) non-Christians have such a relationship with Christ. Although it is rather easy to speak of such individuals having a transcendent relationship to an eternal God, it is more difficult to account for how they (or any person removed from the Holy Land dur-ing the early part of the first century!) can relate to the particular per-son Jesus of Nazareth. Rahner's proposed solution is the "searching Christology," which is perhaps even more *anthropo*logical than christo-logical:

> A person who is searching for something which is specific and yet unknown has a genuine existential connection, as one alert and on the watch, with whatever he is seeking, even if he has not yet found it ... [T]he search is brought about by grace, which has found its historically tangible expression and its irreversible force in Jesus. This means that if the search is caused by this grace, a person engaged on such a quest is directed in some measure to this goal.[95]

While it is not explicitly mentioned, the notion of Christ as *das Real-symbol* of grace is central to Rahner's explanation. The human person, enlivened by God's grace, seeks her goal—and the goal itself is the full realization of that very grace, which simply is Jesus, *the* exteriorization of God's self-communication into the world. On Rahner's anthropology and Christology, there is an intimate connection between the seeker

---

94. "The One Christ and the Universality of Salvation," *TI* 16:220.
95. Ibid., *TI* 16:221.

and the Sought, who are bound together by grace. His concept of *das Realsymbol* serves as a conceptual bridge binding the two together, but this conceptual move is also inextricably bound to his person-centered soteriology. Salvation occurs through one's intimate relationship to Jesus, who is every person's *telos*.[96]

Notably, it is the issue of making Jesus present to spacio-temporally distant persons which emerged prominently in the conclusion of *E latere Christi*. The task of offering an account of this presence was a constant undertaking throughout Rahner's career—from his theology dissertation to the above account of "searching Christology" penned during the final decade of his life. Splitting the difference between these two moments, a 1954 essay called "Advent" takes up the same theme, offering an even more person-centered account of Christ, the blessed, and time itself.[97] The following passage is worth quoting at length:

> Through the work of God in Christ, time has become what it was supposed to be. Time is no longer the bleak, empty, fading succession of moments, one moment destroying the preceding one and causing it to become "past," only to die away itself, clearing the way for the future that presses—itself already mortally wounded. Time itself is redeemed. It possesses a center that can preserve the present and gather into itself the future, a nucleus that fills the present with a future that it already really effected, a focal point that coordinates the living present with the eternal future. The advent of the incarnate God, of the Christ who is the same yesterday and today and eternity (Heb 13:8), from whom neither the things of the present nor of the future can separate those who believe in him and who are united with him in love (Rom 8:38, 39)—this advent has penetrated into this time that is to be redeemed. . . . The believer does not only have certain thoughts and opinions about something, thoughts which remain separate from the [Christ-]event thought about. His "outlook on life" does not merely look upon something that remains external to him and that should be represented [*vertreten*] in him only by his thoughts about it. In faith the believer "thinks" not only his "thoughts." Faith is more than this: in and through us and our freedom, faith is God's grace working to assimilate the very reality of the event thought about. By means of faith the salvation of the believer really takes place in the

96. "Because a man engaged upon the Christological quest is prepared without conditions or qualifications to accept the goal wherever and however it can be found, this Christological search is in fact directed to Jesus, for it is Jesus who in reality is its proper goal. This means that the Christological quest possesses a relationship to Jesus, even if a man does not know how to call him by his proper name" (ibid., *TI* 16:222).

97. "Advent," in *The Great Church Year*, 3–7, originally in *Kleines Kirchenjahr: Ein Gang durch den Festkreis* (Munich: Ars Sacra, 1954), 11–16.

believer himself. Salvation itself comes out from the past into his present, into him . . . Christ lives in him. . . . In a mysterious way he becomes a contemporary of the incarnate Son of God. He dies and lives with him.[98]

This Christ at the center of time and history is related in such a way to the individual Christian that he is present "with him" and even "in him." Another remarkable element of this treatment of the issue is how Rahner simply uses "salvation" and "Christ" interchangeably. Whereas Rahner's typical articulation of the issue concerns how *Jesus* can be accessible from spatio-temporal distance, here, he declares, "*Salvation itself* comes out from the past into [the believer's] present, into him." This identification of Christ with salvation itself makes perfect sense for a theology in which Christ is the locus of salvation.

The Centrality of "Love of Christ" to Rahner's Theology and Spirituality

Finally, let us consider one more late account of understanding Christ's presence throughout time—namely, that in *Was heißt Jesus lieben?* (1982). This text, which Andreas Batlogg has situated well within Rahner's Christology, soteriology, and spirituality,[99] begins with Rahner's suggestion that one of the greatest dangers in contemporary Christology is treating Jesus "as an idea." That is, Rahner worries that too often theologians render Jesus a mere cog within a conceptual system. Lurking in the background is Rahner's awareness that his own Christology-soteriology of Christ as *das Realsymbol*, taken in a certain way by itself, is insufficient—even dangerous[100]: "Jesus Christ, ever so easily, is but a kind of algebraic symbol for God's absolute self-bestowal upon the world, so that if you do not arrive at this figure, or if you substitute

---

98. "Advent," in *The Great Church Year*, 3–4.
99. Batlogg, *Die Mysterien des Lebens Jesu bei Karl Rahner: Zugang zum Christusglauben* (Innsbruck: Tyrolia, 2001), 322ff.
100. Indeed, when considered in isolation from other parts of Rahner's thought, his *Realsymbol* soteriology ("God's absolute self-bestowal upon the world") seems especially vulnerable to precisely this criticism. Rahner seemed well-aware of this fact late in his career as he was composing *Was heißt Jesus lieben?* Factors within Rahner's overall though which safeguard against this sort of critique include, first and foremost, his meditational and devotional writings, especially those concerning Jesus's Sacred Heart (see below). Within his writings which are more properly theological, the person-centered aspects explored in this chapter stand as important elements which militate against Jesus' reduction to a conceptual cog. Nevertheless, Rahner's overall thought could be further protected from this vulnerability by making better use of narrative theology, particularly in his exegesis. On this point, see R. Krieg, "The Crucified in Rahner's Christology: An Appraisal," *The Irish Theological Quarterly* 50 (1983–1984), 151–67; on narrative and Christology more broadly, Krieg, *Story-Shaped Christology: The Role of Narratives in Identifying Jesus Christ* (New York: Paulist Press, 1988).

another quantity for it, you have not actually lost anything. We forget: It is precisely in this concrete Jesus, and only in him, that what this symbol refers to has actually come to pass."[101] Jesus cannot be treated as a placeholder for an "idea," but rather, any theological "idea" about Jesus must be sincerely rooted in a person to whom we have devoted ourselves: "our relationship to Jesus must involve more than an abstract idea of Christ—otherwise we should be simply hypnotized by our own idea of him and riveted to that, instead of loving a concrete, actual human being."[102]

Here, Rahner's perennial question arises once more: *How can we love this concrete, actual human being?* After all, precisely this particularity places us at an enormous distance from him. Rahner begins his answer with an analysis on the nature of love, which he understands to render the lover and the beloved "in" one another. Using language which harkens to his earlier writings on *das Realsymbol*, Rahner writes that "human beings necessarily commit themselves, entrust themselves, to others, and . . . indeed they must do so. . . . Only if one thus abandons oneself, and lovingly sinks into the other, does one succeed in finding oneself."[103] Rahner explains that this idea is perhaps most easily observable in married couples, but that it applies to (and is even paradigmatic in) knowing Christ as well. Such knowing, he says, certainly requires the "grounds" of rational considerations, such as those occasioned by exegesis of the gospels, historical analyses, and psychological evaluations of the disciples after Good Friday. But in the end, a true knowledge of Christ requires that we *love* him (and not just an idea about him), thus existing *in him* and becoming "fully ourselves" in the process.[104] The confluence of Rahner's *realsymbolisch* language of self-realization and the logic of representation is unmistakable here.

---

101. *The Love of Jesus and the Love of Neighbor*, 16. The surrounding text reads, "I readily admit that when I was young I read Paul more than the synoptics – precisely because there, in Paul, the magnificent Christ-idea was to be seized in all its clarity and immediacy. In Paul, in John, the eternal Word of God comes right down from heaven. Here is the one who has created the world from the beginning and holds it in his hand. And now this Absolute Logos, the World-Reason, appears concretely in Jesus of Nazareth, bears witness to itself, and accomplishes the deed of redemption on the cross, thereupon to return to the glory of God the Father. And there it more or less disappears, indistinguishable from the absolute God. Jesus Christ, ever so easily, is but a kind of algebraic symbol for God's absolute self-bestowal upon the world, so that if you do not arrive at this figure, or if you substitute another quantity for it, you have not actually lost anything. We forget: It is precisely in this concrete Jesus, and only in him, that what this symbol refers to has actually come to pass. And forgetting this, we find it easy to present Jesus Christ as, for example, the Omega of a cosmic evolutionary process" (ibid., 15–16).
102. Ibid., 18.
103. Ibid., 16–17.
104. Ibid., 17–18.

Nevertheless, this explanation simply brings us back to our question: *How* is this love for such a distant figure even *possible*?[105] In other words, is not loving the *idea* of Christ ultimately inevitable? Rahner answers to the negative in two parts. First, he explains, one might counter that Christ is risen, and thus alive with God.[106] Indeed, Christ is not only risen, but his body (as recounted in the resurrection appearance stories recorded in the gospels) seems not to be restricted by space and time in the manner which it was prior to his resurrection.[107] Such an answer, according to Rahner, certainly stands as one legitimate way to address the concern. But the bulk of his answer rests on a more fundamental insight about the nature of love itself. Echoing Thomas Aquinas,[108] Rahner states that love occurs "when, despite their diversity, two persons succeed in existing in such mutual exchange of themselves, such mutual communication and sharing, that it can be said that their love makes them *one*."[109] We can best address the concern about spatio-temporal distance between lover and beloved, Rahner advises, by first analyzing the unity they share:

> When we observe human love, we see that this same basic diversity between two people, this basic division separating them, obtains even when they are very near one another, even when they actually seek to unite themselves bodily. They are different, they are distinct. Their respective existence is not a given a priori as if it sprang from one source and origin. With all their physical and physiological proximity, the two remain diverse, distinct. They fall back, or at least they seem to fall back, into separation again, even when, in the act of supreme love, they seem to have achieved unity, a oneness. But (and now we come to the point) even through this basic diversity obtains between two lovers, indeed abides in the very basis of their love, and yet does *not* cause their love not to be—difficult as it may be to explain the coexistence of diversity and unity in love speculatively—then neither can a seemingly great distance in space and time between two persons who seek to love, and actually do love, beto-

105. "But after all – or so it seems at first – the concrete Jesus is cut off from us, is he not, by geographical space, by the distance of history and culture, and by the span of two thousand years. Can one love a person in earnest when that person is that far away?" (ibid., 18).
106. Ibid., 18–20.
107. Cf. Jesus's mysterious entry into rooms (Luke 24:36ff), even if the doors were shut (John 20:26) and locked (John 20:19), his instantaneous disappearance from the table on the journey to Emmaus (Luke 24:31), and his apparent ability to appear in distance locations within very short periods of time (Luke 24:33–34; shortly after Jesus disappeared from the table, the eleven in Jerusalem report that he had just appeared to Simon Peter).
108. Thomas speaks of two individuals, when united by the bond of love, becoming "one person" (*ST* I–II, q. 87 a. 7 co.) or "quasi" one person (*De veritate* q. 29 a. 7 s.c. 3, ad 11; see Thomas Aquinas, *Truth*, 3 vols. [Chicago: H. Regnery Co., 1952–4]).
109. *The Love of Jesus and the Love of Neighbor*, 21.

ken an impossibility for love. After all, even before its encounter with this spatial and temporal difficulty, love must face a much more radical difference—and experience shows it is perfectly capable of doing so. For this earlier, greater difference is actually to be reaffirmed in this love—for the lover love and affirms the other precisely *as* other, certainly not seeking simply to absorb the beloved into his or her own peculiar way of being.[110]

In other words, the concern about spatio-temporal diversity impeding a genuine love between two people would, pushed to its logical conclusion, end up undermining *any* genuine instance of love. After all, all people, and thus any set of lover and beloved, exist in spatio-temporal diversity (to some degree) from one another. However, if love exists at all (and Rahner is wagering here that it does), it can create a genuine *unity* of persons despite their spatio-temporal diversity. The most perplexing part of love is, Rahner points out, the *unity* of diverse persons which it occasions—and if we are willing accept this perplexity, a larger *degree* of spatio-temporal diversity should not present any great difficulty.

Thus, in the last years of his life, Rahner provides the existence of *love itself* as a response to the question of how Jesus can be present to the contemporary Christian. His soteriology cannot be adequately summarized by simply positing Jesus as the primal communicator of grace within a *realsymbolisch* conceptual framework. Rather, it must be understood in a more person-centered way which turns on our loving this particular historical individual in order that he, as our Representative, can in fact be *one* with us: "you're actually only really dealing with Jesus when you throw your arms around him and realize right down to the bottom of your being that this is something you can still do today. . . . I think one can and must love Jesus, in all immediacy and concretion, with a love that transcends space and time, in virtue of the nature of love in general and by the power of the Holy Spirit of God."[111]

Before leaving *Was heißt Jesus lieben?*, it is worth reiterating that Rahner's remarks within it (on being "in" Jesus through love) amount to the notion of "representation." As is also the case with his dictionary entry and his *de facto* response to Balthasar's excursus ("Reconciliation and Vicarious Representation"), Rahner begins his reflections here by insisting that human beings cannot be understood in an individualistic manner. Rather, they can only be truly themselves in relation to

110. Ibid. (emphasis original.)
111. Ibid., 23.

another. Moreover, the culminating moment of this inter-relationality is the love of Jesus, with whom we become "one." Such an argument, I would wager, is yet another (at least in part) response by Rahner to Balthasar's excursus on his soteriology, which claimed that Rahner was opposed to any idea of Christic representation.

There are several indicators that this is the case—namely, points within *Was heißt Jesus lieben?* at which Rahner explicitly addresses other concerns raised in Balthasar's excursus. One such instance concerns Rahner's "from-below" Christology, which leads (epistemologically, at least) from Christ's perfect life/death for our salvation to the doctrine of the hypostatic union. Why, Balthasar asks, should this not render the immaculate Mary hypostatically united with God as well?[112] Without mentioning Balthasar by name, Rahner ponders a very similar objection in *Was heißt Jesus lieben,*[113] answering by more or less acknowledging the limitations of a purely "from-below" methodology and grounding Jesus's uniqueness in God's loving act of "condescension."[114] An exchange on this particular matter with an unnamed interlocutor within two years of *Theo-Drama* IV (of which, we have seen, Rahner was acutely aware) is one indication that *Was heißt Jesus lieben?* was written with Balthasar's soteriological critique on Rahner's mind.

Another piece of evidence that Balthasar's excursus lurks in the background of *Was heißt Jesus lieben?* is what appears to be a counter-attack upon Balthasar's own soteriology in the second part (though again, Rahner never explicitly names Balthasar here). Balthasar's soteriology, articulated most famously in *Mysterium Paschale* but in more detail in his later volumes of *Theo-Drama* (especially the fourth and

---

112. "Why is Jesus' self-surrender to death on the cross regarded as absolutely unique? . . . [W]e would have to ask why the death of Mary (and her life, which was a preparation for it) did not lead to the same hypostatic union? . . . [S]ince she was perfect, was her death not of the same quality as that of Jesus?" (*TD* 4:280).

113. "The following objection, after all, could be raised: Suppose some person, wherever he or she might be, to be in fact indissolubly united to God and, in virtue of an absolute predestination, to remain so. This person could then be loved with the unconditional love that we appear to reserve for Jesus alone. We have only to think of Mary. Such an unconditional love can, then, it would seem, rest on other grounds than we have required in Jesus in the hypostatic union" (*The Love of Jesus and the Love of Neighbor*, 43).

114. "To be sure, the definitiveness of a human being's union with God opens the way for a true definitiveness of love for him or her (even where one's love for someone else may be greater on other grounds). But on what does the definitiveness of the union with God which forms the basis of such love *rest*? It rests on God's love-creating condescension. But this love-creating condescension has become unequivocally accessible and irreversible in the salvation history of the world only in Jesus. For it when God has affirmed and bestowed his concrete love (not in a theorem) on the world in the form of a love that is irreversible from his side that the unconditional reliability and utter self-assurance of a love for a human being is possible. But this affirmation and bestowal is available only in Jesus" (ibid.).

fifth), is centered upon the Trinitarian love between the Father and the Son encompassing (and hence, redeeming) all of reality, and act which is particularly effected in the Son's descent into dark realm of sin and godlessness, hell itself.[115] In the second part of *Was heißt Jesus lieben?*, Rahner distinguishes between "pure-Chalcedonian" and "neo-Chalcedonian" Christologies. The latter, he explains,

> understand the oneness of divinity and humanity as the ground of salvation so emphatically *as* oneness that, while maintaining the Chalcedonian doctrine of the nonconfusion, or non-commingling, of divinity and humanity in Jesus, they nevertheless proceed to regard Jesus' history and lot as the history and lot of God *as God*. They thus interpret the Chalcedonian dogma in the manner of Cyril of Alexandria: God has suffered; the eternal Word of God has himself undergone our condition and our death and thereby our condition and our death are saved and redeemed; the Word of the Father has personally taken on our condition, with its mortgage of sin and death, and thereby redeemed it.[116]

To be clear, Rahner recognizes that many truths, even those (such as the communication of idioms) which "belong *per se* to Catholic Christianity's deposit of faith," exist within the Neo-Chalcedonian approach to soteriology. However, he also believes that this kind of soteriology stands in danger of exaggerating and distorting those truths, excessively restricting itself to such truths, to the exclusion of other crucial theological factors.

Speaking of this view's "representatives in theology today" and without naming names, he writes that they end up rendering the soteriological action a completely *divine* drama, one which disrespects the proper division of attributes (in constant danger of rendering the *communication* of idioms an *identity* of idioms) and occluding the humanity of Christ. The final part of his critique, which he calls an "excursus" on neo-Chalcedonian soteriology, comes across as an especially pointed message to Balthasar: "We would then have the eternal, impassible God, who transcends all history—in a spirit of gnosticism or Schellingism or what you will—suffering in himself, suffering as God. We would be positing the redemption of our condition as occurring in

115. On Balthasar's soteriology, particularly with respect to the descent, see Steffen Lösel's "A Plain Account of Christian Salvation? Balthasar on Sacrifice, Solidarity, and Substitution," in *Pro Ecclesia* 13, no. 2 (2004), 141–71; Alyssa Lyra Pitstick's *Light in Darkness: Hans Urs von Balthasar and the Catholic doctrine of Christ's descent into Hell* (Grand Rapids, Mich.: William B. Eerdmans Pub. Co., 2007), and Pitstick's debate over the matter with Edward T. Oakes, "Balthasar, Hell, and Heresy: An Exchange," in *First Things* 168 (2006), 25–32.
116. *The Love of Jesus and the Love of Neighbor*, 55 (emphasis original).

virtue of a transposition of that condition to the interiority of God him-self."[117] A quarter-century later, Alyssa Pitstick would similarly criti-cize Balthasar for his treatment of divine passibility and the (lacking) soteriological consequence of Jesus's humanity.[118] Moreover, in a rare instance which occurred during an interview, Rahner *explicitly* names Balthasar when articulating this criticism in virtually the same terms. Regarding those who critique his soteriology, Rahner states,

> If I wanted to launch a counterattack, I would say that there is a modern tendency (I don't want to say theory, but at least a tendency) to develop a theology of the death of God that, in the last analysis, seems to me to be Gnostic. One can find this in Hans Urs Von Balthasar. . . . To put it crudely, it does not help me to escape from my mess and mix-up and despair if God is in the same predicament. . . . In Moltmann and others I sense a theology of absolute paradox, of Patripassianism, perhaps even of a Schelling-like projection into God of division, conflict, godlessness, and death.[119]

Although the content of Rahner's critique is certainly worthy of atten-tion, my interest concerns the *fact* that Rahner makes it within *Was heißt Jesus lieben?* When one considers the nature of the critique, Rah-ner's choice to describe it as an "excursus," and its similarity to a crit-icism explicitly directed at Balthasar elsewhere, it seems quite likely that *Was heißt Jesus lieben?* stands, at least in part, as a rejoinder to Balthasar's excursus. Rahner's exchange over the issue of Mary by way of self-apology only increases this likelihood. If *Was heißt Jesus lieben?* indeed stands as such a rejoinder, Rahner's heavy focus on loving the person of Christ unto unity with and "in" him may function as a fur-

---

117. The majority of the entire critique is as follows: adherents of neo-Chalcedonian soteriology "understand redemption as a matter of God's having suffered, God's having died, and thereby hav-ing redeemed us. While not forgetting that we are dealing with a mystery here, the neo-Chal-cedonian understands the expression 'Jesus was obedient unto death' of the divinity itself, as well as of the humanity. A representative of pure-Chalcedonianism, however, while continuing to maintain the hypostatic union of divinity and humanity in Jesus, will insist here that, in this union of divinity and humanity, the nonconfusion must also be safeguarded. Death and finitude belong only to the creaturely reality of Jesus. They remain 'this side' of the infinite distance sep-arating God and creature; they remain on the creaturely side of the one 'God-man.' The eternal Word, in his *divinity*, can undergo no such historicity nor any 'obedience unto death.' Pure Chal-cedonianism is ever wary of the other soteriology, fearing it will make the surreptitious transition from a *communication idiomatum*, a communication or exchange of concrete attributes (in the two natures) precisely to an *identity* of concrete attributes (of both natures). We would then have the eternal, impassible God, who transcends all history—in a spirit of gnosticism or Schellingism or what you will—suffering in himself, suffering as God. We would be positing the redemption of our condition as occurring in virtue of a transposition of that condition to the interiority of God him-self" (ibid., 56).

118. See Pitstick, *Light in Darkness*, 131ff, 196, 238, 305–6.

119. *Karl Rahner in Dialogue*, 126–27. The passage is taken from an interview with Albert Raffelt in Freiburg in 1974.

ther apology on his own behalf, specifically to the effect of showing how "representation," understood in the authentic way that we have seen him insist upon (i.e., *Repräsentation* rather than *Stellvertretung*) is present in his own person-centered Christology and soteriology.

Rahner's Person-Centered Soteriology: Christ's Being Our Salvation

As mentioned above, Rahner demonstrates himself to have a person-centered soteriology in two ways. The first, just considered, argues that a relationship with the person of Jesus is central to our salvation. The second and final way in which we will consider how Rahner exemplifies the third, person-centered marker of representative soteriology is by focusing upon how he understands Christ not simply to *do* our salvation, but to *be* our salvation.

Before proceeding any further, and at the risk of beating a dead horse, it bears repeating that a person-centered, representative soteriology does not understand Jesus to simply effect our redemption by merely in coming into existence—that is, the incarnation is not the sole moment of import for such a soteriology, as is the case with the "physical" model of redemption. Certainly, the event of the incarnation carries great soteriological weight. Indeed, a person-centered, representative soteriology holds that *all* of Jesus's acts carry soteriological consequence since they facilitate our union with him, the one who is salvation's locus as well as author and agent.

To speak of Christ *being* our salvation is not to suggest that a representative soteriology supplants Jesus's saving activity with ontological considerations. Both Jesus's "being" and his "doing" are salvific—their *configuration* is the issue. The person-centered claim is that Jesus's "being" is *not* simply a means to an end—the incarnation is not about establishing an agent who goes on to perform a monumental and otherwise unachievable task. And such a claim by no means denies the soteriological bearing that particular events—whether his incarnation, ministry, death, resurrection, and so on—have on establishing and rendering accessible the locus of salvation, namely, Jesus himself. In other words, to be person-*centered*, or to speak of Christ "being" our salvation, is not to be act-*exclusive*.

One of the most salient person-centered components of Rahner's mature soteriology is his insistence upon Christ being our salvation. Nevertheless, this component is in large part absent from secondary summaries of his soteriology, like those considered in the first chapter. One notable exception comes from Mark Fischer, who not only recognizes this component but even connects it with Irenaeus of Lyons. Fischer writes,

> The Christology of Rahner holds that Jesus saves humanity, not just by what he did, but by who he is. Christ, the absolute savior, comprises and thus saves the whole of reality. This teaching, which goes back to the theory of recapitulation, reflects the Greek-influenced world of Irenaeus of Lyons. Donald Gelpi implied that it is an example of inflated metaphysics.[120] Rahner accepted the inflated metaphysical claim that the whole of creation stands under the influence of Christ. But that is not just Greek metaphysics, but Christian doctrine. Rahner, with his teaching about Christ as the absolute savior, was expressing the faith of Christians.[121]

In agreement with Fischer's analysis, I will set out below to demonstrate Rahner's emphasis on Christ's being our salvation by considering how he unites Christology and soteriology, his explicit theological statements to this effect in *Foundations of Christian Faith*, and explicit spiritual statements, particularly some concerned with the devotion to Jesus's Sacred Heart.

Unity of Christology and Soteriology: Jesus as Our Salvation

The best place to begin this demonstration is with Rahner's entry on "Salvation" in *Sacramentum Mundi*. There, he laments that too often Catholic theologians have unduly separated Christology (who Christ is) from soteriology (how Christ effects salvation). "Soteriology and Christology form a closer unity than normally appears in the handbooks of theology. . . . We now see more clearly . . . that the best approach to the Christological dogmas is the recognition that Jesus is the historical, eschatological gift of God's salvation to us, the absolute bringer of salvation."[122] Indeed, if *who* Jesus is stands as a central rationale for *how*

---

120. Donald L. Gelpi, *The Firstborn of Many: A Christology for Converting Christians*, 3 vols. (vol. 1: *To Hope in Jesus Christ*; vol. 2: *Synoptic Narrative Christology*; vol. 3: *Doctrinal and Practical Christology*), Marquette Studies in Theology, no. 20 (Milwaukee: Marquette University Press, 2001); see especially 3:270, 330–415.

121. Fischer, "Karl Rahner's Transcendental Christology," presentation at the Catholic Theological Society of America annual convention in Miami, 8 June 2013, http://karlrahnersociety.com/wp-content/uploads/2013/05/Transcendental-Christology-06.08.13.docx.doc.

122. "Salvation," *SM* 5:436.

he brings about salvation, Christology and soteriology are, in fact, two sides of the same coin.

As he makes this claim, Rahner is sure to avoid possible misunderstandings by providing a number of clarifications. First, the unity of Christology and soteriology *cannot* be construed in such a way as to exclude Christ's *life and acts* from having saving significance. Writing about this unity earlier in the entry, Rahner makes this first warning explicit.

> Kerygmatically it inevitably leads to misunderstandings if in soteriology the person and the work (death) of Christ are too sharply separated. If in an incarnational doctrine of redemption it is emphasized too one-sidedly that mankind was redeemed by the fact of the divine Logos assuming a human nature as member of the one mankind ("quod assumptum est, redemptum est"), then redemption is one-sidedly envisioned only under cosmic and objective aspects and Scripture is not taken seriously when it sees the redemptive event in Jesus' love and obedience even to the Cross.[123]

Once again, the specter of "physical redemption" makes an appearance and Rahner is certain to distance himself from this troubled soteriological category.

Following this first warning, Rahner makes a second, even stricter warning about overemphasizing Christ's acts (especially his death) to the exclusion of his *being*, which cannot simply exist as a necessary precursor.

> If only the . . . act is taken into consideration in a "staurological soteriology" (cf. 1 Cor 1:18), and the incarnation regarded merely as the constitution of a subject who is *capable* of redeeming *if* he posits the requisite action, then soteriology inevitably falls into the purely juridical concepts of an exclusive "satisfaction theory". The incarnation no longer appears as an intrinsic constituent of the redemptive event itself, redemption remains in a purely 'moral' domain and its profoundly world-transforming character is obscured.[124]

I refer to this warning as "stricter" since, while Rahner here says that Christ's *being* cannot simply exist at the service of his eventually performing a saving act, he leaves open the converse—namely, that Christ's actions were done at the service of facilitating our union with

---

123. Ibid., 427–28.
124. Ibid., 428, emphasis original.

his saving person. In fact, I would suggest that this latter possibility is precisely what Rahner believes to be the case.

Evidence for this suggestion can be seen in Rahner's synthesis, which follows his two warnings in this *Sacramentum Mundi* entry about improperly emphasizing Christ's being (the "ontic" dimension) and Christ's acts (the "moral" dimension). Rather than staking salvation entirely in one or the other of these dimensions, Rahner advises that we center it upon the self-realizing *person* of Jesus.

> A theology of the personal subject and of freedom, the specifically personal unity of nature and activity . . . , would have to show that the assumption of a human "nature" by the Logos is the assumption of a "nature" necessarily working in freedom towards its destiny. The incarnation itself is a divine movement which is fully deployed only in the death and resurrection of Jesus Christ (cf. John 3:17; 1 Tim 11:15; *D* 86: the *descensus* is itself *propter nos homines et propter nostram salutem*)"[125]

Here, Rahner reemphasizes the saving significance of Jesus's incarnation. In fact, he accounts for the saving significance of Jesus's acts as *extensions* of it, as further moments in which God's gracious movement in the incarnation is "fully deployed." In other words, the *person* at the center of Christian soteriology is genuinely free, and so, the exercise of that freedom is part and parcel of this locus of our salvation. If "physical redemption" could be depicted as a single point at which salvation is effected, the person-centered soteriology for which Rahner advocates here can be depicted as an *interval* or line-segment at which salvation occurs. Accordingly, it is neither a singular performative act nor the bare metaphysical fact of his existence by which Jesus brings about human salvation, but rather, his entire person in all of its particularity, freedom, and temporal-spacial extension. Jesus himself *is* our salvation.

Theological Rationale: Combating Individualistic Tendencies of the West

Although this person-centered soteriology is extant and detectable throughout Rahner's mature corpus, nowhere is it more salient than in a soteriological discussion within his *Foundations of Christian Faith* (1976). There, Rahner explicitly critiques the standard categories

125. Ibid.

according to which Christians, or at least those in the West, understand the idea of redemption. The solution, he suggests, is a renewed appreciation for how Christ's *being* itself saves us. Let us turn to the context and then the passage itself.

The sixth chapter of *FCF*, titled simply "Jesus Christ," is quite lengthy (it comprises nearly one-third of the nine chapter work) and treats a variety of issues.[126] Subsection 7, "The Content, Permanent Validity and Limits of Classical Christology and Soteriology" contains Rahner's discussion of classical and official christological doctrines and their accompanying concepts. This discussion (parts of which have been considered in the chapters above) includes the concepts of "nature," "hypostatic union," and *"hypostasis,"* along with the various ways that these concepts can be misconstrued. (Rahner worries most about a contemporary overreaction to Nestorianism which would deny a created "subjectivity," and perhaps even a created will, to Christ in virtue of his being a single divine person.)[127] Among his other concerns are an improper utilization of the classical communications of idioms (namely, if one treats the "is" in terms of strict identity, in a monophysite manner)[128] and his perennial objection that a Christology done purely "from above" risks being regarded as excessively mythological and also rendering Jesus's humanity a mere "livery" donned by God's Word.[129] As he does in "Current Problems in Christology" (1954), Rahner here insists that while these normative, classical notions can never be disregarded and possess ongoing value, new expressions within contemporary Christology should not only be permissible, but are, at times, even necessary.[130]

In a sense, one might be surprised to see this section cited as evidence for Rahner favoring a person-centered soteriology. Rahner expresses serious concern about the way "person" language is used by theologians to describe Christ; especially since "person" today typically means "center of consciousness," talk of Christ's (divine) person can result in a conception of the human Jesus as a puppet of sorts. Moreover, in this subsection, Rahner mentions the "physical redemption" often associated with the fathers only to, in obvious disapproval, "prescind" from any substantive discussion of it.[131] However, the per-

---

126. *FCF*, 176–321.
127. *FCF*, 287, 292.
128. *FCF*, 291.
129. *FCF*, 290.
130. *FCF*, 289.
131. *FCF*, 288, cf. chapter 4 above.

son-centered soteriology which Rahner has in mind is not physicalist, and it does not center on the divine Logos simply garnering a new metaphysical property (namely, subsisting in a new, created human nature) in the incarnation. Rather, as we saw in *Sacramentum Mundi*, it understands Christ's *being*, which is fully human, fully free, and extended in space and time, as the locus of salvation.

This point about Christ's being our salvation is made explicit as he closes this seventh subsection of his chapter on Christ. In his final and culminating item on a list of shortcomings in classical christological expressions (or at least, in how they are frequently understood today), Rahner offers a critique, worth quoting at length, of Western act-centered soteriological thinking:

> In its explicit formulation the classical Christology of the Incarnation does not give expression in a clear and immediate way to the *soteriological* significance of the Christ event. This is especially true of western Christianity's understanding. Perhaps because of western individualism, the idea of an "assumption" of the *whole* human race *in* the individual human reality of Jesus is rather foreign to their way of thinking. Within this horizon of understanding, then, the hypostatic union is the constitution of a person who *performs* redemptive activity, provided that his actions are moral and that his accomplishment is accepted by God as representative [*stellvertretend*] for the human race. But he does not mean in his very *being* salvation, redeemer and satisfaction [*nicht aber selbst schon in ihrem* Sein Heil *als solches bedeutet (Erlöser, Genugtuung)*]. But from the perspective of scriptural statements and of our own understanding today, it would be desirable to have a formulation of the Christological dogma which indicated and gave immediate expression to the *salvific* event which Jesus Christ himself *is*, and which did this prior to explicit and special soteriological statements. Then the selected formulations could help to avoid more easily a monophysitic and hence a mythological misunderstanding.[132]

A few remarks are in order. First, it should be made clear that by referring to "an 'assumption' of the *whole* human race *in* the individual human reality of Jesus," Rahner is not advocating for an idea of the hypostatic union according to which the Word mechanically assumes humanity *in general*, rather than a single, specific human nature.[133] As the foregoing material in subsection seven demonstrates, Rahner understands Christ as fully human, like us in all things but sin (and

---

132. *FCF*, 293, emphasis original.
133. Cf. Thomas Aquinas's treatment of this possibility in *ST* III q. 4 a. 5. According to Harnack's reading, such a view is espoused by Gregory of Nyssa (cf. chapter 3 above).

thus, having one human nature, not every instance of human nature *in toto!*). What I believe Rahner *does* envision is the possibility for each human being, in the authentic exercise of her freedom, coming to participate in the unique person of Christ, her fully human brother, and thus being able to share in God's own saving life (cf. 2 Pet 1:4). It is precisely this free (rather than a purely metaphysical and mechanical) sharing in another which Rahner sees as unduly ignored by theologians in the West; his talk of "the *whole*" "*in*" the individual reality is best understood as shorthand for this larger, free process of "sharing in" which is best encapsulated by the term "representation."

Furthermore, the representation which Rahner has in mind is *not* that of Christ's accomplishment simply being "credited" to humans whose own freedom is left out of the process. This alternative idea of "representation," which we have seen Rahner frequently criticize, is raised and again censured under the descriptor "*stellvertretend*," and furthermore associated with a soteriology based on Christ's "*perform*[ing] redemptive activity." The authentic idea of representation for which Rahner advocates is one which considers Christ's *being* not as a necessary precursor, in the sense that an act requires an agent, but one which holds that "Jesus Christ *is*" the "*salvific* event," that Jesus is "in his very *being* salvation." Although Rahner does not here explicitly point to his own Christology and soteriology as an exemplary instance which realizes this theological *desideratum*, the many instances in his corpus which testify to his person-centered, representative soteriology indicate that he made a serious effort to shape his Christology along these lines. Moreover, Rahner indicates elsewhere that he has tried to unite Christology and soteriology in precisely this way.[134]

---

134. "It is true that traditional textbook theology devoted too little attention to the unity of Christology and soteriology. It was not Luther but we Catholic, neoscholastic textbook theologians who had developed a Christology of the hypostatic union, the communication of properties, and so on, which initially had nothing at all to do with soteriology, with 'Christ for us.' After this Christology we turned over the page to a new treatise entitled *De Deo redemptore*. We cannot do it this way anymore of course, and not just because people today are so convinced of their own importance and central position, and so on, that they cannot imagine a theology which does not constantly talk about human beings and their needs. This kind of mentality is, when all is said and done, highly questionable, even though nowadays it gives the appearance of being terribly obvious. But we do confess: *qui propter nos homines et propter nostram salutem descendit de caelis* [who for us and for our salvation came down from heaven]. From the outset Christology must be soteriology. The simple implication of this is of course that we have every right in the light of the New Testament or other more speculative viewpoints to attempt a formulation of the nature and meaning of Jesus which is from the outset a soteriological statement and at the same time really expresses the 'nature' of Jesus Christ in a truly orthodox way. It is my considered opinion that a reasonable ontology (or whatever else you want to call it) can and should be convinced from the outset that statements of function and statements of essence do not necessarily contradict one another. But from this it follows that one can quite properly construct a Christology which is called functional in full

Finally, Rahner couches his call for a person-centered soteriology as a response to an excessive individualism that has infiltrated Western Christianity. Recall, Rahner voiced a remarkably similar complaint about the "individualization" of Western Christian spirituality four decades earlier in *E latere Christi*, a work which is infused with patristic, Irenaean soteriology of recapitulation and focuses on Jesus as the New Adam.[135] In this remark, it is clear that Rahner has not left behind the past patristic insights he engaged as a young scholar. Rather, in his mature years, he levels the same complaint, and remarkably, suggests the matching solution—a return to what can be accurately be summarized as a *fons vitae* Christology of Jesus "being" our salvation.

Spiritual Rationale: The Sacred Heart and Our Salvation

As we come to the conclusion of considering the person-centered dimension of Rahner's soteriology, and having just considered his theological rationale for emphasizing Christ's being our salvation, it seems fitting to return once more to Rahner's spiritual motivations for the same idea. Recall, Joseph Wong has convincingly argued that Rahner's Ignatian spirituality was the primary force behind his theology of *das Realsymbol*. Likewise, Rahner's thought regarding the devotion to Jesus's Sacred Heart intersects with his soteriological considerations. Indeed, some of Rahner's earliest scholarship, especially *E latere Christi*, was driven by his desire to make theological (and especially, soteriological) sense of this devotion and its historical development. Accordingly, let us take a final look at Rahner's spiritual writing on this topic.

As we did before, let us split the difference between Rahner's writing of *E latere Christi* and his works of his final years, turning to years in which Rahner was first gaining widespread international renown. Included within Rahner's *Kleines Kirchenjahr* (1954) is a meditation for the feast of Jesus's Sacred Heart, titled "Herz-Jesu-Fest," as well as one for the cross and Good Friday, "Karfreitag."[136]

Although it was written a few years before *Kleines Kirchenjahr*, "Herz-

---

awareness that in so doing one has also constructed the essential Christology of classical church doctrine. I have already suggested a small example of such a formulation. But I cannot go into this in detail here" ("Brief Observations on Systematic Christology Today," *TI* 21:233–34 [1980]).

135. See the treatment of *E latere Christi* (in particular, its fifth chapter and conclusion) in chapter 4 above.

136. "Karfreitag" was first published in *Kleines Kirchenjahr*, 68–74 (ET available as "Good Friday: 'Behold the Wood of the Cross . . .'," in *The Great Church Year*, 149–54). "Herz-Jesu-Fest," (ET available as "The Mystery of the Heart," in *The Great Church Year*, 239–44), was first published as "Geheimnis des Herzens," *Geist und Leben* 20, no. 3 (1947), 161–65.

Jesu-Fest" (1947) stands as a helpful complement to "Karfreitag," which was first published in 1954. Rahner begins "Herz-Jesu-Fest" with a general discussion of the human person's "heart" and her "center," in which she fully possesses herself. Echoing the realsymbolisch themes which he associates throughout his career with the idea of "heart,"[137] Rahner explains that the human person is mysterious in that she only truly possesses herself by going outside of herself, giving herself away, seeking the other in order to return to and fully realize herself. What/ who is this "other" into which/whom our own hearts go out in order to fully self-realize, the other who thus exists as somehow "interior" to each of us? While many answers could be given, Rahner explains that, in a most basic and fundamental sense, the ultimate other in whom we self-realize is God.[138]

However, Rahner immediately cautions against too quickly settling for "God" as an answer to this question about the center of our own hearts. After all, such a proposal is rather disconcerting—God is uniquely infinite, uniquely one, uniquely perfect, and fundamental Mystery. To propose that we, as imperfect and finite beings, have such a reality as our very center seems not only hubristic, but terrifying: Does such a God, residing in our own flawed hearts, appear as swift justice or tender mercy?[139] Moreover, positing an inscrutable, ineffable God as our "heart of hearts" hardly begins to answer the question about who we are. As Rahner puts it, "Just when we want to use his heart so that the needed calculation of our heart will come out right, we write the enigmatic number of his ambiguous infinity and the figuring of our heart becomes all the more a really insoluble riddle."[140] And yet, Rahner puzzles, the "center of our hearts has to be God."[141]

The resolution to this dilemma about God as our "heart of hearts"

---

137. Cf. "Theology of the Symbol" (TI 4:221–52), "'Behold This Heart! Preliminaries to a Theology of Devotion to the Sacred Heart" (TI 3:321–30), "Some Theses for a Theology of Devotion to the Sacred Heart" (TI 3:331–52), "The Theological Meaning of the Veneration of the Sacred Heart" (TI 8:217–28), "Unity-Love-Mystery" (TI 8:229–47) and "Devotion to the Sacred Heart Today" (TI 23:117–28).

138. "[God] is the central point, the heart of the world, in whom all reality is gathered up and yet is not pressed together in a stifling corner. . . . He is not, as we are, merely the heart of one solitary person, but the heart of all reality, the all-in-one inwardness of all things" ("The Mystery of the Heart," The Great Church Year, 241–42).

139. "[E]ven if we say that God is the mystery of our hearts, the salvation of our heart's need, then, if we reflect rightly, it may appear to us in fear and trembling that it is most frightful to have God as the center of our center. For is not his own infinity, in which everything is the same, bearable only for him? . . . [F]or us and for our narrowness it is precisely this that is frightful and terrifying, it is just this that causes all the seams of our finiteness to sag apart. He is always his whole self" (ibid., 242).

140. Ibid., 243.
141. Ibid.

occurs in virtue of the God's incarnation in Jesus, whose heart, both fully God and fully human, is at the center of our own.[142] Our own fulfillment as humans occurs in our coming to dwell *in* the heart of Jesus Christ, where we come to fully realize ourselves, and thus, our salvation—life with God himself, whose posture toward a sinful world is ultimately that of love.[143]

> If he is our heart, our diversity can enter into the apartness of God without being burned to nothing in it. In him our dispersion can be collected without being confined and constricted, our heart can gush forth into the expanse of the world without being lost. The heart of Jesus is God's heart in the world, in which alone the world finds its God as its blessed mystery, in which alone God becomes the heart of our hearts, in which our being finds its center: at one and the same time unified and all-embracing.[144]

Thus, Jesus himself, as a person (and not simply an agent), stands as the central nexus point between the world as it is brought to its final salvation in the presence of God. Our salvation—and thus, our *telos* and true selves—lies within Christ's own Sacred Heart.

Having established within *Kleines Kirchenjahr* this approach to soteriology which is at once devotional, theological, and anthropological, we can better observe how Rahner's soteriological meditation on Good Friday in "Karfreitag" serves as a powerful testimony to his person-centered representative soteriology. Rahner begins this meditation with the Good Friday liturgy, during which the priest unveils a cross, intoning, "Behold, the wood of the cross, on which is hung our salvation. O come, let us adore!"[145] In doing so, Rahner underlines from the outset the identity of our salvation with the person of Jesus, who hangs on the cross ("on which is hung our salvation"). (In good Johannine fashion, he will close with this *inclusio* as well.) Continuing, Rahner asserts that this ritual of unveiling the cross is a "shadowy image" of something which occurs throughout all of human history, for the "cross of

142. God "make[s] at the center of our being a heart that is really the heart of the infinite God, and that *nonetheless* is a heart that is not everything. . . . For the mortal fear over his ambiguous infinity and for the need of our hearts to depart from us, he has to let his heart become finite. . . . He must let it enter into our narrow confines, so that it can be the center of our life without destroying the narrow house of our finitude, in which alone we can live and breathe. And he has done it. And the name of his heart is: Jesus Christ! It is a finite heart, and yet it is the heart of God" (ibid.).
143. "Our heart becomes calm and rests in this heart, in his heart. . . . In him the enigmatic mystery of the world's heart which is God becomes the crimson mystery of all things, the mystery that God has loved the world in its destitution" (ibid)
144. Ibid., 244.
145. "*Seht, das Holz des Kreuzes, an dem das Heil der Welt gehangen, kommt, laßt uns anbeten!*" (*Kleines Kirchenjahr*, 68; cf. "Good Friday: 'Behold . . .'," *The Great Church Year*, 149).

Christ has cast its shadow over all time. To be sure, historically speaking, the cross was erected only once in a definite place . . . and at a definite time. . . . But all time had waited for this moment that seems so short. All that had gone before flowed together into this moment."[146] And this moment, Rahner declares, stands as the "deciding word" in which God has definitively established his relationship to a world in need, a world filled with people who are thus oriented toward this decisive moment and exist in a *de facto* procession toward the cross which has been unveiled before them.[147]

Rahner then turns to a series of reflections on how the various members of the human race today—the dying, suffering, children, elderly, homeless, lonely, grieving, lovers, scholars, priests, and even agnostics—react to their encounter with the cross. Do we scoff, pass by, or remain vigilant at its foot? As we process up toward the cross over the course of our lives, lives which are encapsulated by the procession in the liturgy, what is our demeanor toward it?

Given the structure of the meditation (beginning with the priest's unveiling and intonation), these reflections occur as Rahner is nearing the cross itself during his own liturgical/life procession. As he approaches, he wonders at the many things which this cross means for us and offers a host of ways that the crucified Christ brings about our salvation. The themes he mentions include forgiveness and covenant renewal,[148] Christ's obedience to the Father,[149] satisfaction theory,[150] ritual sacrifice,[151] testimony to God's love,[152] and the Omega who "fulfilled all things."[153] Finally, he comes to his final soteriological theme—Jesus's Sacred Heart.

At this point in the essay, Rahner is "at" the unveiled cross, having

---

146. Ibid.
147. "Yes, the ages before Christ were overshadowed by the cross. They were mysteriously mapped out to be a part of that divine and universal drama of the history of humankind, in which the cross of Christ, the glorification of the Lord on the cross, is the deciding word. . . . But before the word was actually spoken from the cross, no one knew what answer God would give to all the words of human history, to the cries of guilt and of need, of yearning and of complaint, and of urgent petition. Before the cross, no one knew definitively and equivocally what God would say to us. Now, however, God has spoken his final word in this world and in its history, the word that is the cross of his Son. And in the two thousand years since the cross, human beings have been advancing in a never-ending, drab procession to meet this unveiled cross – whether they knew it or not – in all the tangles and meaningless twisting of their path through life" (ibid. 150).
148. ". . . him who forever stretches his hands out toward a stubborn and rebellious people" (ibid., 153).
149. Ibid.
150. ". . . the righteousness which the Son has satisfied" (ibid.).
151. ". . . to be close to the Son of the Father, close to their dead brother who sacrificed himself for them . . . the sacrifice that alone penetrates through all heaven" (ibid.).
152. Ibid.
153. Ibid., 154.

completed his procession and now disposing himself toward the cross before him. Simultaneously plumbing the theological implications of the Crucified One and offering a glimpse into his own inner, spiritual monologue, Rahner gives us perhaps the best look at the motivation behind his soteriology. Turning to the cross directly in front of him, he prays,

> Do I kneel thus below the cross for the three hours of my life. . . ? Am I one with the crucified? My soul thirsts for God my savior. I want to rise up and I want to see him who has drunk the most bitter cup of this world. . . . I want to kiss his bloody feet, the feet that pursued me even into the most monstrous inextricability of my sins. I want to see the pierced side of him who has locked me in his heart and who therefore took me with him when he went home, passing over from this world through death to the Father, so that I, too, am now where only God can be. I want to see the wood of the Cross, on which the salvation of the world, my salvation, hung. Come let us adore him.[154]

Within this intensely personal spiritual reflection, the heart of Rahner's own soteriological writings emerges into full view. Christ is God our savior and brother, the person *in* whom salvation is realized, and with whom Rahner thirsts to be "one." For this is the person whose side has been opened to us, in whose own heart we have been secured, and thus, carried into the intimate, saving presence of God.

Conclusion: Rahner's Person-Centered Soteriology

Testimonies to the person-centered character of Rahner's soteriology in his mature work can be divided into two major groups, one which emphasizes the necessity of relating to the saving person of Jesus and one which underlines Christ's very being as salvific. Regarding this first group, Rahner discusses the believer's relationship with Christ in a number of ways. First, Rahner states that Jesus's soteriological import does not lie in his being the origin of a particular act, but in being the one *to whom* one relates in order to realize salvation. This import is apparent when Rahner speaks of Jesus *constituting* our salvation by being "one with us"; in both its purely "ontic" and act-focused dimensions, soteriology is for Rahner about Christ uniting with us to effect our redemption. Second, this person-centered import is also apparent in Rahner's "searching Christology," which posits Christ as the *telos* of

154. Ibid.

every human being; in fact, Christ is the full realization of the same grace which drives every person to question and search for life's meaning. Finally, Rahner emphasizes how crucial it is for Christians to love the person (rather than the idea) of Jesus, and how such love allows us to participate *in* Jesus himself.

The second group consists of various ways in which Rahner underlines the salvific value of Christ being (and not just doing) our salvation. In *Sacramentum Mundi*, Rahner warns against improperly emphasizing either the beginning or end of Christ's life. Rather, he advises, the central emphasis should be placed on the person of Jesus, who in his entire, free, and authentically human life "fully deploys" the grace inaugurated in the incarnation. In *Foundations of Christian Faith*, Rahner chides Western theologians for limiting their christologies and soteriologies to models according to which Christ *performs* our salvation, so that the hypostatic union exists only as a necessary precursor to a saving act. Rahner proposes that theologians in the West would be better served with christologies which acknowledge Christ's *being itself* as already salvific. Finally, Rahner's spiritual writings in *Kleines Kirchenjahr* demonstrate the connection between his person-centered soteriology and his devotion to Jesus's Sacred Heart. Jesus's Heart, he explains in "Herz-Jesu-Fest," exists as our own "heart of hearts," through which we can have God himself as our "center." Moreover, in "Karfreitag," Rahner presents human life as a procession to the Crucified One, *in* whom we find our salvation. Jesus brings us into God's presence by "locking" us within his Sacred Heart, which is open to us through his pierced side.

As this chapter has shown, the theology written by Rahner in the latter half of his career contains numerous instances which testify to a representative soteriology. That is, even in his mature writings, Rahner understands salvation to be effected in a person-centered way by Jesus, who is both God's presence to the world as well as the one human being who sums up all others in himself. Although the excerpts above were divided according to these three markers of representative soteriology, we saw how many instances overlap and interact with the other two categories as well. Recall, Rahner's idea of Christ *creating* (rather than simply *opening*) heaven with his resurrection not only explains how Christ mediates God's presence to us, but it centers upon his person and depends on our participating in that person, our Representative. Likewise, his definitions of *Repräsentation* underscore how the person of Christ constitutes the entire network of human solidarity, as well as how *Repräsentation* accounts for the possibility of God's presence to finite beings. Finally, his person-centered reflections on the salvific value of Jesus's Sacred Heart posit Jesus as the mediator through which God becomes the center of our lives, as well as the one who gathers the human race together in his bosom. For Rahner, as was the case with Irenaeus and others of the church fathers, these three markers coalesce in a single, representative soteriological vision. And although Rahner's direct engagement with the fathers dwindled as his theological career advanced into its second half, their shared soteriological framework—readily apparent in early works like *E latere Christi*—continued to impact Rahner's theology well into final years.

Conclusion

As this study of Rahner's soteriology comes to its end, I would like to conclude not by itemizing the various findings and theses which we have seen in the foregoing chapters, a task which has been completed (albeit in piecemeal fashion) in those chapters themselves, but rather, by recapitulating its central thesis, and then, briefly suggesting several points for further reflection and study which arise in light of it. My central thesis can be framed in response to Balthasar's "excursus" on Rahner's soteriology, part of which insisted that for Rahner and his theory of sacramental causality, "it is not Christ who, in virtue of his uniqueness, embraces and contains mankind in order to reconcile it to God through his suffering—for we have already heard that such 'representative' action [*Stellvertretung*] is inconceivable."[1] Although it is fair to say that Rahner has serious qualms with the term *Stellvertretung* (qualms which, however, do not prevent him from approving the term[2] and even using it[3] in a qualified manner), the suggestion that Rahner's Christ does not "embrace and contain" humankind in order to bring about reconciliation with God, ultimately through Christ's death and resurrection, is egregiously mistaken.[4] For Rahner, God not only "reconciled the world to himself in Jesus the crucified," but Jesus Christ

---

1. *TD* 4:276.
2. Recall, Rahner affirms that the statement, "the human race is redeemed by the 'vicarious' suffering of Jesus [«*stellvertretende*» *Leiden Jesu*]," as well as "the human race is vicariously represented by Christ [*Stellvertretung des Menschen durch Christus*]," is "thoroughly valid [*durchaus legitimen*]" ("The Christian Understanding of Redemption," *TI* 21:239–54, at 248).
3. "Jesus Christ, the *Mediator, is *the* supreme representative of mankind in his vicarious redemption [*der absolute Repräsentant der Menschheit in seiner stellvertretenden Erlösung*]" (*Theological Dictionary* (New York: Herder and Herder, 1965), 405).
4. To be fair, many of the texts which cited here on this topic were written subsequent (and in all likelihood, at least partly in response) to Balthasar's critique. However, as I hope to have argued throughout the course of this work, the representative character of Rahner's soteriology pervades his entire career.

himself "has become our reconciliation."[5] Rahner's soteriology is a person-centered, representative one, with Christ as the True Human in
whom all the blessed freely and eternally participate. The representative quality of Rahner's soteriology can be traced back to his early fascination with patristic theology (particularly that of Irenaeus of Lyons
and his idea of recapitulation), and this soteriology can only be fully
appreciated when his idea of *das Realsymbol* is supplemented by that of
Repräsantation.

In light of this thesis, there are several points for further study
and reflection which, in good Rahnerian fashion, I would like to raise
but not sufficiently explore at this time. The first has to do with the
relationship of theology and spirituality. In his masterful work on a
spirituality of liberation, Gustavo Gutiérrez has lamented a fourteenth-
century divorce "between theology and spirituality that was to be
harmful to both."[6] Moreover, Gutiérrez explains, the fallout of this
divorce included an individualizing and privatizing of Christian spirituality,[7] which at its heart should be understood as stemming from a
communal encounter with the person of Christ.[8] It is safe to say that
Rahner, who once told Harvey Egan, "Beware the Christians with no
devotions"[9] and who speaks of a similar privatization in the final pages
of *E latere Christi*, shares Gutiérrez's perspective on both counts. Rahner's own theology is best viewed in light of his Jesuit spirituality, and
in particular, with an eye toward his devotion to Jesus's Sacred Heart.[10]
Thankfully, as noted in chapter 4, a movement to better appreciate the
importance of Rahner's spirituality is blossoming. As a contribution to
this movement, I would add that Rahner's devotion to Jesus's Sacred
Heart cannot be fully appreciated without paying serious attention to
the patristic *fons vitae* thinking which he explores in *E latere Christi*, and

---

5. "Christians know full well that God's forgiving and reconciling love that encompasses all guilt has
entered the world in such a way that it can never be revoked. This love has revealed itself in the
cross of Jesus Christ who has become our reconciliation. . . . God's forgiving love has reached its
historically visible culmination in Jesus' death on the cross, because this love has become irrevocable and has found its acceptance in a human being. . . . God has reconciled the world to himself
in Jesus the crucified. . . . [I]t also becomes reality for its part when human beings accept it" ("Reconciliation and Vicarious Redemption," *TI* 21:255–69, at 261).
6. Gutiérrez, *We Drink from Our Own Wells: The Spiritual Journey of a People* (Maryknoll: Orbis, 1984), 36.
7. Ibid., 14–15.
8. Ibid., 33–34.
9. Egan, "Foreword," in Callahan, *Karl Rahner's Spirituality of the Pierced Heart: A Reinterpretation of
Devotion to the Sacred Heart* (Lanham, MD: University Press of America, 1985), iv–viii, at vi.
10. Cf. Rahner's remark, "*Ut apertum core . . . piis esset requies et poenitentibus pateret salutis refugium . . .*
(so that opened heart . . . might be a resting place for the pious and be open to the penitent as
a refuge of salvation. . .). Such words are not just vague pious phrases and sentimentalities; they
form an absolutely exact statement which academic theology has not yet been able to surpass"
("The Eternal Significance of the Humanity of Jesus," *TI* 3:35–46, at 46).

thus, to his representative soteriology. As he laments the privatization of the "church as Second Eve" type and posits the Sacred Heart as a contemporary analogue to this type as it functioned for the fathers, Rahner calls for a retrieval of their person-centered *fons vitae* theology-spirituality, insisting that we "can learn something from the early church."[11] If we are going to better understand Rahner's theology in light of his spirituality, we need to more seriously attend to his early, formative, and intense engagement with the theology of the church fathers.

A second suggestion concerns theological conversations about the Christ's atonement during the last couple of decades. Shortly after Rahner's death in 1984, a variety of theologians began to critique traditional notions of atonement centered upon the crucifixion, especially in light of insights connecting the atonement doctrine with abuse.[12] Taking these concerns seriously, Kathryn Tanner has responded by suggesting that a patristic, nonphysicalist, and incarnation-based soteriology is the best option for responsibly retrieving the doctrine of Christ's atonement.[13] Moreover, as noted toward the end of chapter 3, a variety of other theologians have begun advocating for similar, patristic-inspired representative soteriologies. As the trend of retrieving recapitulation as a helpful contemporary category for rethinking atonement continues to advance, Karl Rahner's soteriology should be part of the conversation.

One final suggestion is not restricted to his soteriology, but instead, concerns his overall approach to theology. Whether one wants to refer to Rahner as "systematic," "constructive," or "speculative," it should have become evident throughout the course of this book that Rahner is also a deeply historical theologian. That is, Rahner's thought is pro-

11. *E latere Christi: Der Ursprung der Kirche als zweiter Eva aus der Seite Christi des zweiten Adam, eine Untersuchung über den typologischen Sinn von Joh 19, 34*, in *SW* 3:1–84, at 84.
12. E.g., Rita Nakashima Brock, "And a Little Child Will Lead Us: Christology and Child Abuse," in *Christianity, Patriarchy, and Abuse: A Feminist Critique*, eds. Joanne Carlson Brown and Carole R. Bohn (New York: Pilgrim, 1989), 42–61; J. Carlson Brown and Rebecca Parker, "For God So Loved the World?," in *Christianity, Patriarchy, and Abuse*, eds. Brown and Bohn, 1–30; Delores S. Williams, *Sisters in the Wilderness: The Challenge of Womanist God-Talk* (Maryknoll: Orbis, 1993), especially 161–67; Elisabeth Schüssler Fiorenza, *Jesus: Miriam's Child, Sophia's Prophet* (New York: Continuum, 1994), especially 97–128; Rosemary Radford Ruether, *Introducing Redemption in Christian Feminism* (Sheffield: Sheffield Academic Press, 1998), especially 95–107; Regula Strobel, "New Ways of Speaking About the Cross: A New Basis for Christian Identity," in *Toward a New Heaven and a New Earth: Essays in Honor of Elisabeth Schüssler-Fiorenza*, ed. Fernando F. Segovia (Maryknoll: Orbis, 2003), 351–67; Stephen Finlan, *Problems with Atonement: The Origins of, and Controversy About, The Atonement Doctrine* (Collegeville: Liturgical Press, 2005); J. Denny Weaver, *The Nonviolent Atonement*, 2nd ed. (Grand Rapids: Eerdmans, 2011).
13. Tanner, "Incarnation, Cross, and Sacrifice: A Feminist-Inspired Reappraisal," *Anglican Theological Review* 86, no. 1 (2004), 35–56.

foundly shaped by his robust knowledge of and concern for the theology and overall Christian tradition which has preceded him. To use buzzwords in use around the time of the Second Vatican Council, Rahner's approach to theology is not only one of *aggiornamento* ("updating"), but also one of *ressourcement* ("retrieval"). Though such terms are often coupled with bifurcations such as *Concilium* and *Communio*, "liberal" and "conservative," and so on, and though Rahner's name itself has for various reasons become somewhat of a point to or against which various tribes of Catholic theologians rally, Rahner is, in fact, a bit of a misfit when it comes to predominant contemporary factions.

On this point, it is worth recalling the suspicion with which many curial officials viewed Rahner at the outset of Vatican II. As noted in the beginning of chapter 1, this suspicion even led to all of Rahner's writings being censored at the outset of the council. However, as these critics engaged Rahner and learned more about him, he began to defy their preconceptions, eventually gaining a profound respect and even friendship with him.[14] One of his most decisive opponents prior to the council, Dutch dogmatic theologian Sebastian Tromp, remarked after working with Rahner at the council, "This Rahner is remarkable—when he starts talking *Latin*, then you can understand him."[15] Similarly, I would suggest that Rahner may find supporters in unlikely places if they had the opportunity to encounter (especially the deeply historically informed) aspects of his thought which are not part and parcel of his popular reputation. Indeed, this man who was at once the editor of Denzinger and a creative force behind reform at Vatican II, the theologian who chided the subsequent generation of theologians for both

14. "During this period [beginning with the close of the first session in Dec. 1962] Rahner acquired a high reputation among those Roman theologians who were, objectively speaking, his opponents. He had a perfect mastery of the Latin language. He possessed an enormous knowledge of the patristic and Scholastic traditions. He could understand his opponents' arguments from within. He opposed them with a striking logical sharpness. He left no doubt in anyone's mind that he was concerned with the pastoral needs of the Church. And so he moved towards a resolution of his conflict with the Holy Office. In February 1963 during a break between sessions he talked with Cardinal Ottaviani about the censorship measure taken against him. Ottaviani explained to him that the measure had been taken out of friendship for him, that it had been wrongly interpreted, that it was for his defense, in short that it should have been regarded as a privilege. Rahner replied that he would willingly renounce such a privilege. In May 1963 the Jesuit General told Rahner that in the future he, the General, would choose Rahner's censors, as before. With this the Holy Office retreated, and from then on until his death Rahner was spared further canonical penalties. In fact he came to have a genuinely friendly relation with his former enemies, and contributed essays to the *Festschriften* for Ottaviani and Parente" (Vorgrimler, "Karl Rahner: The Theologian's Contribution," in *Vatican II Revisited: By Those Who Were There*, ed. Alberic Stacpoole (Minneapolis: Winston, 1986), 32–46, at 43–44). On Rahner's friendship with Ottaviani, cf. *Karl Rahner in Dialogue: Conversations and Interviews*, eds. Paul Imhof and Hubert Biallowons (New York: Crossroad, 1986), 261, 300.
15. Ibid., 299.

their "whoring after relevance"[16] and their lack of ingenuity,[17] should challenge all of us today to be simultaneously better grounded in the church's heritage and more creative in our thinking.

16. "Rahner criticizes those who discard the past too quickly. He complained on more than one occasion that those 'whoring after relevance' by jettisoning precious elements in the church's tradition had replaced these elements with nothing and created an un-Christian vacuum in so many lives" (Egan, "Foreword," in Callahan, *Karl Rahner's Spirituality of the Pierced Heart*, vi.).
17. In "The Present Situation of Catholic Theology" (1979), Rahner observes, "In this earlier phase new ground was broken with a certain enthusiasm. Today one can speak of patient continuation at the most. In this second period everything has become a little more pallid. There is unmistakably a certain resignation, almost a danger of the actual Christian-ecclesial life no longer operating in the field of theological discipline but wandering off into other fields, and of scientific theological reflection becoming something like a withered branch on the tree called Church. . . . Perhaps one cannot deny that the generation of theologians associated with the groundbreaking of the new theology, men like von Balthasar, Chenu, Congar, Daniélou, de Lubac, Malmberg, Schillebeeckx, Schoonenberg, has now grown old. They have – I hope I am wrong – not really found successors of the same stature" (*TI* 21:70–77, at 74–75). Rahner goes on to ask whether "theology in the Church today is less vibrant and active than it was in the first phase of the new theology?," notes "a certain stagnation of ecumenical theology" and "a dearth of high-level theology which would bring Christianity to unbelievers of our time" (ibid., *TI* 21:75). He concludes, "All things taken into consideration I really do feel that Catholic theology today by and large does not rate a higher mark than Grade C" (ibid.).

Bibliography

Primary Literature by Karl Rahner (arranged alphabetically)

"The Abiding Significance of the Second Vatican Council." In *Theological Investigations*. Vol. 20, *Concern for the Church*, 90–102. Translated by Edward Quinn. New York: Crossroad, 1981.

"Advent." In *The Great Church Year: The Best of Karl Rahner's Homilies, Meditations, and Sermons*, edited by Harvey D. Egan, 3–7. New York: Crossroad, 1993.

"The Angels (2 October)." In *The Great Church Year: The Best of Karl Rahner's Homilies, Meditations, and Sermons*, edited by Harvey D. Egan, 356–58. New York: Crossroad, 1993.

"Anonymous Christianity and the Missionary Task of the Church." In *Theological Investigations*. Vol. 12 *Confrontations 2*, 161–78. Translated by David Bourke. New York: Seabury, 1974.

"Augustin und der Semipelagianismus." *Zeitschrift für katholische Theologie* 62, no. 2 (1938): 171–96.

"A Basic Theological and Anthropological Understanding of Old Age." In *Theological Investigations*. Vol. 23, *Final Writings*, 50–60. Translated by Joseph Donceel and Hugh M. Riley. New York: Crossroad, 1992.

"'Behold This Heart!': Preliminaries to a Theology of Devotion to the Sacred Heart." In *Theological Investigations*. Vol. 3, *The Theology of the Spiritual Life*, 321–30. Translated by Karl H. Kruger and Boniface Kruger. Baltimore: Helicon Press, 1967.

"Brief Observations on Systematic Christology Today." In *Theological Investigations*. Vol. 21, *Science and Christian Faith*, 228–38. Translated by Hugh M. Riley. New York: Crossroad, 1988.

"A Brief Theological Study on Indulgences." In *Theological Investigations*. Vol. 10, *Writings of 1965-67, 2*, 150–65. Translated by David Bourke. New York: Seabury, 1977.

269

"Christian Dying." In *Theological Investigations*. Vol. 18, *God and Revelation*, 226–56. Translated by Edward Quinn. New York: Crossroad, 1983.

"The Christian Understanding of Redemption." In *Theological Investigations*. Vol. 21, *Science and Christian Faith*, 239–54. Translated by Hugh M. Riley. New York: Crossroad, 1988.

"Christology Today." In *Theological Investigations*. Vol. 21, *Science and Christian Faith*, 220–27. Translated by Hugh M. Riley. New York: Crossroad, 1988.

"'Coeur de Jésus' chez Origene?" *Révue d'Ascetique et de Mystique* 15 (1934): 171–74.

"The Comfort of Time." In *Theological Investigations*. Vol. 3, *The Theology of the Spiritual Life*, 141–57. Translated by Karl H. Kruger and Boniface Kruger. Baltimore: Helicon Press, 1967.

"The Concept of Mystery in Catholic Theology." In *Theological Investigations*. Vol. 4, *More Recent Writings*, 36–73. Translated by Kevin Smyth. Baltimore: Helicon Press, 1966.

"Concerning the Relationship Between Nature and Grace" In *Theological Investigations*. Vol. 1, *God, Christ, Mary and Grace*, 297–317. Translated by Cornelius Ernst. Baltimore: Helicon Press, 1961.

"The Consecration of the Layman to the Care of Souls." In *Theological Investigations*. Vol. 3, *The Theology of the Spiritual Life*, 263–76. Translated by Karl H. Kruger and Boniface Kruger. Baltimore: Helicon Press, 1967.

"Considerations of the Active Role of the Person in the Sacramental Event." In *Theological Investigations*. Vol. 14, *Ecclesiology, Questions in the Church, the Church in the World*, 161–84. Translated by David Bourke. New York: Seabury, 1976.

"Current Problems in Christology." In *Theological Investigations*. Vol. 1, *God, Christ, Mary and Grace*, 149–200. Translated by Cornelius Ernst. Baltimore: Helicon Press, 1961.

De Gratia Christi: Summa Praelectionum in usum privatum auditorum ordinata. Oeniponte, 1937–38.

"Der Begriff der ecstasis bei Bonaventura." *Zeitschrift für Aszese und Mystik* 9 (1934): 1–19.

"De termino aliquo in theologia Clementis Alexandrini, qui aequivalet nostro conceptui entis 'supernaturalis.'" *Gregorianum* 18, no. 2–3 (1937): 426–31.

"Devotion to the Sacred Heart Today." In *Theological Investigations*. Vol. 23, *Final Writings*, 117–28. Translated by Joseph Donceel and Hugh M. Riley. New York: Crossroad, 1992.

"Die deutsche protestantische Christologie der Gegenwart." *Theologie der Zeit* 1 (1936): 189–202.

"Die geistliche Lehre des Evagrius Ponticus. In ihren Grundzügen dargestellt." *Zeitschrift für Aszese und Mystik* 8 (1933): 21–38.

"Die Illuminationstheorie des heiligen Augustinus." In *Karl Rahner: Sämtliche Werke.* Vol. 1, *Frühe spirituelle Texte und Studien,* edited by Karl Lehmann and Albert Raffelt, 277–304. Freiburg: Herder, 2014.

"Die Lehre von der Glückseligkeit bei Aristoteles und Thomas." In *Karl Rahner: Sämtliche Werke.* Vol. 1, *Frühe spirituelle Texte und Studien,* edited by Karl Lehmann and Albert Raffelt, 255–73. Freiburg: Herder, 2014.

"Die Liebe zu Gott." *Korrespondenz des Priester-Gebetsvereines "Associatio perseverantiae sacerdotalis"* 59, no. 6 (1938): 74–80.

"The Doctrine of the 'Spiritual Senses' in the Middle Ages." In *Theological Investigations.* Vol. 16, *Experience of the Spirit: Source of Theology,* 104–34. Translated by David Morland. New York: Seabury, 1979.

"Dogmatic Questions on Easter." In *Theological Investigations.* Vol. 4, *More Recent Writings,* 121–33. Translated by Kevin Smyth. Baltimore: Helicon Press, 1966.

"Easter: A Faith that Loves the Earth." In *The Great Church Year: The Best of Karl Rahner's Homilies, Meditations, and Sermons,* edited by Harvey D. Egan, 192–97. New York: Crossroad, 1993.

"Ein messalianisches Fragment über die Taufe." *Zeitschrift für katholische Theologie* 61, no. 2 (1937): 258–71.

E latere Christi: Der Ursprung der Kirche als zweiter Eva aus der Seite Christi des zweiten Adam, eine Untersuchung über den typologischen Sinn von Joh 19, 34 [From the Side of Christ: The Origin of the Church as Second Eve from the Side of Christ the Second Adam, An Examination of the Typological Meaning of John 19:34]. PhD diss., University of Innsbruck, 1936.

Encounters with Silence. Translated by James M. Demske. Westminster, MD: Newman Press, 1960.

"Es ist merkwürdig bei einem Konzil." *Stimmen der Zeit* 9 (2012): 590–96.

"The Eternal Significance of the Humanity of Jesus for our Relationship with God." In *Theological Investigations.* Vol. 3, *The Theology of the Spiritual Life,* 35–46. Translated by Karl H. Kruger and Boniface Kruger. Baltimore: Helicon Press, 1967.

"The Eternal Word of God Is Our Companion at Table." In *The Great Church Year: The Best of Karl Rahner's Homilies, Meditations, and Sermons,* edited by Harvey D. Egan, 248–50. New York: Crossroad, 1993.

The Eternal Year. Translated by John Shea. Baltimore: Helicon, 1964.

"The Eucharist and Suffering." In *Theological Investigations.* Vol. 3, *The Theology of the Spiritual Life,* 161–70. Translated by Karl H. Kruger and Boniface Kruger. Baltimore: Helicon Press, 1967.

Faith in a Wintry Season: Conversations and Interviews with Karl Rahner in the Last

Years of His Life. Edited by Paul Imhof and Hubert Biallowons. Translated by Harvey D. Egan. New York: Crossroad, 1990.

"Feast of St. Augustine (28 August)." In *The Great Church Year: The Best of Karl Rahner's Homilies, Meditations, and Sermons*, edited by Harvey D. Egan, 353–55. New York: Crossroad, 1993.

"First Mass." In *Mission and Grace: Essays in Pastoral Theology*, vol. 3, 211–20. Translated by Cecily Hastings and Richard Strachan. London: Sheed & Ward, 1966.

"Following the Crucified." In *Theological Investigations*. Vol. 18, *God and Revelation*, 157–70. Translated by Edward Quinn. New York: Crossroad, 1983.

"Forgotten Dogmatic Initiatives of the Second Vatican Council." In *Theological Investigations*. Vol. 22, *Humane Society and the Church of Tomorrow*, 97–105. Translated by Joseph Donceel. New York: Crossroad, 1991.

Foundations of Christian Faith: An Introduction to the Idea of Christianity. Translated by William V. Dych. New York: Crossroad, 2007.

"Geschichte und Geschichtserkenntnis im Geiste thomistischer Metaphysik." In *Karl Rahner: Sämtliche Werke*. Vol. 1, *Frühe spirituelle Texte und Studien*, edited by Karl Lehmann and Albert Raffelt, 245–54. Freiburg: Herder, 2014.

"Gnade als Mitte menschlicher Existenz. Ein Gespräch mit und über Karl Rahner aus Anlaß seines 70. Geburtstages." *Herder-Korrespondenz* 28 (1974): 77–92.

"Good Friday: 'Behold the Wood of the Cross . . .'" In *The Great Church Year: The Best of Karl Rahner's Homilies, Meditations, and Sermons*, edited by Harvey D. Egan, 149–54. New York: Crossroad, 1993.

"Good Friday: Gratitude for the Cross." In *The Great Church Year: The Best of Karl Rahner's Homilies, Meditations, and Sermons*, edited by Harvey D. Egan, 159–63. New York: Crossroad, 1993.

Grace in Freedom. Translated by Hilda Graef. New York: Herder & Herder, 1969.

The Great Church Year: The Best of Karl Rahner's Homilies, Meditations, and Sermons. Edited by Harvey D. Egan. New York: Crossroad, 1993.

Hearer of the Word: Laying the Foundation for a Philosophy of Religion. Translated by Joseph Donceel. Edited by Andrew Tallon. New York: Continuum, 1994.

"Hidden Victory." In *Theological Investigations*. Vol. 7, *Further Theology of the Spiritual Life 1*, 151–58. Translated by David Bourke. New York: Seabury, 1971.

"The Ignatian Mysticism of Joy in the World." In *Theological Investigations*. Vol. 3, *The Theology of the Spiritual Life*, 277–93. Translated by Karl H. Kruger and Boniface Kruger. Baltimore: Helicon Press, 1967.

"Immanent and Transcendent Consummation of the World." In *Theological Investigations*. Vol. 10, *Writings of 1965-67, 2*, 273–89. Translated by David Bourke. New York: Seabury, 1977.

I Remember: An Autobiographical Interview with Meinold Krauss. Translated by Harvey D. Egan. New York: Crossroad, 1985.

"Jesus Christ in the Non-Christian Religions." In *Theological Investigations.* Vol. 17, *Jesus, Man, and the Church,* 39–50. Translated by Margaret Kohl. New York: Crossroad, 1981.

"Jesus Christ—The Meaning of Life." In *Theological Investigations.* Vol. 21, *Science and Christian Faith,* 208–19. Translated by Hugh M. Riley. New York: Crossroad, 1988.

Karl Rahner in Dialogue: Conversations and Interviews. Edited by Harvey D. Egan. New York: Crossroad, 1986.

Karl Rahner: Spiritual Writings. Edited by Philip Endean. Maryknoll, NY: Orbis, 2004.

"Laienheiligkeit im christlichen Altertum." *Stimmen der Zeit* 135 (1939): 234–51.

"The Life of the Dead." In *Theological Investigations.* Vol. 4, *More Recent Writings,* 347–54. Translated by Kevin Smyth. Baltimore: Helicon Press, 1966.

The Love of Jesus and the Love of Neighbor. Translated by Robert Barr. New York: Crossroad, 1983.

"The Man with the Pierced Heart." In *Karl Rahner: Spiritual Writings,* edited by Philip Endean, 120–31. Maryknoll, NY: Orbis, 2004.

"The Meaning of Frequent Confessions of Devotion." In *Theological Investigations.* Vol. 3, *The Theology of the Spiritual Life,* 177–89. Translated by Karl H. Kruger and Boniface Kruger. Baltimore: Helicon Press, 1967.

Mission and Grace: Essays in Pastoral Theology. Translated by Cecily Hastings and Richard Strachan. 3 vols. London: Sheed & Ward, 1964–66.

"The Mystery of the Heart." In *The Great Church Year: The Best of Karl Rahner's Homilies, Meditations, and Sermons,* edited by Harvey D. Egan, 239–44. New York: Crossroad, 1993.

"Nature and Grace." In *Theological Investigations.* Vol. 4, *More Recent Writings,* 165–88. Translated by Kevin Smyth. Baltimore: Helicon Press, 1966.

"The One Christ and the Universality of Salvation." In *Theological Investigations.* Vol. 16, *Experience of the Spirit: Source of Theology,* 199–224. Translated by David Morland. New York: Seabury, 1979.

"One Mediator and Many Mediations." In *Theological Investigations.* Vol. 9, *Writings of 1965–67,* 169–84. Translated by Graham Harrison. New York: Seabury, 1972.

On Prayer. Collegeville, MN: Liturgical Press, 1993.

On the Theology of Death. Translated by C. H. Henkey. New York: Herder & Herder, 1965.

"On the Theology of the Incarnation." In *Theological Investigations.* Vol. 4, *More*

Recent Writings, 105–20. Translated by Kevin Smyth. Baltimore: Helicon Press, 1966.

Opportunities for Faith: Elements of a Modern Spirituality. Translated by Edward Quinn. London: SPCK, 1974.

"The Parish Priest." In *Mission and Grace: Essays in Pastoral Theology*, vol. 2, 35–52. Translated by Cecily Hastings and Richard Strachan. London: Sheed & Ward, 1964.

The Practice of Faith: A Handbook of Contemporary Spirituality. New York: Crossroad, 1983.

Prayers for a Lifetime. Edited by Albert Raffelt. New York: Crossroad, 1984.

"The Presence of the Lord in the Christian Community at Worship." In *Theological Investigations*. Vol. 10, *Writings of 1965-67, 2*, 71–83. Translated by David Bourke. New York: Seabury, 1977.

"The Present Situation of Catholic Theology." In *Theological Investigations*. Vol. 21, *Science and Christian Faith*, 70–77. Translated by Hugh M. Riley. New York: Crossroad, 1988.

"Priestly Existence." In *Theological Investigations*. Vol. 3, *The Theology of the Spiritual Life*, 239–62. Translated by Karl H. Kruger and Boniface Kruger. Baltimore: Helicon Press, 1967.

"The Prison Pastorate." In *Mission and Grace: Essays in Pastoral Theology*, vol. 3, 74–97. Translated by Cecily Hastings and Richard Strachan. London: Sheed & Ward, 1966.

"Problems Concerning Confession." In *Theological Investigations*. Vol. 3, *The Theology of the Spiritual Life*, 190–206. Translated by Karl H. Kruger and Boniface Kruger. Baltimore: Helicon Press, 1967.

"The Prospects for Dogmatic Theology." In *Theological Investigations*. Vol. 1, *God, Christ, Mary and Grace*, 1–18. Translated by Cornelius Ernst. Baltimore: Helicon Press, 1961.

"Purgatory." *Theological Investigations*. Vol. 19, *Faith and Ministry*, 181–93. Translated by Edward Quinn. New York: Crossroad, 1983.

"Reconciliation and Vicarious Representation." In *Theological Investigations*. Vol. 21, *Science and Christian Faith*, 255–69. Translated by Hugh M. Riley. New York: Crossroad, 1988.

"Remarks on the Dogmatic Treatise *De Trinitate*." In *Theological Investigations*. Vol. 4, *More Recent Writings*, 77–102. Translated by Kevin Smyth. Baltimore: Helicon Press, 1966.

"Remarks on the Theology of Indulgences." In *Theological Investigations*. Vol. 2, *Man in the Church*, 175–202. Translated by Karl H. Kruger. Baltimore: Helicon Press, 1963.

"Repräsentation." In *Lexikon für Theologie und Kirche*, vol. 8, edited by M. Buchberger, J. Höfer, K. Rahner, and H. Brechter, 1244–45. Freiburg: Herder, 1963.

"Resurrection." (editor) In *Sacramentum Mundi: An Encyclopedia of Theology*. Vol. 5, *Philosophy to Salvation*, 323–42. New York: Herder & Herder, 1970.

Sacramentum Mundi: An Encyclopedia of Theology. (editor) 6 vols. New York: Herder & Herder, 1968–70.

"Salvation." In *Sacramentum Mundi: An Encyclopedia of Theology*. Vol. 5, *Philosophy to Salvation*, 405–38. New York: Herder & Herder, 1970.

"See, What a Man!" In *Theological Investigations*. Vol. 7, *Further Theology of the Spiritual Life 1*, 136–39. Translated by David Bourke. New York: Seabury, 1971.

"Sin as Loss of Grace in the Early Church." In *Theological Investigations*. Vol. 15, *Penance in the Early Church*, 23–53. Translated by Lionel Swain. New York: Seabury, 1982.

"Some Implications of the Scholastic Concept of Uncreated Grace." In *Theological Investigations*. Vol. 1, *God, Christ, Mary and Grace*, 319–46. Translated by Cornelius Ernst. Baltimore: Helicon Press, 1961.

"Some Theses for a Theology of Devotion to the Sacred Heart." In *Theological Investigations*. Vol. 3, *The Theology of the Spiritual Life*, 331–52. Translated by Karl H. Kruger and Boniface Kruger. Baltimore: Helicon Press, 1967.

Spirit in the World. Translated by William Dych. New York: Continuum, 1994.

"The 'Spiritual Senses' According to Origen." In *Theological Investigations*. Vol. 16, *Experience of the Spirit: Source of Theology*, 81–103. Translated by David Morland. New York: Seabury, 1979.

"The Status of the Sacrament of Reconciliation." In *Theological Investigations*. Vol. 23, *Final Writings*, 205–18. Translated by Joseph Donceel and Hugh M. Riley. New York: Crossroad, 1992.

"The Student of Theology." In *Mission and Grace: Essays in Pastoral Theology*, vol. 2, 146–81. Translated by Cecily Hastings and Richard Strachan. London: Sheed & Ward, 1964.

Theological Investigations. Vol. 1, *God, Christ, Mary and Grace*. Translated by Cornelius Ernst. Baltimore: Helicon Press, 1961.

Theological Investigations. Vol. 2, *Man in the Church*. Translated by Karl H. Kruger. Baltimore: Helicon Press, 1963.

Theological Investigations. Vol. 3, *The Theology of the Spiritual Life*. Translated by Karl H. Kruger and Boniface Kruger. Baltimore: Helicon Press, 1967.

Theological Investigations. Vol. 4, *More Recent Writings*. Translated by Kevin Smyth. Baltimore: Helicon Press, 1966.

Theological Investigations. Vol. 5, *Later Writings*. Translated by Karl H. Kruger. Baltimore: Helicon Press, 1966.

Theological Investigations. Vol. 7, *Further Theology of the Spiritual Life 1.* Translated by David Bourke. New York: Seabury, 1971.

Theological Investigations. Vol. 8, *Further Theology of the Spiritual Life 2.* Translated by David Bourke. New York: Seabury, 1977.

Theological Investigations. Vol. 9, *Writings of 1965-67.* Translated by Graham Harrison. New York: Seabury, 1972.

Theological Investigations. Vol. 10, *Writings of 1965-67, 2.* Translated by David Bourke. New York: Seabury, 1977.

Theological Investigations. Vol. 12 *Confrontations 2.* Translated by David Bourke. New York: Seabury, 1974.

Theological Investigations. Vol. 13, *Theology, Anthropology, Christology.* Translated by David Bourke. New York: Seabury, 1975.

Theological Investigations. Vol. 14, *Ecclesiology, Questions in the Church, the Church in the World.* Translated by David Bourke. New York: Seabury, 1976.

Theological Investigations. Vol. 15, *Penance in the Early Church.* Translated by Lionel Swain. New York: Seabury, 1982.

Theological Investigations. Vol. 16, *Experience of the Spirit: Source of Theology.* Translated by David Morland. New York: Seabury, 1979.

Theological Investigations. Vol. 17, *Jesus, Man, and the Church.* Translated by Margaret Kohl. New York: Crossroad, 1981.

Theological Investigations. Vol. 18, *God and Revelation.* Translated by Edward Quinn. New York: Crossroad, 1983.

Theological Investigations. Vol. 19, *Faith and Ministry.* Translated by Edward Quinn. New York: Crossroad, 1983.

Theological Investigations. Vol. 20, *Concern for the Church.* Translated by Edward Quinn. New York: Crossroad, 1981.

Theological Investigations. Vol. 21, *Science and Christian Faith.* Translated by Hugh M. Riley. New York: Crossroad, 1988.

Theological Investigations. Vol. 22, *Humane Society and the Church of Tomorrow.* Translated by Joseph Donceel. New York: Crossroad, 1991.

Theological Investigations. Vol. 23, *Final Writings.* Translated by Joseph Donceel and Hugh M. Riley. New York: Crossroad, 1992.

"The Theological Meaning of the Veneration of the Sacred Heart." In *Theological Investigations.* Vol. 8, *Further Theology of the Spiritual Life 2,* 217–28. Translated by David Bourke. New York: Seabury, 1977.

"The Theology of the Symbol." In *Theological Investigations.* Vol. 4, *More Recent Writings,* 221–52. Translated by Kevin Smyth. Baltimore: Helicon Press, 1966.

"Thoughts on the Possibility of Belief Today." In *Theological Investigations.* Vol. 5, *Later Writings,* 3–22. Translated by Karl H. Kruger. Baltimore: Helicon Press, 1966.

"The Transfiguration of the Lord (6 August)." In *The Great Church Year: The Best of Karl Rahner's Homilies, Meditations, and Sermons*, edited by Harvey D. Egan, 340–42. New York: Crossroad, 1993.

The Trinity. Translated by Joseph Donceel. New York: Crossroad, 1997.

"The Two Basic Types of Christology." In *Theological Investigations*. Vol. 13, *Theology, Anthropology, Christology*, 213–23. Translated by David Bourke. New York: Seabury, 1975.

"Unity-Love-Mystery," In *Theological Investigations*. Vol. 8, *Further Theology of the Spiritual Life 2*, 229–47. Translated by David Bourke. New York: Seabury, 1977.

"Vom Sakrament der Nächstenliebe." *Kirchenanzeiger St. Michael* 5, no. 37–38 (September 1934): 151–52, 154–55.

"Warum uns das Beten nottut." *Leuchtturm: Monatsschrift der neudeutschen Jugend* 18 (1924–25): 310–11.

"Zur Geschichte der Lehre von den fünf geistlichen Sinnen." In *Karl Rahner: Sämtliche Werke*. Vol. 1, *Frühe spirituelle Texte und Studien*, edited by Karl Lehmann and Albert Raffelt, 305–35. Freiburg: Herder, 2014.

Rahner, Karl, and Herbert Vorgrimler. *Theological Dictionary*. Edited by Cornelius Ernst. Translated by Richard Strachan. New York: Herder & Herder, 1965.

Secondary Literature on Karl Rahner

Bacht, Heinrich. "Theologie in Valkenburg (1929–1933)." In *Karl Rahner - Bilder eines Lebens*, edited by Paul Imhof and Hubert Biallowons, 22–23. Zürich: Benziger, 1985.

Balthasar, Hans Urs von. *The Moment of Christian Witness*. Translated by Richard Beckley. San Francisco: Ignatius Press, 1994.

_____. *Theo-Drama*. 5 vols. San Francisco: Ignatius Press, 1988–98.

Barron, Robert. *The Priority of Christ: Toward a Postliberal Catholicism*. Grand Rapids: Brazos, 2007.

Batlogg, Andreas R. *Die Mysterien des Lebens Jesu bei Karl Rahner: Zugang zum Christusglauben*. Innsbruck: Tyrolia, 2001.

_____. "Karl Rahner in Innsbruck: Aus der Wissenschaftsbiographie eines Jesuitengelehrten-zugleich ein Stück Fakultätsgeschichte." *Zeitschrift für Katholische Theologie* 129, no. 3 (2007): 397–422.

_____. "Karl Rahners Theologische Dissertation 'E latere Christi': Zur Genese eines patristischen Projeckts (1936)." *Zeitschrift für Katholische Theologie* 126, no. 1 (2004): 111–30.

Beaton, Rhodora E. *Embodied Words, Spoken Signs: Sacramentality and the Word in Rahner and Chauvet.* Minneapolis: Fortress Press, 2014.

Buckley, James. "On Being a Symbol: An Appraisal of Karl Rahner." *Theological Studies* 40, no. 3 (1979): 453–73.

Burke, Patrick. *Reinterpreting Rahner: A Critical Study of His Major Themes.* New York: Fordham University Press, 2002.

Callahan, Annice. *Karl Rahner's Spirituality of the Pierced Heart: A Reinterpretation of Devotion to the Sacred Heart.* Lanham, MD: University Press of America, 1985.

Carr, Anne E. "Stephen M. Fields, S.J., Being as Symbol: On the Origins and Development of Karl Rahner's Metaphysics." *Journal of Religion* 82, no. 3 (2002): 484–85.

Caponi, Francis J. "Karl Rahner: Divinization in Roman Catholicism." In *Partakers of the Divine Nature: The History and Development of Deification in the Christian Tradition,* edited by Michael J. Christensen and Jeffery A. Wittung, 259–80. Madison, NJ: Fairleigh Dickinson University Press, 2007.

Clasby, Nancy. "Dancing Sophia: Rahner's Theology of Symbols." *Religion & Literature* 25, no. 1 (1993): 51–65.

Dych, William V. *Karl Rahner.* Collegeville, MN: Liturgical Press, 1992.

Edwards, Denis. *What Are They Saying About Salvation?* New York: Paulist Press, 1986.

Egan, Harvey D. "Karl Rahner: Theologian of the 'Spiritual Exercises.'" *Thought* 67, no. 3 (1992): 257–70.

Endean, Philip. *Karl Rahner and Ignatian Spirituality.* Oxford: Oxford University Press, 2001.

Farmer, Jerry T. "Four Christological Themes of the Theology of Karl Rahner." In *The Myriad Christ: Plurality and the Quest for Unity in Contemporary Christology,* edited by T. Merrigan and J. Haers, 433–62. Leuven: Leuven University Press, 2000.

Fields, Stephen. *Analogies of Transcendence: An Essay on Nature, Grace, and Modernity.* Washington, DC: Catholic University of America Press, 2016.

_____. *Being as Symbol: On the Origins and Development of Karl Rahner's Metaphysics.* Washington, DC: Georgetown University Press, 2000.

_____. "Symbol." In *Cambridge Dictionary of Christian Theology,* edited by Ian McFarland, David A. S. Fergusson, Karen Kilby, and Iain R. Torrance, 489–90. New York: Cambridge University Press, 2011.

Fischer, Mark F. *The Foundations of Karl Rahner: A Paraphrase of the Foundations of Christian Faith, with Introductions and Indices.* New York: Crossroad, 2005.

_____. "Karl Rahner's Transcendental Christology." Presentation at the Catholic Theological Society of America annual convention, Miami, June 8, 2013.

Fritz, Peter Joseph. "Karl Rahner, Friedrich Schelling, and Original Plural Unity." *Theological Studies* 75, no. 2 (2014): 284–307.

_____. *Karl Rahner's Theological Aesthetics.* Washington, DC: Catholic University of America Press, 2014.

Grün, Anselm. *Erlösung durch das Kreuz. Karl Rahners Beitrag zu einem heutigen Erlösungsverstandnis.* Münsterschwarzach: Vier-Türme Verlag, 1975.

Haight, Roger. *Jesus: Symbol of God.* Maryknoll, NY: Orbis, 1999.

Hilberath, Bernd Jochen, and Bernhard Nitsche. "Das Symbol als vermittelnde Kategorie zwischen Transzendentalität und Geschichte in der transzendentalen Theologie Karl Rahners." In *Erfahrung-Geschichte-Identität: Schnittpunkt von Philosophie und Theologie,* edited by Matthias Laarmann and Tobias Trappe, 239–60. Freiburg: Herder, 1997.

Kasper, Walter. *Mercy: The Essence of the Gospel and the Key to Christian Life.* New York: Paulist Press, 2014.

Kelly, Geffrey B., ed. *Karl Rahner: Theologian of the Graced Search for Meaning.* Minneapolis: Fortress Press, 1992.

Kilby, Karen. *Karl Rahner: Theology and Philosophy.* New York: Routledge, 2004.

Kress, Robert. *A Rahner Handbook.* Atlanta: John Knox, 1982.

Krieg, Robert A. "The Crucified in Rahner's Christology: An Appraisal." *Irish Theological Quarterly* 50, no. 2–4 (1983): 151–67.

_____. "A Fortieth-Anniversary Reappraisal of 'Chalcedon: End or Beginning?'" *Philosophy and Theology* 9, no. 1 (1995): 77–116.

Lowery, Mark. "Retrieving Rahner for Orthodox Catholic Catholicism." *Faith & Reason* 17, no. 3 (1991): 251–72.

Mansini, Guy. *The Word has Dwelt Among Us: Explorations in Theology.* Ave Maria, FL: Sapientia Press, 2008.

McCool, Gerald, ed. *A Rahner Reader.* New York: Seabury, 1975.

McDade, John. "Catholic Theology in the Post-Conciliar Period." In *Modern Catholicism: Vatican II and After,* edited by Adrian Hastings, 422–43. New York: Oxford University Press, 1991.

Molnar, Paul D. "Can We Know God Directly? Rahner's Solution from Experience." *Theological Studies* 46, no. 2 (1985): 228–61.

Neufeld, Karl-Heinz. *Die Brüder Rahner: Eine Biographie.* Freiburg: Herder, 1994.

_____. "Editionsbericht." In *Karl Rahner: Sämtliche Werke.* Vol. 3, *Spiritualität und Theologie der Kirchenväter,* edited by Andreas R. Batlogg, Eduard Farrugia, and Karl-Heinz Neufeld, xiii–xvi. Freiburg: Herder, 1999.

_____. "Karl Rahner: Predigten zur Verkündigungstheologie 1938." *Zeitschrift für Katholische Theologie* 129, no. 2 (2007): 183–206.

Nichols, Aidan. "Rahner and Balthasar: The Anonymous Christianity Debate

Revisited." In *Beyond the Blue Glass: Catholic Essays on Faith and Culture*, vol. 1, 107–28. London: Saint Austin Press, 2002.

O'Donovan, Leo J., ed. "A Changing Ecclesiology in a Changing Church: A Symposium on Development in the Ecclesiology of Karl Rahner." *Theological Studies* 38, no. 4 (1977): 736–62.

_____. *A World of Grace: An Introduction to the Themes and Foundations of Karl Rahner's Theology*. Washington DC: Georgetown University Press, 1995.

Ogden, Schubert M. *Is There Only One True Religion or Are There Many?* Dallas: Southern Methodist University Press, 1992.

O'Meara, Thomas. *God in the World: A Guide to Karl Rahner's Theology*. Collegeville, MN: Liturgical Press, 2007.

Pekarske, Daniel T. *Abstracts of Karl Rahner's Theological Investigations 1–23*. Milwaukee, WI: Marquette University Press, 2002.

Peterson, Brandon R. "Critical Voices: The Reactions of Rahner and Ratzinger to Schema XIII (*Gaudium et Spes*)." *Modern Theology* 31, no. 1 (January 2015): 1–26.

Peterson, Brandon R., and James B. South. "Karl Rahner on Patristic Theology and Spirituality." *Philosophy & Theology* 27, no. 2 (2015): 499–512.

Power, David N. "Sacraments in General." In *Systematic Theology: Roman Catholic Perspectives*, edited by Francis Schüssler Fiorenza and John P. Galvin, 461–96. Minneapolis: Fortress Press, 2011.

Pryor, Adam. "Comparing Tillich and Rahner on Symbol: Evidencing the Modernist/Postmodernist Boundary." *Bulletin of the North American Paul Tillich Society* 37, no. 2 (2011): 23–38.

Rahner, Hugo. "Eucharisticon fraternitatis." In *Gott in Welt. Festgabe für Karl Rahner*, vol. 2, edited by Johann Baptist Metz et al., 885–99. Freiburg: Herder, 1964.

Ratzinger, Joseph. *Principles of Catholic Theology: Building Stones for a Fundamental Theology*. San Francisco: Ignatius Press, 1987.

Reno, R. R. "Rahner the Restorationist: Karl Rahner's Time has Passed." *First Things* no. 233 (May 2013): 45–51.

Roberts, Louis. *The Achievement of Karl Rahner*. New York: Herder & Herder, 1967.

Sheehan, Thomas. *Karl Rahner: The Philosophical Foundations*. Athens: Ohio University Press, 1987.

Siebenrock, Roman A. "Christology." In *The Cambridge Companion to Karl Rahner*, edited by Declan Marmion and Mary E. Hines, 112–27. Cambridge: Cambridge University Press, 2005.

_____. "Gratia Christi. The Heart of the Theology of Karl Rahner: Ignatian Influences in the Codex De Gratia Christi (1937/38) and Its Significance for the

Development of His Work." *Revista Portuguesa de Filosofia* 63, no. 4 (October–December 2007): 1261–72.

Van Nieuwenhove, Rik. "'Bearing the Marks of Christ's Passion': Aquinas' Soteriology." In *The Theology of Thomas Aquinas*, edited by Rik Van Nieuwenhove and Joseph Wawrykow, 277–302. Notre Dame: University of Notre Dame Press, 2005.

———. "St Anselm and St Thomas Aquinas on 'Satisfaction': Or how Catholic and Protestant Understandings of the Cross Differ." *Angelicum* 80 (2003): 159–76.

Vass, George. *A Pattern of Doctrines 2: The Atonement and Mankind's Salvation.* Vol. 4 of *Understanding Karl Rahner*. London: Sheed & Ward, 1998.

Vorgrimler, Herbert. *Karl Rahner: His Life, Thought and Works.* Translated by Edward Quinn. Glen Rock, NJ: Deus Books, 1966.

———. "Karl Rahner: The Theologian's Contribution." In *Vatican II Revisited: By Those Who Were There*, edited by Alberic Stacpoole, 32–46. Minneapolis: Winston Press, 1986.

———. "Soteriologie." In *Karl Rahner: Gotteserfahrung in Leben und Denken*, 218–22. Darmstadt: Primus, 2004.

———. *Understanding Karl Rahner: An Introduction to His Life and Thought.* New York: Crossroad, 1986.

Walsh, Michael J. *The Heart of Christ in the Writings of Karl Rahner: An Investigation of Its Christological Foundation as an Example of the Relationship between Theology and Spirituality.* Rome: Università Gregoriana Editrice, 1977.

Wassilowsky, Günther. *Universales Heilssakrament Kirche: Karl Rahners Beitrag zur Ekklesiologie des II. Vatikanums.* Innsbruck: Tyrolia, 2001.

Wong, Joseph H. "Anonymous Christians: Karl Rahner's Pneuma-Christocentrism and an East-West Dialogue." *Theological Studies* 55, no. 4 (1994): 609–37.

———. *Logos-Symbol in the Christology of Karl Rahner.* Rome: LAS, 1984.

Zahlauer, Arno. *Karl Rahner und sein "produktives Vorbild" Ignatius von Loyola.* Innsbruck: Tyrolia, 1996.

Ancient, Patristic, and Medieval Literature

Aquinas, Thomas. *Summa Theologica.* Translated by Fathers of the English Dominican Province. 3 vols. New York: Benziger Brothers, 1947.

———. *Truth* [De Veritate]. Translated by Robert W. Mulligan, James V. McGlynn, and Robert W. Schmidt. 3 vols. Chicago: H. Regnery, 1952–54.

Aristotle. *Physics.* In *The Complete Works of Aristotle: The Revised Oxford Translation*, vol. 1, edited by Jonathan Barnes, 315–446. Princeton: Princeton University Press, 1984.

Athanasius. *Against the Arians*. In *Nicene and Post-Nicene Fathers: Second Series*. Vol. 4, *St. Athanasius: Select Works and Letters*, edited by Philip Schaff and Henry Wace, 306–447. New York: Christian Literature Publishing, 1892.

———. *On the Incarnation*. Crestwood, NY: St. Vladimir's Seminary Press, 2002.

Augustine. *Against Julian* [Contra Julianum]. Vol. 16 of *Writings of Saint Augustine*. Translated by Matthew A. Schumacher. Washington, DC: Catholic University of America Press, 1974.

———. *Confessions* [Confessiones]. Translated by F. J. Sheed. Indianapolis: Hackett, 1993.

———. *Expositions on the Psalms, 1-32*. Translated by Maria Boulding. Edited by John E. Rotelle. The Works of Saint Augustine 3, book 15. Hyde Park, NY: New City Press, 2000.

———. *Expositions on the Psalms, 33-50*. Translated by Maria Boulding. Edited by John E. Rotelle. The Works of Saint Augustine 3, book 16. Hyde Park, NY: New City Press, 2000.

———. *Expositions on the Psalms, 121-150*. Translated by Maria Boulding. Edited by John E. Rotelle. The Works of Saint Augustine 3, book 20. Hyde Park, NY: New City Press, 2004.

———. *Lectures or Tractates According to the Gospel of St. John*. In *Nicene and Post-Nicene Fathers: First Series*. Vol. 7, *St. Augustin*, edited by Philip Schaff, 7–452. New York: Christian Literature Publishing, 1888.

———. *Sermons (94a-147a)*. Translated by Edmund Hill. Edited by John E. Rotelle. The Works of Saint Augustine 3, book 4. Brooklyn, NY: New City Press, 1992.

———. *Sermons (184-229z)*. Edited by John E. Rotelle. The Works of Saint Augustine 3, book 6. Brooklyn, NY: New City Press, 1993.

Chrysostom, John. *Baptismal Instructions*. Edited and translated by Paul W. Harkins. Ancient Christian Writers 31. New York: Newman Press, 1963.

———. *De Laude Maximi et Quales Ducendae Sint Uxores*. In *Patrologiae Cursus Completus: Series Graeca*, vol. 51, edited by Jacques-Paul Migne, 225–42. Paris, 1862.

Clement of Alexandria. *Exhortation to the Heathen*. In *The Ante-Nicene Fathers*. Vol. 2, *Fathers of the Second Century*, edited by Alexander Roberts and James Donaldson, 171–206. Buffalo, NY: Christian Literature Publishing, 1885.

———. "Hymn to Christ the Saviour." In *The Seventh Book of the Stromateis*, edited by Matyáš Havrda, Vit Hušek, and Jana Plátová, 319–22. Leiden: Brill, 2012.

———. *The Instructor* [Pædagogus]. In *The Ante-Nicene Fathers*. Vol. 2, *Fathers of the Second Century*, edited by Alexander Roberts and James Donaldson, 207–98. Buffalo, NY: Christian Literature Publishing, 1885.

_____. *The Stromata*. In *The Ante-Nicene Fathers*. Vol. 2, *Fathers of the Second Century*, edited by Alexander Roberts and James Donaldson, 299–567. Buffalo, NY: Christian Literature Publishing, 1885.

Cyril of Alexandria. *Commentary on the Gospel According to S. John*. Edited by P. E. Pusey and T. Randell. 2 vols. London: W. Smith, 1874–85.

Irenaeus of Lyons. *Against Heresies* [Adversus Haereses]. In *The Ante-Nicene Fathers*. Vol. 1, *The Apostolic Fathers with Justin Martyr and Irenaeus*, edited by Alexander Roberts and James Donaldson, 315–567. Buffalo, NY: Christian Literature Publishing, 1885.

Methodius. *The Banquet of the Ten Virgins; or, Concerning Chastity* (*Symposium*). In *The Ante-Nicene Fathers*. Vol. 6, *Gregory Thaumaturgus, Dionysius the Great, Julius Africanus, Anatolius and minor writers, Methodius, Arnobius*, edited by Alexander Roberts and James Donaldson, 309–55. Buffalo, NY: Christian Literature Publishing, 1888.

Migne, Jacques-Paul, ed. *Patrologiae Cursus Completus: Omnium SS. Patrum, Doctorum Scriptorumque Ecclesiasticorum Sive Latinorum, Sive Graecorum*. Paris, 1844.

Tertullian. *A Treatise on the Soul* (*De Anima*). In *The Ante-Nicene Fathers*. Vol. 3, *Latin Christianity: Its Founder, Tertullian*, edited by Alexander Roberts and James Donaldson, 181–235. Buffalo: Christian Literature Publishing, 1887.

Other Literature

Altaner, Berthold. "Augustinus und Irenäus, eine quellenkritische Untersuchung." *Theologische Quartalschrift* 129 (1949): 162–72.

Atz, Karl, and Stephen D. Beissel. *Die kirchliche Kunst in Wort und Bild*. Regensburg: Manz, 1915.

Aulén, Gustaf. *Christus Victor: An Historical Study of the Three Main Types of the Idea of Atonement*. New York: Macmillan, 1969.

Balthasar, Hans Urs von. *Mysterium Paschale: The Mystery of Easter*. San Francisco: Ignatius Press, 2000.

Barth, Karl. *Church Dogmatics*. Edited by G. W. Bromiley and T. F. Torrance. 5 vols. London: T&T Clark, 2010.

Bavinck, Herman. *Reformed Dogmatics: Sin and Salvation in Christ*. Edited by John Bolt. Translated by John Vriend. Grand Rapids: Baker Academic, 2006.

Brock, Rita Nakashima. "And a Little Child Will Lead Us: Christology and Child Abuse." In *Christianity, Patriarchy, and Abuse: A Feminist Critique*, edited by Joanne Carlson Brown and Carole R. Bohn, 42–61. New York: Pilgrim Press, 1989.

Brondos, David A. "The Redemption of 'Man' in the Thought of Irenaeus." In

Fortress Introduction to Salvation and the Cross, 49–63. Minneapolis: Fortress Press, 2007.

Carlson Brown, Joanne, and Rebecca Parker. "For God So Loved the World?" In *Christianity, Patriarchy, and Abuse: A Feminist Critique*, edited by Joanne Carlson Brown and Carole R. Bohn, 1–30. New York: Pilgrim Press, 1989.

Catechism of the Catholic Church. 2nd ed. Vatican City: Libreria Editrice Vaticana, 2000.

Cessario, Romanus. *The Godly Image*. Petersham, MA: St. Bede's Publications, 1990.

Chenu, Marie-Dominique. "Le plan de la Somme théologique de saint Thomas." *Révue Thomiste* 45 (1939): 93–107.

———. *Toward Understanding St. Thomas*. Chicago: Henry Regnery, 1964.

Clifford, Richard J., and Khaled Anatolios. "Christian Salvation: Biblical and Theological Perspectives." *Theological Studies* 66, no. 4 (2005): 739–69.

Daley, Brian. "'He Himself Is Our Peace' (Ephesians 2:14): Early Christian Views of Redemption in Christ." In *The Redemption: An Interdisciplinary Symposium on Christ as Redeemer*, edited by Stephen T. Davis, Daniel Kendall, and Gerald O'Collins, 149–76. New York: Oxford University Press, 2004.

———. *The Hope of the Early Church: A Handbook of Patristic Eschatology*. Cambridge: Cambridge University Press, 1991.

Denzinger, Heinrich, ed. *The Sources of Catholic Dogma*. Translated by Roy J. Deferrari. Fitzwilliam, NH: Loreto Publications, 2007.

Dupuis, Jacques. *Toward a Christian Theology of Religious Pluralism*. Maryknoll, NY: Orbis Books, 1997.

Finlan, Stephen. *Problems with Atonement: The Origins of, and Controversy about, the Atonement Doctrine*. Collegeville, MN: Liturgical Press, 2005.

Flannery, Austin, ed. *Vatican Council II: The Basic Sixteen Documents*. Northport, NY: Costello, 1996.

Green, Joel B., and Mark D. Baker. *Recovering the Scandal of the Cross: Atonement in New Testament and Contemporary Contexts*. Downers Grove, IL: InterVarsity Press, 2000.

Gutiérrez, Gustavo. *We Drink from Our Own Wells: The Spiritual Journey of a People*. Maryknoll, NY: Orbis, 1984.

Harnack, Adolf. *History of Dogma*. Translated by Neil Buchanan. 7 vols. New York: Dover Publications, 1961.

Hart, Trevor. "Irenaeus, Recapitulation and Physical Redemption." In *Christ in Our Place: The Humanity of God in Christ for the Reconciliation of the World*, edited by Trevor A. Hart and David P. Thimell, 152–81. Exeter: Paternoster Press, 1989.

Hegel, Georg Wilhelm Friedrich. *Lectures on the Philosophy of Religion*. Translated by E. B. Speirs and J. Burdon Sanderson. 3 vols. New York: Humanities Press, 1962.

Hettrick, Jane Schatkin. "Musical Settings of Clement's 'Hymn to Christ the Saviour.'" In *The Seventh Book of the* Stromateis, edited by Matyáš Havrda, Vit Hušek, and Jana Plátová, 323–39. Leiden: Brill, 2012.

Kasper, Walter. *Jesus the Christ*. New York: Paulist Press, 1977.

Kelly, J. N. D. *Early Christian Doctrines*. Rev. ed. San Francisco: Harper & Row, 1978.

Klager, Andrew P. "Retaining and Reclaiming the Divine: Identification and the Recapitulation of Peace in St. Irenaeus of Lyon's Atonement Narrative." In *Stricken by God? Nonviolent Identification and the Victory of Christ*, edited by Brad Jersak and Michael Hardin, 422–80. Grand Rapids: Eerdmans, 2007.

Krieg, Robert A. *Story-Shaped Christology: The Role of Narratives in Identifying Jesus Christ*. New York: Paulist Press, 1988.

Künstle, Karl. *Ikonographie der christlichen Kunst*. 2 vols. Freiburg: Herder, 1926–28.

Ladd, George Eldon. *A Theology of the New Testament*. Rev. ed. Grand Rapids: Eerdmans, 1993.

Loewe, William. "Irenaeus' Soteriology: *Christus Victor* Revisited." *Anglican Theological Review* 67, no. 1 (1985): 1–15.

_____. "Irenaeus' Soteriology: Transposing the Question." In *Religion and Culture: Essays in Honor of Bernard Lonergan, S.J.*, 167–79. Albany: State University of New York Press, 1987.

Loofs, Friedrich. *Leitfaden zur Studium der Dogmengeschichte*. 4th ed. Halle: Niemeyer, 1906.

Lösel, Steffen. "A Plain Account of Christian Salvation? Balthasar on Sacrifice, Solidarity, and Substitution." *Pro Ecclesia* 13, no. 2 (2004): 141–71.

Löser, Werner. *Im Geiste des Origenes: Hans Urs von Balthasar als Interpret der Theologie der Kirchenväter*. Frankfurt: Knecht, 1976.

Lubac, Henri de. *Catholicism: Christ and the Common Destiny of Man*. Translated by Lancelot C. Sheppard and Elizabeth Englund. San Francisco: Ignatius Press, 1988.

_____. *The Mystery of the Supernatural*. Translated by Rosemary Sheed. New York: Herder & Herder, 1998.

_____. *Surnaturel: études historiques*. Paris: Aubier, 1946.

Ludlow, Morwenna. *Gregory of Nyssa, Ancient and (Post)modern*. Oxford: Oxford University Press, 2007.

Marshall, Howard. "The Theology of the Atonement." In *The Atonement Debate*, edited by Derek Tidball, David Hilborn, and Justin Thacker, 49–68. Grand Rapids: Zondervan, 2008.

Masson, Robert. "Interpreting Rahner's Metaphoric Logic." *Theological Studies* 71, no. 2 (June 2010): 380–409.

McBrien, Richard P. *Catholicism*. Rev. ed. San Francisco: HarperSanFrancisco, 1994.

———. *The Church: The Evolution of Catholicism*. New York: HarperOne, 2008.

McDermott, Brian O. *Word Become Flesh: Dimensions in Christology*. Collegeville, MN: Liturgical Press, 1993.

Meconi, David Vincent. *"O Admirabile Commercium*: The True Christmas Exchange." *Homiletic and Pastoral Review* 111, no. 3 (December 2010): 47–50.

Modras, Ronald. "Catholic Substance and the Catholic Church Today." In *Paul Tillich: A New Catholic Assessment*, edited by Raymond F. Bulman and Frederick J. Parrella, 33–47. Collegeville, MN: Liturgical Press, 1994.

Moell, C. J. "Sacred Heart, Devotion to." In *New Catholic Encyclopedia*. Vol. 12, *Ref–Sep*, 490–92. 2nd ed. Detroit: Gale, 2003.

Mongrain, Kevin. *The Systematic Thought of Hans Urs von Balthasar: An Irenaean Retrieval*. New York: Crossroad, 2002.

Mulcahy, Eamonn. *The Cause of Our Salvation: Soteriological Causality According to Some Modern British Theologians 1988-1998*. Rome: Editrice Pontificia Università Gregoriana, 2007.

Nichols, Aidan. *Divine Fruitfulness: A Guide Through Balthasar's Theology Beyond the Trilogy*. London: T&T Clark, 2007.

Oakes, Edward T., and Alyssa Lyra Pitstick. "Balthasar, Hell, and Heresy: An Exchange." *First Things* no. 168 (2006): 25–32.

O'Collins, Gerald. *Jesus Our Redeemer: A Christian Approach to Salvation*. New York: Oxford University Press, 2007.

Osborne, Kenan B. "Tillich's Understanding of Symbols and Roman Catholic Sacramental Theology." In *Paul Tillich: A New Catholic Assessment*, edited by Raymond F. Bulman and Frederick J. Parrella, 91–111. Collegeville, MN: Liturgical Press, 1994.

Peterson, Brandon R. "Paving the Way? Penalty and Atonement in Thomas Aquinas's Soteriology." *International Journal of Systematic Theology* 15, no. 3 (July 2013): 265–83.

Pitstick, Alyssa Lyra. *Light in Darkness: Hans Urs von Balthasar and the Catholic Doctrine of Christ's Descent into Hell*. Grand Rapids: Eerdmans, 2007.

Placher, William. "How Does Jesus Save? An Alternative View of Atonement." *Christian Century* 126, no. 11 (2009): 23–27.

Rahner, Hugo. *Fons Vitae. Eine Untersuchung zur Geschichte der Christusfrömmigkeit in der Urkirche. 1.-3. Jahrhundert*. Diss., University of Innsbruck, 1930.

———. *A Theology of Proclamation*. New York: Herder & Herder, 1968.

Rahner, Hugo, and Karl Rahner. *Prayers for Meditation.* Translated by Rosaleen Brennan. New York: Herder & Herder, 1962.

———. "Über die Gnade des Gebetes in der Gesellschaft Jesu. Nach P.Hieronymus Nadal S.J." *Mitteilungen aus den deutschen Provinzen [der Gesellschaft Jesu] (Eupen)* 13 (1935): 399–411.

Ramelli, Ilaria. "*Stromateis* VII and Clement's Hints at the Theory of *Apokatastasis.*" In *The Seventh Book of the* Stromateis, edited by Matyáš Havrda, Vit Hušek, and Jana Plátová, 239–57. Leiden: Brill, 2012.

Ratzinger, Joseph. *Introduction to Christianity.* Translated by J. R. Foster. New York: Herder & Herder, 1970.

———. "Introductory Article and Chapter 1: The Dignity of the Human Person." In *Commentary on the Documents of Vatican II.* Vol. 5, *Pastoral Constitution on the Church in the Modern World,* edited by Herbert Vorgrimler, 115–63. New York: Herder & Herder, 1969.

———. *Jesus of Nazareth: From the Baptism in the Jordan to the Transfiguration.* San Francisco: Ignatius Press, 2008.

———. "Stellvertretung." In *Handbuch theologischer Grundbegriffe,* vol. 2, edited by Heinrich Fries, 566–75. Munich: Kösel, 1963.

Reimherr, Otto. "Irenaeus Lugdunensis." In *Catalogus Translationum et Commentariorum: Mediaeval and Renaissance Latin Translations and Commentaries,* vol. 7, edited by Virginia Brown, Paul Oskar Kristellerd, and F. Edward Cranz, 13–54. Washington, DC: Catholic University of America Press, 1992.

Ruether, Rosemary Radford. *Introducing Redemption in Christian Feminism.* Sheffield: Sheffield Academic Press, 1998.

Schillebeeckx, Edward. *Christ, the Sacrament of the Encounter with God.* New York: Sheed & Ward, 1963.

———. *De sacramentele Heilseconomie: theologische bezinning op. S. Thomas' sacramentenleer in het licht van de traditie en van de hedendaage sacramentsproblematiek.* Antwerp: Nelissen, 1952.

———. "Sakramente als Organe der Gottbegegnung." In *Fragen der Theologie heute,* edited by Johannes Feiner, 379–401. Einsiedeln: Benziger 1957.

Schineller, J. P. "Christ and Church: A Spectrum of Views." *Theological Studies* 37, no. 4 (1976): 545–66.

Schumacher, Michele M. "The Concept of Representation in the Theology of Hans Urs von Balthasar." *Theological Studies* 60, no. 1 (1999): 53–71.

Schüssler Fiorenza, Elisabeth. *Jesus: Miriam's Child, Sophia's Prophet.* New York: Continuum, 1994.

Semmelroth, Otto. *Die Kirche als Ursakrament.* Frankfurt: J. Knecht, 1953.

Sölle, Dorothee. *Christ the Representative: An Essay in Theology after the 'Death of God.'* Philadelphia: Fortress Press, 1967.

Steenberg, Matthew C. *Irenaeus on Creation: The Cosmic Christ and the Saga of Redemption.* Leiden: Brill, 2008.

_____. *Of God and Man: Theology as Anthropology from Irenaeus to Athanasius.* London: T&T Clark, 2009.

Strobel, Regula. "New Ways of Speaking about the Cross: A New Basis for Christian Identity." In *Toward a New Heaven and a New Earth: Essays in Honor of Elisabeth Schüssler Fiorenza,* edited by Fernando F. Segovia, 351–67. Maryknoll, NY: Orbis, 2003.

Tanner, Kathryn. *Christ the Key.* Cambridge: Cambridge University Press, 2010.

_____. "Incarnation, Cross, and Sacrifice: A Feminist-Inspired Reappraisal." *Anglican Theological Review* 86, no. 1 (2004): 35–56.

Tillich, Paul. "Dimensionen, Schichten und die Einheit des Seins." In *Gesammelte Werke.* Vol. 4, *Korrelationen: die Antworten der Religion auf Fragen der Zeit,* edited by Ingeborg C. Henel, 118–29. Stuttgart: Evangelisches Verlagswerk, 1961.

_____. *Dynamics of Faith.* New York: Harper & Row, 1957.

_____. *The Protestant Era.* Translated by James Luther Adams. Chicago: University of Chicago Press, 1948.

_____. *Systematic Theology.* 3 vols. Chicago: University of Chicago Press, 1951–63.

Viller, Marcel. *Aszese und Mystik in der Väterzeit.* Edited and translated by Karl Rahner. Freiburg: Herder, 1939.

Vogel, Jeffrey A. "The Haste of Sin, the Slowness of Salvation: An Interpretation of Irenaeus on the Fall and Redemption." *Anglican Theological Review* 89, no. 3 (2007): 443–59.

Weaver, J. Denny. *The Nonviolent Atonement.* 2nd ed. Grand Rapids: Eerdmans, 2011.

Williams, Delores S. *Sisters in the Wilderness: The Challenge of Womanist God-Talk.* Maryknoll, NY: Orbis, 1993.

Wolf, William J. "Atonement." In *The Encyclopedia of Religion,* vol. 1, edited by Mircea Eliade, 9–14. New York: Macmillan, 1987.

Zachhuber, Johannes. *Human Nature in Gregory of Nyssa: Philosophical Background and Theological Significance.* Leiden: Brill, 1999.

Index of Names

Alfaro, J., 3

Anatolios, K., 105–7

Anselm of Canterbury, 4, 10, 30,
36–38, 42, 103, 202, 251, 259

Aristotle, 14, 54, 59–60, 68–69, 72,
84, 93, 157, 208, 214

Athanasius of Alexandria, St., 42,
44, 122, 125–28, 140

Augustine of Hippo, St., 12, 29–30,
42, 44, 55–56, 128–32, 143, 150,
151, 157–58, 161, 179–80, 190,
208

Aulén, G., 118, 136, 138, 200, 204–5

Bacht, H., 150

Balthasar, Hans Urs von, soteriology of, 231, 247–48; evaluation
of Rahner's soteriology, xiii,
3–6, 26–27, 218–22, 246, 263; on
physical redemption, 139;
polemics with Rahner, xiv,
218–19, 246–48; Rahner's
responses to, 218–19, 245–48

Barron, R., 62

Barth, K., 3, 40–41, 77, 214

Batlogg, A., 47, 90, 148ff, 165, 193,
242

Beaton, R., 52

Bonaventure, St., 154, 159, 163, 181

Bonhoeffer, D., 40

Blondel, M., 3, 146

Brondos, D., 107–8, 137–38

Buckley, J., 165

Burke, P., 62

Cajetan, T., 92

Callahan, A., 147–48, 165, 194

Caponi, F., 97, 196

Carr, A., 72

Černušková, V., 122–23

Cessario, R., 139–40

Chenu, M.-D., 67, 267

Clasby, N., 54

Clement of Alexandria, 122–25, 150,
153, 172–73, 189

Clifford, R., 105–7

Congar, Y., 204, 239, 267

Cyril of Alexandria, 42, 44, 122, 133,
247

Daley B., 42ff, 97, 103, 112, 115

Daniélou, J., 3, 204, 239

De Lubac, H., 58, 92, 267

Döpfner, J., 1

Dupuis, J., 13, 110–11

Dych, W., 62, 146

289

Ludlow, M., 135

Mansini, G., 6–8
Marcion of Pontus, 105, 110
Maréchal, J., 68, 146–47
Mary, mother of Jesus, xi, 9, 75, 172, 246
Masson, R., 62
McBrien, R., 24, 41, 58
McCool, G., 62, 71, 146, 162
McDade, J., 195
McDermott, B., 13, 41, 122, 127, 137, 140
McIntyre, J., 33
Meconi, D. V., 129
Methodius of Olympus, St., 177
Migne, J. P., 98, 150–51
Modras, R., 75
Moell, C. J., 51
Molnar, P., 25
Moltmann, J., 3, 248
Mulcahy, E., 31–33

Neufeld, K.-H., 47, 147, 148ff, 153–54, 165, 191, 198
Nichols, A., 2, 199
Nitsche, B., 165

Oakes, E. T., 247
O'Collins, G., xiii, 13–14
O'Donovan, L., 146
O'Meara, T., 146
Ogden, S., 13–14, 84, 238
Origen of Alexandria, 42, 123, 154, 158–60, 172, 177, 187, 189, 202
Osborne, K., 74
Ottaviani, A., 1, 266

Pannenberg, W., 3
Paul, the Apostle., xiii, 38, 40, 43–45,

105–6, 110, 116–17, 121, 142, 167–68, 172, 202, 206, 219, 230, 232, 243
Pekarske, D., 231
Peter Lombard, 69, 181
Peterson, B., 82, 139, 146, 218
Pinnock, C., 41
Pitstick, A. L., 247–48
Placher, W., 41, 138, 140, 142, 205
Pryor, A., 74–76

Rahner, H., 49, 61, 149, 152–53, 156ff, 164; on methodological differences with Karl, 155, 158, 192, 203
Ratzinger, J., 2, 11, 41, 137, 184, 204, 218, 239; on *Stellvertretung*, 37
Reimherr, O., 123, 126, 128
Reno, R. R., 47
Roberts, L., 162
Rousselot, P., 68, 146
Ryan, R., 21–23

Schelling, F., 67, 247–48
Schillebeeckx, E., 3, 15, 57–58, 204, 239
Schineller, P., 13, 163
Schleiermacher, F., 62
Schumacher, M., 37
Scotus, 21
Semmelroth, O., 57
Sheehan, T., 146–47, 162
Siebenrock, R., 84, 148, 189–90
Sölle, D., 33, 40, 142
Steenberg, M., 104–5, 107, 110, 113–18, 122

Tanner, K., 41, 140–42, 265
Teilhard de Chardin, P., 2

Index of Subjects

Anonymous Christian, the, 2, 8, 240
anthropology: theological, xiv–xv,
  25–26, 59–60, 91ff, 240
Arianism, 125ff
atonement, xiii; critiques of, 265;
  see reconciliation

Christ. *See* Messiah
church, 57–59, 69, 124, 163–64,
  166ff; as "New Eve," 172ff, 179
causality: final, 5, 84, 214; sacramental and symbolic, 5, 7, 11,
  20, 22, 24, 31–32, 54, 79, 83–84,
  214, 224; formal and quasi-formal, 24–25, 54, 87; instrumental,
  56–57, 69, 213
covenant, 109–11, 259
creation: theology of, 21, 24, 65, 67,
  92, 107, 109ff, 117, 190, 192;
  human infancy and maturation,
  115–16
cross. *See* death, of Jesus

death, of Jesus, 15, 22, 82, 84, 88–91,
  221–22, 239; theology of, 89–91,
  94

divinization (theosis), 45, 96, 103,
  113, 126–31, 192, 195–96, 217,
  231
Docetism, 109, 174

economy, divine. *See* creation, theology of
E latere Christi (Rahner's theology
  dissertation), 39, 47–48, 58–61,
  73, 152–54, 162–88, 193–94, 196,
  241, 256, 264

freedom: human, 22, 29, 39, 219,
  223. *See also* redemption, self-;
  divine, 25, 85–87; as related to
  grace in direct (rather than
  inverse) proportion, 35, 216,
  220, 228

Gnosticism, 104–5, 108, 110, 115,
  133–35, 171, 173–74, 178, 189,
  247–48
God: as Trinity, 53, 55, 111, 120,
  130–31; as "he-who-is-always-
  reconciled," 4, 30, 79, 82–83;
  immutability of, 4, 7–8, 13, 30,
  247; mercy and love of, 30, 37,
  82, 257; wrath or anger of, 4, 7,